The Untold Story of
John Steinbeck and the CIA

STEINBECK:
CITIZEN SPY

Brian Kannard

Grave Distractions Publications
Nashville, TN

STEINBECK:
CITIZEN SPY

Grave Distractions Publications
Nashville, Tennessee
www.gravedistractions.com
© 2013 Brian Kannard

ISBN-13: 978-0-9890293-9-1
Library of Congress Control Number: 2013934251
In Publication Data
Kannard, Brian
Steinbeck: Citizen Spy
Categories:
1. Political Science 2. Intelligence and Espionage

Editor-in-chief of body text: Alice Sullivan (www.AliceSullivan.com)
Cover by Barry Edwards (Barry can be contacted via Grave Distractions Publications)

Printed in the United States

Table of Contents

AA: Alcoholics Anonymous

AG: Attorney General

ACLU: American Civil Liberties Union

ACP: Automatic Colt Pistol

BATF: Bureau of Alcohol, Tobacco, Firearms, and Explosives

BJs: Beach Jumpers

CIA: Central Intelligence Agency

CIAA: Coordinator of Inter-American Affairs

CIG: Central Intelligence Group

CAT: Civilian Air Transport

CCF: Congress of Cultural Freedom

COI: Coordinator of Intelligence

COINTELPRO: Counterintelligence Program

DCI: Director of Central Intelligence

DD/P: Deputy Director of Plans, CIA

DP: Directorate of Plans, CIA

DI: Directorate of Intelligence, CIA

DDI: Deputy Director of Intelligence, CIA

DDO: Deputy Director of Operations, CIA

DoD: Department of Defense

DOJ: Department of Justice

FBI: Federal Bureau of Investigations

FBIS: Foreign Broadcast Information Service. Also referred to as the Foreign Information Service (FIS).

FOIA: Freedom of Information Act

GRU: Soviet Main Intelligence Directorate; from the Russian, *Glavnoye Razvedyvatel'noye Upravleniye*

HUAC: House Committee for Un-American Activities

HTLINGUAL: A CIA domestic mail surveillance program conducted from 1952 to 1973.

IPAC: International Press Alliance Corporation

IRS: Internal Revenue Service

JAG: Judge Advocate General of the United States Navy

KGB: Soviet Committee for State Security, from the Russian *Komitet Gosudarstvennoy Bezopasnosti*

MDR: Mandatory Declassification Review

MPAA: Motion Picture Association of America

MoMA: Museum of Modern Art

NARA: National Records and Archives Administration

NATO: North Atlantic Treaty Organization

NCS: National Clandestine Service, CIA

NCFE: National Committee for a Free Europe

NGO: Non-Governmental Organization

NKVD: Soviet People's Commissariat for Internal Affairs, from the Russian *Narodnyy Komissariat Vnutrennikh Del*

NSA: National Security Agency

NTSB: National Transportation Safety Board

OCCCRBAR: Office for Coordination of Commercial and Cultural Relations between the American Republics

OIAA: Office of Inter-American Affairs

ONI: Office of Naval Intelligence

ORE: The CIA's Office of Reports and Estimates

OSS: Office of Strategic Services

OWI: Office of War Information

POW: Prisoner of War

SDI: Strategic Defense Initiative

SIS: Special Intelligence Service, FBI

SOS: United States Army Service of Supply

UAW: United Auto Workers

NDRC: National Defense Research Committee

USIA: United States Information Agency

USIS: United States Information Service

VE Day: Victory in Europe Day (May 8, 1945)

VOA: Voice of America

WPA: Works Progress Administration (renamed in 1939 as the Works Project Administration)

There are times when everyone experiences a slight hesitation between approaching a doorway and actually knocking on the door. No matter what is behind that door, the reason one raps is to have a question answered. *Are you giving me the job I'm interviewing for? Could she be "the one"? Doctor, what were the test results?* The hesitation between intent and action is fobbed off on checking to make sure a fly is zipped or lunch's garlic-laden falafel has been purged from one's breath. But the real reason for the pause is to allay any fears that crop up right around the time one first forms a fist. *What if my boss finds out I'm interviewing? She must be going out with me as penance for some horrible sin. The tests are going to be positive.* The doorway for this text came, in the parlance of my father, in an ass-backwards manner.

Not to bury the lede, but the conclusion of this book is that John Steinbeck was a CIA asset during the 1950s and '60s. This text supports that hypothesis, but there are some elements of the tale where the story of how I performed my research crosses over with my findings. First and foremost is the interaction I had with John's son, Thomas. One might have thought that in starting out with the insane-sounding premise that John Steinbeck was a CIA spy would begin with the world's one true Steinbeck expert. While there are men and women who have spent their professional lives examining John's life and works, they are experts in Steinbeck's wake. Thomas represents the single person alive who truly knew the Nobel Prize–winning author.

It was because of his intimate knowledge that Thomas was the last person I spoke with about this project. One does not call up someone's son to say, "I've got this wild theory that your dad was a spy. What do you say about that?" At least, not without proof. Before contacting Thomas, I had to have enough evidence to convince a best-selling author of my interpretation of the "truth" about an area of his father's life Thomas likely knew nothing about. So after receiving a pair of letters from the CIA in August of 2012, I set out to compile my prior research and write this book's manuscript. What better way in forming an argument to present to Thomas than putting everything down on paper?

In late February of 2013, my manuscript made enough sense to a select group of readers that I felt it was time to contact Thomas about my suspicions. I had spoken with Thomas in autumn of 2008 about John's fascination with Arthurian lore and the works of Sir Thomas Malory. At that time, I had become convinced that there was an untold story in the work of John's research assistant, Chase

Horton. The enigmatic co-owner of Greenwich Village's Washington Square Bookstore had been an integral part of the research for what would become Steinbeck's posthumously published *The Acts of King Arthur and His Noble Knights*. On that occasion, Thomas and I spoke for over an hour about his father, Horton, and the quest for the Holy Grail. From that conversation, I came away thinking that there was something in Steinbeck's life overlooked by the literary critics, biographers, and scholars. So for the next few years, I picked at the problem as one might fiddle with a loose tooth. Somewhere between November of 2008 and sometime a few years later, that notion became the untold story of Steinbeck and the CIA.

So standing at my own metaphorical doorway on a February morning, I sent Thomas a purposely obfuscated email. There was no mention of spies or the CIA; I simply reminded him that we had spoken a few years back and that I had obtained documents via the Freedom of Information Act (FOIA) about his father that were not public knowledge. The next day I received a response from Thomas's wife and gatekeeper Gail, saying she would be interested in speaking with me. I called her the next day and explained the documentation I had and other supporting evidence for my theory. Throughout the conversation, Gail would interject questions and at no time dismissed me out of hand. At the end of my spiel, I asked Gail rather bluntly if she thought I was a nutter.

"No. There's something to this and you've done your research. You really need to talk to Thom, but why are you not just publishing what you have now?"

I explained to Gail that beside some legal concerns I had about elements of the book, I couldn't just let Thomas find out about this by picking up a newspaper. If you had found out that your father was a spy, wouldn't you want a heads up before it became public knowledge? Going about this without speaking with Thomas simply wasn't the right thing to do. Gail agreed and after another thirty minutes of chatting, she told me that Thomas would be calling me in the next few days. Indeed a couple of days later, I faced the only critic of this work that truly mattered.

The conversation with Thomas started out as rather one-sided. He didn't remember speaking with me in 2008, and I could find no real foothold in easing into the topic at hand. So I launched into my hypothesis by simply explaining my research, the CIA documents, and finished with a letter I received from the FBI stating that they had destroyed elements of John's official file. I paused to take a breath and Thomas, who had been silent through my discourse, asked me if I believed the FBI had actually destroyed his father's file. Never having had much of a verbal filter, I blurted out, "No, Thom. It's horseshit." I half expected Thomas to call me a loon before disconnecting the call. After a short pause, Thomas agreed and said that J. Edgar Hoover had always hated John and he felt there was much more in their [FBI] files than the public had ever seen. There was another hesitation in Thomas's next statement, and I think the words surprised me as much as they did him.

"I always knew my father was up to something," Thomas said.

For the remainder of that conversation, I fleshed out how and why I had gotten to the point of presenting my material to him. Like his wife, Thomas was curious as to why I had bothered contacting him before going to press. I reiterated that I didn't want him to be blindsided by one of his buddies telling him there was a book out accusing his father of being a CIA spy. Thomas's reaction portrayed all the angst and pride a man living "in the shadow of the big man" could muster.

Thomas Steinbeck. Courtesy of the Paladin Group.

"My father has been dead and buried for over forty years. Anything that comes out now won't matter to him. What matters is the truth."

At that, Thomas and I spoke more about the finer points of my research and he rang off with the promise to call me back after fully digesting my message.

I have spoken with Thomas a number of times since that February night. Gail had warned me that Thomas keeps "writer's hours" and every couple of weeks, Thomas would call well after the end of PM newscasts. The aim of his calls was sometimes to tell me an episode he'd remembered from his childhood that might be useful to my work. Other times, the calls were much less calculated and Thomas would talk about his own memoir that he is currently writing. He was always quick to point out that his work was in no way a biography of his father, but what it was like to live with the man. We would speak about Thomas's memories of his childhood and the points where they intersected with my own efforts. A great number of stories Thomas told me had nothing to do with my own work, but I believe were born out of a need for Thomas as he reevaluated his relationship with his father.

Thomas's tales ran the gambit of his formative years. There was the six- or seven-year-old Thomas being called into his father's study to meet someone. To Thomas, that someone looked much like a transient. His hair was unkempt. The stranger was missing a sock and didn't have a first-rate odor about him. The new face was seated upon Thomas's arrival and opened his arms to Thomas, bidding the youth to come closer. Thomas walked over and the man picked him up and placed the lad on his knee. At that John said, "Thom, I'd like you to meet Albert Einstein." In a later conversation, Thomas was a teenage boy and his brother John IV had brought a letter to him. It was something John IV had found on the elder Steinbeck's desk and it sported a State Department letterhead. Thomas, who admittedly was more interested at the time with the mysteries of girls than those of his father, had discounted his brother's find. John IV was always "the nosy little brother," Thomas told me.

At other times, Thomas's stories were darker and difficult to listen to. He told of the day he had received his draft notice for Vietnam. John was in the hospital recovering from back surgery and Thomas went to the hospital to relay the news. After telling his father, Thomas tried to make a deal with John: If the elder Steinbeck would use his influence to keep Thomas from going to Vietnam, Thomas would agree to an additional year in the Army. According to Thomas, he had no dilemma about going to war; he had a problem with going to war with "people he hadn't been properly introduced to." John did not share his son's views on service in Vietnam and wanted his son to visit Arlington National Cemetery to remind him that all those there had given their lives so Thomas could ask such a question. Needless to say, Thomas pulled his tour in Vietnam.

In Thomas and John IV's minds, the elder Steinbeck was pushing his sons into the possibility of dying in a Vietnamese rice paddy when he had never been in the line of fire himself. (The danger John was exposed to as a war correspondent in the Second World War was not considered by his sons, because John never spoke of the inherent hazards of his assignments.) The two brothers could not understand why their father had pushed them into service and at the time, felt it was a cruel thing for their father to do. Thomas sounded discomforted in telling me that story. The probability that John had been risking his life on a regular basis for the CIA meant that many of Thomas's views and opinions of his father had been skewed for the last forty-five years. Not that the possibility made matters "all right" by any means, but Thomas had simply not fully understood the motivations of his father. Then again, what child fully understands the decisions a father makes on behalf of his offspring?

One of those choices John made for his sons was to never tell them of his work with the CIA. One might think that this would have angered Thomas. On the contrary, Thomas is quite proud that his father reached out to the CIA. There were flashes in our conversations that Thomas regretted not putting the pieces together himself, such as on the night Thomas called me to talk about their 1954 trip to Paris. Each Thursday, John would take Thomas and his brother to "get lost in and around Paris." (This story is covered fully in chapter ten.) Thomas now feels that these trips could have been used for John to meet with Agency contacts. After telling me the story, I asked Thomas if he remembered any specific people they might have met on the Thursday treks. Thomas said that he was just beginning to discover girls and he did not recall the names of anyone they might have met. There was a pause after Thomas answered and I knew what he was thinking. I told him that there's no way he could have known about John's covert life. The CIA is, arguably, the best espionage outfit the world has ever seen and ferociously guards their secrets. The Agency's assets and intelligence officers are, by extension, the best spies in the colorful history of espionage. I reminded Thomas of these facts and asked him how a pre-teen boy could possibly have picked up on any additional agenda for the Thursday trips. Thomas lowly said that he knew and dropped the subject.

The details of John's service weren't the most important part of the story to Thomas. In all my discussions with Thomas Steinbeck, talk of CIA redactions to John's FBI file, or if publisher Frederick Praeger had been one of Steinbeck's handlers, was not nearly as important to Thomas as why John would have enlisted with the CIA. To that score, Thomas stayed resolute in the conclusion that John had been involved on a deeper level with the government than just doing Radio Free Europe interviews and providing counseling (in Thomas's lifetime) to presidents Kennedy and Johnson. In talking to Thomas, there seems to have been the same tickle, as I have had, in the back of his mind that John had a covert agenda.

After reviewing the manuscript for this book, Thomas pointed out that I had not addressed the question of John's agenda adequately.[1] I admitted to Thomas that I had shied away from speculating too much about a man's motivations I had never met. Although I did have a feeling that I knew John Steinbeck as well as any man could know another from copious research, I had never been "properly introduced" to John. There is a discussion of my take on John's motivations in chapter two, and Thomas's mindset closely mimics my own.[2]

As stock and as simple as it may sound, the Cold War and John's intense sense of patriotism are what Thomas would attribute to John's covert life. After being too young to enlist in the First World War and turned down for uniformed service during the Second World War, John had a desire to contribute to his country in a way equal to those who had been combat veterans. As the Cold War ramped up in the years after the Second World War, if offered the opportunity to serve covertly for his country, Thomas believes that John would have jumped at the chance. This type of service would have fulfilled everything the elder Steinbeck had wanted—to very literally put his life on the line for the American ideal.

One has to remember that what some might see as clichéd 1950s idealism was John Steinbeck's reality. It is difficult for those who never lived through the Cold War to understand that terms like "mutually assured destruction," "brinksmanship," and "nuclear proliferation" were not academic theories. From the time the Soviets detonated their first nuclear device in August of 1949, to the fall of the Soviet Union in 1991, a misstep in any of the previously mentioned terms would have resulted in the end of civilization. With the introduction of ICBMs, burning in a nuclear fireball could happen in the span of ordering a home delivery pizza. The perception of the threat was never far from the minds of those living through those years.

I recall watching *The Day After* the night before I turned eleven and asking my father if the Russians would target our home in Nashville. Dad, always the realist with me, reminded me that with Fort Campbell to the north and Nashville as the state capitol, the coordinates of Music City were surely programmed into more than a few Russian nukes. What was an eleven-year-old boy going to do for thirty minutes after the missiles started flying? I didn't know, but the prospect scared me witless. And who was the cause of my fright? It was not my father for telling me the truth—it was the Russians.

Thomas told me that his father held much the same view of Soviet-style Communism. John didn't have a problem with American Communists because, according to Thom, John believed they "couldn't get out of bed early enough to attend protests." The real threat was with the true believers in the Soviet Union—the Party thugs who euphemistically "purged" their ranks of dissidents, and unapproved words on a page meant a one-way ticket to a Siberian prison camp. This, coupled with the constant threat of nuclear war, was more than enough reason for John Steinbeck to enlist with the CIA.

The revisionist history of the Cold War would paint the United States military industrial complex as the true villains of the period. To increase profits, the weapon-mongers created the Soviet boogieman threat when in reality, the Soviets would eventually collapsed under the weight of a failed political/economic system. The merits of such a point-of-view are arguable, but should not diminish the heroism of any covert service Steinbeck performed. Any American acting to undermine a threat to one's country through means of subterfuge, rather than violence, shows a special measure of heroism. Certainly, John Steinbeck's many accomplishments are surrounded by invisible laurel wreaths unseen while Steinbeck was living. The American public has the right to know that one of our greatest authors can be counted as one of our greatest heroes as well.

A month or so after my February conversation with Thomas, he called me and our discussions turned toward my own motives. Thomas and I both agreed that this book is bound to cause controversy. It has never been my intention to stir the pot, but to start a conversation. The suggestion that one of America's treasured authors had an association with the CIA will change the way we view the life of John Steinbeck. I hope that a discussion of Steinbeck's life and the role of secrecy in America's intelligence services will emerge from the evidence and conjecture presented within. Ultimately there are far more questions that will be asked in this book than answers given. While this doesn't seem like a proper way to go about writing a book, I am left with little recourse. The only definitive answers to any of the questions I have raised about John Steinbeck's involvement with the CIA lie locked in the recesses of their headquarters.

The CIA has made it abundantly clear that they "can neither confirm nor deny" the existence of any other documents (than those presented in chapter two of this text) in their possession related to a relationship with Steinbeck. My sincere hope is that by publishing this information, public support will cause the veil of secrecy to be lifted somewhat. Even if my central thesis is incorrect, the public will never have a true answer to the Steinbeck question until the CIA releases additional documentation proving otherwise. Unfortunately, I believe those documents will not come out without some pressure from the public.

Another matter that I hope this book brings to the public's attention is the destruction of historical documents by the FBI. One of the primary sources of information for my claims is John Steinbeck's FBI file. The document is readily available to anyone visiting the FBI's "FOIA Vault" website. Once there, anyone can access the FBI files of not only John Steinbeck, but those of a multitude of other entertainers, writers, and politicians. One would think that if a file has been archived in this fashion, the FBI would have preserved corollary documents related to that file as well. As I have come to find out, this is not the case. A number of redacted pages and the text of classified sections of Steinbeck's FBI file were destroyed in 2005.[3] In a digital age, there is no excuse for any governmental agency to destroy any documents, let alone documents relating to a historical figure, such as Steinbeck.

After encapsulating these reasons to Thomas during the same phone call, I felt that he only politely accepted my reasons for writing this book. There still was some unfinished business in my mind and in his. Thinking back on everything I had discovered about John Steinbeck as a person, I realized that my reasons didn't really matter that much. It's easy to view a celebrated author by only citing his or her works and the trigger points in their lives. But that method doesn't fully give one the measure of "who a person is." I felt that Thomas wanted to know how well I really understood the psyche of John Steinbeck. I would shortly find out if I truly had the measure of his father as I offered another explanation to Thomas.

"Enough time has passed; the information can't be used against you or anyone else he cared about." Searching for mutual understanding, I continued, "I think John would have wanted this to come out."

There was an audible sigh from Thomas as he replied, "I've been waiting for you to say that."

Thomas was kind enough to offer a short commentary on this work. I believe it is fitting to end this section of the introduction with the words of the man who knew John Steinbeck as only a son can:

As a Vietnam-era journalist, I am quite aware that there has always been something of a special, though predominately clandestine, relationship between the press corps and national security organizations of various descriptions. However, as his oldest son, I can honestly testify that John Steinbeck played his cards very close to the chest when it came to any relationship—good, bad, or indifferent—that he might have maintained with government agencies of any category, including, of course, the FBI and the Internal Revenue Service. One must accept the standard principle that if one wishes to keep an important secret, the very first rule is not to tell the children, and at the time this particular subject matter was in play, we were indeed children.

Though we often traveled together as a family, I must assume our father, who enjoyed the occasional innocent deception, brought his sons along because we made very believable domestic camouflage. Bickering, troublesome children lend a certain verisimilitude if one is claiming to be traveling with the family for pleasure. Though we journeyed to quite a few exotic and colorful destinations, any number of which were experiencing domestic complications of one kind or another, my father never once even hinted that he might have had focused motives when choosing our destinations. As far as I know, not even my stepmother knew anything about my father's mixed agendas. It now occurs to me that he obviously didn't even trust his third wife, Elaine. She was even worse than we were at keeping secrets, especially if she believed they were really important and would make an impression on the listener. This was particularly important where her sisters were concerned.

My final comment is based on curiosity alone. John Steinbeck was a relatively controversial figure throughout his professional life. This time Steinbeck will make a much softer target; having been dead for over forty years means he can't argue the point, nor do I think he would honor the challenge. As far as he is concerned, the whole question is moot, and not worth his time or effort.

I can't wait to hear what his public is going to say about Mr. Kannard's revelations.

Thomas Steinbeck

Tradecraft

As much as I appreciate the support of Thomas and Gail in this project, I would be remiss if I did not mention one more person integral to this text. In a number of places in this text, I make reference to an unnamed source as "TC." This person is a decorated CIA intelligence officer who served with the Agency from the Eisenhower to Reagan administrations. TC's work was mainly clandestine and being the consummate spy, TC has no wish for his name to be in the public domain. TC is one of the thousands of CIA officers who will never be able to publicly acknowledge their ties with the Agency. Even after retirement from the CIA, the vast majority of intelligence officers sign an agreement that they will never "out" themselves to the public. There is also a very real danger that by printing TC's real name, either he or I could be in violation of the Espionage Act of 1917. At the time of this publication, the Obama administration has prosecuted twice the number of individuals for breaking silence on security matters than have all other presidents combined, since the law's inception. (At the time of publication, the fate of National Security Agency (NSA) whistleblower Edward Snowden is still in limbo.) Most recently, ex-CIA operative John Kiriakou was charged with violating the Espionage Act for disclosing covert operatives' names to journalists.[4]

Even though TC has not been an active intelligence agent since before my voice changed, in respect for TC and the agents who are in similar positions, I will hold TC's identity in confidence until sometime after his death (which, I hope for TC's sake, is many years from now). I understand that there will always be the charge by some naysayers that TC is a figment of my imagination or a glory seeker leading me down the primrose path. I hold ample proof that TC is not only a very real person, but also one whose credibility is not in question.

I would also like to make it clear that TC never discussed specifics about any CIA operations during our conversations. The only names that TC mentioned were of CIA officers who are already known to the public as such. (The William Colbys and E. Howard Hunts of the spook world.) TC also made it a point of being very general in any discussion about CIA operations. There was never a time when TC told me dates, locations, or operation names. TC did intimate that he utilized members of the media as assets during his tenure with the Agency. Any precise knowledge about the names, method of contact, or other specific information of any of TC's assets were never discussed. TC did provide background to my own research and helped me understand some of the nuances of Walter Bedell Smith's response to Steinbeck's 1952 letter, and to overall CIA operations during the 1950s and '60s. TC's assistance was invaluable to this project and I appreciate all the time TC spent with me.

The residents of New York's East 72nd Street awoke on the morning of January 28, 1952, to a staccato ticking sound emanating from the windowpanes of their bedrooms. No two residents of East 72nd Street who were roused by the auditory annoyance had come to the same initial solution of the problematic tick-tick . . . tick-tick. A cross father awoke thinking the ticking sound was a suitor throwing pebbles against his teenage daughter's window. Seeing that it was daylight, the father dismissed the notion and went back to sleep. A college student three doors down from the protective father heard the ticking and concluded his hangover had amplified the usually quiet movements within his alarm clock. He, too, decided that going back to sleep was the best practice, given his current state.

Across the street from the college student lived a writer who would have easily sympathized with the young man's plight. Too many mornings the writer got out of bed feeling as if his tongue had gotten cold during the night and pulled on a wool sweater for warmth. Luckily this morning the writer was free of a fashionably dressed tongue or a brigade of Kaiser-helmeted microbes using the lining of his skull as a trampoline. He had decided there simply was too much to do today to lay on this week's cocktail of choice, Hawaiian Punch and vodka.

As fate would have it, the writer was the only one on 72nd Street to suss out the ticking sound that had confounded his neighbors. Tiny pellets of ice were being driven into the windowpanes from a twenty-five-mile-an-hour northerly wind. As the writer pulled back his curtains to confirm his hypothesis, he was glad to see that the falling snowflakes had the courtesy to move out of the way of their more dense brothers in precipitation. Nature following its own version of Emily Post had slightly reaffirmed the writer's faith in the universe. The true test of cosmic civility would rest on if the icebox held any more eggs.

Bounding down the stairwell, the single-purposed writer almost didn't notice his wife sitting in the living room. Before he had a chance to engage his words, his third wife Elaine spoke.

"Good morning, Dear. I got up early to go to the bodega for some eggs."

He crossed the room and kissed his wife's forehead before speaking, "You do love me."

"With the weather this morning, you're safe to say that I do."

After cupping his hand on her shoulder, he headed toward the kitchen. Reaching into the icebox, he removed a single egg. Carefully cracking the shell down the egg's centerline, the writer began a seesaw motion to separate the yolk from the white. After a dozen or so transfers from shell-half to shell-half, he opened the trashcan and chucked out the yolk. Unceremoniously he poured the whites into the percolator and then crunched up the shell, letting the white particulates fall into the pot as well. Water and coffee were placed in their appropriate places within the percolator.

While waiting for the egg-enriched coffee to brew, the writer noticed the new *Life Magazine* on the counter. The cover held the picture of a beautiful raven-haired Phyllis Newell who couldn't make up her mind for a career path. Model? Pianist? Artist? Maybe she'd just get married. The writer didn't care to find out what her choice was and flipped through the pages. There was little in the way of substance in *Life Magazine*, but the pictures were nice to look at while the percolator performed its alchemy.

The Korean War had been going on for a year and a half and *Life* had managed to avoid the topic entirely. The conflict had ground to a stalemate the summer before, and there was little hope that would change in the near future. It was an election year and *Life* had added a healthy dose of advice for the Republicans in their editorials.

"They'll need all the help they can get," mumbled the writer as he read on.

There was talk of Dwight Eisenhower running for president in the fall. The country wasn't sure if Ike was a Democrat or Republican until a few weeks before. He had pulled off the D-Day invasion at Normandy, and by all accounts was a hell of a guy. Wasn't that enough for a man to be a good president, no matter which party he belonged to? The writer didn't think so. Any man who only read cowboy novels couldn't hold much promise for the country's future. The Democratic ticket would do him just fine, thank you.

The percolator's sputtering had come to the point where the writer knew he could extract a measure of its contents. He had learned to tip the pot slowly as he poured so the chunks of eggshells wouldn't end up in his mug. Before taking a sip, the writer lit his first cigarette of the day and inhaled the nicotine and caffeine nearly simultaneously. The perfection of the moment was shattered by the business of marriage.

"I've already called the travel agency this morning. They're willing to work with us on rerouting the first leg of the trip. The revolt in Egypt has scared a number of their customers from going over there."

"Hmmm . . . half of Cairo burning does shake out the faint of heart. Let's talk about any itinerary changes next week. I need to check on something and think about the . . . logistics of the trip."

"Just let me know. *Whither thou goest, I will go!*"

The couple chatted about their impending trip over the breakfast table and after their morning routines were played out, the writer snuck away to his desk where he pulled a sheet of stationary from a top drawer and found a suitable writing instrument to capture his thoughts. He abhorred typing and shunned the practice whenever possible. The recipients of his letters would have rather the writer taken up the habit. The cursive script he employed was generally viewed as an exercise in decryption rather than correspondence.

The stationery's heading—"John Steinbeck * Office: 206 East 72nd Street * New York 21, N.Y."—lay awaiting his words. After a moment's consideration, the writer filled the page with block script, to avoid any confusion his cursive penmanship might have caused as to his intent. He then took out an envelope, neatly filled in the return address, and then wrote, "Director of Central Intelligence, Walter Bedell Smith; Central Intelligence Agency; 2430 East Street NW, Washington DC."[1]

For the last five years, I've known that many things about John Steinbeck's life simply did not add up. In reading the major biographies of the Nobel Prize–winning author, there were too many times that there was no explanation for his actions or the actions of those around him. Why did the House Committee for Un-American Activities (HUAC) never call Steinbeck to the stand? Why did John start a TV production company in 1947 when all those around him begged him not to? Why did Steinbeck push his publisher and literary agent so hard to publish *The Short Reign of Pippin IV: A Fabrication*, but seemingly gave up on his rewrite of Sir Thomas Malory's *Le Morte d'Arthur*? What exactly did John do during the early days of the Second World War and why was he denied a Silver Star on false pretences? Why did the CIA redact portions of Steinbeck's FBI file and why did the spy agency request information about John? Many of these questions have never fully been explored, simply because there is not enough hard evidence for the academic community to make comment. Tenured professors and Ph.D. candidates are not known for "going out on a limb." I, on the other hand, have no compunction about casting theories into the fray. I am fortunate enough to answer only to myself, my wife, and to my readers for the content I publish.

Five years ago, I turned hunting down these questions about Steinbeck into a hobby. Where some might take a two-day getaway trip to the beach or mountains, I would go to archives. Stanford University, the New York Public Library, and the National Steinbeck Center's musty rooms of special collections replaced sand and sun for me. There is something of a thrill in actually holding a letter penned by the great author. It is as if the ink might magically transfer a bit of Steinbeck's talent through the protective acid-free plastic coverings into my own fingertips. On each trip, my romantic notions were quickly erased as I furiously scribbled notes and strained to decipher John's horrid handwriting. The only magic that could be found in the letters and journals was the sorcery of perseverance.

During the trips and hours spent combing through any available resources I had, there was no discernible pattern to answer my questions about Steinbeck's life. In mid-2011, I decided to go back and review Steinbeck's FBI file, which can be easily accessed at the Bureau's "Vault" website.[1] Steinbeck's file was released under the Freedom of Information Act (FOIA) during the early 1980s. I had reviewed the FBI's findings on Steinbeck half a dozen times for the file's facts. But this time, I decided to examine all the information in Steinbeck's FBI file that had nothing to do with Steinbeck. Who were the people generating the reports on Steinbeck? Where was the information about Steinbeck coming from? What could the bureaucratic notations on the FBI file tell me about the FBI's interest in John? To understand these aspects of John's FBI file, I first had to unlock the language of documents released under the FOIA.

Passed into law in 1966, the FOIA "provides that any person has a right, enforceable in court, to obtain access to federal Agency records, except to the extent that such records (or portions of them) are protected from public disclosure by one of nine exemptions or by one of three special law enforcement record exclusions."[2] The preceding statement taken from the Department of Justice would make it seem that government documents are as easy to obtain as checking out a book from a local library. Nothing could be farther from the truth. In order to make an FOIA request, one must know exactly what one is looking for, and which governmental Agency has the information. There is no FOIA center that forwards requests to the correct Agency or assists the public in making requests. Furthermore, each Agency sets up their own rules for accepting and processing FOIA requests. In some cases, a specific document number must be given in the FOIA request. But how does one know what document number to request on a specific topic in these cases? Why, by filing an FOIA request for documents on that topic, of course! The circular bureaucratic logic is enough to make one's head spin.

Once a request is received by a government Agency, that Agency has to acknowledge they have received the request within forty-five days. However, there is no statutory time period in which an Agency must fulfill a FOIA request. Theoretically, a request could languish literally for years after someone has been notified that the request is being processed. One of the reasons why there is no timetable forcing the government to fulfill a request is that different agencies' operations that are mentioned in the respondent documents must be reviewed for exclusions. For example, let's say the FBI holds a file on Mr. Allen. Mr. Allen has previously been under investigation by the Bureau of Alcohol, Tobacco, Firearms, and Explosives (BATF). Since the FBI file mentions BATF operations, any pertinent sections of Allen's file must be cleared by the BATF before being released under the FOIA.

As different agencies review files for release, there are those pesky exceptions to the FOIA statute. Government agencies can withhold all or some of a document based on the following:

Exemption (b1) - National security information.
Exemption (b2) - Internal personnel rules and practices of an Agency.
Exemption (b3) - Information exempt under other laws.
Exemption (b4) - Confidential business information.

Exemption (b5) - Inter or intra Agency communication that is subject to deliberative process, litigation, and other privileges.

Exemption (b6) - Personal privacy.

Exemption (b7) - Law enforcement records.

Exemption (b8) - Financial institutions.

Exemption (b9) - Geological information.[3]

If a document has a redacted portion, the exception code (b1, b2, etc.) is usually listed beside the hidden text. While redacted text is infuriating to researchers, there are instances when the exclusion is necessary for matters of national security. The recipe for the carbon polymers that make up the skin of the B-2 stealth bomber would be a reasonable example of a b1 exemption.

Thankfully, there is a slight boon to the exemption process. If other agencies have reviewed a document and made exclusions, many times that Agency will be listed as making the exclusion. One also has the slight advantage of knowing a ballpark reason the information was excluded. Then again, some FOIA requests are denied in the spirit of b1 exclusions, but offer no real reasonable explanation at all.

The CIA has continually pushed the limit of the b1 exclusion since the early 1970s. After *The Los Angeles Times* broke the 1975 *Glomar Explorer* story, the Agency was flooded with FOIA requests about the mission. In March of 1968, a Russian Golf II ballistic missile submarine designated K-129 experienced distress and sank 1,560 nautical miles northwest of Hawaii. The CIA embarked on an ambitious plan to recover the submarine without the Soviets detecting a salvage mission. The Hughes Corporation was contracted to build a ship specifically designed for raising the K-129 to the surface. The salvage ship was christened the *Glomar Explorer* and the hope was to recover missiles, propulsion systems, codebooks, or any other salvageable intelligence left on the vessel. Since the operation was still technically ongoing, these requests were denied by responding: "The Agency can neither confirm nor deny the existence of your requested records." Acting on the *Los Angeles Times'* story, the American Civil Liberties Union (ACLU) sued the Department of Defense (DoD) and the CIA for violations of the FOIA. After a number of appeals, the ACLU eventually lost the case. The courts upheld that the "neither confirm nor deny" line was reasonable given that even acknowledging the existence of the *Glomar Explorer* would damage national security. The ruling coined the terms "Glomar exemption" and "Glomarization" to be synonymous with that type of doublespeak.

The courts often err on the side of secrecy in our post-September 11th world. In 2011, another lawsuit was filed against the CIA to make public two volumes of the CIA's *Official History of the Bay of Pigs*. George Washington

A Soviet Golf II class submarine, taken October 1, 1985. Image courtesy of the US Navy.

University's National Security Archives took up the mantle to have the chronicle of the botched 1961 invasion of Cuba released. In this case, the CIA argued that this text was a draft and an incomplete analysis of the invasion. Federal judge Gladys Kessler ruled in favor of the CIA, keeping the volume secret, citing that the history

> . . . would have a chilling effect on current CIA historians who might be reluctant to try out "innovative, unorthodox or unpopular interpretations in a draft manuscript" if they thought it would be made public.[4]

Basically the CIA argued that the American public is not bright enough to interpret the volume—and won.

The genuinely intriguing tale of previously classified documents is the text scratched out with a black marker hiding the portions we *cannot* read. The truly "juicy bits" of information are to be found in the redacted sections of any document. Applying what I'd found out about the ins and outs of the FOIA process, I took a fresh look at the redacted sections of Steinbeck's FBI file. In the 120-page file, there are twenty paragraphs and two separate pages that have been redacted under exclusion b1 (national security issues). The FOIA describes exemption b1 as it:

> Allows for the withholding of national security information concerning the national defense or foreign policy that has been properly classified in accordance with the substantive and procedural requirements of the current national security classification executive order.[5]

There's an easy explanation for using John Steinbeck and national security in the same sentence. It is common knowledge that from 1940–1942, John worked for the Office of War Information (OWI) and other government agencies. While it is difficult to believe, there are still documents from the Second World War that are classified.

To give some perspective on how long it takes to declassify some information, in 2011, the CIA finally made public the recipe for invisible ink used during the First World War. The big secret the 1917 documents held was that one can use lemon juice to create invisible writing.[6] The earth-shattering technology has been available to any third grader who has read an Encyclopedia Brown story, but the CIA had to be compelled by a lawsuit to declassify the "sensitive" material.[7]

In another instance, the FBI's *History of the SIS*, published by the Bureau in 1946, deals with the FBI's counterintelligence efforts in Latin America during the Second World War. The text was released in 2004, and the redacted portions of the FBI's five-volume set are appointed to be declassified in 2029.[8]

Looking back on the timeline of the redacted sections of the FBI file, I was more than a little dismayed that the sections redacted under b1 did not seem to match up with the period of 1940–1942. The reports generated from the FBI generally follow in chronological order. Using the file's timeline as a benchmark, none of the redactions were from the time John was in the OWI. The b1 redactions in Steinbeck's file were from 1944 onward. More curious still was that five of those b1 exemptions, including the two full pages of redacted text, were listed as "per CIA." All that tells us is that the CIA was interested in John Steinbeck. Given that there have always been questions as to Steinbeck's politics during the 1930s and '40s, one could see why the CIA might have reviewed Steinbeck's FBI file before its public release.

Following that logic, if politics was the reason for the redactions, there must be other people of the same time period whose FBI files had CIA redactions. I set to work combing through other FBI files of those in the entertainment industry from 1940–1970 to find out if CIA redactions were a

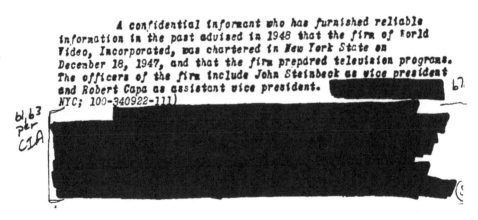

Example of a CIA b1 and b3 redaction in Steinbeck's FBI file.

common practice. The files of Desi Arnaz, Pearl S. Buck, Walt Disney, Ernest Hemingway, Lillian Hellman, Bettie Page, and John Updike were all examined. A number of these files contained b1 exceptions, which is not surprising. Desi Arnaz had ties with the Cuban community, which would have interested the CIA in the early 1960s. Hemingway ran a Cuban spy network in 1942 for the FBI. Walt Disney had done work for the Office of Inter-American Affairs (OIAA) during the Second World War. Lilly Hellman and Pearl S. Buck were blacklisted as Communists in the 1950s. Influential novelist and journalist John Updike could have registered a blip on the CIA's radar. And Bettie Page was just plain scandalous. All of these people were likely candidates for CIA attention via the FBI. Redactions were found in these files from the State Department, Army, Navy, and even Congress, but none of these files contained a single overt redaction from the CIA.[9]

I then set out to find other FBI files from 1940–1970 that did have CIA redactions. Surely there had to be CIA redactions in Albert Einstein's file. The man who arguably triggered the Manhattan Project via a letter to President Roosevelt in 1939, and who in 1952 had been asked to become Israel's president, would have some passing interest to the CIA. Einstein's file also must have bounced around Washington for a few months before it was released. There are notations for redactions or clearance of information from the Department of Energy, Army, Navy, Air Force, Congress, and the State Department. However, in over 1,500 pages of the FBI's file on Einstein, the CIA made only three redactions. One was a full-page redaction[10] and the other two totaled a few sentences.[11] In context, the two smaller redactions blot out information about the International Relief Association, of which Einstein was a member.

The comparison of redactions only proves that Steinbeck's FBI file held more information the CIA wanted redacted than Einstein's, or the other subjects', files. The lack of redactions in these subjects' files from the CIA can mean one of two things. First, these persons' FBI files contained no information that warranted the CIA censors to examine their files. The second possibility is that Steinbeck's activities were more closely connected to the CIA than the other subjects. Further muddying the waters, the two conditions are not mutually exclusive.

Another unnerving aspect of Steinbeck's FBI file is found in the reference slips inserted between the main documents. In FBI files, these reference pages act as a bibliography for the main documentation. Instead of pointing to books, FBI reference slips list other documents that make up the main document. Thankfully the FBI has a file number system that makes the sea of numbers make some sense. Each file number has a prefix that acts as an offense code for that particular file.[12] For example, file number 9–4583 listed in Steinbeck's file is related to extortion. This fits because Steinbeck had notified the FBI about a plot to discredit him by means of force. In a letter to Carlton Sheffield, John speaks of an insurance policy he has just taken out to stymie any would-be extortionists. John says that he "placed certain information in the hands of J. Edgar Hoover" that should any ill come of him, the FBI would know where to begin their investigations.[13]

The difficulty in utilizing the reference slips to link a file type to a specific event or time period in Steinbeck's life, is that many of the documents in his FBI file sometimes cover decades of the author's life. What is disconcerting is the range and type of offense codes that make up the bibliography of Steinbeck's file.

The majority of offense codes in Steinbeck's file fall under Domestic Security, which seems to be a catch-all category. The following list is of other offense codes and the number of times unique files with that offense code are seen in Steinbeck's file:

Treason: 24
Espionage: 17
Miscellaneous-Nonsubversive: 14
Foreign Counterintelligence: 4
Foreign Miscellaneous: 4
War Labor Dispute Act: 4
Administrative Matters and Applications: 2
Extortion: 2
Loyalty of Government Employees: 2
Passport and Visa Matters: 2
Special Inquiry, State Department, Voice of America: 2
Hatch Act: 1
Interstate Transportation of Stolen Property: 1
Research Matters: 1

The "offense code" isn't always, but can be, what one may think of as a crime, and a number of the topics listed make perfect sense as to why they would be included in John's FBI file—i.e., Passport and Visa Matters, Loyalty of Government Employees, etc. The addition of Foreign Counterintelligence, Espionage, and Treason are *not* things one would expect to find in John Steinbeck's file. Given that Espionage and Treason are the top two frequent offense codes found on the reference slips, we can assume one of two things: either John Steinbeck was investigated for being a foreign spy, or events in Steinbeck's life related to cases of espionage and treason. When one adds in the redactions in Steinbeck's FBI file from the CIA, one begins to see a pattern. There was only one way to fit the puzzle together.

In the first week of January 2012, I sent off an FOIA request to the CIA. The request included information on everything they might hold on Steinbeck. At that point, I was not quite sure what I would get back, if anything. Over the course of the next few weeks, I received a letter from the CIA's FOIA coordinator advising me that my request had been received and the Agency was reviewing the request. Then in late April, the CIA informed me that information related to my request would be granted, but that it could take an indefinite amount of time to gather the records. The CIA's response sounded like the times during my single years I asked a girl out, only to be rebuffed with the "I'm washing my hair that night" line.

There was still hope that I could find out what I had secretly thought. Could John Steinbeck have been an interest to the CIA because he had worked for them? The thought had crossed my mind after reexamining Steinbeck's FBI file, but the jump in

Example of a reference or search slip in Steinbeck's FBI file.

logic was one that I really didn't like to consider. It was not that working for the CIA would diminish Steinbeck, or his works, in my eyes. To be quite honest, I was afraid I had jumped off the conspiracy theorists' ledge into the abyss of drawing unfounded connections on index cards, linked with different colored yarn. After all, it was quite absurd to think of John Steinbeck skulking around alleyways in a trench coat, passing off secret documents.

But that absurd thought became a bizarre reality when I received this letter from the CIA. Enclosed with that letter were two other pieces of paper. They read:

August 3, 2012
Mr. Brian Kannard
Reference: F-2012-00585

Dear Mr. Kannard:

This is a final response to your 9 and 30 January 2012 Freedom of Information Act (FOIA) requests pertaining to John Ernest (sic) Steinbeck. We processed your request in accordance with the FOIA, 5 U.S.C. § 552, as amended, and the CIA Information Act, 50 U.S.C. § 431, as amended. Our processing included a search for records as described in our 13 April 2012 acceptance letter.

We completed a thorough search for records responsive to your request and located one document, consisting of three pages, which we can release in segregable form with deletions made on the basis of FOIA exemption (b)(3). The document is enclosed.

With respect to records that would reveal a classified connection between the CIA and your subject, in accordance with section 3.6(a) of Executive Order 13526, the CIA can neither confirm nor deny the existence or nonexistence of records responsive to your request. The fact of the existence or nonexistence of requested records is currently and properly classified and relates to intelligence sources and methods information that is protected from disclosure by section 6 of the CIA Act of 1949, as amended, and section 102A(i)(l) of the National Security Act of 1947, as amended. Therefore, this portion of your request is denied pursuant to FOIA exemptions (b)(1) and (b)(3). I have enclosed an Explanation of Exemptions for your reference and retention.

Although our searches were thorough and diligent, and it is highly unlikely that repeating those searches would change the result, you nevertheless have the legal right to appeal the above decisions. As the CIA Information and Privacy Coordinator, I am the CIA official responsible for these determinations. You have the right to appeal this response to the Agency Release Panel, in my care, within 45 days from the date of this letter. Please include the basis of your appeal. In accordance with our regulation, as a matter of administrative discretion, the Agency has waived the fees for this request.

Sincerely, Michele Meeks
Information and Privacy Coordinator

Central Intelligence Agency

Washington, D.C. 20505

August 3, 2012

Mr. Brian Kannard

██████████████████

Reference: F-2012-00585

Dear Mr. Kannard:

This is a final response to your 9 and 30 January 2012 Freedom of Information Act (FOIA) requests pertaining to John Ernest Steinbeck. We processed your request in accordance with the FOIA, 5 U.S.C. § 552, as amended, and the CIA Information Act, 50 U.S.C. § 431, as amended. Our processing included a search for records as described in our 13 April 2012 acceptance letter.

We completed a thorough search for records responsive to your request and located one document, consisting of three pages, which we can release in segregable form with deletions made on the basis of FOIA exemption (b)(3). The document is enclosed.

With respect to records that would reveal a classified connection between the CIA and your subject, in accordance with section 3.6(a) of Executive Order 13526, the CIA can neither confirm nor deny the existence or nonexistence of records responsive to your request. The fact of the existence or nonexistence of requested records is currently and properly classified and relates to intelligence sources and methods information that is protected from disclosure by section 6 of the CIA Act of 1949, as amended, and section 102A(i)(l) of the National Security Act of 1947, as amended. Therefore, this portion of your request is denied pursuant to FOIA exemptions (b)(1) and (b)(3). I have enclosed an Explanation of Exemptions for your reference and retention.

Although our searches were thorough and diligent, and it is highly unlikely that repeating those searches would change the result, you nevertheless have the legal right to appeal the above decisions. As the CIA Information and Privacy Coordinator, I am the CIA official responsible for these determinations. You have the right to appeal this response to the Agency Release Panel, in my care, within 45 days from the date of this letter. Please include the basis of your appeal. In accordance with our regulation, as a matter of administrative discretion, the Agency has waived the fees for this request.

Sincerely,

Michele Meeks
Information and Privacy Coordinator

Enclosures

After reading Ms. Meeks' letter, I assumed that two pages of documents wouldn't hold anything of real value. I couldn't have been more mistaken as I read the next two sheets of paper.

Jan 28, 1952

Dear General Smith:

Toward the end of February I am going to the Mediterranean area and afterwards to all of the countries of Europe not out of bounds. I am commissioned by *Collier's Magazine* to do a series of articles—subjects and areas to be chosen by myself. I shall move slowly going only where interest draws. The trip will take six to eight months.

If during this period I can be of any service whatever to yourself or to the Agency you direct, I shall be only too glad.

I saw Herbert Bayard Swope recently and he told me that your health had improved. I hope this is so.

Also I wear the "Lou for 52" button concealed under the lapel as that shy candidate suggests.

Again—I shall be pleased to be of service. The pace and method of my junket together with my intention of talking with great numbers of people of all classes may offer peculiar advantages.

Yours sincerely,

John Steinbeck

Home REgent 7-5515

Office REgent 7-3442

John Steinbeck   •   Office: 206 East 72nd Street   •   New York 21, N.Y.

Jan 28, 1952

Dear General Smith:

Toward the end of February I am going
To the Mediterranian area and afterwards To all of the countries
of Erope not out of bounds. I am comissioned by Colliers
magazine to do a series of articles — subjects and areas To
be chosen by myself. I shall move slowly going only
where interest draws. The trip will take six To eight months.

If during this period I can be of any service
whatever To yourself or to the agency you direct, I shall
be only Too glad.

I saw Herbert Bayard Swope recently and
he told me that your health had improved. I hope
This is so.

Also I wear the "Ike for 52" button conceaaled
under the lapel as that shy candidate suggests.

Again — I shall be pleased To be of
service. The pace and method of my junket
To gether with my intention of talking with great
numbors of people of all classes may offer peculiar
advantages

Yours sincerely

John Steinbech

6 February 1952
Mr. John Steinbeck
206 East 72nd Street
New York 21, New York

Dear Mr. Steinbeck:

I greatly appreciate the offer of assistance made in your note of January 28th.

You can, indeed, be of help to us by keeping your eyes and ears open on any political developments in the areas through which you travel, and, in addition, on any other matters which seem to you of significance, particularly those which might be overlooked in routine reports.

It would be helpful, too, if you could come down to Washington for a talk with us before you leave. We might then discuss any special matters on which you may feel that you can assist us.

Since I am certain that you will have some very interesting things to say, I trust, also, that you will be able to reserve some time for us on your return.

Sincerely,
Walter B. Smith
Director

O/DCI:REL:leb
Rewritten: LEBecker:mlk
Distribution:
Orig – Addressee
2 – DCI (Reading Official) ["w/Basic" has been handwritten beside this line and scratched out]
1 – DD/P [a check mark and w/Basic handwritten in]
1 – Admin [This has been scratched out] handwritten is "w/ Basic"

ᴸᴿ 2-5603

(b)(3)

6 February 1952

Mr. John Steinbeck
206 East 72nd Street
New York 21, New York

Dear Mr. Steinbeck:

I greatly appreciate the offer of assistance made in your
note of January 28th.

You can, indeed, be of help to us by keeping your eyes
and ears open on any political developments in the areas through
which you travel, and, in addition, on any other matters which
seem to you of significance, particularly those which might be
overlooked in routine reports.

It would be helpful, too, if you could come down to
Washington for a talk with us before you leave. We might then
discuss any special matters on which you may feel that you can
assist us.

Since I am certain that you will have some very interesting
things to say, I trust, also, that you will be able to reserve
some time for us on your return.

Sincerely,

Bedell Smith

Walter B. Smith
Director

O/DCI:REL:leb
Rewritten: LEBecker:mlk
Distribution:
    Orig – Addressee
    2 – DCI (Reading
         Official)
    1 – DD/P ✓ w/Basic
    1 – Admin. Files

APPROVED FOR
RELEASE DATE:
18-Jul-2012

The offer Steinbeck makes to the CIA, and the CIA's response, are nothing short of astounding. On one hand, the Agency is "neither confirming or denying" that Steinbeck had a connection with the CIA, and on the other, I had just been sent two letters that all but confirm John worked with the Agency. I can only guess as to why the letters from Steinbeck and Smith were declassified. The material in both letters held no specific information about CIA operations or covert operatives. Given whatever guidelines the CIA has for FOIA requests, these letters could have just squeaked past the CIA censorship rules. Thank you, Ms. Meeks.

The original FOIA request had been no more than a shot in the dark for information on Steinbeck. I had actually expected that I would receive a polite letter telling me that I should shine up my tin foil hat because the Agency's interest in Steinbeck was circumstantial. Instead I was holding a CIA authenticated, previously unknown, letter by John Steinbeck asking to become a spy. To be quite honest, for the first few moments after reading the letters, there was almost that feeling of giddy dread that comes when preparing for a first date. I'd been asked to the prom, so to speak, and the first thing one does after being asked out is to call their best friend. So I promptly fumbled with my cell phone and jabbed the autodial for my wife, Laura.

According to her, the only thing I could get out initially was, "I got it. I got it . . . " She had no idea what I was ranting about and hoped I had not caught the West Nile Virus. After a few stern admonishments that I was making no sense, I was able to convey the news. All of the questions I'd been dancing around for years finally came into sharp focus for both of us. God love my wife because she's endured me talking about Steinbeck for years and has steadily spurred on my efforts. I recall Laura letting out a girly squeal after I was able to speak, coherently followed by a stream of, "I knew you were right all along." After our conversation, the only thought I was left with was that this changed everything we thought we knew about Steinbeck.

Steinbeck's life and works, from at least 1952 onward, now have to be viewed in a different light. The rest of this text will examine a number of situations in which Steinbeck's relationship with the CIA could bring about a totally different interpretation of his actions and writings. Before those questions are asked, an examination of the transaction between the CIA and John Steinbeck in 1952 is in order. To understand exactly what John was offering and, more importantly, what the CIA expected out of Steinbeck, the context of the letters must be examined.

When a civilian offers information to the CIA, that person is interviewed by an intelligence officer. The interviewing officer evaluates the civilian, not only as a onetime source of information, but their suitability as a long-term informant, known in Agency speak as an asset. If the volunteer is a suitable candidate, they will be turned over to the clandestine services for grooming as a field asset.[14] One might think that calling up the CIA with the offer to be an intelligence asset is something straight from an airport paperback. In the 1950s, the use of volunteers was not only an accepted practice by the CIA, but the service of civilians was something the Agency actively looked for. Before Walter Bedell Smith's restructuring of the CIA, the Agency was well behind the proverbial eight-ball on intelligence gathering.

In the early 1950s, Congress had never allocated enough funds to the Agency to achieve a mission of properly obtaining all of America's intelligence. Civilians represented a cost-effective and relatively low-risk investment of CIA resources. Most of the civilian operatives employed by the CIA volunteered out of a sense of patriotic duty and required no payment for their services. The Agency also had the advantage of picking from the nine percent of Americans who had served in uniform during the Second World War.[15] Specialized skill sets taught in military service could be highly valuable in a potential asset.

The Agency also prized assets who had technical, scientific, journalistic, or academic backgrounds. Persons in these job classifications often had traveled outside of the country and were likely to have contacts with foreign colleagues. Those with technical and scientific backgrounds could also provide a glimpse into a country or foreign business' level of technology. In an age where technologies we now take for granted were emerging, insight on the advancements of our friends and enemies greatly interested the CIA. Academics were sought out for similar reasons, if they were involved with hard sciences or engineering. Humanities-related academics were also in demand. Classroom discussions often lead to political talk and a professor could take the pulse of youthful "rabble-rousers." Journalists are naturally inquisitive and normally do not raise suspicion when asking situationally unusual questions.

Would the CIA have actually used Steinbeck as an asset? According to TC, the former CIA intelligence officer I consulted during my research, it would not have surprised him. While TC did not have direct knowledge of Steinbeck working for the Agency, he did admit that the use of civilian assets in the 1950s was business as usual for the CIA. Furthermore, assets in the book publishing and journalism fields were commonplace in the ranks of civilian assets. "We [the CIA] had a large number of reporters working for us and most of them volunteered," said TC.[16] The ranks of those wishing to do a good turn for Uncle Sam were common enough by the mid-1950s that the Agency referred to volunteers as "walk-ins." The exact number of citizen spies utilized during the 1950s and '60s will likely never be known outside those with security clearances. The Agency maintains a policy of not disclosing specifics of covert operations, methods, or personnel utilization.[17] As frustrating as the CIA's stance on disclosure is, in some cases, what we might consider ancient history can have forward-echoing consequences to present-day operations. For example, let's say next week the Agency releases a document that names the recently deceased Saeed as an asset used during the CIA's 1950s operations to topple the Iranian government. In light of present political tensions between Iran and the United States, it is likely that the SAVAK (Iran's Organization of Intelligence and National Security and analogous to the CIA) would question any living family and friends of Saeed. The interrogations, which would probably not be a tea and crumpets chat, may lead the SAVAK to discover that Saeed had recruited others who are still actively providing the United States with intelligence. At best, two assets can no longer provide information to the CIA. At worst, both assets are found guilty of espionage and are executed for their crimes against the state.

Even as prevalent as "walk-ins" were, the CIA did not sit idly by and wait for volunteers to gather intelligence. The Agency actively recruited assets during the 1950s. If a member of the private sector was brought to the attention of the Agency as being useful, an intelligence officer would approach the potential asset. The assignment could be for a onetime event, or as an ongoing relationship with the Agency. Suppose, for example, that an intelligence officer catches wind that next month there will be an international aerospace engineering conference in Copenhagen. The CIA might be interested in loose chatter of developments in the field or in a specific foreign company's current projects. That officer would draw up a list of candidates who could pass information along to the Agency about predetermined topics. The asset would then report on the requested information or any other topics the asset felt would be salient to his handler. This might be the only time the Agency would use this particular asset. With the volume of information being gathered by the untold number of assets, like our helpful aerospace engineer, analysts would generate an aggregate picture of any topic the CIA might be interested.

No matter into what pigeonhole the Agency placed an asset, a majority of the assets used by the CIA in the 1950s were passive intelligence gatherers in foreign countries. The asset would simply report on things they saw or overheard from the local populace. Information like this may sound trivial, but every bit of information gathered by CIA assets can be put together to form an overall picture of a given geographic area. The process works something like this. Let's say that Larry is a CIA asset and he's on a business trip to Portugal. After a day's work, Larry visits the local pub where he strikes up a conversation with a mid-level manager of a tungsten mine. Larry's newfound friend is drinking the night away because there's been an accident in one of the tunnels. The mine's output will decrease by 15 percent over the next six months, and Larry's drinking buddy won't be getting his Christmas bonus. The company has paid off the local newspaper to keep the accident on the QT so as not to shake the customers' confidence in the mine's operation. Larry dutifully reports this seemingly trivial bauble of information to his case officer. As it happens, the Russians purchase a great deal of tungsten from this mine to forge rocket engine nozzles. It looks like the Russians won't be producing as many rockets in the next six months as CIA analysts had previously estimated.

Steinbeck volunteered for the same type of intelligence gathering as our mythical Larry. It would be incorrect to think of John Steinbeck as a "spy" at this point. The distinction between spy and asset is necessary to make in understanding what John would initially be doing for the Agency. It would be fair to say that later evidence in this text will show that Steinbeck would cross the line from an informant to achieving active covert intelligence goals. While this might be an exercise in semantics, for the fledgling CIA of the 1950s and '60s, Steinbeck could be considered a "spy." In the context of modern-day espionage, a "spy" is a professional operative who runs intelligence networks or performs covert paramilitary actions. Spies will embed themselves within a location or specific group with the goal of recruiting assets. The spy/asset relationship is necessary from the standpoint of any intelligence agency. If an asset smuggles the top-secret plans for a new aircraft design out of a factory and gets caught, a "plausible deniability" exists. The spy would then be extracted from the post and the politicians have an easy way to talk themselves out of an international incident.

"You say your engineer smuggled aircraft plans out of your facility? That's too bad. He said that he was selling the plans to us? That's news to us. Do you have any proof? You don't. Gee whiz, maybe it was the Canadians."

The above scenario is an over simplification of the espionage world, but serves to give the basics of how international intelligence games are played. In a majority of situations, assets are in immediate danger of being pinched for collecting intelligence, not spies. That is not to say that being a covert operative is risk free. The process of developing an asset and operating on foreign soil leaves a spy exposed to an array of dangers. The 103 stars chiseled into the marble wall at the CIA's headquarters in Langley, Virginia, are a grim testament to that fact.[18] Each star represents a nameless intelligence officer who has lost his or her life in service to the citizens of this country. The stars represent the real cost of intelligence work and not the popular fiction representation of spies. There is very little parachuting into hidden island bases to plant explosive charges in the real world. Intelligence operations are slow, delicate affairs in which the spy has no desire to bring attention to themselves

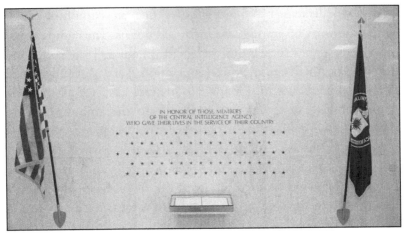

The Memorial Wall at the CIA's Headquarters in Langley, Virginia.
Photo from the CIA.

or the Agency's goals. In reality, stakeouts are infinitely more common than explosions, but the dangers are ever present and the consequences of missteps are very genuine.

There would be dangers for Steinbeck working with the CIA as well. There was always the chance that John could have been seen by a foreign intelligence officer while speaking with his CIA case officer. If the CIA agent was known to a rival intelligence Agency, John's cover could be blown.

During the 1950s, there was still something of a gentleman's code among intelligence operatives, and it is unlikely a blown cover would have resulted in physical danger for the author.[19] But there are worse threats than bodily harm for a public figure like Steinbeck. Outing John as a CIA operative would have been a public relations nightmare for the Agency and had a lasting effect on Steinbeck's career. The personal repercussions of a *Pravda* headline reading, "John Steinbeck, Spy for the Capitalist Overlords," is a matter of mental war gaming. Steinbeck's image with the American public could have skyrocketed with the revelation. In this case, the *New York Times* rebuttal of the *Pravda* headline could have read, "Steinbeck Fights the Reds by Working for CIA." Equally as likely during the height of the Red Scare could have been the American public seeing Steinbeck as a snitch. Had the wind blown south, a *Washington Post* headline could have read, "Steinbeck Rats out Red Friends to the CIA."

Hero or villain, John's personal life would have paid a high price for any recognition that he worked for the CIA. Many of Steinbeck's friends, acquaintances, and associates had been either called before the HUAC or had been blacklisted by publications like *Red Channels* as being a Communist. How would they have viewed John as being a CIA informant? Would Steinbeck's family understand why he had to keep his association with the CIA secret and would they have trusted him afterward? There would be a personal price for John to pay, had his involvement with the CIA become public knowledge, and John would have been ardently aware of the outlay.

The fact remains that John *did* volunteer, but why? The simplest answer was that being eyes and ears for the CIA would have been viewed by John as a fight against the oppressive totalitarianism practiced by Communism governments. In particular, John was outraged by the treatment of artists and writers under the Communist system.

Steinbeck's feelings are summed up in a July 1950 letter to his close friend, Swedish painter Bo Beskow:

> I have been horrified at the creeping paralysis that is coming out of the Kremlin, the death of art and thought, the death of individual. When I was in Russia a couple of years ago I could see no creative thing.

Steinbeck continues in the same letter:

> I can't think that wars can solve things but something must stop this thing or the world is done and gone into a black chaos that makes the dark ages shine.[20]

Steinbeck had no distain for the Russian people, but he despised the stranglehold the Soviet government had over its citizens. The situation is little different than John's crusade for migrant workers' rights in *The Grapes of Wrath*. In the fields of California or the Ukraine, oppression is a universal issue. The difference for Steinbeck was that under Communism, there was no chance for change. The same public outcry over working conditions of migrant workers would have resulted in a stay at the Gulag in the Soviet Union. Steinbeck's work with the CIA was his blow against a governmental system that systematically subjugated an entire citizenry.

The not-so-simple answer to "Why did John want to be a CIA asset?" had to do with John's activities during the Second World War. In the early days of the war, John worked for the Office of War Information (OWI), Office of Strategic Services (OSS), and other government agencies as an unpaid consultant. From 1941–43, John fought for a commission in the United States Army, which was never given to him. Feeling that he would never be able to directly participate in the war, John found a workaround by becoming a *New York Herald Tribune* war correspondent. During his time as a correspondent, John would spend nearly two months with Douglas Fairbanks Jr.'s top-secret Beach Jumper (BJ) unit. While Steinbeck was embedded with the BJs, their mission was to conduct a campaign of deception to draw the Germans' attention away from real Allied troop movements. The vast majority of these missions relied on stealth, rather than firepower, to accomplish the BJ's goals. Steinbeck saw firsthand the value of covert operations in a strategic context.

Volunteering for work with the CIA would have been a way Steinbeck could be "in the fight" against Communism. The early Cold War presented a different type of combat than John had seen as a war correspondent in 1943. The direct warfare between the United States and Russia would take the form of propaganda bombs and cultural strafing runs. As each super power attempted to convince the populaces of countries that their ideological system was superior to the other, John was in the thick of things. There were no Cold War bonds that John could buy. John couldn't join an Army that would push the Soviets out of Eastern Europe. Steinbeck only had his talent for writing and an uncanny penchant for observation to offer in this war. One may only speculate at John's reasons for offering his services to the CIA and we are left with looking to his letter to Smith for any other clues the correspondence offers.

One of the most striking elements of Steinbeck's letter to Smith was the casual tone it took. Smith was the United States' ambassador to the Soviet Union when John and Robert Capa visited the country in 1947. A few days after Steinbeck and Capa arrived in Moscow, Smith invited the pair to dinner at the American Embassy.[21] The meeting is briefly mentioned in Steinbeck's account of the trip, *A Russian Journal*. The details of the dinner party with Smith take up less than a paragraph, but it establishes a basis for contact between the two men. Steinbeck's 1952 letter makes no introductions and launches into his intent, indicating the two men had at least a nodding familiarity with each other. Steinbeck was a straightforward person, but he was not one to dispense with social pleasantries. In a 1943 letter to his old friend Toby Street, John announces his wedding date to Gwyn and begins the letter by speaking of travel plans.

> We are going to New Orleans to be married. Gwyn is going next
> week and I'll go down about the 27th if I can get a plane.

Here John wastes no time stating his purpose, just as in the letter to Smith. In contrast, John writes to 20th Century Fox about their changes to his script of the Alfred Hitchcock film *Lifeboat*. The situation is of grave concern to Steinbeck, but he is addressing an unknown recipient:

> Dear Sirs:
> I have just seen the film *Lifeboat*, directed by Alfred Hitchcock and
> billed as written by me. While in many ways the film is excellent
> there are one or two complaints I would like to make.[22]

The beginning of each letter conveys a different tone. The letter to Street is picking up where a previous conversation left off, while the 20th Century Fox letter is officious. These are just two examples of Steinbeck's letter writing styles, but the 1952 letter to Smith takes on more of the characteristics of the Street letter, than that of the 20th Century Fox letter.

The next section of the letter contains a reference to "Herbert Bayard Swope" that is intriguing on a number of levels. Swope was the epitome of a New York journalist. His wildly successful 1917 series "Inside the German Empire" had won Swope the Pulitzer Prize and landed him the editorship of the *New York World* in the early 1920s. The *New York World*, under Swope's leadership, pushed the boundaries of journalistic endeavors of the day. Often accused of pioneering "yellow rag" style journalism, the *New York World* equally transformed the landscape of journalism in the twentieth century. Swope created the op-ed piece which has been followed by American newspapers ever since. The *New York World* also broke ground in investigative journalism by exposing the secrets of the Ku Klux Klan in 1921. Swope's paper serialized the exposé over twenty-one editions and fifteen other major newspapers throughout the country syndicated the *New York World*'s feed. Serialization and syndication were not a new concept to the newspaper business, but the success of the Klan story cemented the convention as a standard business practice.

One of the privileges of being the *World*'s editor was access to the movers and shakers of New York society. Saying Swope was "well connected" would discredit the term. Swope was a social and political hub in which the rich and famous revolved around him. The savvy editor massaged his relationships with newsmakers by throwing lavish parties at his home during the roaring '20s. Described by Swope's wife Margret as, "an absolutely seething bordello of interesting people," the parties were attended by such notables as Bernard Baruch, George Gershwin, Robert Moses, the Marx Brothers, Irving Berlin, Vanderbilts, Whitneys, and Harrimans. To give one an idea of the scope of these parties, they are thought to have been the basis for scenes in F. Scott Fitzgerald's *The Great Gatsby*.[23] The social gatherings at the Swope home would have served a dual purpose for Swope. Not only did these functions increase Swope's social currency, parties invariably lead to loose talk. By the end of any given affair, one can be assured that Swope would have heard every bit of gossip that had been spread. The curse of good journalists is that they never stop asking questions and are always listening to find the next big scoop.

Swope's achievements in journalism were lightly overshadowed by his prowess as a gambler. The tales of Swope's gambling binges are nearly as legendary as his parties. One story has a cub reporter Swope ditching work for days, chasing a hot streak at a two-dollar craps game. Swope allegedly got fired from the job, but cushioned the blow by winning $6,000 at the table. In a 1923 trip to Palm Springs, Swope got embroiled in a two-day poker game with oil baron Joshua Cosden; Florenz Ziegfeld, of Follies fame; and steel magnate J. Leonard Replogle. Swope walked away from this venture $470,300 richer.[24] Had there ever been a Pulitzer Prize for gambling, Swope would have had another for his collection.

Swope officially retired from the newspaper business in 1929 and held a number of advisory positions in state and federal governments. Appropriately Swope served as the head of New York's Racing Commission for a time. His real talent post-journalism would manifest in the form of public relations. In the mid-1930s, Swope signed his first client, financier and presidential advisor Bernard Baruch. The arrangement allowed Swope to have access to the Washington corridors of power, but Swope always tried to stay in the shadows. He understood that to be effective at public relations, the focal point had to be on the client. In comparison to his days in journalism, very little has been documented about Swope's life after 1929. The main biography of Swope, *The World of Swope*, published in 1965, spends less than an eighth of the text dealing with Swope's later life.

Steinbeck dropping Swope's name in the letter to Smith is a slight quandary. Steinbeck and Swope's only known association was through the Society of the Silurians. The organization was created in 1924 as a haven for distinguished New York journalists. By distinguished, the early members of the Society of the Silurians described themselves as a "bunch of old geezers" who had been in New York's journalism scene for over thirty years.[25] The term Silurian, tongue-in-cheek applied for the Society's use, comes from the geological period 440 million years ago, when marine life evolved sufficiently to take its first steps on dry land. The Society still exists in a modified form of the "good old boys of journalism" club it was originally intended to be. Swope and Steinbeck could have had contact via this organization, but Steinbeck did not become a member until the winter of 1952–53.[26] Swope's membership into the reporter's club is a bit of a mystery to *Silurian News* editor Eve Berliner. She knew that Swope had been a member, but could not put a date on his membership.[27]

Steinbeck and Swope could have met through any number of New York social occasions or clubs the two would have attended. One of the crossover points between the two men was New York's posh Stork Club. The nightclub was a fixture for New York socialites from the end of prohibition until the club's decline in the 1960s, and both Swope and Steinbeck were club regulars.[28] As an aside, the Stork Club did have at least one connection with the CIA on its own. Alexander Irwin Rorke, the son-in-law of the Stork Club's owner Sherman Billingsley, has long been suspected as being a CIA operative. Rorke had reportedly been involved with anti-Castro operations in Cuba and in September of 1963, Rorke received media attention for conducting a bombing raid over Cuba. The next month, Rorke disappeared after his twin-engine Beechcraft took off from Mexico and was never seen again. It is widely believed that Rorke's plane went down over Cuba where he either died or was executed.[29]

The connection between Steinbeck and Swope is not as puzzling as why Steinbeck would make his connection to Swope known to Smith. Steinbeck could simply have said that he had heard Smith's health was improving and been done with it. The connection with Swope is quite deliberate. Steinbeck's reasons for bringing up Swope could have been an understated hint at Steinbeck's access to well-connected persons. This resume by accomplishment was a tactic Steinbeck would employ in a June 1962 letter to President Kennedy about a plan to diffuse the Berlin Wall situation. John reminds Kennedy of his plans assisting OSS (Office of Strategic Services) operations in occupied Denmark during the Second World War.[30] The self-deprecating Steinbeck is selling himself as a creator of successful ideas to Kennedy in the same way Steinbeck's mention of Swope has given Smith a reason to believe the author will have access to similar persons in Europe.

Another less likely scenario on Steinbeck's mention of Swope to Smith is that Swope could have suggested Steinbeck offer his services to the CIA. Swope was never known to have direct involvement with the Agency, but his counsel was, at times, sought after and other times given unsolicited in Washington circles. Nuremburg trial prosecutor Robert Jackson had sought Swope's advice on publicity for the hearings. Swope had a laundry list of methods that would give Nuremburg an air of legitimacy, including having the British and French

counsel in their traditional garb.[31] On another occasion, Swope had advised President Eisenhower in 1954 on a public relations scheme to legitimize the new Guatemalan government. The CIA had supported a coup of Guatemala's pro-Marxist government in favor of a democratic government. Swope's suggestion ended up on Secretary of State John Foster Dulles' desk and was sent back slightly

An East German girl looks through the wire at friends in Steinstücken. The photo was taken during October of 1961 and is from the booklet *A City Torn Apart: Building of the Berlin Wall*. Photo from the CIA.

modified to Eisenhower.[32] Swope also served as a delegate to the United Nations Atomic Energy Commission in 1947 with Bernard Baruch and would have included a security clearance. These are just a few examples of Swope's veiled influences in Washington circles. Through any of these connections, Swope could have been privy to the CIA's need of volunteers and knew to be on the lookout for candidates.

Aside from Swope's Washington connections, there are several other circumstantial links with Swope and the Agency. Swope was on the board of directors of CBS from 1932 to 1949, which has long been rumored to have an association with the CIA.[33] Swope, unlike many board members, took an active part in the day-to-day business of CBS. Chief executive William S. Paley commonly had contact with Swope about broadcasting matters. Swope was a type "A" personality who would dig at Paley for slight missteps. Many mornings Paley would walk into his office to find a note from Swope about a mispronounced word or other gaffe from the previous evening's broadcasts.[34] The intervention of Swope would have been unnerving to Paley, who had been involved with CBS since its inception.

Paley's father and brother-in-law purchased an unprofitable Philadelphia radio network of sixteen stations in 1927 that would become CBS. The junior Paley revamped the advertising structure of the stations and grew the business venture to 114 stations by 1937. During the Second World War, Paley was drafted to work with the Office of War Information's (OWI) psychological warfare branch. One of Paley's tasks early in the war was to expand CBS's shortwave radio coverage in Latin America to counter Nazi propaganda. Later in the war, Paley would work directly under General Dwight Eisenhower, coordinating radio traffic in North Africa and reestablishing radio services in liberated countries.[35]

During the Cold War, Paley has been fingered by a number of sources as providing the CIA with access to CBS resources.[36] One of the more famous incidents was Paley allowing the CIA to use CBS's booth at the United Nations in 1959. Intelligence officers camped out in CBS's real estate to read the lips of Russian Premier Nikita Khrushchev's delegation during the Premier's first trip to the United States. The CBS/CIA relationship was not limited to that one event or Paley's influence. CBS news director Sig Mickelson, who would head Radio Free Europe after leaving CBS, was said to have had a direct phone line to CIA headquarters that bypassed the CBS switchboard.[37] The relationship was both insidious and benign in the same stroke. CBS would obtain story leads from the CIA and the CIA would utilize CBS to its advantage. The micromanaging Swope, being a Washington insider and CBS board member, is likely to have known of the relationship between CBS and the CIA.

As tenuous a link between the CIA and Swope via CBS is, another organization under Swope's watchful eye has links to the intelligence community, since Swope was one of the founding members of the non-governmental organization (NGO) Freedom House. According to Freedom House's website:

> Freedom House was established in 1941 in New York City. Its creation was a result of a merger of two groups that had been formed, with the quiet encouragement of President Franklin D. Roosevelt, to encourage popular support for American involvement in World War II at a time when isolationist sentiments were running high in the United States . . . Having been created in response to the threat of one great totalitarian evil, Nazism, Freedom House took up the struggle against the other great twentieth century totalitarian threat, Communism, after the end of World War II.[38]

Eleanor and Belle Roosevelt, Dorothy Thompson, Rex Stout, Wendell Willkie, and a handful of other notables were also involved with Freedom House's beginnings. To support "American involvement in World War II," Freedom House produced a counter-Nazi propaganda radio serial from 1942–43, *Our Secret Weapon*, written by Rex Stout. Predictably, the serial was aired on the Swope-influenced CBS radio networks. After the war, Freedom House shifted its gaze from Nazis to Commies by endorsing the Marshall Plan and NATO.[39] In a move that would seem wholly opposed to combating Communism, Freedom House would also take a stand against McCarthyism during the 1950s and actively campaign for the Civil Rights movement during the 1960s.

Making a connection between Freedom House and the CIA is largely a circumstantial case. A common tactic of the CIA is to utilize both private companies and NGOs for their own purposes. The ease in which a connection between Freedom House and the CIA could have been made becomes more likely when one considers the two Roosevelts on Freedom House's original board. The implication of having a First Lady on Freedom House's board speaks for itself. The lesser-known Belle Roosevelt was literally one degree of separation from the Agency. Her son, Kermit Roosevelt Jr. (grandson of President Teddy Roosevelt), was the head of CIA covert operations in the Middle East during the 1950s. Kermit is best known for organizing a CIA-backed Iranian coup in 1953.[40] Of particular interest to a possible link between the CIA and Freedom House, Kermit also served in some executive capacity of pro-Israel institutions during the late 1940s and early 1950s. The Institute of Arab American Affairs Incorporated, the Committee for Justice and Peace in the Holy Land, and the American Friends of the Middle East were all organizations Kermit Roosevelt served on as advisory board member, executive secretary, and director/founder respectively. Of these groups, the American Friends of the Middle East is known to have been funded directly by the CIA.[41] Also of note, Dorothy Thompson was a founding member of both Freedom House and the American Friends of the Middle East. If the motive for Freedom House assisting the CIA is not present, certainly the method and opportunity of CIA involvement with the NGO exist.

The use of NGOs, private foundations, and front companies are a prominent page from the CIA playbook. From 1950 to the mid-1970s, the CIA is known to have directly controlled or heavily financed a number of NGOs, private foundations, and shell companies for intelligence purposes. The vast majority of CIA shill organizations are used to develop agents' cover stories and to fulfill other mission roles. Possibly the best-known example of CIA links to outside the Agency's entities is that of Air America and sister company Civilian Air Transport (CAT). Founded in the early 1950s for the purposes of indirect support of Southeast Asian countries under Communist siege, Air America and CAT flew airlift and direct combat missions in a number of countries. Operations in many of these countries were in unclear legal waters and the activities of "private" companies placed distance between the CIA, and the president for that matter, and legal entrapments. The debate still exists as to the extent of the Executive Branch when committing military or paramilitary units on foreign soil. Article I, Section 8, Clause 11 of the United States Constitution affords Congress the ability to declare war. The contention over discretionary presidential use of military force not approved by Congress has raged since the time of Air America and is now an ever-present forethought in the War on Terror. Warfare by private company proxy has turned into a workaround of the letter of the law, if not the law's spirit.

Not all CIA fronts are utilized in the arena of armed conflict. During the first two decades of the Cold War, the CIA utilized front organizations to wage a cultural war with the Soviets. One tends to think of the Cold War in terms of ballistic missiles and mutually assured destruction, rather than modern art and symphonies, but the Cold War was a titanic struggle of diametrically opposed ideologies. The theory behind cultural warfare is

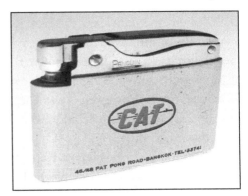

A Civil Air Transport (CAT) lighter from the Hong Kong-to-Bangkok inaugural flight of CAT on July 20, 1957. Photo from the CIA.

that if in Communist countries, one could sell the idea that Capitalism was a better way of life, the populace would eventually change forms of government internally. NGOs and private foundations were the CIA's foot soldiers in the trenches of "hearts and minds." A number of examples exist from the era of organizations doing their part against the Red Horde. From prime movers of CIA funds in the cultural war, from the Ford Foundation to the Congress of Cultural Freedom (CCF), various NGOs and private foundations were also approached by the CIA to chip in on the Cold War effort.[42]

The CCF and Ford Foundation seem to be the primary sources of funding for secondary institutions that assisted the CIA during the Cold War. Both organizations were "outed" as having CIA ties by *Ramparts Magazine* in 1967 and scholarship in recent years has confirmed the links.[43] The funding web worked, to put distance between the CIA and any of their front organizations. A bogus individual would donate money to a foundation, which could then directly fund a CIA-driven initiative, or that foundation could subsidize yet another CIA front institution. By the time funds were dispersed to their intended recipients, the trails were so convoluted there was little chance of tracking money back to the CIA. In many cases in the cultural Cold War, the individual artists or writers never knew the funds came from the Agency. A struggling artist would open their mailbox one day and find they had been selected to receive a grant from the Ford Foundation. The artist would be able to continue their work, which advanced the CIA's long game of promoting American artistic endeavors as superior to that of the Soviet Union.

Steinbeck was also a beneficiary of the CIA's largesse during the cultural war. John was issued a grant from the CCF[44] and attended a CCF-funded writer's conference in Mexico City.[45] The Ford Foundation also kicked in to promote Steinbeck's work. From 1952–61, the Ford Foundation produced the television series *Omnibus*. Hosted by Alastair Cooke, *Omnibus* featured everything from discussions about the arts to productions of original works. Three episodes of *Omnibus* featured Steinbeck's work. Also the Ford Foundation–sponsored TV series *Play of the Week*[46] ran Steinbeck's play *Burning Bright* in 1959. The stage production of *Burning Bright* had been produced in 1950 and was, by all means, a theater flop, having only thirteen stage performances.[47] It is doubtful that the documentation to prove or disprove that the support Steinbeck received from the CCF or Ford Foundation was a CIA-driven exercise will ever be made available to the public. However, the possibility does go to show another potential link between the Agency and Steinbeck. The other question that CIA funding via the CCF and Ford Foundation of Steinbeck's work brings up is if it was a *quid pro quo* for his work with the CIA. Given the manner in which the CIA dispersed funds to support the cultural Cold War, John likely did not know at all.

One of the more peculiar examples of the CIA utilizing fronts in the cultural Cold War was the Agency partnering with the Museum of Modern Art (MoMA). In this case, individual artists never knew that their work was being subsidized by the Agency. The CIA was interested in the ramifications of abstract expressionist art as a sign of unfettered American creativity in the face of stoic art being produced in Communist countries. By exhibiting abstract expressionist art throughout the world, the seeds of Americanism could be planted in the minds of those living in Communist-controlled countries. To that end, the CIA indirectly supported abstract expressionists Pollock, de Kooning, and Motherwell by funding MoMA exhibitions through the CCF, the Rockefeller Foundation, and other privately owned foundations. (Interestingly enough, CBS executive William Paley was also on the board of MoMA during this time period.) So keen was the CIA on the idea of artistic expression being used as a propaganda tool, they set up operative Tom Braden, best known as the author of *Eight Is Enough*,[48] as executive secretary of MoMA in 1949. Braden recounts that:

> We wanted to unite all the people who were writers, who were musicians, who were artists, to demonstrate that the West and the United States was devoted to freedom of expression and to intellectual achievement, without any rigid barriers as to what you must write, and what you must say, and what you must do, and what you must paint, which was what was going on in the Soviet Union. I think it was the most important division that the Agency had, and I think that it played an enormous role in the Cold War.[49]

One such CIA covert art operation was a 1958 exhibition at London's Tate Gallery. An abstract expressionist exhibition was nearing an end in Paris and the Tate Gallery was keen to be the exhibit's next stop. At the time, Tate did not have the funds to transport the art from Paris. The CIA backed the millionaire MoMA board member Julius Fleischmann to provide the funds through the Fairfield Foundation that would enable the Tate Gallery to conduct the exhibit. Setting up beard foundations on the fly was not as difficult as one might imagine. According to Braden:

> We would go to somebody in New York who was a well-known rich person and we would say, "We want to set up a foundation." We would tell him what we were trying to do and pledge him to secrecy, and he would say, "Of course I'll do it," and then you would publish a letterhead and his name would be on it and there would be a foundation. It was really a pretty simple device.[50]

Now MoMA understandably distances themselves from any influence the CIA had over MoMa exhibits. In a 2011 interview with Jay Levenson, MoMA's Director of International Programs, he commented on the relationship between the CIA and MoMA.

> Whether that political dimension led the Museum to favor AbEx [abstract expressionist] artists, as some commentators have claimed, is another question altogether. It's actually been argued that the CIA was itself behind the exhibition program, but the Agency's influence is hardly needed to explain the initiative.[51]

The MoMA/CIA liaison exemplifies all the benefits and pitfalls front organizations undertook when securing Agency funding. In the case of MoMA, it would seem that the CIA provided resources for an end goal of promoting abstract expressionist art abroad. This fit neatly into MoMA's goal of supporting American artists when and wherever they could. MoMA's risk was the sigma of "Agency money" tainting the integrity of artistic endeavors. Where the CIA's directives end and MoMA's methods of promotion begin may never be fully known. We simply can see through the example of the CIA's interest in MoMA how front organizations were used to further the Agency's goals.

Freedom House also fits well within the mold of organizations influenced by the CIA in some fashion. The tacit connections of Freedom House's founders to the Agency have been born out in recent years, as Freedom House has come under scrutiny by news organizations and United Nations representatives as being a front for the CIA. The Zimbabwean newspaper *The Sunday Mail* ran a story entitled "CIA's Freedom House: A House of Destruction" on August 25, 2012. The article charges that a public opinion poll by Freedom House was skewed to cast aspersions on the Zimbabwean government.[52]

During hearings into the consulate status of various NGOs at the United Nations in 2001, the Cuban representative leveled charges that Freedom House was a CIA instrument by stating there were links

> . . . between the NGO [Freedom House] and Frank Garcon, former head of Cuba-related programs at the CIA. Also, the instructions given to the NGO's emissaries to Cuba were clearly of a secret conspiratorial nature, primarily because the NGO was aware of the illegal activities it carried out. For Cuba and for global public opinion, Freedom House was nothing but a façade for the special services of the United States.[53]

The Cuban government had come to this conclusion partially from a Freedom House–funded program, Friends of Cuban Libraries. The benignly titled organization was co-founded by New York Public Librarian Robert Kent to establish independent Cuban libraries in 1998. Most of the libraries were little more than persons lending books out of their personal collections. The dissemination of ideas outside of state control was not welcome in Castro's island kingdom and fourteen independent librarians were convicted of "mercenary activities and other acts against the independence and territorial integrity of the Cuban state."[54] The Cuban government branded Kent as being "Roberto X," a CIA agent bent on assassinating high-level party officers. When asked about being in the service of the CIA, Kent has been quoted as saying, "I'm still trying to figure out who's cashing all my CIA paychecks."[55]

Accusations do not create CIA front companies and Freedom House has always denied any links between their organization and the CIA. In a separate incident of Cuba's insistence of CIA/Freedom House links, Freedom House President Adrian Karatnycky countered:

> . . . another pathetic attempt by the Cuban Communist regime to deflect attention from its dismal human rights record. For the record, Freedom House does not engage in espionage, although we have extended assistance to democratic dissidents in Cuba and elsewhere.[56]

Just as Cuban accusations do not create certainty of CIA links, Freedom House's outrage does not ensure the links with the Agency do not exist. The fact that institutions like Freedom House are perfect covers for covert operations will always cast doubt on their motivations. No NGO that is acting in concert with the CIA would ever openly blow their cover, and probing the probable is the best one can accomplish. When examining Freedom House, one must weigh the circumstantial evidence, accusations, and denials in deciding if there is a covert connection. If a link does, in fact, exist, Steinbeck's mention of Swope in the 1952 Smith letter would then take on a different meaning than that of a casual conversation piece. At a dinner party or other social gathering, Swope could have easily mentioned to Steinbeck that the CIA was looking for information from men of his caliber. To seal the deal, Swope could have told Steinbeck, "Write a letter to 'Beetle' Smith telling him about your trip to Europe and be sure to mention my name."

Swope would have been the perfect person to bird dog potential assets for the Agency. Aside from having served as an unofficial presidential advisor, Swope's one official governmental posting was that of a delegate to the United Nations Atomic Energy Commission in 1946. The assignment would have required Swope to undergo a rigorous security clearance process that would enable him to be briefed on America's nuclear capabilities. Having been cleared for the Holy Grail of secrecy in 1946, scouting assets for the CIA would not have been a security issue. Swope's wide range of social and professional contacts would have given the ex-journalist an extensive pool of potential assets to send to Langley. Once again, we are faced with a circumstantial case for Swope's association with the CIA. Between the known link between CBS and the CIA and the potential link between Freedom House and the CIA, Swope's mention in the Steinbeck letter places him as a prime candidate for working with the Agency.

Steinbeck's statement about "Lou for 52" is a little more enigmatic than that of Swope. The moniker refers to President Truman's Defense Secretary from 1949–50, Louis A. Johnson. An ardent Truman supporter, Johnson had briefly been given the nod to run as the 1952 Democratic presidential candidate. At a dinner honoring Johnson, the day he was sworn in as the Secretary of Defense in April of 1949, a well-timed cry of "Lou for 52" rang through the room.[57] Johnson's short-lived campaign for President even ramped up enough to produce "Vote for Lou in 52" thimbles,[58] though his campaign and public service is little more than a footnote today and would have been something of a joke in 1952.

Louis Johnson had rambled around Washington since Franklin D. Roosevelt's administration. Johnson had been FDR's Assistant Secretary of War from 1937–40 and advocated expanding America's military capabilities in light of Germany's war footing. This was in direct opposition to Secretary of War Henry Hines Woodring's isolationist views on the developments in Europe during Johnson's tenure. Woodring's shortsightedness cost him his job with the fall of France in June of 1940, and Johnson felt he was a shoo-in for his former boss' position. FDR felt differently and named Henry Stimson the new Secretary of War. Johnson's name had also been bandied about in the press as FDR's running mate in the 1940 election. To placate Johnson after being bypassed for the Secretary of War job, FDR's staff let Johnson think he would be on the 1940 presidential ticket. The hope of becoming vice president also extended to twelve others at the Democratic National Convention that year. Johnson came away from the convention with exactly one vote as FDR's running mate and realized he'd been led down the garden path. A little over a week after the convention ended, Johnson put in his resignation and returned to his Washington law practice.[59]

Years later, Johnson saw an opportunity to get back into politics during Harry Truman's 1948 campaign. Using what political clout he could muster, Johnson became Truman's chief fundraiser while trying to position himself for being named Secretary of Defense.[60] Johnson's chance would come when Truman fired James Forrestal from the position over defense budget cutbacks in 1949. Truman had a pre-World War II view on defense spending that had

Louis Johnson (left of the photograph's center) greets William R. McLand along with other military personnel at Pope Air Force Base, January 13, 1950. Courtesy of the Harry S Truman Presidential Library.

little basis on potential military threats to the United States, while Forrestal had realized that the timbre of warfare had changed with the Second World War and that in future wars, the United States would not have the luxury of years, or even months, of preparation.[61] Wishing to give the President the cutbacks he wished, Johnson's tenure as Secretary of Defense was marked by selling or scrapping much of the surplus arms from World War II and quashing new weapons programs.

Johnson's political career and any other aspirations ended with the beginning of the Korean War in 1950. America's initial response to the North Korean invasion of South Korea was to send a weak and ill-equipped unit that would become known as Task Force Smith in honor of its commander Lieutenant Colonel Charles B. Smith. The theory was that by simply seeing American troops on the ground, it would give the North Koreans pause and the offensive would simply go away. But the North Korean Army took no notice of an American unit with worn-out rifles and no artillery or tanks.

On July 5, 1950, Task Force Smith engaged elements of the North Korean 107th Tank Regiment of the 105th Armored Divisions near Osan with disastrous results. The American troops did not have the equipment to fight tanks and withdrew from the battlefield the next day. One hundred fifty-three American soldiers lost their lives in the Task Force Smith debacle[62] and Louis Johnson resigned two and a half months later. Even though Johnson was following Truman's guidance on defense spending, Johnson was held accountable for the needless deaths of those 153 men. There would be no reviving a political career after Task Force Smith, so Johnson again retreated to his law firm and practiced until his death in 1966.

Steinbeck's invoking the political spirit of Louis Johnson is truly an oddity. As 1952 was an election year, Eisenhower had just come out of the political closet as a Republican a few weeks before Steinbeck's letter to Smith. Neither

Steinbeck nor Smith supported Eisenhower's presidential bid. Smith was an ardent supporter of Eisenhower in his military roles and had served as Ike's chief of staff during the Second World War. Smith's feelings on Eisenhower as president were quite clear:

> It is my conviction that the necessary and wise subordination of the military to civil power will best be sustained . . . when lifelong professional solders, in the absence of some obvious and overriding reasons, abstain from seeking high political office.[63]

There was no real enmity between Smith and Eisenhower other than Smith constantly living in Ike's shadow during the war. Being the good soldier Smith was, he left the CIA to accept Eisenhower's appointment as the Under Secretary of State in 1953.

Smith was also first and foremost a military man. Having enlisted in the Indiana National Guard at the age of sixteen in 1911, Smith spent the majority of his life in the Army. A veteran of World War I, Smith served under Eisenhower with distinction through the end of World War II. Smith's military career and contributions to the United States Army require their own text, but it is hard to conceive of Smith supporting Louis Johnson as president. While serving as ambassador to the Soviet Union in 1949, Smith supported rearming Europe as a bulwark against the Soviets.[64] Johnson's dismantling of the military would have distressed Smith greatly, especially after the initial failures in Korea. Why then did Steinbeck mention backing a nonexistent presidential candidate that was sure to rub Smith the wrong way?

It would be easy to fall off the conspiratorial cliffs and assign the cryptic statement as a coded message. There is always that possibility. If Herbert Swope had suggested John contact the CIA, the "Lou for 52" business could have been a recognition code. Specific phrases are used in spycraft in conjunction with someone's name to confirm a message's source. These tactics are employed in everyday life in much the same way. For example, you ask a friend if she knows a competent and reasonably priced plumber. Your friend tells you about a guy she knows who works for a contracting outfit that does jobs off the books. As she gives you his phone number, there are some further instructions: "Tell him that I sent you and that he still owes me for those tickets I got him on the fifty-yard line." The covert world uses similar recognition codes when setting up meetings with unknown entities.

The tone of the letter still suggests familiarity over first contact, so it is doubtful the "Lou for 52" section is some sort of code. The reference also could not have been born out of Steinbeck's meeting with Smith at the American Embassy in Moscow during the 1947 trip. At that time, Louis Johnson was fundraising for Truman's campaign. Johnson's political future was on shaky ground at best, and depended on the outcome of the 1948 elections. The other option is that Steinbeck is attempting a joke with the DCI Smith, much in the same way a Republican might rib a yellow-dog Democrat by saying, "Romney is looking forward to your vote this November." If this is the case, Steinbeck was likely in contact with Smith since 1947. One does not joke with the head of the CIA unless one knows it will be taken in good humor.

As we move to the CIA's response to Steinbeck, the body of Smith's reply to Steinbeck is nearly as stunning as Steinbeck's letter to Smith. The CIA is giving Steinbeck the opportunity to become an asset. There is no indication in Smith's letter that the Agency initially wanted John to perform the duties of a "spy." DCI Smith is simply telling Steinbeck that his offer of assistance as a passive intelligence gatherer has been accepted. This does not mean that the Agency might not have directed Steinbeck to speak with certain people about certain topics or perform other intelligence duties. As we examine Steinbeck's 1952 trip to Europe, there is evidence that the Agency did play an invisible role in his movements throughout Europe.

Undoubtedly there will be those who read the exchange between Steinbeck and Smith and come to a totally different conclusion on the contents of Smith's reply. There is the possibility that Smith was trying to appease the influential author much in the same way a parent going on a business trip placates a child. "Little Johnny, I can't take you with me this time. Who is going to take care of your mother while I'm gone?" To that end, Smith might have felt that shunning Steinbeck would have future repercussions. In addition to being a novelist, John was a respected journalist with political ties. Snubbing someone of Steinbeck's stature might not have been in the best interest of the Agency. The letter then could have been a showpiece and the CIA did not take Steinbeck's offer seriously. While this is one explanation of it, there are clues within Smith's reply that make the placation theory improbable. We must first look at all the information the letter contains before examining the actual syntax of Smith's reply.

The first items of note in Smith's letter are the alphanumeric combination "ER 2-5603" at the top of the page. One possibility is that "ER 2-5603" was a CIA telephone number. In the golden days of telephone technology, the first two letters of a phone number corresponded with the first two letters of a specific phone exchange. These two digits were in line with the first two digits of the phone number using the same letter/number combinations found on telephones today. For example, an exchange in Nashville was the Tucker exchange and when dialing 885-1342 one would tell the operator they wanted to call Tucker 5-1342. It is likely that "ER 2-5603" was a either a direct line to the DCI's office, or another direct phone line to an active CIA office, as

An artist's rendering of the CIA headquarters in Langley, Virgina, during the building's early planning stages. Image courtesy of the CIA.

the main phone number for the CIA was "EX (or the Executive exchange) "3-6115."[65] Had the Agency considered Steinbeck a crackpot, the phone number given would have been the main switchboard where the telephonic gatekeepers could have indefinitely stymied the author contacting anyone of authority in the Agency. Anyone who has complained to a bank or retail chain store and asked for a regional manager's phone number knows the difficulty of securing direct access to an executive. Government circles are no different than corporate America. When was the last time you called your Senator or Congressman's office and were "put right through"?

A second possibility exists for "ER 2-5603." The designation could also have been a reference number for the letter. The CIA tracks documents like a bookkeeper follows a chart of accounts. The "ER" prefix was used to denote a document flagged as an "Executive Record" for the DCI. This would mean that Smith's letter, and any other documents relating to this letter, would be handled by the DCI's office and not shuffled off to someone lower in the CIA's chain of command.[66] In either the phone number or Executive Record interpretation of "ER 2-5603," it is evident that there was a genuine reason for the DCI to be kept in the loop for developments related to Steinbeck.

One also might notice that Smith's reply to Steinbeck is missing any sort of letterhead. Any reference to an address of Smith's office appears to have been redacted via a b3 exclusion at the top right of the letter. This is not surprising since in 1952, the CIA did not operate from a single office. There was an official CIA headquarters located at 2430 E Street NW in Washington, D.C. The E Street building was publicly known during the 1950s, but before the construction of the present CIA campus in Langley, Virginia, the CIA operated out of at least forty different offices scattered throughout Washington.[67] The majority of those locations were classified at the time and still are. Any address information on the letterhead could have been the physical location of a secondary office or a catch-all letter drop address for the Agency. In either case, the CIA has no intention of disclosing this information sixty years after the fact. The redaction is telling in that since the E Street compound is well known, there would be no need for a redaction of the address. This could indicate the location of a secondary CIA office that the Agency was willing to share with Steinbeck and this would point to a relationship between the Agency and Steinbeck prior to January of 1952.

Just below Smith's signature are the letter's "reference initials." The practice of using reference initials has diminished to the point of extinction with the advent of email and requires some deciphering. Reference initials were used in the dark ages when the boss would call his secretary into his office to "take down a letter." The initials provided a trail to the persons who had a part in distributing the letter. Uppercase reference initials were used to denote the letter's author. Lowercase initials showed who typed the piece of mail. If there was an error in the letter, our olden-times authority figure would know exactly who to discipline for screwing things up. If the person writing the letter also typed it, there was no need to use any reference initials. This is not the case with Smith's letter. A number of people have been involved in Smith's response to Steinbeck. Taken line by line, we can read the reference to mean:

> **O/DCI:REL:leb**: Someone with the initials "REL" from the Office of the Director of Central Intelligence (General Smith) penned the letter. The letter was typed by someone with the initials "leb."
> **Rewritten: LEBecker:mlk**: The original text of the "REL" letter was modified by L.E. Becker and typed by someone with the initials "mlk."

From the context of the reply to Steinbeck, we cannot identify who "REL" is. Most likely, "REL" was a CIA officer assigned as an administrative assistant to the DCI. That the same initials show up as the author of a hastily written

```
O/DCI:REL:leb
Rewritten:   LEBecker:mlk
Distribution:
    Orig - Addressee
       2 - DCI (Reading
                Official)
       1 - DD/P  w/Basic
       1 - Admin. Files
```

A close-up of the reference initials in Becker/Smith's reply to Steinbeck.

note on a 1953 letter from Alaska Senator Edward Bartlett to General Smith, further supports that "REL" was someone professionally close to Smith.[68] We can reasonably identify "leb" as L.E. Becker by the "rewritten" line of the reference initials. L.E. Becker could only be the Deputy Director of Intelligence (DDI) at the time, Loftus E. Becker.

Smith had started restructuring the CIA shortly after taking the position of the DCI. Prior to Smith's tenure as DCI, the flow of information and cooperation between the different departments of the CIA had become an impediment to providing accurate intelligence. The lack of organization of the CIA was evidenced by the Agency's failure to predict the North Korean invasion of South Korea in June of 1950.[69] Smith had taken the office of DCI a few months after the hostilities started in Korea and had no wish for the Agency to repeat past mistakes.

To achieve this goal, Smith had to streamline the CIA's analytical efforts. Since the Agency's inception, intelligence analysis was conducted by a single department called the Office of Reports and Estimates (ORE). The mission of the ORE was never well defined and analysis was performed by anyone whose desk a project landed on. Smith's military mindset called for a more specialized analysis structure. Between 1950 and 1952, Smith created six different offices of analysis within the CIA. The different departments each had a set area of focus and the entire structure was renamed the Directorate of Intelligence (DI). The findings of the DI were distilled into the Central Intelligence Bulletin, which has been delivered to the president daily since 1952.[70]

On January 21, 1952, Smith's executive assistant Loftus Becker was named the Agency's first DDI. A lawyer by trade and an Army Intelligence veteran, Becker took a hands-on approach to his new post. His function as DDI was a bit more than simply insuring the geeks of the CIA were doing their jobs. Becker was tasked with creating a line of communication between the symbiotically related DI and the clandestine services of the Directorate of Plans (DP).[71] In the infancy of electronic surveillance, and before satellite technology, agents in the field supplied a majority of the CIA's raw data. In order to perform effective clandestine duties, field operatives had to receive accurate and timely overviews about the regions in which they worked. In late January/early February of 1952, Loftus Becker would have been a man looking for opportunities to strengthen relationships between the two arms of the CIA and Steinbeck's letter would have presented just that opportunity.

Given the timing of Steinbeck's letter and the flurry of reference initials, we can piece together a promising scenario. Possibly being Smith's new executive assistant, "REL" was tasked with screening Smith's mail. "REL" reads the letter and pens what he thinks is a nice thank-you letter from Smith. Before showing the letter to Smith, "REL" takes it to his buddy Loftus Becker for a read over. The two men had probably worked together in the DCI's office a week before and "REL" didn't want to make a mess of things right out of the gate. Becker types "REL"'s response as he's reading it and something about the content is wrong. Either "REL" had not seen the opportunity of Steinbeck's offer and blew the famous author off, or the response was not written in such a way that would entice Steinbeck to work for the Agency. No matter what the situation was, Becker rewrites "REL"'s reply to Steinbeck and gives it to "mlk" to type up. Becker then presents the letter to Smith for review. Smith literally signs off on the idea

Walter Bedell Smith ca. 1956. Photo courtesy of the Harry S Truman Presidential Library.

and authorizes the letter to be sent out. Becker has an early win as DI and the Agency has a high-profile civilian asset that was provided by the DI and could be run by the DP.

The distribution section of the CIA's response to Steinbeck further supports the above scenario. First of all, a copy was sent to the DD/P (Deputy Director of Plans). This position has changed names a few times during the Agency's history and was originally called the Deputy Director of Operations (DDO). In January of 1951, the title changed to DD/P and reverted back to the DDO in March of 1973.[72] In 2005, the CIA did some slight restructuring, and the position is now the Director of the National Clandestine Service (NCS). No matter which title one is discussing, the current designation encapsulates the job's responsibilities. As previously mentioned, the DD/P was the person who oversees the CIA's clandestine agents. One can infer that Smith, and/or Becker, would not have sent a copy of Steinbeck's letter to the DD/P unless the Agency was serious about using him as an asset.

At the time Steinbeck's letter was sent, Frank Wisner was the DD/P. Wisner was an overworked micromanaging neurotic who fiercely defended his clandestine operations powerbase. Serving in the Second World War with the Office of Strategic Services (OSS), Wisner was one of the many OSS agents who would find their way into the ranks of the fledgling CIA after the Agency's formation in 1947. The OSS handled everything from basic intelligence gathering to inserting agents into German-occupied territories to assist local resistance groups. Wisner headed up OSS operations in southeast Europe and performed a minor miracle during the August 1944 Romanian royal coup.

The traditional monarchy of Romania, headed by King Michael, rallied pro-Allied units within the Romanian army to overthrow the country's Nazi puppet regime. The Soviets used the opportunity to focus their advance toward Romania to exploit the situation. In the midst of the coup, Wisner called on King Michael to allow an operation designed to free American prisoners of war (POW) held by the Germans in Romania. In the chaos of Royalist Romanians and Soviets fighting with pro-Nazi Romanians supported by German forces, over 1,700 American POWs were flown out of the country.

Wisner would leave the OSS in 1946 and return to Washington to practice law. Like many ex-OSS agents, a civilian life would be short-lived for Wisner. In 1947, he was offered the job of heading up covert operations for the newly formed CIA. The job title eventually morphed into the DD/P, a position Wisner would hold in 1952. On the pallet of operations Wisner created from circa 1947–1950, Operation MOCKINGBIRD would seem to apply to Steinbeck. Under the guise of MOCKINGBIRD, Wisner sought out journalists as both active and passive assets for the CIA. The scope of Operation MOCKINGBIRD will be discussed later in this text. But to give one an idea of how massive an undertaking MOCKINGBIRD was, over four hundred journalists were reported to have been involved with the CIA.[73] The participation of journalists with the CIA spanned a quarter of a century and ranged from the aforementioned intelligence gathering to outright propaganda.

Steinbeck would have neatly fit into Wisner's already established MOCKINGBIRD. In fact, Steinbeck may have already been involved with MOCKINGBIRD before 1952. In Steinbeck's letter to Smith, he specifically states that his legend is writing for *Collier's Weekly* as if John was well aware this would be an acceptable cover story. Given the celebrity status Steinbeck held, it is easy to reason that his point of contact would be DCI Smith's bailiwick. Even if Smith was not directly involved with running Steinbeck as an asset, the Agency might certainly wish to give Steinbeck that impression. Regardless of that, DD/P Wisner would be the person at the CIA who would have operational oversight for Steinbeck and therefore would have been informed of the author's intent. Had Smith's office not taken Steinbeck seriously, there would be no need to forward the letter to Wisner and Steinbeck's letter would have made its way into the nearest trash bin.

The final item on the distribution list gives a final glimpse of how the CIA handled Steinbeck. This recipient is listed as "Admin" and has been lined through. No bureaucracy can function without mountains of paperwork, and the CIA is no different than local animal control centers in this respect. Normally when a civilian volunteered to become a CIA asset, the final link in the process was to create a file on that individual. This was especially critical in cases where a civilian turned out not to be of use to the Agency. The members of the DI did not have time to waste on those presenting frivolous information. A simple note in John Doe's file stating, "He's a nutter and claims his grandmother is a dangerous Commie from Mars," would save DI officers hours of interviews and investigations. In the instances where a civilian was accepted as an asset, a file was generated like any other organization's personnel file. All of these functions were carried out by the CIA's Administrative Office.

On the administrative level, the CIA operates just like a corporation. In a corporation, employee files are commonly accessed by accounting, human resources, or management teams. Pay increases, changes in 401(k)s, and performance reviews all have to be routinely jacketed in one's file. The CIA operates with many of the same administrative burdens as a private enterprise, but differs in one respect. Even the most mundane records of certain individuals can tell a savvy admin clerk as much about someone's function within the Agency as full disclosure from the DCI. Even an intelligence officer performing a simple name search of CIA records could compromise a sensitive asset. To ensure that accidental disclosure of an asset did not happen, not everyone had a file sent down to the secretarial pool.

An asset like Steinbeck would have warranted special records treatment. The CIA's response to Steinbeck would have, by default, been listed for distribution to the administrative offices. The inclusion of the administrative offices in Smith's letter would therefore have been standard operating procedure from the letter's typist "mlk." Had Becker's reply to Steinbeck been meant as a hollow offer to placate a famous author, the transaction between Smith and Steinbeck would have ended up in an admin file with a notation for future officers to simply smile and nod if Steinbeck contacted the Agency again. The fact that Smith, and/or Becker, took the administrative offices out of the loop meant that Steinbeck's service was to be "off the books." Records of Steinbeck's work with the Agency would be kept in the offices of the DD/P or DI in a need-to-know capacity.[74]

Outside of the Becker/Smith response to Steinbeck, there is another bit of trace evidence that the CIA had accepted Steinbeck's offer. On March 18, 1952, the FBI responded to a file check on Steinbeck from the State Department.[75] The check was to include all information the Bureau had obtained on Steinbeck from February 13, 1948, to the present. Given the arbitrary backdate of February 13, 1948, we can assume the name check was for the last four years and was made on February 13, 1952. The request from the State Department could have been related to John obtaining visas for his upcoming trip. The name check could also have resulted from John's involvement with the Voice of America (VOA). In 1952, VOA operations were under the purview of the State Department and would not transfer to the United States Information Agency (USIA) until the Agency's creation in August of 1953. Neither visas nor VOA interviews are unlikely to have caused an FBI name check for Steinbeck. While applying for visas does sometimes trigger an FBI background check, John had already left for Europe when the FBI's check came back to the State Department.

A bust of Steinbeck on Monterey's Cannery Row. Photo courtesy of the Library of Congress.

Any visas John would have needed to enter the countries on his itinerary would have been well in hand before Steinbeck had left the United States. Likewise, VOA interviews tripping a background check are not probable because the VOA had aired interviews with Steinbeck on January 31st and February 11th and 26th of 1952.[76] If the State Department had some concerns about airing Steinbeck's views on VOA, the results of the name check would have been reviewed before the interviews were broadcast. It would seem that the VOA interviews or visa applications did not trigger an FBI background check on Steinbeck.

The timing of the State Department's request for an FBI name check does coincide with the CIA performing background checks on Steinbeck. We can assume that Steinbeck sent some sort of reply back to the CIA after receiving the Becker/Smith letter dated February 6th. Estimating a two-day postal delivery time between Washington and New York, the CIA's response would not have reached John until Saturday the 8th at the very earliest. Had John penned a second acceptance letter to Smith on that Saturday and posted it the same day, the second letter would not have arrived at CIA headquarters until Monday the 11th or Tuesday the 12th. If Steinbeck had phoned Smith to make arrangements for a meeting, it would not have been until the next working day of Monday the 11th. In either case, a four-year background check initiated by the CIA on February 13th fits perfectly in the timeline.

No matter what celebrity or social station one has, background checks are inevitable when performing classified work. By running an FBI name check on John through the State Department, no one at the FBI could make a connection between the CIA and Steinbeck. The employee originating the background check would likely have been a CIA officer with an official cover in the State Department. Diplomatic posts have always been rife with spies. In perusing the State Department's 1951 Foreign Service lists, there is a veritable "who's who" list of spooks. William Colby and E. Howard Hunt are two of the more recognizable spies listed in this text in their official cover capacity with the State Department.[77] One can then assume that the CIA utilized an agent with an official State Department cover to initiate the background check.

Understanding the background of the CIA's response to Steinbeck, we can now fully appreciate the content of the letter. Undoubtedly the Agency is accepting Steinbeck's offer, but there are parts of the letter that offer additional glimpses into the relationship between Steinbeck and the intelligence community. Steinbeck's letter to DCI Smith seemed to take the same familiar tone as the Becker/Smith reply to Steinbeck. It is almost as if Becker/Smith doesn't have to screen Steinbeck for asset work or even give him basic instructions for his mission. Steinbeck is told, "It would be helpful, too, if you could come down to Washington for a talk with us before you leave." The statement could simply be phrased as a polite request instead of an issuance of an order. Steinbeck would have had to meet with someone from the CIA before leaving for Europe. At the very least, Steinbeck would have to be given reporting procedures to use during his trip. Assets in Western Europe during the 1950s were usually given a secure phone number to call if they had something to report. The asset was then told when and where to meet an officer from the nearest CIA station to relay their information. Assets were sometimes given the backup of sending letters to a CIA-rented post office box with their findings. But this method was not preferred because of the chance a letter could be intercepted before being received by an intelligence officer.[78]

Steinbeck was living in New York in 1952 and a round-trip to Washington could have been made in a long day without rousing any questions to those around him. There are no records of John visiting Washington during February or March of 1952. The Agency would not have wanted John to broadcast a trip to CIA Headquarters. It would have been necessary for John to either disappear for a day or construct a convincing cover for a day trip to Washington. Steinbeck does mention in an April 13, 1956, letter to his publisher and friend, Pat Covici, that on that day he was going to Washington and he hadn't "been there since the war."[79] If Steinbeck's statement about not having been in Washington since the 1940s is accurate, it does not mean that Steinbeck did not go through with an assignment with the CIA. A CIA officer could have easily been assigned to meet Steinbeck in New York to make any necessary arrangements for the author's covert work.

The other possibility is that John simply lied to Covici about not having been in Washington since the Second World War. The logistics of a meeting in Washington aside, it might have been unnecessary for John to meet with anyone prior to the European trip. John is told by Becker/Smith that he can be of help ". . . in addition, on any other matters which seem to you of significance, particularly those which might be overlooked in routine reports." From the text, it sounds as if Becker/Smith knew Steinbeck would already have some idea of what "routine reports" would include. John did work for a number of government agencies during the Second World War, but this would not account for a basic knowledge of what current information the CIA was interested in John obtaining. That is unless there was a reason for John to have some background knowledge of intelligence gathering. Would this indicate that Steinbeck's involvement with the intelligence community was not limited to the Europe trip in 1952?

One set of documents within Steinbeck's FBI file dated April 12, 1957, might be the key to that question.[80] These twelve pages give an overview of the FBI's findings on Steinbeck to-date and appear to have been requested by the CIA. The page immediately preceding the FBI's report has been redacted under FOIA exemptions b1 (national security issues) and b3 (information exempt under other laws). I suspect this redacted page is the CIA's request for the FBI to generate a findings report on Steinbeck. At the head of the report's first page is a notation: "original to [redacted] Office of Security, CIA 4/15/57 [initials] AJP." The first two-and-a-quarter lines of this report have been redacted "per CIA b1, b3." To remove any doubt that the CIA wanted this document, typed at the bottom of the page is "Orig & dupl to CIA." If the CIA did not request the information from the FBI, they certainly received it. (This document and others mentioned in this text can be found in the Appendix of this book.)

The report goes on to chronicle basic biographical data on Steinbeck and other sources that mention Steinbeck. These other sources include publications, the House Committee on Un-American Activities (HUAC) and confidential informant reports on Steinbeck. The FBI's findings are roughly in chronological order and contain FBI b1 redactions that line up with events in the years 1944 and 1947. The CIA has one b1 and b3 redaction of an event that happened between December 1947 and May 1948. The next redaction from the CIA is a missing full page immediately before an FBI report sent to the CIA's Office of Security on April 12, 1957. The "what" sometimes answers the "why" in government documents. What exactly did the CIA's Office of Security do in 1957? According to the CIA, the Office of Security is described as follows:

> Security is an integral part of the CIA mission. DS [Directorate of Support, under which the Office of Security falls in the present organization of the CIA] Security officers are responsible for the protection of our organization's people, mission, facilities and information. Security officers are involved in a wide range of activities, from the vetting of personnel for positions of trust with the Agency and access to sensitive information, to protecting our facilities and information systems.[81]

Security hasn't changed much since 1957 and a CIA security officer from that time would nod in approval with how the current description fits with their duties in the 1950s.

Knowing the function of the Office of Security, there would be little reason for anyone there to request the FBI file if John was not either involved with the Agency in 1957, or recognized as a security threat. I doubt that John turned from an asset in 1952 to a threat to national security in 1957.

Six months before the FBI file was released, John was named a member of President Eisenhower's "People to People" program. The Presidential initiative was designed to encourage Americans to adopt foreign pen pals as a grassroots export of American ideals. Steinbeck, along with William Faulkner, Saul Bellows, and William Carlos Williams, were picked by Eisenhower as literary poster children for the program.[82] Someone suspected as being a security threat

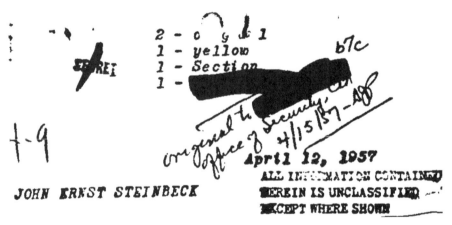

Top portion of the April 12, 1957, FBI reply to the CIA's Office of Security. The letters CIA can be seen after the cursive "Office of Security" and have been half covered by the redactions.

would not have been placed in a position of prominence in a foreign letter–writing campaign. Additionally, John was never called before HUAC and his post–World War II travel to foreign countries was never restricted. These tactics were commonly employed to those thought to be subversive during the Red Scare. Steinbeck's friend, Robert Capa, had his passport revoked in the early 1950s simply for traveling to Russia in 1947.[83] Oddly enough, Capa had traveled to Russia as the photographer for *A Russian Journal* with John, but the same fate never befell Steinbeck's passport.

There is an alternative theory as to the CIA's 1957 request of FBI documents on Steinbeck. John was the subject of the CIA's domestic mail-opening campaign codenamed Operation HTLINGUAL. The program ran from 1952 until approximately 1975 with a goal of finding Soviet agents operating within the United States. The goals of HTLINGUAL were achieved by stationing agents at postal sorting centers. With the full knowledge of the Postmaster General and local postal employees, these agents would work overnight pulling the mail of subjects on a predetermined "watch list." Early in the program, only the exterior of envelopes were copied for sender/receiver information. A few years into the operation, agents were cleared to extract and copy the contents of a subject's mail.

Steinbeck was supposedly targeted because of both his travel and correspondence behind the Iron Curtain. The Office of Security did initially run HTLINGUAL, but turned control of the operation over to James Jesus Angleton's Counterintelligence Office staff in 1955.[84] Agents from the Office of Security did stay involved with HTLINGUAL after 1955, but simply supplied the manpower to open and photograph the subjects' mail. Members of the Counterintelligence Office analyzed the letters' data and managed the day-to-day business of HTLINGUAL.[85] Had the 1957 request for FBI information on Steinbeck been regarding HTLINGUAL, the call would have come from Counterintelligence and not the Office of Security.

HTLINGUAL also explains why the CIA was not worried about directly requesting FBI documents about Steinbeck in 1957. The FBI also had a mail-opening program running concurrently with HTLINGUAL. The Bureau called their program Operation COINTELPRO (yet another clever government acronym for *Counterintelligence Program*) and started opening mail in 1956. Both the CIA and FBI were fully aware of the other's efforts to gather intelligence from domestic mail sources. Any request the CIA might have made of the FBI for information about an American citizen could be flagged for use with HTLINGUAL without raising any questions at the FBI. The CIA would even use HTLINGUAL as a cover for their interest in Steinbeck during the 1975 Church Commission. Steinbeck was mentioned, along with publisher Frederick Praeger and playwright Edward Albee, as being subjects of HTLINGUAL. In this case, the public admission of opening Steinbeck's mail would actually obfuscate the use of Steinbeck as an asset. The CIA had created a plausible denial for any interest the Agency showed in the author, should anyone during the Church Commission dig into prior history.

If HTLINGUAL or Steinbeck being a security risk did not trigger the Office of Security's request to the FBI, we can reasonably assume that Steinbeck was still working with the Agency in 1957. The timing of the CIA's request falls in line with this theory.

On March 25, 1957, John and his wife Elaine set sail from New York to Naples. The timing of the trip and the April CIA Office of Security request to the FBI are likely not happenstance. Once again, Steinbeck travels to Europe, and once again, the Agency digs into Steinbeck's background. Given that the Office of Security does the "vetting of personnel for positions of trust with the Agency," had John been chosen for a mission that required an additional security clearance? Unfortunately we may never know for sure without further document declassification.

The relationship between Steinbeck and the CIA doesn't end at 1957, and would appear to continue to at least 1964. Steinbeck's FBI file contains another document request by the CIA on February 27, 1964. This time the CIA has requested a summary of all Steinbeck's files sent by the FBI to the CIA. Included in this listing are the following FBI reports on Steinbeck sent to the CIA:

> Your attention is directed to the following reports and memoranda which have been sent to your agency;
>
> 1. Memorandum dated April 12, 1957, captioned "John Ernst Steinbeck" sent April 15, 1957.
>
> 2. Report dated August 24, 1959, by SAA[86] (name redacted) at New York captioned "Bulgarian Funds, New York Division" sent August 31, 1959.
>
> 3. Memorandum dated May 26, 1960, Chicago, Illinois, captioned (redacted), Internal Security-PO sent June 8, 1960.
>
> 4. Report dated February 14, 1964, at New York, by SA [Special Agent] (name redacted) captioned "Russky Golos Publishing Company."[87]

Unlike the April 1957 CIA request to the FBI, there is no indication as to which office of the CIA any of the aforementioned reports are sent. Even the FBI's file summary to the CIA in March of 1964 does not include any additional hints as to whom in the CIA the report was being sent. The

Your attention is directed to the following reports and memoranda which have been sent to your agency:

1. Memorandum dated April 12, 1957, captioned "John Ernst Steinbeck" sent April 15, 1957.

2. Report dated August 24, 1959, by SAA ███████ ████████ at New York captioned "Bulgarian Funds, New York Division" sent August 31, 1959.

3. Memorandum dated May 26, 1960, Chicago, Illinois, captioned ████████████████████ Internal Security-PO" sent June 8, 1960.

4. Report dated February 14, 1964, at New York, by SA ██████████████████ captioned "Russky Golos Publishing Company."

(100-106224-10, 65-34794-239, 105-81470-7, 100-39588-276)

Enclosure

Original & 1-CIA
Request Received-2-27-64

A portion of the February 27, 1964, FBI report sent to the CIA.

distribution list simply says, "Original & 1-CIA" and the request date. The individual instances of FBI files sent to the CIA in 1964 will be covered later in this text, but for the moment, we can be assured that the CIA was interested in Steinbeck at least until 1964.

There were too many holes in the FBI file to create a definitive picture of the CIA's interest in Steinbeck from 1952–1964. To fill in the redacted sections of Steinbeck's FBI file, I had previously sent the Agency an application for a Mandatory Declassification Review (MDR). The MDR process allows one to ask government agencies to review material for declassification that has been previously classified. Many government agencies and departments have set guidelines for declassifying documents that relate directly to the amount of time that has passed since the document was created. My request was filed before the CIA had cleared Steinbeck's 1952 letter for dispersal. At the time, I had hoped an MDR of Steinbeck's FBI file would help confirm or deny my suspicions as to whether the FOIA request to the CIA was a blind alley. Within the MDR request, I specifically cited sections that had been redacted by the CIA along with all other redactions of Steinbeck's FBI file. Since Steinbeck's FBI file was released in the 1980s, there was a chance that an MDR might force the FBI to reveal some of the redacted sections. The sticking point with an MDR is that, by law, a government Agency has up to a year to respond.

I was rattled when I received a reply from the FBI within a month of sending my MDR. The the response I received follows on the next page. Of note, copies original FBI and NARA letters in this chapter are to be found in this text's Appendix. The transcriptions, at times, have had redundant or unnecessary information (specific addresses and the like) truncated.

FOIPA Request No.: 1189085-000

Subject: STEINBECK, JOHN ERNST (MDR)

Dear Mr. Kannard:

This is in response to your Freedom of Information/Privacy Acts (FOIPA) request. In order to respond to our many requests in a timely manner, our focus is to identify responsive records in the automated and manual indices that are indexed as main files. A main index record carries the names of subjects of FBI investigations. Records which may be responsive to your FOIPA request were destroyed February 15, 2005. Since this material could not be reviewed, it is not known if it was responsive to your request. The retention and disposal of records is governed by statute and regulation under the supervision of the National Archives and Records Administration (NARA), Title 44, United States Code, Section 3301 and Title 36, Code of Federal Regulations, Chapter 12, Sub-chapter B, Part 1228. The FBI Records Retention Plan and Disposition Schedules have been approved by the United States District Court for the District of Columbia and are monitored by NARA.

Additionally, a search of the Central Records System maintained at FBI Headquarters indicated that potentially responsive records have been sent to NARA. If you wish to review these potentially responsive records, send your request to NARA at the following address using file number 100-HQ-145 as a reference: . . .

You may file an appeal by writing to the Director, Office of Information Policy (OIP). . . Your appeal must be received by OIP within sixty days from the date of this letter in order to be considered timely. The envelope and the letter should be clearly marked "Freedom of Information Appeal." Please cite the FOIPA Request Number assigned to your request so that it may be identified easily. Enclosed for your information is a copy of the FBI File Fact Sheet.

Very truly yours, David M. Hardy, Section Chief, Record/Information, Dissemination Section, Records Mgt. Division

The letter's closure should have read, "Very truly yours, we destroyed the documents." The FBI knowingly destroyed documents on a person of historical and literary importance. I quickly found out this isn't the first time the FBI has been party to the destruction of historical documents.

Washington, D.C.'s, J. Edgar Hoover Building serves as the national headquarters for the FBI. Image courtesy of the FBI.

In 2009, *USA Today* reported that they had filed an FOIA request for Walter Cronkite's FBI file after his death in July of 2007. The newspaper received a notice very similar to mine stating that Cronkite's FBI file had been destroyed in October of 2007. One might be able to forgive the FBI if this was a onetime *mea culpa*. Unfortunately the FBI has also destroyed Rosa Parks' file despite having a policy to work "with the National Archives to try to ensure historically important records are preserved."[88] *USA Today* was not the only media outlet to who tried to obtain Cronkite's FBI file. The *Gawker* website sent a request to the FBI for Cronkite's file, but got a slightly different response. There does seem to have been a file that mentioned Cronkite in relation to an extortion case. Since Cronkite was not the subject of the investigation, the FBI didn't consider it historically relevant.[89] The public will never know if that particular document had historical value.

The oddity about the MDR of Steinbeck's FBI file is that it has been digitally archived on the FBI's own website.[90] Anyone may go to the FBI's "Vault" website (http://vault.fbi.gov/John%20Steinbeck) to view a PDF of Steinbeck's file. Given the FBI's response to the MDR, it would seem that the FBI scanned Steinbeck's redacted file and chucked out the original. If the redacted file was important enough to be digitally archived and publicly displayed, shouldn't the file in its entirety also have historical worth? I decided to put that question to the FBI. Under the FOIA laws, a refusal of an MDR can also be appealed. This is an excerpt of my basis for my appeal to Melanie Ann Pustay (Director of Information Policy, DOJ) on May 24, 2012:

> . . . I am appealing the denial of this FOPIA request on the grounds
> of the unsurity of the FBI's assertion that the documents in my MDR
> request were specifically destroyed and that the destruction of these
> documents could potentially violate internal policies of the FBI, thus
> increasing the likelihood these documents do still exist.

To the first point of my appeal, the language in the denial does not indicate that the documents were, in fact, destroyed. The phrasing which I emphasized in the previous quotation points to there being some question as to the status of these documents. The denial states that the documents were not found within the FBI's main index file. Mr. Steinbeck's file contains information from the 1940s and '50s. It is reasonable to assume that these specific documents may not have been indexed. According to the denial of an unrelated request, the FBI stated that their main indexing of files from this time frame were in the process of being scanned and may not be found within the index at this time.

I would argue that given Mr. Steinbeck's position within the literary community and American history, all efforts should be made to ascertain the precise disposition of these documents.

The historical nature of these documents brings me to the second point of my appeal. John Steinbeck was not only considered one of America's greatest authors, he was the recipient of the Nobel Prize for Literature and the United States Medal of Freedom. The merits of Mr. Steinbeck's contribution to American society and history are abundantly apparent.

According to a 2009 *USA Today* interview with former FBI legal counsel Scott Hodes on the destruction of CBS news anchor Walter Cronkite's FBI file, Mr. Hodes states that, "All FBI records on such a prominent person should have been saved under the FBI's policies." Not being privy to FBI internal policies, I can only assume that Mr. Hodes' statements are accurate and truthful. If this is the case, the destruction of portions of Mr. Steinbeck's FBI file would have, at very least, not been in the best interest of American history. At worst, the destruction of these documents could violate the policies outlined by Mr. Hodes' statement.

If this is the case, the FBI has shown that they recognize Mr. Steinbeck as a person of historical interest. The FBI has provided Mr. Steinbeck's FBI file on their webpage entitled "The Vault." By inclusion in this group of documents, the FBI has recognized the merits of preserving Mr. Steinbeck's file and presenting it to the public. Since Mr. Steinbeck's FBI file was preserved electronically on 31 Aug 1999 (according to the origination date of the PDF of Mr. Steinbeck's FBI file downloaded from "The Vault"), I find it highly unlikely that portions of this document were destroyed 5 years later.

I would respectfully appeal the decision of the FBI in this matter. The historical value of gaining a deeper understanding into the life of Mr. Steinbeck warrants a closer look into the disposition of the documents held within my request. Should the documents in question be found, I would ask that my initial MDR request for these documents be reinstated. Please contact me if there is additional information.

The response I received is below. The FBI basically told me I didn't understand what "we destroyed the documents" means:

August 9, 2012

Re: MDRA 2012-0000

Request No. 1189085

KWC:SKV

You appealed from the action of the Federal Bureau of Investigation on your Mandatory Declassification Review (MDR) request for certain records concerning John Steinbeck.

By letter dated May 4, 2012, the FBI informed you that records which may have been responsive to your request were destroyed on February 15, 2005, and that further potentially responsive records are maintained by the National Archives and Records Administration. Because the FBI did not withhold any classified information, there is no action for the Department Review Committee (DRC) to consider on appeal.

If you construe this response as a denial of your request, you may appeal to the InterAgency Security Classification Appeals Panel pursuant to Section 5.3 of Executive Order 13526.

Sincerely, Mark A. Bradley, DRC Chairman

cc: Federal Bureau of Investigation

I have a feeling that Mr. Bradley thought my appeal was as asinine as I regarded Bradley's denial. There was really no need in pursuing the issue of Steinbeck's FBI file with the DOJ any further. If the files have been destroyed, the FBI could not magically resurrect the information I was looking for. If I succeeded in filing a lawsuit against the DOJ, a Federal judge could not order the FBI to produce documents that officially don't exist. However, in a digital age, it is unconscionable that any government agency should destroy any documents, especially those with historical importance.

Currently, the millions of pages of bureaucratic Shakespeare that local, State, and Federal government bodies generate every year is somewhat regulated by the National Archives and Records Administration's (NARA) 168-page tome entitled the *Disposition of Federal Records: A Records Management Handbook*.[91] The handbook is more "Hints from Heloise" than the Ten Commandments where documents of historical importance are concerned. The head of each government department/agency sets their own guidelines to schedule the disposition or disposal of documents. In turn, each department/agency names an official historian who is tasked with ensuring schedules are adhered to. Files that have historical significance fall into the category of "permanent records" and appear to be flagged as such by the individual department/agency historians. Permanent records are then turned over to the NARA to ascertain if they are indeed permanent-record worthy.

The NARA admits that the process of determining if a record is worthy of being permanent is "complex." One of the litmus tests the NARA suggests that historians follow is:

> The importance of records, especially permanent records, in documenting and preserving the memory of an agency, the Federal Government, and American society.[92]

Rosa Parks, Walter Cronkite, or John Steinbeck would certainly fall into the category being of "important to American society." So then why has the FBI destroyed documents related to their life? The system for oversight into documents that are actually flagged for destruction seems to be nonexistent. NARA's main concern is that record-keeping schedules are approved and kept to date. There appears to be nothing like a list of persons or events that government departments/agencies are given by the NARA as items of historical merit. In the *Disposition of Federal Records: A Records Management Handbook* section on "Appraisal Guidelines for Permanent Records" the NARA states:

> Because of the wide variety of records accumulated by the Government and because of differences in agency organizations, functions, and recordkeeping systems, these guidelines cannot include all the records that may be eligible for permanent retention.[93]

The guidelines give the individual agencies/departments wide latitude for interpreting what is a permanent record. What's worse, there are no real consequences if a department/agency does destroy a historical document, as long as the NARA schedule has been followed. The current Federal law that governs everything from removing to destroying public documents references records that *should be kept on hand*, given the NARA's destruction schedule.[94] The law does not address documents that have been intentionally or "mistakenly" mis-categorized and destroyed. The end result is that if any arm of the government waits long enough, they can destroy whatever documents they wish with no legal repercussions. Undoubtedly the records officer for a department/agency would have some sort of reprimand placed in their employee file, but public embarrassment after the fact appears to be the only accountability in the process.

The issue of record retention is a larger issue than my personal quest to obtain a true picture of John Steinbeck's covert life. The NARA regulations actually give government agencies/departments a statute of limitations for their misdeeds. Let's hypothetically consider what may have been in Walter Cronkite's FBI file. The public is not privy to the FBI's record schedule, so let's arbitrarily give FBI files a thirty-year shelf life. The other condition in this equation is that FBI files cannot be released to the public until a person's death. In our hypothetical FBI file on Cronkite, there are records of the FBI opening Cronkite's mail as part of their illegal domestic surveillance program COINTELPRO. This particular domestic surveillance program was canceled after the Church Commission findings in the mid-1970s, and Cronkite died in 2009. The FBI cleans house and destroys the portion of Cronkite's FBI file containing references to COINTELPRO after the thirty-year mark. Since Cronkite outlived the thirty-year document statute of limitations, no one making a FOIA request of Cronkite's file after his death will ever see mention of COINTELPRO. The FBI has technically done nothing wrong because they have followed the NARA-approved record retention schedule and the public is none the wiser to a violation of Cronkite's civil rights. Once again, the example of Cronkite's FBI file is for the sake of argument, but it does illustrate how government agencies can play games with the FOIA process.

For the next few weeks, I stewed over the FBI letters as I started working on the manuscript for this book. I had still not requested FBI file 100-HQ-145 from the National Archives as suggested in the original FBI denial. I wasn't even sure what that file might have contained, but according to the FBI, the documents were "potentially responsive records" to my request for a MDR on Steinbeck's FBI file. So in late August, I sent this portion of the following letter to the National Archives on August 30, 2012:

> Under the Freedom of Information Act, 5 U.S.C. subsection 552, I am requesting information or records on FBI File 100-HQ-145. This request is pursuant to FOIPA Request 1189085-00 of the Department of Justice (Federal Bureau of Investigations) suggestion that I seek this document within your holdings. The original request was related to FBI file numbers 9-4583 and 100-106224 on John Ernst Steinbeck (SSN: xxx-xx-xxxx). . .

> If you deny all or any part of this request, please cite each specific exemption you think justifies your refusal to release the information and notify me of appeal procedures available under the law. . .

I actually received two letters back from the NARA for this request.

November 6, 2012

Dear Mr. Kannard:

This is in further response to your Freedom of Information Act (FOIA) request of August 30, 2012 (our case number NW 38734) for access to Federal Bureau of Investigation (FBI) Headquarters Case Files 9-4583 and 100-106224 regarding John Ernst Steinbeck. In our previous letter dated November 6, 2012, we stated that file 9-4583 was microfilmed, but we believed that the microfilm was still in the FBI's custody. Today the FBI informed us, after checking thoroughly, that the file is not included on their microfilm.

Sincerely, Mary Kay Schmidt, Archivist, Special Access

(and)

November 17, 2012

Dear Mr. Kannard:

This is in response to your Freedom of Information Act (FOIA) request of August 30, 2012, which was received in this office on September 29, 2012. Your request has been assigned case number NVV 38734. You requested access to FBI Headquarters Case Files 9-4583 and 100-106224 regarding John Ernst Steinbeck. These files are part of Record Group 65, Records of the FBI.

We conducted a search for the files but could not locate them among our holdings. After contacting the FBI to request additional information, we learned that file 100-106224 was listed as "destroyed" on February 15, 2005. File 9-4583 was microfilmed, but we believe that the microfilm is still in the custody of the FBI. For your information, we noticed that the FBI has digitized these two files and made them available on their Website. You may view the files at http://vault.fbi.gov/John%20Steinbeck...

This concludes the processing of your FOIA request.
Martha Wagner Murphy, Chief Special Access and FOIA

One might notice that there is no mention of FBI file 100-HQ-145 anywhere in the NARA's response. Mrs. Murphy seems to have misread my request believing that I was requesting access to Steinbeck's FBI file. The level of frustration I felt at Mrs. Murphy's response is not something a polite person puts in print; however there was a silver lining to this bureaucrat's lack of attention to detail. The second letter from Mrs. Murphy states that as far as the NARA was concerned, part of Steinbeck's FBI file (#9-4583) was still being held by the FBI. In trying to follow the logic of government document retention regulations set by the NARA, one possibility leaps forward. If the NARA knew of the existence of file 9-4583, then someone at the FBI had to have notified the NARA that the file was categorized "permanent."[95] If this is the case, we are left wondering why the FBI destroyed a permanent record.

The irresistible force of history meets the immovable wall of government. Currently there are still a number of FOIA appeals and further requests pending in various government offices, all with a subject line of John Steinbeck. Perhaps one day we will have the full story of John Steinbeck and the CIA. Until then, the open-ended possibilities of Steinbeck's 1952 letter to the CIA require viewing Steinbeck's life with an approach based on astronomy.

On April 21, 1992, two radio astronomers, Aleksander Wolszczan and Dale Frail, made the first confirmed discovery of planets outside our solar system. Astronomers before that point knew within a good degree of certainty that other stars had planets, just as ours does, but were never able to prove other planets existed. Compared to stars, planets are too small and dark to observe with ground-based optical telescopes so Wolszczan and Frail took an indirect approach to their planet search. The star the astronomers focused on was a pulsar, which rotates and emits a predictable burst of radio waves. A planet that orbits a pulsar will slightly change the radio wave emissions of the pulsar when the planet comes between the star and the Earth. Wolszczan and Frail succeeded and were able to demonstrate that two planets were orbiting the pulsar by looking for the slight anomalies in the star's regular patterns. No one had seen the two planets, but we knew they were there.[96]

In the case of John Steinbeck and the CIA, we are left with an incomplete picture in which we have to focus on the anomalies in John's life. Much like Wolszczan and Frail, the examination of the association between the CIA and Steinbeck has to be charted by out-of-place actions and personal connections. It is my contention that John Steinbeck worked with the United States intelligence community from 1940 to at least 1964. Either through document classification or destruction, we are left with few other options than postulations that will create a discernible pattern. The destruction of documents by the FBI and the Glomar exclusion of CIA files is a setback in understanding the complete story of John Steinbeck's life, but it is not an end point. Although they would never admit it, I would bet the family farm there are more documents related to John Steinbeck in some CIA storage facility. It may take another fifty years for the CIA to release those documents to the public, but asking open-ended questions and making theories from the information we have available is the first step.

Another hurdle in viewing Steinbeck through the lens of the CIA also leaves us bereft of logic's handiest tool, Occam's Razor. The principle states, "Entities should not be multiplied unnecessarily." All things being equal, the more complex the theory, the less likely that theory is correct. When dealing with espionage, it is difficult to follow the centuries-old tenet of logic. Espionage is built on a solid foundation of secrecy and deception; neither lend themselves to looking for simple answers in a multipart equation. We are left with little more than a treasure hunt within the limits of what is publicly known about Steinbeck.

My conclusions might not be your conclusions on the other materials presented within this text. I'm sure Steinbeck scholars will present their opinions based on obscure evidences

Steinbeck and his son, John IV, meet with President Johnson at the White House in 1966. Image courtesy of the LBJ Library and Museum.

that have long languished outside the public's view. I also do not say this as a hedge against any of the research I have done for this book. In preparing this text, I have tried to utilize as many references that are openly available to generate the discussion about Steinbeck and the CIA. There is an implicit compact between writer and reader that states, "If you read what I've written, you will get something for your time." Stephen King's readers get to sleep with a nightlight for a period after reading most of his books, for example. What I hope to achieve with this text is a starting point for your own examination into the topic. This book embodies the quest of the "every man" and "every woman." I think John would have liked it that way.

Most of us learned in a biology or psychology class that there are two scientific explanations relating to how humans develop a personality. The first is that nature almost predestines our personalities via our genetic makeup. On the other side of the fence is the theory of nurturing. Those residing in that camp believe we are born with a blank slate and our life experiences create a distinct personality. The literary world ascribes to the nurturing aspect of human development. The average literary commentator measures why an author writes a particular work and bases it on the influences and events in his or her life. These critics feel the B.F. Skinner approach is the way an outsider can come to terms with the life of a creative person. Since we cannot ride the double helix of the human genome, one's life story is the best information most of us have to work with.

The "nurture theory" is often applied to the lives of great authors because the lives of these men and women are usually well-documented affairs. There is an inherent need to understand an author's work by dissecting their lives. One has to look no further than a freshman literature class as proof. Professors boil any author's works down to a simple, almost formulaic recipe. Take a pint of a dysfunctional family, fold in wartime trauma, and then sprinkle a healthy dose of alcoholism to taste. Bake the ingredients with a few bad marriages and *voilà*—one has the works of Ernest Hemingway. William Faulkner's and Flannery O'Connor's tales were written because of their experiences as Southerners. Herman Melville and Charles Dickens were longwinded because they were paid by the word. To keep this work at a "PG" rating, we will not get into the motivations behind Henry Miller and Anaïs Nin's work.

A backwards engineering of the "recipe" theory is commonly true of fans of great authors. Hardcore readers reverse the author's creative process as a way of backtracking the author's life. We visit the houses and haunts of those who have written works that have influenced our lives, and that process gives us some tangible connection to their creative process. Like the literary critic, the fan struggles to understand the motivations of putting pen to paper.

Mystery is a hard pill to swallow for those wishing to create a mental stew for resolving an author's works. Take, for example, the public's treatment of J.D. Salinger. The famous recluse was hounded by those wishing for five minutes of his time to explain the mysteries of *Catcher in the Rye*. Shortly after his death, the UK's *Guardian* newspaper published a picture of the reclusive Salinger. A reporter had taken it upon himself to drive into the Salinger compound hoping to snag the Holy Grail of literary interviews. What our meddling media hound came away with was an iconic photograph of a frightening looking Salinger beating on the reporter's car window.[1] The need for the intrusive journalist to trespass on Salinger's property, and self-imposed exile, was fueled by the public's wish to understand the "recipe" behind one of the twentieth century's most influential novels.

I must confess to indulging in a type of the aforementioned behavior. If one were to look at my travel log, one would see trips to Paris, New York, and Monterey. To the uninitiated, these trips might seem to be simply for the pleasure of the experience. Those who know me understand that *The Short Reign of Pippin IV* and *Sweet Thursday* prompted the side excursions to Number One Avenue de Marigny, Harry's New York Bar, The Algonquin, and Cannery Row. Much as a psychometrist would discern the events of a person's life by holding a wedding ring, these pilgrimages were all in an attempt to pick up a feeling for John Steinbeck. The travels were made to fulfill a hope that something in the ether surrounding these near-sacred places would jump out at me. The possibility existed that these places were like Steinbeck's description of Cannery Row: "A poem, a stink, a grating noise, a quality of light, a tone, a habit, a nostalgia, a dream."[2]

The description of Cannery Row can also be used to understand an almost imperceptible facet of Steinbeck's life. Like a hint of sulfur that taints the air after a match is lit, there is an undercurrent of a love of secret things that flows concurrently with the early documentation of his life story. The elements of secrecy are easily overlooked in the pursuit of understanding Steinbeck's work, but the goal here is to examine a man's life primarily outside his writing. In our context, Steinbeck's ever-present mysticism and furtive references in his novels are a reflexive glance of a man who volunteered for work with the CIA. Examining the class distinctions in *The Winter of Our Discontent*, the eternal struggle between good and evil in *East of Eden*, and the political satire of *The Short Reign of Pippin IV* overshadows references to the Knights Templar, Freemasonry, and a lost Merovingian line within these same books. We therefore see Steinbeck as a man driven by the larger motivations and forget that he truly was a man who first loved hidden things and intentionally parceled the infatuation with the *sub rosa* into his work. A foundation for a love of the concealed started with a fascination with King Arthur early in life.

Imagine looking backwards in time to a pre-adolescent John Steinbeck having problems reading. There was no physical impairment that made reading difficult for John. His eyesight was fine and the lad did not suffer from an ailment, such as dyslexia, that made reading taxing. The Steinbeck's house was full of books and his mother had even been a trained as a teacher. John's mother Olive would instruct the boy for hours at a time, but something in John's mind did not adapt to the written word. It was not a matter of the material being boring to the student. The Steinbecks' son enjoyed listening to stories that were read to him. Yet nothing his parents did seemed to make an impact on John's reading abilities.

Had John's parents asked the schoolboy, he would have no doubt expressed a certain amount of angst over mastering the written word. In the introduction to *The Acts of King Arthur and His Noble Knights* John states, "I remember that words—written or printed—were devils, and books, because they gave me pain were my enemies."[3] The thought of a Nobel Prize–winning author having a near phobia of books is inconceivable. Certainly John's early mental block against the written word has been glossed over by some Steinbeck biographers. The oversight is tragic in a biographical setting because the solution to young John's reading problem would drive him to seek out the hidden.

John's maternal aunt, Molly, simply gave her nephew a copy of Thomas Malory's *Le Morte d'Arthur*. The books in the Steinbeck home were community property. Everyone in the house had access to any of the volumes, but the book Aunt Molly gave John was *his*. The distinction of actually owning a book gave way to a curiosity in John to understand what the words on the pages said.

John would later use another ploy to stimulate reading with his own sons. There was a locked chest in John's library and the elder Steinbeck told his sons that they could read anything in the library except the books in that box. The illicit books were too much of a temptation for the Steinbeck boys and they voraciously read whatever text was locked away. John directed what he wanted his sons to read by the ruse. John confirmed the strength of the forbidden fruit gambit one night at a dinner party when he overheard his son Thomas discussing one of the banned books with a guest.[4]

Just as Thomas had found a niche with discussing a book with a dinner guest, John found that Malory's text had cracked the reading code. The archaic English of Malory not only started to make sense to John, but the prose became a secret language that only he understood. Chivalry, quests, sword fights, magic, and fair maidens are mental candy for a preadolescent boy. Steinbeck was hardly the first to come under the spell of Arthurian legend and will by no means be the last. But secrets aren't much fun to hold alone and John let his sister Mary into the world he had discovered. The siblings cavorted in the Gabilan Mountains outside of Salinas. The mountain peaks played the part of a far-away castle backdrop. John would make up Arthurian stories and the pair would act those tales out.[5] This was possibly the first time in Steinbeck's life that he had a creative outlet. John's sister would revel in the tales John weaved and relished that her big brother would involve her in the games.

The words of Malory would be a touchstone and fascination that held John for the rest of his life. The author would spend the better part of the mid-1950s researching Malory in an effort to modernize *Le Morte d'Arthur*. The influence Malory's work had on John is often underemphasized because aside from a few concrete cases, Malory is difficult to track in John's own writing. It is difficult to tangibly link the writing style between an author writing in modern English to that of Malory's Middle English. *Cannery Row, Sweet Thursday*, and *Tortilla Flats* are the closest thematically and structurally to the works of Malory. Each of these works is more a combination of linked vignettes that complete a fable-like novel. Unfortunately each of these books is *summarily* dismissed as minor works in the light of *The Grapes of Wrath* and *East of Eden* and Malory's influence is not given the attention it deserves.

The true influence that is missed in Steinbeck's affinity for Malory is within John's own character. One of the greatest tenants of the chivalric ideal is that of the strong championing the weak. Little has to be said in this regard in light of Steinbeck's work to bring the plight of migrant farm workers to the public's attention. John was a tad more realistic and critical of his own need to serve the greater good than that of the idyllic King Arthur. Lancelot was the comparison John actually made to himself of all of the Knights of the Round Table. The relationship between John and Lancelot is often chalked up to John's self-deprecating view of his character and talents. Like his characters, Steinbeck is a flawed man. Given to excessive drink, adultery in his first marriage, manic periods, and an understated temper, it is easy to see why Steinbeck would associate himself with the imperfections of King Arthur's greatest knight. While the reasons for Steinbeck identifying with Lancelot are accurate, John would have another reason to find a kindred spirit with the disgraced knight.

In the Grail Cycle, Lancelot's indiscretion with Guinevere nearly destroys Arthur's kingdom. Camelot sprang into being because it was Arthur's will. Even with the intrigue and imperfections of his Round Table, the illusion of Camelot persists as long as Arthur believes the kingdom is an idyllic place. To Camelot, and Arthur, from disintegrating from within, Lancelot adds the sin of deception to his next confession's list. In "Sir Lancelot and Queen Guinevere," Malory recounts the kidnapping of Arthur's queen by Sir Mellygaunce. Lancelot comes to Guinevere's rescue, but initially the queen asked Lancelot to spare Mellygaunce's life. In their parlay, Mellygaunce becomes suspicious that Guinevere is having an affair with Lancelot. The sly Mellygaunce tries to trap Lancelot by playing on his honorable nature. Mellygaunce's plan is to force Lancelot into a confession by shifting the blame to one of ten other knights. Knowing that Lancelot would never intentionally say anything to dishonor his fellow knights, Mellygaunce feels sure Lancelot will shoulder the blame. Lancelot recognizes the gambit and unexpectedly crafts a lie that not only clears the other knights, but him as well. Mellygaunce's plan to rat out Lancelot and Guinevere falls short and Camelot is saved for the moment.

"He is tested, he fails the test and is still noble," said Steinbeck in a 1959 letter to his editor Elizabeth Otis about Lancelot.[6] The sentiment sums up Steinbeck's feelings about Lancelot and by extension himself. The lie Lancelot told to Mellygaunce was uttered to maintain the illusion of Camelot in Arthur's eyes and therefore save the entirety of the kingdom. John's own double life as an asset with the CIA is an analogy to Lancelot's duplicity that would not have been overlooked by Steinbeck. There would be times John would have to lie to the people closest to him in order to maintain his cover. "Honey, I'm going out to get a pack of smokes," is a harmless lie used to cover up a meeting with John's handler. The dishonesty might be small, but the sin is the same. The difference in John's Lancelot-tinted eyes was that the deception assisted those keeping his loved ones and country safe at night.

On the flipside of a necessity for dishonesty, John learned at an early age that certain truths can only be stated to the correct audience. A little-known event in Steinbeck's life was described in the short story "The Wool Gatherer." The story was penned by John's son Thomas in the anthology *Down to a Soundless Sea*.[7] To make money during the summertime, a teenage John would work as a ranch hand on Big Sur's Post Ranch. The ranch was far enough away from the nearest train station that John would ride horseback to reach the cattle farm. While riding out for his first day of work during the summer of 1920, John's mount became agitated. Thinking the horse had caught wind of a predator, John steadied his steed and surveyed the trail ahead.

A scan of the area did not raise an alarm to the seventeen-year-old Steinbeck. But his horse's actions betrayed that John must have missed something. Looking more closely at a rise to the side of the trail, John finally clued into the source of the mare's discomfort. Fighting the horse's bucking and kicking, John discerned movement on the embankment. The motion became a shape and the shape slowly morphed into the form of a bear. Rising up on its hind legs, the beast looked down at John and his mount. John came to realize this was not your run-of-the-mill California brown bear; nor was the creature a grizzly bear. The sight of either animal would have been frightful enough, but John had come upon something that shouldn't exist. The animal was enormous and was described as being "big enough to have taken a whole steer and walk off with it still kicking."[8] John believed he had encountered the legendary Great Sur Bear. Campfire stories of these giant bears circulated Big Sur and the Salinas Valley about the great-grandfathers of John's generation hunting the bears to extinction.

While the bear made no aggressive moves toward John, his horse was not going to take the chance on the bear changing its mind. John's mount flew down the treacherous trail for a couple of miles before the lad could get her under control. The ordeal wasted half the morning's travel time and caused John to be late for his first day at work. When the young Steinbeck explained his tardiness to his fellow hands and Mr. Post, a wave of ridicule followed. The bookish lad was seen by his compatriots as making up the tale as a fanciful cover for his tardiness. Undone by the derision, Steinbeck spent every free minute searching Big Sur for tracks of the monster bear. He craved some physical evidence to prove that he had actually seen the creature. The quest cut into John's work time and even cost him the use of his horse. After venturing far off a trail, John's mount lost her footing and skidded down an embankment. The medical care for the horse bankrupted the teen of the entire summer's wages. At the end of the summer, John would have to borrow money from Mrs. Post to hire a stagecoach for the return trip to Salinas.

John never found the evidence that would vindicate his belief that the Great Sur Bear had crossed his path. Of the story's veracity, Thom Steinbeck did not doubt that his father believed he had seen the giant bear.

> My father told me that story a thousand times, and swore it was true. He always began the story with, "The only thing worse than telling a lie, and getting caught, is telling the truth and having no one believe you."[9]

What is not fully examined in "The Wool Gatherer" is the inevitable fallout from the other ranch hands. We are given a small taste of the condemnation John received at telling the story of the Great Sur Bear on the first day of work. Teenage boys can be merciless in their teasing, and every time John went out to look for evidence of the bear, a miniature version of the first day of work followed. One can wonder if the tenor of Curley's cruelty in *Of Mice and Men* was born out of the ridicule John received at the hands of the boys.

In sighting the Great Sur Bear, Steinbeck found out that the truth always comes with a price. Telling one's boss that her new blouse is a travesty in polyester might be the truth, but bluntly verbalizing that fact might not be in one's best self-interest. John would be reminded of honesty's penalty when *The Grapes of Wrath* was published. The vicious attacks on Steinbeck's character and validity of migrant farmer's poor living conditions could easily have turned Steinbeck into a J.D. Salinger–type recluse. However, through the censure that percolated from *The Grapes of Wrath* and the event that shaped "The Wool Gatherer," John held fast because he had spoken the truth. When it came time for John to decide to pursue work with the CIA, the price of truth would once again be high. The juxtaposition of relaying accurate observations would be met

The short-faced bear, or *Arctodus*, closely resembles the description of the Great Sur Bear. *Arctodus* became extinct 11,000 years ago and folk tales of these giant bears likely spawned the legend of the Big Sur Bear. *Arctodus'* size is seen here relative to a six-foot-tall man.*

with the need for secrecy about his association with the CIA. The lesson from "The Wool Gatherer" would be that the price for telling friends and family of his assignments for the CIA was too costly for Steinbeck to bear. John's honor would have been tarnished by allowing those close to him to know the truth, and it is likely that the same people would have been hurt by John obfuscating the association with the Agency. The key to balancing the price of truth with the need for secrecy was another lesson a young Steinbeck would learn of, in all places, a fraternal organization in which he was a member.

On the second Tuesday night of every month, John's father would have donned his Sunday best before leaving the house for the rest of the evening.[10] Being a quizzical lad, John would have questioned where his father was going. The inquiry would have been made not because John didn't know where his father was going, but because John didn't understand what his father accomplished on his monthly, and sometimes weekly, outings. Understanding the need for John's quiz, his father would have likely answered, "John, you know I'm going to a Lodge meeting." John's father was a prominent member of Salinas' Freemasonic Lodge and his mother was a member of the Order of the Eastern Star.[11] Like most children of Masons, John would have grown up with his parents going to meetings and discussing veiled references to their affiliations. The young Steinbeck would have been entranced with the trappings of his parents' involvement in Masonic organizations. The precocious John would have had a litany of unanswerable questions when the regalia of Masonry caught his eye. Rings, aprons, and lapel pins festooned with arcane symbols are a gold mine for a young boy's imagination.[12]

The fraternity of Freemasons has been in existence from at least 1717, when the first Grand Lodge was formed in England. There is evidence that the institution is much older than the first Grand Lodge. The Lodge of Edinburgh (Mary's Chapel) #1 holds minutes of Masonic Meetings taking place from 1599 onwards.[13] The accepted history of Masonry is that the fraternity grew out of medieval stonemason guilds. At different levels of proficiency, a mason would be taught a secret word and handgrip that was given to paymasters for the appropriate level of wages. Those in the building profession of that time also closely guarded their methods of erecting structures, which necessitated workers clinging to a strict code of silence. Builders and architects during the medieval period also believed there was a spiritual aspect to their work. The mathematical components that allowed Europe's grand cathedrals to be erected were, in a sense, the language of God. The principles of earthly architecture mirrored the philosophy of God's universal architecture. The more mystical component of the stonemason guilds began to attract the patrons of buildings around the late fifteenth century. Those who were not actual builders were given the honorary title as speculative masons within the guild system. Moral lessons were coupled with an architectural motif and what were once stonemasons guilds became the fraternity we know as modern-day Freemasonry.[14]

While today's Freemasonry is primarily a charitable fraternity, the same aspects of the secrecy permeating stonemasons guilds still exist. The proceedings of a Masonic Lodge cannot be spoken of to those outside the fraternity. The secrecy is in place to protect the free speech of those attending a Lodge. Freemasonry utilizes a system of morality plays called "degrees" that teach specific lessons to that degree's candidate. Masonry, in all its forms, utilizes visual/oral symbols and sometimes legendary historical examples to teach universally accepted moral lessons. The concepts of hard work, toleration, balance in one's life, and basic moral virtues are presented within the workings of a degree. These rituals are also kept behind the closed door of the Lodge in the same way medieval building techniques were guarded.

Another foundation of Freemasonry is that all men are equal. The notion of equality seems sophomoric in the twenty-first century, but in the fifteenth century, the concept was revolutionary. Regardless of social station or economic status, each man's voice carries the same weight in a Lodge meeting. The sheriff, sharecropper, baker, and banker all have equal worth and voice as Masons. The translation outside of a Lodge is that no matter where a man falls in the social strata, he has the same collective rights as the next man. A Mason is viewed by his actions and moral standing rather than by the balance of his bank account. The concept of equality in Masonry is known as being "on the level." The familiar phrase is generally used as a question. "Are you on the level?" is a question asked when we wish to ascertain someone's truthfulness. The term is one of the many Masonic phrases that have crept into common usage. "Are we square?" "Giving someone the third degree," "Being hookwinked," and "Blackballed" all have their origins within Masonic Lodges.

Freemasonry would prove to be an important part of Steinbeck's life. As a teenager, he was initiated into the Order of DeMolay. Open to boys aged twelve to twenty-one, DeMolay is something of the Boy Scouts of Freemasonry. Young men are taken through a group of rituals that tell the story of the last Grand Master of the Knights Templar, Jacque DeMolay. The Templars were a group of warrior-monks who were an ever-present force during

1800s wood cut depicting some of Freemasonry's most recognizable symbols.

the Crusades. Acting not only as a military force, the Templars also provided shipping and banking services to Crusaders from the beginning of the twelfth century until the end of the conflict at the tail end of the thirteenth century. Throughout the invasions of the Holy Lands, the Templars had become an incredibly wealthy and politically influential organization. It has been said that at the height of the Templars' power, no royal court in Europe was without a Templar representative and half of Europe's farmable lands were owned by the knights. At the time DeMolay was elected the Grand Master of the Order in 1292, the Crusades were all but over. With the fall of Acre in 1291, the last major Crusader stronghold in the Middle East had forced a retreat to Cyprus. Without a foothold in the Holy Lands, The momentum of the Crusading spirit had been quashed in the minds of the Pope and Europe's royal courts. The potent Templars were left without a purpose and many of Europe's royal courts had borrowed large sums of money from Templar banks. France had found their treasuries overcapitalized to the Templars and King Philip the Fair had no way to repay his debt to the Templars. Rather than face the collapse of France, should the Templars call their loans, Philip trumped up charges of heresy against the Knights and had the members of the order arrested on

Friday, October 13, 1307.[15] DeMolay along with at least fifty other Templars were taken by the king's sheriffs. The majority of these men would be burned at the stake after a series of trials carried out by the French crown and the Papacy. DeMolay remained in prison for seven years only to face a similar fate, and was put to the flame with his second in command Geoffroi de Charney on March 18, 1314.

The story of the Knights Templar and DeMolay would have been seen as something of an epiphany to the young Steinbeck. The Templars were the real-life version of Malory's Knights of the Round Table to Steinbeck. Even as powerful as the Templar organization was in 1307, the warrior-monks were still the victims of a corrupt legal system that allowed trials based on the pragmatic needs of a monarch. This is likely the first time in Steinbeck's life that questions of social justice had taken a historical context for the young man. Tales of Arthur's knights had given Steinbeck a theoretical grasp of fair play and honorable actions, but the visions of DeMolay roasting in front of jeering crowds gave a face to injustice.

Many of the lads who are involved with the Order of DeMolay join Masonic Lodges and Steinbeck was no different. The author became a Master Mason at Salinas Lodge #204 in May of 1929.[16] The discussion of Steinbeck's membership in a Masonic Lodge has nothing to do with a Dan Brown–inspired conspiratorial view of Masonry. The thought that Masonry is directly linked with Steinbeck's service with the CIA is asinine. A Georgetown coffee shop is more likely to breed shadowy deals that affect our government than Masonic Lodges. Neither did Steinbeck's Masonic membership somehow directly lead to clandestine service.

The point of Steinbeck's membership into Masonry is twofold. First to a Mason, keeping secrets is a matter of honor. The ability to remain silent about the rituals and contents of a Lodge meeting are an integral part of the fraternal bonds that develop between Masons. Second, Masonry was an ever-present influence in Steinbeck's life. Although later in life Steinbeck did not technically belong to a Lodge, the fact he was a Mason was a point of pride for the author. According to a source within Salinas Lodge #204, John carried his membership and a proof of leaving the Lodge under amicable terms (this instrument is known as a dimit card within Masonry) in his wallet until the day he died.[17] John's son Thom recalls the elder Steinbeck pointing out the importance of stonemasons' marks on the blocks that made up Edinburgh Castle.[18] The engravings were unique to each stonemason and were used so the master of the work could hold his workforce accountable. Thom also remembered that "throwing the Masonic handshake opened a lot of doors" at the Imperial War Museum in London.[19]

Steinbeck's work also shows how important an influence Masonry was throughout his writing career. Nearly all of Steinbeck's novels contain some overt or covert reference to Masonry. Adam Trask in *East of Eden* and Ethan Allen Hawley from *The Winter of Our Discontent* are two characters from Steinbeck's body of work who are mentioned as being Masons.[20] Sprinkled throughout John's writing is some of the previously discussed Masonic phraseology. "On the level" makes an appearance in *Pastures of Heaven* and "being blackballed"

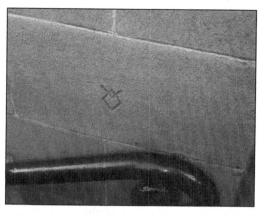

A mason's mark at Edinburgh Castle. Photo by author.

from the United States Army is used in a personal correspondence with Toby Street. An observant eye will catch many other Masonic phrases throughout a majority of Steinbeck's work. There is a discussion in *The Grapes of Wrath* about how "lodges and service organizations" are not living up to their avowed charitable nature.[21] This possibly contains the clue as to why Steinbeck withdrew from the Salinas Masonic Lodge in 1933. For all of the good works any Masonic or charitable organization does, each institution can take on the imperfections of their membership. In Masonry, one of the central themes is that of equality, regardless of social standing. It is not difficult to believe that Steinbeck's views of equality and those of his fellow Lodge brothers might not have coincided.[22] The difference between the Masonic ideal and the practice of individual members may well have led to the passage in *The Grapes of Wrath* and his departure from the Salinas Lodge. Equally as likely is that John demitted from the Salinas Lodge when moving to New York, intending to join a Lodge in New York, but never did.[23] Whatever the reasons, it is clear from discussing Masonry with Thom Steinbeck that his father always considered himself a Mason, no matter what his reasons were for demitting.[24]

For the purposes of our discussions about Steinbeck's involvement with the CIA, Masonry would have given John an early lesson in the security of secrets. One of the difficulties that both Masons and intelligence officers face is the desire to share that part of their lives with loved ones. For the Mason, telling one's wife a discussion that happened during a stated meeting violates personal honor. In the case of an intelligence officer, breaking silence can threaten the lives of fellow Americans. While the penalties are vastly dissimilar, the need to share is equal in both cases. Masons learn to curb this need as intelligence officers do. Years of being circumspect about aspects of being a Mason would have aided John in not "slipping up" when it came to his cover activities.

Freemasonry also tends to draw those who are in altruistic careers. The ranks of firefighters, police officers, and military men of the "greatest generation" were particularly high compared to other fraternal organizations.[25] The conspiratorial view that being a Mason is somehow a requirement to admission for these career paths is the exact opposite of reality. A man who would enter into selfless job roles is exactly the type of person that would be attracted by Masonry. One can then assume that during the time period, there were a great number of Masons within the intelligence community.[26] It would have been likely that John would have come in contact with fellow Masons who were in the intelligence community. The commonality of experience would have also given Steinbeck a slight advantage in entering the covert realm. Once again, there is no prerequisite in membership in any fraternal organization for entry into any government agency. Trust more easily exists between those with common experiences; much in the same way as two Eagle Scouts or persons belonging to the same branch of the military might have. Had John dealt with any fellow Masons within the Agency, it would have given him an element of trust that might not have existed from a non-Masonic candidate.

Discussions of King Arthur, magical bears, and a pseudo-secret society in relation to one's work with the world's largest covert agency may sound fantastical. One has to remember that these improbable elements are part of a man's formative years and have direct bearing on how Steinbeck came to a duplicitous life. Honor, candor, and secrecy are all hallmarks of what Americans should expect out of those in our intelligence services. At times since the CIA's inception, the Agency's actions have fallen far below the mark of the ideal. It is difficult to marry honor with projects like MK-ULTRA, which sought to control the mind by way of LSD, or the Agency utilizing drug or weapons trafficking to fund operations. The miscues of an organization do not always tell the story of the individuals who operate within its structure—just as the atrocities at My Lai do not reflect on the whole of the United States Army. For Steinbeck, we will see that working with the intelligence community began far earlier than 1952 and represented a patriotic duty. His early lessons would have provided him a touchstone to keep that perspective.

Tucked neatly in the corners of preparation for the holidays, December is a month of reflection. Thoughts of the windfalls and blights of the past eleven months peek around the edges of presents and the promise of a new year's change. John Steinbeck would have been especially mindful of the events of 1939 that December. Looking back on the year, John would have realized that nothing could get the author in trouble faster or open more doors than putting a pen to paper. The publication of *The Grapes of Wrath* in mid-April of 1939 achieved both conditions. Simultaneously Steinbeck was lauded and vilified by different sectors of the American public for exposing the plight of migrant farm workers. The subtle sting of the word "Communist" followed John in the months since *The Grapes of Wrath* hit bookstore shelves. The same Americans who were horrified to see newsreel footage of books burning at Nuremberg, lined up sparking flint and steel to copies of *The Grapes of Wrath*. John stayed ahead of the Red Wake that followed *The Grapes of Wrath* as best as any man could. He had avoided being discredited by being set up for a phony rape charge by a farmer's association in Los Gatos and for charges of being part of a vast Jewish conspiracy by an overzealous Baptist preacher. Unbeknownst to John, literary critics would forever hold John's future works in comparison to *The Grapes of Wrath*.

The cosmos has a way of finding an equilibrium point in events on galactic to quantum scales and the publication of *The Grapes of Wrath* followed the universe's tendencies. Both President Roosevelt and First Lady Eleanor had taken notice of the work. John's editor Pat Covici had sent a prerelease copy of the book to the White House hoping FDR would see that the New Deal had not solved all of the Great Depression's ills. Covici's ploy coupled with the flap about the book had served its purpose. Eleanor Roosevelt took enough notice that she traveled to California in the early spring of 1940 with hopes of touring the migrant farms with Steinbeck.[1] The meeting would not happen because by that time, John had moved on from the stink of *The Grapes of Wrath* to a glorified fishing expedition. John had taken to the high seas with marine biologist and longtime friend Ed Ricketts. The pair had mustered up a boat and crew and set sail around the Baja peninsula collecting specimens for Ricketts' Pacific Biological Laboratory.

The collection voyage would be later chronicled in *The Log from the Sea of Cortez* and marks the start of Steinbeck's personal entry into the Second World War. One of the details of the voyage Steinbeck had to hammer out were the legal aspects of collecting specimens. The majority of the gathering would take place in Mexican waters and no one wanted to land in a Mexican jail, pinched for an obscure infraction of maritime law. John sought the assistance of renowned microbiologist Paul de Kruif in late 1939. The scientist held connections in Washington and might be able to minimize the red tape factor. The seminal events of John's life often revolved around the sound of a clacking typewriter or a fountain pen scraping across the surface of his letterhead. The side offer in the de Kruif letter was no different than the publication of *The Grapes of Wrath* as a life-changing event. In both cases, a cluster of words on twenty-four-pound paper started chain reactions that would resonate through the breadth of John's life.

A bust-style statue of Ed Ricketts off Monterey's Cannery Row.*

Upon receiving John's letter, de Kruif must have felt the request for assistance was out of his depth and forwarded Steinbeck's letter to Basil O'Connor. The New York lawyer had been FDR's legal advisor since the 1920s and headed up the National Foundation for Infantile Paralysis, which would be renamed in 1979 as the March of Dimes Foundation. O'Connor and de Kruif had become acquainted via their work fighting polio.[2] O'Connor, in turn, forwarded Steinbeck's request on to FDR's personal assistant on December 8, 1939.[3] In true Washington bureaucratic fashion, no one seemed to know what to do about an American author wishing to collect sea urchins off the Mexican coast. The FDR Library and Museum holds the cascade of letters generated by Steinbeck's request and each could easily have read, "Hell, I don't know what to do with this. Why don't you send it to . . . " The letter bounced around until it was finally fobbed off to the State Department and an official at the Smithsonian Museum. Aside from a quirky exposé of FDR's staffers, there is one gem in the mix. The Steinbeck quandary landed on the desk of FDR's Naval Attaché Captain, D.J. Callaghan, on December 13, 1939. Callaghan's response to receiving the Steinbeck issue was in part:

The President asked me to consider with ONI [Office of Naval Intelligence] the possibility of using Mr. Steinbeck in connection with information for ONI. Admiral Anderson tells me that he will investigate this matter with a possibility of using Mr. Steinbeck and his associate for this purpose.[4]

The "purpose" in Captain Callaghan's letter is never outlined and the memo is marked "Confidential." Following up on December 18th, Callaghan sends these further remarks to FDR's personal assistant:

I am returning the letter addressed to you by Mr. Basil O'Connor, having noted that the President has approved Dr. Schmitt's interest in obtaining specimens for the National Museum. Should ONI desire to avail itself of Dr. (sic) Steinbeck's services while in Mexican territory they will undoubtedly forward him the necessary credentials for that purpose.[5]

It is fairly clear that FDR had some sort of mission in mind for Steinbeck that dovetailed with a specific need of the ONI. It has often been said that Steinbeck had made an offer to look for German or Japanese submarines during the Baja expedition. This does not seem to be the case. The only known point of reference FDR or Callaghan had in regards to Steinbeck's Baja trip was the letter sent by Basil O'Connor. At no time in O'Connor's December 8th letter does O'Connor indicate Steinbeck offering to gather information for the ONI or any other intelligence organization. Unless there were additional communications from O'Connor that have not been made public by the FDR Library and Museum, FDR wants to use Steinbeck on a mission for the ONI. FDR obviously not only held Steinbeck in some regard, but felt that Steinbeck would be amicable to carrying out the ONI's "purpose."

By December of 1939, Roosevelt was grasping at any intelligence asset he could get his hands on. As early as June of 1939, FDR recognized the abject lack of the country's intelligence resources and urged the FBI, ONI, and Army Intelligence to coordinate their efforts.[6] The scramble was to ascertain Axis intentions on American interests and plan accordingly. In relation to Steinbeck, the most logical conclusion is that the ONI was compiling information on Japanese interests in the Baja peninsula. Japanese fishing companies and farming consortiums had been a heavy presence in Mexico since at least 1908.[7] The capabilities of maintaining fishing fleets could be translated into supporting Japanese naval units and therefore would have been of interest to the ONI. FDR's intent for Steinbeck may have been nothing less than using a cover story to tour the larger Japanese-held fisheries that dotted Baja's coast. This would explain the need for Steinbeck "to obtain credentials" as pointed out in Callaghan's December 18th memo to the White House. Unfortunately we do not know if the ONI contacted Steinbeck and what mission the author could fulfill for the intelligence organization. There simply is not enough information to support or disprove a position on Steinbeck and the ONI during the Baja expedition. The importance of Steinbeck's consideration for performing a task for the ONI is actually not in whether ONI utilized Steinbeck or not. Either way, John Steinbeck's name had been associated with intelligence work for FDR. Six months later, FDR would definitely open the gateway into the intelligence world for Steinbeck.

Steinbeck returned home from the Baja expedition on April 22, 1940, with just enough time to recuperate and pack up for another trip to Mexico in late May. For the May Mexican trip, marine biology had been replaced with a filming of Steinbeck's fable *The Forgotten Village*. The hour-long documentary-style tale described the resistance of a rural Mexican village to modern medical practices. Steinbeck would be in Mexico for a little over a month overseeing the film's production. During his month south of the border, it became evident to John that Germany's influence within the country could pose a serious problem to the United States. Germany had enjoyed a brisk trade relationship with Mexico since the late 1920s and there had been a significant German emigration to Mexico to support that trade. The role of Mexico and other Latin American countries in the Second World War has been generally obscured by historians' focus on the battlefronts in Europe. On a military and political level, the entry of any of the Latin American countries on the side of the Axis would have been disastrous for the Allies. America would be faced with fighting a three-front war and disruption of Latin American raw materials supplied to the United States.

Steinbeck's Mexican observations were slanted toward the Germans, but he failed to recognize the cooperation between Russia and Germany. Given the ferocity of German advances in Russia during Operation BARBAROSSA in June 1941, it's hard to remember the Germans and Soviets maintained friendly relations early in the Second World War. Neither country was satisfied with the outcome of the First World War, which left the Germans in financial ruins and Russia with territory losses in Eastern Europe. The purposes of the Soviets and Germans aligned for a short time in 1939. That year the countries signed the Molotov–Ribbentrop Nonaggression Pact which called for the Russians not entering into a European conflict against the Germans in return for both countries carving up pieces of Romania, Poland, Lithuania, Latvia, Estonia, and Finland. The agreement was sealed in blood as both the Germans and Soviets invaded Poland in September of 1939. Until the German invasion of Russia in 1941, the two countries traded in both material goods and secrets. Mexico was one place where the two countries' intelligence services intersected.[8]

While the Germans were primarily concerned with securing raw materials in Mexico, the Soviets had a different objective there. Both countries increased their intelligence networks in Mexico in early 1940, partially to keep their eyes on America's interests. The Soviet's true prize in Mexico was Leon Trotsky. A leader of the *glorious* 1917 Russian Revolution had fallen afoul of the Communist Party in the late 1920s and was exiled from Russia in 1929. After being bounced around Europe's different countries as a political hand grenade, in December of 1936, Trotsky and his family took up residence in the Mexico City home of muralist Diego Rivera.[9] Rivera had given the Communist Party in Mexico the kiss of life in the early 1920s and the Party, in turn, dumped Rivera in 1928 for his pro-Trotsky views. Nevertheless, Rivera lobbied the government to allow his embodiment of the Communist ideal, Trotsky, asylum.[10] The idea seemed to be good at the time, like many ideas in Rivera's life. A year after Trotsky was exiled, Rivera's mural in the entrance to Rockefeller Center was facing a similar artistic fate as Trotsky. Rivera's Rockefeller Center mural conveyed an overt Communist imagery, and striking an artistic blow for the cause in the very heart of capitalism was a lofty plan. Public outrage over the mural's themes, complete with an image of Lenin, had led to the mural's public removal in February of 1934. Mirroring the fate of the Rockefeller Center mural, Rivera's personal life was nearly destroyed by the grand idea of inviting Trotsky into his home. Trotsky would have an affair with Rivera's wife, artist Frida Kahlo, and the couple divorced in December 1939.[11]

As the soap opera of Trotsky, Kahlo, and Rivera developed in 1937, another drama was unfolding in Russia. Stalin had started his purge of political rivals by public "show trials." Anyone not in line with Stalin's regime was put through a carefully crafted prosecution for crimes against the state. The outcomes of the trials were predetermined and if the defendant refused to admit guilt in the legal theater, they were quietly executed. Trotsky was tried and convicted by Stalin's courts in absentia on charges of conspiracy to assassinate government officials. The sentence by the court was death for Trotsky and fifteen other co-defendants who were tried in Russia. The Soviets did not see Trotsky's immigration to Mexico as a stumbling block in carrying out the sentence and increased their intelligence assets in Mexico to hunt down the dissident.

Stalin was very clear on his feelings that Trotsky posed an impediment to the world's Communist community. In a statement to Russia's Interior Minister and head of the Soviet security, Stalin said:

> . . . without Trotsky's elimination [. . .] we won't be able to trust our allies in the international Communist movement when the Imperialists attack the Soviet Union. If they have to worry about Trotskyite infiltrations in their ranks, their international role of

destabilizing the enemy's rear guard through sabotage and guerilla warfare will face major impediments.[12]

The Germans had a different axe to grind with Trotsky. At the end of World War I, Trotsky had supported the formation of a Communist Party in Germany. The hopes Germans would throw off the shackles of their imperialist masters were crushed by German anti-Communist paramilitary groups of World War I veterans, but the seeds of Communism would resurge in 1923. As the Weimar Republic began to waiver in favor of the Nazi party, Trotsky became a vocal opponent of Adolph Hitler.[13] Trotsky's stance on Hitler would not only make him an enemy of Hitler, but of Joseph Stalin as well. Stalin believed that Hitler

Leon Trotsky, 1918

could be managed through treaties and trade where Trotsky saw Hitler's brand of Fascism as a security risk to the Soviet Union. The German Communist Party sided with Stalin's stance and for their complacency, Hitler would blame the party for the 1933 Reichstag fire. The reaction of the Nazi party was to effectively stamp out any vestige of Communism in Germany. In 1940, only Trotsky remained as Communism's voice against the Nazi regime. Even after being tried as a traitor in the Soviet Union, Trotsky was an ideological candle for many Communists throughout the world. The German government feared an unfettered Trotsky could rekindle opposition to Hitler elsewhere in the Communist world. Only Trotsky's blood would satiate both Hitler and Stalin.

Adding to the growing list of Trotsky detractors, Diego Rivera had something of a show trial for Trotsky himself. The charge of sleeping with Rivera's wife carried a sentence of exile for the deposed Communist leader yet again. Unceremoniously, Rivera threw the Bolshevik out of his house. Rivera had also come to grow disdainful of Trotsky's political stances on Mexico and Trotsky of Rivera's. Trotsky had gone as far as to denounce Rivera as one of Stalin's Mexican agents.[14] The betrayals of Trotsky had mounted to a point of personal crisis for Rivera. Over the last few years, the muralist's great political mentor had become nothing more than a sniping home wrecker, and the Mexico he loved was in danger of the machinations of German-Soviet interests. To Rivera, there was no other choice but to blow the whistle by holding a press conference late in 1939. During the forum, Rivera accused Mexican politicians of a relationship with Soviet agents that had entered Mexico at the end of the Spanish Civil War. He supplied a list of Communist moles within the government and reported sixty political assassinations by officially ordered death squads. Rivera's final accusation was that the Soviets were using Mexico as an infiltration point for Soviet intelligence agents into the United States.[15] Finally Rivera reported that the Mexican Communist Party was being primarily financed north of the border.[16]

In a separate public appeal in December of 1939, Rivera wanted the German ocean liner, SS *Columbus*, seized and searched for war materials. The ship had weighed anchor with two others in Mexican territorial waters. One of Rivera's contacts had passed along that the *Columbus* was secretly refueling Nazi U-Boats in the Caribbean. In a letter to the Mexican newspaper, *Hoy*, Rivera outlined the German plot and threw the gauntlet down to the Mexican government. If the ship was not at least searched, Rivera claimed that proved the government was actively supporting Germany's war effort. Within twenty-four hours of the letter being published, the *Columbus* and the two other ships left Mexican waters. In two days' time, the *Columbus* would be challenged four hundred miles off the coast of Virginia jointly by British and American ships. Rather than be boarded, the captains of all three German ships scuttled the vessels.[17] Rivera considered the scuttling as proof that his claims were founded, but no one within the Mexican government seemed to listen.[18] Rivera turned to the only other entity in Mexico that had an interest in the Soviet and German presence, the United States government. Upon contacting the American Embassy in Mexico City, Rivera was given Consul Robert McGregor as his point of contact.[19] The German-Soviet threat in Mexico was larger than Rivera could keep a handle on himself, and McGregor prompted Rivera to expand his network. The Communist-turned-American-asset eventually created a network of thirty agents to assist him in monitoring the Germans and Soviets in Mexico.[20]

Less than a day after Steinbeck stepped onto the tarmac of Mexico City's airport on May 23, 1940, Soviet intelligence presence in Mexico City would become more than Rivera's conjecture. In the early hours of the morning of May 24th, Russian NKVD[21] officer Josef Grigulevich led a raid with members of the Mexican Communist Party on Trotsky's new home, a few blocks away from the Rivera residence. With assistance from one of Trotsky's bodyguards, the group gained entry into the home and proceeded to Trotsky's bedroom. The wetwork team was not very stealthy and alerted Trotsky that something was amiss in the home. Trotsky pushed his wife out of bed and drug her under their bed for cover. The act saved their lives. Carrying Thompson submachineguns, the would-be assassins pumped over seventy rounds into the bedroom without the benefit of a fatal hit.[22] To cover their tracks, the Soviet-led team left a timed explosive in the house and disappeared into Mexico City's night. Trotsky's luck held and the bomb never went off. The only notable injury sustained in the attack was a round to Trotsky's grandson's foot.[23]

Frida Kahlo and Diego Rivera. Photo taken by Carl Van Vechten and courtesy of the Library of Congress.

The Mexican authorities had no tangible leads on who was involved with the assassination attempt on Trotsky. Rivera's fallout with the Russian was well known within the community and that placed the artist as the police's prime suspect. For speaking out against the government, as Rivera had in the last few months, Rivera was convinced the powers that be would use this as an excuse to silence him once and for all. The only option open to Rivera was to go to ground and hope whoever had made the attempt on Trotsky's life would be found. For this strategy to work, Rivera would have to cut ties from his usual circle of friends and vanish from sight. The Mexican authorities were sure to question his known associates and Rivera couldn't take the chance that one of them would divulge his location. Luckily for Rivera, he had an ace in the hole.

A few weeks before the assassination attempt on Trotsky, Hollywood starlet Paulette Goddard had come to Mexico to sit for a painting with Rivera. The former *Ziegfeld Follies* performer had appeared in twenty films since her days as a showgirl and was in serious contention for the role of Scarlett O'Hara in *Gone with the Wind*. She might have gotten the part had it not been for her somewhat scandalous personal life. At the age of fifteen, Goddard had married the older millionaire lumber tycoon Edgar James. The life she had chosen with James was not as she had expected it to be and by eighteen, Paulette was a first-time divorcee. With a generous alimony agreement, Goddard struck out for Hollywood. It was there she would meet the boon and bane to her movie career, Charlie Chaplin. The pair met in 1932 while Paulette was under contract by Hal Roach Studios and became a frequent topic of Hollywood gossip columns. The relationship would yield Goddard's first real critical acclaim staring beside her beau in *Modern Times* (1936). The two would also be secretly married that year. Being married or not, Paulette would always be viewed as a Hollywood "bad girl" and suffered the professional consequences of her perceived lascivious nature.

Two years after their marriage, Paulette and Charlie rented a house on Pebble Beach. Chaplin had always been fascinated with Steinbeck's novels and would drive around Monetary and Pacific Grove trying to place scenes from John's books.[24] One day on a lark, Chaplin unexpectedly went by Steinbeck's house. Steinbeck saw a limousine drive up and went outside to figure out who could possibly be calling. Chaplin popped out of the car and held out his hand to introduce himself. John couldn't quite understand why one of the world's most famous actors would come for a visit, but Charlie quickly explained he was a fan and simply wanted to meet John. The two became fast friends and John also established a long-standing friendship with Paulette.

At the time of Trotsky's assassination attempt, Paulette and Chaplin were on the fringe of breaking up. John had actually attended a party with Chaplin the night before leaving for Mexico in May of 1940.[25] The two had taken a long walk during the party and would have discussed Chaplin's personal life and Paulette's jaunt to Mexico, sitting as Rivera's muse. The day after that, John would fly to Mexico and on his first full day in the country, Paulette Goddard was helping Diego Rivera setup a safe house. We do not know if Goddard and Steinbeck made contact during this time, but it would be likely that they did. John's first wife, Carol, had accompanied him on this excursion and it would have been a natural suggestion that Carol look up Paulette, if Goddard did not already know of the Steinbecks' travel plans. Goddard wouldn't have had much time to socialize with the Steinbecks, but she would have had reasons of her own to seek them out.

The days after Trotsky's assassination attempt would have left Goddard with little else to do than support Rivera. In the uncertainty of the situation, the face of trusted friends would have been a welcome sight for Goddard. No matter how plucky the starlet was, Goddard was still basically alone hiding Mexico's most wanted man. If there had been anyone in the country Goddard trusted to have assisted in aiding and abetting a fugitive, it would have been Steinbeck. John was a known quantity to not only Goddard, but Rivera as well. John had long been an admirer of Rivera's work and the two had met in Mexico in 1937.[26] The only other person who knew of Rivera's whereabouts was his ex-wife Frida, who would not have been much assistance to Goddard. Rumors have always persisted that Goddard and Rivera were romantically involved and if true would have made any contact with the women strained at best.

Goddard and Rivera knew that he could not stay hiding in Mexico indefinitely and the situation required a game-changing move. That opportunity would come in the next few days as Frida was pressured by the Mexican government, and possibly the United States Embassy as well, to furnish Rivera's location. At great reluctance, Frida took the Mexican officials to Rivera's hideout, having been convinced Rivera's life was at risk. The meeting turned out fortunately for Rivera as he noted in his autobiography that he was provided a "passport already prepared for entry into the United States."[27] This had been furnished by the United States Embassy, undoubtedly wanting to protect their newfound intelligence asset. Goddard was roped into hotfooting Rivera across the border into Texas[28] and further escorted Rivera to San Francisco by the second week of June. The stars had aligned perfectly for the artist on the lam as he had been invited in early May to paint a mural at the Golden Gate International Exposition on Treasure Island. While in the Bay area, Rivera frequently took advantage of Goddard and Chaplin's hospitality at the couple's Pebble Beach home.

Paulette Goddard in an early 1930's publicity photo.

The tale of Diego Rivera is one of the many times Steinbeck's orbit passed within active intelligence assets. While there is no record of Rivera and Steinbeck meeting during the first two weeks of Steinbeck's stay in Mexico, an encounter between the two would explain why John was distressed about the influence the Germans in Mexico. John's fears for the country were outlined in an undated letter to his uncle Joe Hamilton. Uncle Joe had been a newspaperman in New York who had gotten John a job with *New York American* in 1926. From New York, Joe had gone on to become an executive with an ad firm in Chicago and then joined the WPA (Works Progress Administration) as an information officer. Hamilton's position allowed him access to the Washington elite including the president. John's letter to Hamilton is currently held by the Franklin D. Roosevelt Library and Museum and had made its way into the president's hands fairly quickly upon being received by Joe. While there is no date on the letter, Steinbeck mentions in closing that at "that moment word came of the capitulation of France." This allusion would indicate the letter was penned on either June 14th or 22nd. On June 14th, the Germans reached Paris and offered an alliance with the French. June 22nd was the day the official armistice was signed between the two countries. Steinbeck would leave

Mexico and travel to Washington, D.C., on the 22nd of June to discuss the Mexican situation with FDR, so the 14th is the likely date for the document.

When described in many contemporary sources, Steinbeck's letter to Hamilton sounds as if it was a note dashed off to voice his concerns about Nazi propaganda. Steinbeck's analysis of Mexican politics is a three-and-a-half page report on everything from graft in the upcoming Mexican election, to shoddy intelligence work by the FBI. The analysis is even more remarkable when one considers Steinbeck was in the country for twenty-two days and burdened with the production of a film. John begins the letter with a chilling overview:

> We are living in a bad Oppenheim novel—spies, counter-spies, arrests, local power drives, little bribes. It is funny and a little bit dangerous.[29]

Steinbeck goes on to talk about the plan to film *The Forgotten Village* with director Herbert Kline. Strangely enough, Kline would receive an Academy Award nomination for the documentary, *Walls of Fire*, about Rivera and fellow Mexican artist David Alfaro. Steinbeck was entrenched in the business of making a film in Mexico and did have frustrating contact with members of the Mexican government. Anyone who has gotten a government permit can appreciate the difficulties of obtaining permits in one's home country, let alone securing permissions in a foreign country. Dealing with bureaucrats would also have afforded John some insight into some of Mexico's internal problems. One universal truth of bureaucracies is that the people holding the permits love to tell you about their problems. One of the issues that would have been of great concern to any bureaucratic types John dealt with was the upcoming elections. Dependant on the outcome of July's presidential elections, some of the functionaries John spoke with could have been out of a job. Of great concern to Steinbeck is General Juan Andreu Almazán's candidacy in the July presidential race. In a scathing assessment of Almazán, Steinbeck states that Almazán had backing from William Randolph Hearst, Harry Chandler, oil companies, and the German propaganda office.[30]

Mexico had nationalized all of the country's oil production facilities in 1938. American and British oil companies lost millions of dollars in equipment. Relations between the United States and Mexico became strained as oil companies lobbied for governmental sanctions to be placed on the Mexican government. The Roosevelt Administration had no real love for oil companies and also feared that sanctions would collapse the fragile Mexican economy. As a hedge against America and Britain finding another source for oil, the Mexicans began selling oil to Germany and Japan in early 1939. By the time of Steinbeck's letter in 1940, FDR was looking for a solution that would keep

Mexican oil out of the hands of the Axis while trying to appease American oil companies that would become strategic resources, should the United States enter the war. American oil companies were simply looking for reparations for the nationalization process and a new president who might reverse the nationalization of their oil fields. Almazán was viewed as malleable enough, given the right incentives, to bend to the oil companies' will.

Hearst and Chandler had separate interests in having Almazán elected. Chandler was invested in oil companies, but his main interests were agriculture in the Mexicali Valley. Chandler's Colorado River and Land Company was a 105,000-acre feudal lord model. The land was rented to farmers by Mexican shills for ten-year increments to plant crops as they wished, while Chandler cashed the rent checks.[31] The issue of further nationalization by the Mexican government would have been a great concern for Chandler's fiefdom in Mexicali and he similarly would back a Mexican president who would be sympathetic toward his business ventures. Hearst had real estate issues of his own in Mexico to protect. His 1.25 million-acre Babicora Ranch in Chihuahua had been taken from him for two years during the days of Pancho Villa's rebellion.[32] Hearst had no wish to repeat the experience with another round of Mexican nationalizations fueled by rebellion.

The hint of a popular uprising in the air around Almazán was concerning. The fashionable opinion was that if Almazán did not win the election, he would openly oppose the new president by force. This could have been another reason the American big business interests were backing Almazán. If he could not legitimately win the election, there was always the safety net of a coup. Steinbeck felt the chances of Almazán taking up arms were quite great.

Steinbeck's astute observations about the situation in Mexico extended to intelligence operations as well. As Steinbeck writes to Hamilton:

> The FBI men arrived lately in Mexico. They are all known and the feeling down here is not nice. In fact they are regarded as spies. They are so obviously FBI men that it is funny. They have dipped their ears in our soup already, and a hammier bunch of flat feet never existed.[33]

Steinbeck's remarks would have raised further concerns with FDR. In June of 1940, the FBI established the Special Intelligence Service (SIS) Division to gather intelligence in Latin America. The oddity is that according to FBI records, SIS undercover agents were not sent into Mexico until July of 1940. At that time, only one agent was sent into Mexico with the cover of being employed by an American company.[34] To further complicate matters, the official record of the SIS also states that operations "in Mexico began in August, 1940, when two undercover Agents were assigned to that Republic for a brief period."[35] Either Steinbeck was mistaken about the FBI presence in Mexico in June of 1940 or the FBI had more agents in play than official FBI records indicate. A third option is that the FBI agents were misidentified by Steinbeck and were intelligence operatives from other countries. The German intelligence service Abwehr had been operating in Mexico since late 1939 and expanded their operations during May and June of 1940. In addition, the Soviets were also ramping up their intelligence efforts in Mexico at the time.[36]

The German interest in Mexico is fairly obvious. The strategic importance of having either a neutral or complicit Mexico would benefit the Germans should the United States enter the war. Mexico was also a grand place to observe shipping and transfers of raw materials into the United States from South America. The Abwehr had a broad base of intelligence in Mexico even before the war started. Germans had established communities in Mexico since the late 1800s and by the mid-1930s, there were six to seven thousand German nationals living in the country. Germany had become entrenched in the Mexican infrastructure by supplying the country with automotive, electrical, construction, and pharmaceuticals.[37] Gathering intelligence from Germans already entrenched in Mexican society was not a difficult task. These efforts were also made somewhat easier by the unexpected ally in the Soviets. The two countries would actually pool their resources in August of 1940 to make right May's botched assassination attempt on Trotsky. Abwehr operatives acted as lookouts for the Soviet team that finally killed Trotsky in August of 1940. The cooperation between the Soviet and German intelligence services was not confirmed until 1994, when Pavel Sudoplatov, director of the KGB's Foreign Intelligence service published his memoirs.[38]

John does mention the possibility of Soviet/German intelligence collaboration in his letter to Hamilton, but goes on to downplay any cooperative links between the two countries based on witnessing a street fight between pro-Nazis and Communists. It is surprising the letter does not mention the assassination attempt on Trotsky. Mexico City was brimming with the news of the attempt on Trotsky and the possibility that Russian spies were behind the caper. Steinbeck is totally invested in describing the German threat and leaves out Soviet entanglements in the country. Steinbeck either did not see the Soviets as being a real player on the Mexican political chessboard, or there was a reason he did not address the Soviet issue.

It is clear at the end of John's letter to Hamilton the contents are to form actionable intelligence. John tells Hamilton of his intent to leave Mexico and immediately go to Washington to speak with Hamilton and "anyone else who is interested."[39] The subtext is that Steinbeck wishes Hamilton to play Paul Revere shouting, "The Germans are in Mexico!" to Hamilton's Washington cronies. Hamilton did forward John's letter to the Oval Office and a transcript of the letter is held by the FDR Library and Museum. The letter in FDR's files has been highlighted for the president's review and there is little doubt FDR knew of the letter's contents before John arrived in Washington on June 24th. Since John's ultimate goal was to sound the alarm about Mexico, we can assume that he was more than a little confident in the letter's sources. Rumors at a café or by permit-wielding Mexican functionaries would not be significant enough to share with Washington. For Steinbeck to have believed in this information enough to lay his reputation on the line with the government, the source had to be solid. That source could very easily have been Diego Rivera.

At any moment during Rivera's two-week disappearing act, the artist was in danger of being arrested or even killed. For all Rivera knew, everyone from the Mexican police to the Germans were on his trail. The only lifeline Rivera had to the outside world was Paulette Goddard. The two would have brainstormed on ways to get Rivera out of his current predicament or at the very least tell someone else what Rivera knew of the German threat in Mexico. Seeking asylum in the American Embassy would have blown Rivera's cover as an informant. John Steinbeck is the only other person in the country both Goddard and Rivera could trust. If left with no other options, Goddard could have arranged for Steinbeck to meet Rivera. Steinbeck would have been the perfect choice as a vessel for Rivera's fears of a Nazi-controlled Mexican government. Rivera, being a Communist himself, would naturally gloss over any Soviet influence within the country. Steinbeck is then left with the impression the Germans are the only hazard to Mexico. All Rivera asks of Steinbeck is that he use any means at his disposal to shed light on these issues. Steinbeck cautiously agrees and over the next week, starts to confirm Rivera's intelligence. Satisfied that Rivera is on the level, Steinbeck is moved enough to write Hamilton and schedule a trip to Washington.

An unpublished June 1945 letter from Steinbeck to Goddard and then-husband Burgess Meredith gives reason to believe Steinbeck had contact with Goddard in Mexico.[40] At the time, John was in Mexico overseeing the filming of *The Pearl*. The letter is little more than Steinbeck letting Goddard and Meredith know where he was staying, should the couple wish to correspond. Steinbeck says, "We don't live at the hotel [Hotel Marik in Cuernavaca] but we get our mail there. I know Paulette knows the place." Steinbeck's comment could have been born out of a conversation with Goddard about hotels around Mexico City. Equally, Steinbeck could have known Goddard had stayed at the Hotel Marik because they had met there in 1941.

The above scenario does go a long way to explain Steinbeck's sudden and passionate feelings on the Germans in Mexico. Steinbeck would have been more likely to go to Washington having Rivera as a direct source, than that of rumors and talk on the streets of Mexico City. Also Steinbeck would not have to have been informed of Rivera's work with the American Embassy. Once Steinbeck told Rivera's story to anyone in the United States government, Rivera could be independently confirmed as a current asset, lending credence to bedtime stories of German spies in Mexico. While we may never know if Diego Rivera is how Steinbeck came about his detailed analysis of German intentions in Mexico, the situation certainly gives pause for reflection. What we are certain of is that Steinbeck's letter to Hamilton landed a meeting with FDR.

Steinbeck left Mexico on June 22nd and traveled straight to Washington. After settling in, John wrote President Roosevelt a truncated version of the Hamilton letter on June 24th. The language Steinbeck utilizes in the three-paragraph letter is dire, as Steinbeck closes with:

> However, if my observation can be of any use to you, I shall be very glad to speak with you for I am sure that this problem is one of the most important to be faced by the nation.[41]

The letter to FDR is reminiscent of the 1952 letter to General Smith. In both letters, Steinbeck takes a humble tone in offering his services to the government. The approach would seem to have worked in both instances. Steinbeck's letter to FDR was immediately seen by the president's administrative assistant James Rowe Jr. who then forwarded the letter to the president and suggested FDR might be interested in speaking with Steinbeck. Piggybacking on Rowe's note to FDR was a further endorsement by the Librarian of Congress, Archibald MacLeish, that Steinbeck's views would be beneficial to the president. Initially it might seem odd that the Librarian of Congress would have been privy to Steinbeck's correspondence with FDR. However MacLeish's role within the Roosevelt administration was not simply limited to running the Library of Congress. MacLeish would set the framework for the OSS's Research and Analysis Branch and after the beginning of World War II, MacLeish was the director of the War Department's Office of Facts and Figures. FDR did not need much convincing to see Steinbeck, considering the President had thought of using Steinbeck as an asset for the Baja expedition earlier that year.

Wedged in-between appointments with former National Recovery Administration head Donald Richberg and FDR's administrative assistant James Forrestal, Steinbeck was given fifteen minutes to meet with the president.[42] The sections marked on Steinbeck's letter to Hamilton would indicate FDR was most interested in one aspect of Steinbeck's observations. Other paragraphs marked on the letter were denoted by a line beside the text. In charcoal gray pencil, a box was drawn around the paragraph in which

Steinbeck suggests that the United States set up a propaganda office. By utilizing radio and motion pictures, the propaganda office would attempt "to get this side of the world together."[43] There are no official records of what the two men actually talked about, but another clue exists. Steinbeck would write FDR on a separate matter on August 13, 1940, and stated that FDR had made a job offer to John that was not accepted.[44] What that particular job was, we do not know.

Most meetings between two people can never be judged by the promises of action in the midst of pleasantries and jolly-glad-hands. The success or failure of any meeting can only be measured by actions taken after the parting handshake. If looking at the results of Steinbeck's meeting with FDR is any indication, Steinbeck's message resonated with the president. A month to the day after Steinbeck and FDR's tête-à-tête, FDR scheduled another fifteen-minute meeting with Nelson Rockefeller seemingly to discuss the formation of the Office for Coordination of Commercial and Cultural Relations between the American Republics (OCCCRBAR).[45] (Someone slightly more sensible shortened the office's name to Office of Inter-American Affairs (OIAA) and the two offices are essentially the same for purposes of this text.) The acronym-heavy office's mission was to improve the infrastructures of Latin American countries to a point where raw materials could easily flow into the United States. As one would expect, programs to modernize transportation, communications, and sanitation were paramount to OCCCRBAR's success south of the border. While overseeing grants to improve rail lines in Mexico turned into the bread and butter of OCCCRBAR's public face, the office's operations reached farther into Latin American environments than infrastructure cosmetics.[46]

OCCCRBAR was to eradicate the desire for Latin American countries to trade goods with Axis nations. Through a two-pronged attack of intelligence and propaganda, OCCCRBAR sought to eliminate competing ideological and business influences. A steady diet of pro-United States propaganda was delivered up to Latin American countries via radio and motion pictures. The brilliance of OCCCRBAR's public relations program was a theme of "sympathetic understanding."[47] Any cultural blunders early in the propaganda efforts could be explained away as part of the learning curve between American and Latin points of view. The strategy also allowed time for OCCCRBAR spin doctors to research what content would win over the populace of Latin America, while still fostering a "getting to know you" attitude. To this end, Rockefeller sent Hollywood executives to Central and South America to understand how best to present media specifically geared toward a Latin American audience.

The economic warfare component of the OCCCRBAR's agenda was by far a more thorny issue than that of infrastructure management or propaganda in Latin America. From OCCCRBAR's inception in August of 1940 to Pearl Harbor in 1941, there was nothing to prevent trade between Axis and Latin American countries. For example, Mexico was selling oil to the Japanese and Germans in 1940 and there was nothing legally the United States could do to prevent the sales. OCCCRBAR's civil programs did present a great incentive for Latin American countries to discontinue trade relations with Axis nations, but that was not enough to ensure compliance with the American agenda. What was needed was an intelligence network that not only identified Axis owned or operated companies in Latin America, but acted to disrupt their operations. As an Axis company was identified, it was put on an OCCCRBAR blacklist and an American company was subsidized to compete. Any vestige of German-held aviation companies in Latin America were dispensed with in this manner.[48]

The intelligence network setup by OCCCRBAR was not limited to the economic battlefield. Largely forgotten in the evolution of the CIA, during the course of the Second World War, OCCCRBAR, and later OIAA, formed one of the five largest intelligence agencies within the United States government.[49] Working closely with the FBI's SIS division, OIAA agents were tasked with counterintelligence duties in Latin America. Many of OIAA's agents would go on to help form the backbone of the CIA. One of the more famous OIAA employees was baseball great Morris "Moe" Berg. After a stint with the OIAA early in the war, Berg was reassigned to the OSS and would take part in Project AZUSA interrogating Italian and German physicists about Germany's nuclear program. Coincidentally in 1952, Berg was employed by the CIA to gather information on the Soviet nuclear program. Berg's spycraft was outshined by his stats on the baseball diamond and the mission provided the CIA with no useful information.[50] The Agency's recruitment of Berg further illustrates the CIA's need for any information during the early 1950s and the crossover potential from OIAA to the larger intelligence world.

Steinbeck is overlooked by historians as having any influence in the creation of OCCCRBAR, who simply ascribe the office's formation as a reaction to the fall of France.[51] Even if the idea of what would become OCCCRBAR had been kicked around the Oval Office before Steinbeck's June 26th meeting with FDR, Steinbeck's firsthand accounts could only have shored up the concept in FDR's mind. The idea of Steinbeck influencing FDR has always been discounted due to Steinbeck saying, "no President has ever taken any of my advice."[52] In deference to John, that does not appear to be the case with setting up a propaganda office for Latin America and OCCCRBAR's subsequent activities. Steinbeck may never have been patted on the back for contributing to the evolution of OCCCRBAR, but discussing the Hamilton letter with FDR and the timing of OCCCRBAR's birth tell a different story.

The public was never given the entire picture of OCCCRBAR's mission and the organization simply seemed to exist for the facilitation of south-of-the-border trade. From Steinbeck's point of view, the meeting with FDR had not yielded any discernible effect. Dejected as Steinbeck may have felt from his first meeting with FDR, the author still had a mind to assist his country in an impending crisis. On August 13, 1940, Steinbeck sent another letter to FDR hinting at a plan that may end the conflict with Germany before it ever happened. This time at bat, Steinbeck had brainstormed with the University of Chicago anatomy professor Dr. Melvyn Knisley and developed a plan "more devastating than many

AMERICANOS TODOS
★
LUCHAMOS POR LA VICTORIA

★ **AMERICANS ALL** ★
LET'S FIGHT FOR VICTORY

Wartime American propaganda poster produced to influence Latin-American countries. Image courtesy of the Library of Congress.

battleships" according to Steinbeck.[53] The actual details of the death stroke to the Nazis were left out of the dispatch to FDR, but Steinbeck promised to FDR that a full accounting would not take too much of the president's time in a face-to-face meeting. The prospect was intriguing enough to pass the tin foil hat test of one of FDR's many administrative assistants, James Rowe. In a memo to FDR, Rowe states:

> If this letter were not from Steinbeck I would handle it as routine. As you know, Steinbeck has a high reputation as an amateur scientist. Certainly he is not a crackpot. Shall I tell Steinbeck anything?[54]

As a hedge, Rowe also sent a memo to General Edwin Watson stating that FDR might fob Steinbeck off on "someone else." A scribbled shorthand note at the top right corner of the memo notes who that someone was: "See Dr. Bush. Bush says in a week send him to proper place."[55] The note's "Dr. Bush" probably was Dr. Vannevar Bush, head of National Defense Research Committee (NDRC). The NDRC formed the backbone of American military research before the United State's entry into the Second World War, performing groundbreaking research that would lead to radar and the atomic bomb. There is no evidence that Steinbeck ever met with Bush as Rowe's prediction was off the mark. FDR was once again intrigued enough to schedule a meeting with Steinbeck on September 12th and a meeting with Bush would have been moot.[56]

The plan Steinbeck and Knisley would outline to FDR couldn't have come from a more unlikely pair. One would have expected a best-selling author and the doctor who developed an instrument to microscopically view capillary blood flow to have plucked plans for a Tesla Death Ray from the ether. In reality, Steinbeck's plan was as straightforward as it was devoid of bloodshed. The United States Treasury Department would print millions of counterfeit Deutsche Marks and collapse the German economy under the weight of phony bills. In economic terms, the counterfeiting scheme is analogous to the use of nuclear weapons. Once used, a country would forever live in fear that the full force of another sovereign nation could employ similar tactics. There was also the sticking point of the legality and ethics of a counterfeiting scheme. With a formal declaration of war against Germany a year away, an economic attack on Germany had implications of an assault on Germany's civilian population. Worthless money translates into a civilian population unsure if their money can be used to purchase even the most basic of necessities. Such ethics were chucked out with yesterday's fish as the war progressed, as the residents of Dresden could attest, but prewar America had the luxury to debate the finer points of warfare.[57]

Even with the downsides, FDR was enamored enough with Steinbeck's plan to pass it along to the Treasury Department. Henry Morgenthau, Secretary of the Treasury, hated the idea, believing that the Treasury Department had no business printing counterfeit bills for any purpose. FDR also consulted the British ambassador on the plan who was as outraged at the thought. Ultimately the nuclear economic option was officially nixed because of the previously mentioned ethical implications and basic operational concerns.[58] How does one smuggle enough counterfeit money into Germany to cause wide-spread panic over the monetary supply? Would the bills be good enough to pass tests devised by the very Germans who printed real Deutsche Marks? Ironically the Germans did not share the same concerns as the British and American authorities and had made plans in 1939 to destabilize the United Kingdom's monetary supply with counterfeit pound notes. The Germans planned to drop the phony notes over English airbases and populated areas. Fortunately for the Brits, it had taken until early 1943 to print enough pound notes to make a dent in the UK's economy. While not totally decided by 1943, air supremacy over the skies of the UK belonged to the Allies and a large-scale airdrop could not have been pulled off by the Luftwaffe. Still not giving up on the idea of somehow utilizing the fake pounds, Germany kept cranking out the notes until the end of the war. It's been estimated that £132 million counterfeit notes were printed before the war's end.[59]

The writer of the Bible's Book of Ecclesiastes was fond of reminding readers that "there is nothing new under the sun" and schemes to collapse governments with counterfeit currency fell in line with the maxim. The CIA did a study on this type of economic warfare in an October 1950 paper entitled "Foreign Economic Intelligence Requirements Relating to the National Security." Under the "Financial Matters" section of the document, it states:

> This would include attempts to dislocate the enemy economy through manipulation of exchange materials, dumping of counterfeit currency to promote inflation, etc.[60]

The CIA report is a part of wargame scenarios Agency geeks play out on paper "just in case" an opportunity arises. The CIA's consideration of counterfeiting would have been an interesting endnote to Steinbeck's foray into dirty-trick warfare, had the author not brought the scheme to the public's eye. Steinbeck comes back around to the story's 1940 starting point by writing "The Secret Weapon We Were Afraid to Use" thirteen years later for *Collier's Weekly*. In the January 10, 1953, edition of the periodical, Steinbeck describes the meeting with FDR in 1940 and presents a fictional account of flooding the Soviet Union with funny money. The tag line for the article read:

> President Roosevelt liked the author's plan, but it shocked the Secretary of the Treasury and infuriated the British Ambassador. We didn't use it. But it's as potent a weapon now as it was then. Will we be equally timid again?[61]

Steinbeck's association with the CIA raises serious questions as to the purpose of "The Secret Weapon We Were Afraid to Use." It's obvious from the 1950 report that the CIA had considered counterfeiting and the team of Steinbeck/Knisley were the originators of the idea in the United States; it would follow that the publication of "The Secret Weapon We Were Afraid to Use" was not happenstance. "The Secret Weapon" was part of the block of articles Steinbeck had contracted with *Collier's Weekly* as mentioned in the 1952 letter to General Smith. As we will see in subsequent chapters, Steinbeck's articles for *Collier's Weekly* took tones of outright propaganda.[62] The Agency would have been fully aware of Steinbeck's hand in the 1940 counterfeiting plan and asked Steinbeck to freshen up the concept for the Cold War. By simply publicizing a counterfeiting plan with a baiting tagline "The Secret Weapon," the contents gave the Soviets another Capitalist threat to defend against. The same disinformation tactic was used by a duped media with the 1980's "Star

Wars" (offically known as the Strategic Defense Initiative) missile-killing satellite system. To sell the fiction of a soon-to-be working missile shield, major news outlets carried Star Wars–related stories throughout the 1980s.[63] If ink wasn't enough to convince the Russians of the technical prowess of the United States, a demonstration of laser technology was the subject of a PBS series *Frontline* in 1983. Without the benefit of special effects, a model of a communications satellite was destroyed by a laser in the show's opening sequences.[64] As with the missile defense system, there had to be a kernel of truth to sell Steinbeck's "Secret Weapon" story.

In confidence scams, nubs of reality are known as "salting," which comes from cons selling phony gold metal mines. Small quantities of gold dust are sprinkled around the mine to create the illusion of a mine full of gold. The salting of "The Secret Weapon" would happen in June/July of 1953. A joint venture of the CIA-subsidized National Committee for a Free Europe (NCFE)[65] and Radio Free Europe used weather balloons to bombard Czechoslovakia with propaganda leaflets.[66] The technique of floating weather balloons filled with a propaganda literature into Iron Curtain countries had been an ongoing CIA operation since 1951.[67] (Children of the 1980s may remember the German musician Nena's hit song, "99 Red Balloons," which was inspired by the CIA operation.) On the nights of July 13–17, 1953, twelve million leaflets were delivered by 6,500 balloons into Czechoslovakia. A third of these leaflets were counterfeits of Czechoslovakia's base currency, the Koruna. The CIA's batch of counterfeit one Koruna notes included a handy message of how the Soviets had failed the Czechoslovakian people.[68] The Czech military was so frustrated with the leaflet bombing they took to using anti-aircraft guns to shoot down the balloons and citizens were compelled to turn the material over to their local police force. Coordinated or not, Steinbeck's "The Secret Weapon" article in conjunction with the fake Korunas gave the Soviet Union a sobering proof that economic warfare was a viable concept. The effects of the boldly counterfeit Korunas on the Iron Curtain nation's monetary supplies have never been documented. However if the Soviet's reaction to the "Secret Weapon" was a hundredth of what Star Wars or was, the Kremlin spent millions of Rubles shoring up their monetary supply.[69]

The uneasy question about Steinbeck's "Secret Weapon" is the possibility that the CIA took advantage of the author's celebrity for propaganda or covert purposes. If Steinbeck and other Operation MOCKINGBIRD journalists did compromise journalistic ethics at the CIA's behest, how are we to judge their actions and their writing? Professional journalism *should* equate to truth in the United States. We depend on journalists to uncover the sins of the government, not to become instruments of the government's agenda. Idealisms

Above: Front of NCFE counterfeit Koruna. The text inset in the bill reads: "MEN CALL THIS THE HUNGER CROWN, A GIFT OF THE SOVIET UNION! It is the proof of the government's helplessness and bankruptcy of the five-year plan, a remembrance of what you have had stolen by the government. It is the appeal to fight, the appeal to direct the people's power against the weakness of the regime and to resist as best you can. The peoples of other countries enslaved by the Soviet Union are writing and will join you in your struggle. The free world is with you. All power belongs to the people!"

Above: Back of NCFE counterfeit Koruna. The text reads: CZECHS AND SLOVAKS! The regime is weakening and is afraid of you. The power is in the people and the people are against the regime. Unite and mobilize your forces! Down with the collective farms! Insist on the rights of the workers! Today demand concessions, tomorrow freedom! Photos and translation courtesy of Sergeant Major Herbert A. Friedman (Retired, US Army) and his website www.psywarrior.com.

over a sterling media are only magnified in a generation of the corporately owned media outlets operating on a twenty-four-hour news cycle. Cynicism over unbiased news reporting has made truth in journalism a rare commodity in the minds of many Americans. The judgment passed on journalists of the World War II and Cold War eras who acted as a state mechanism may therefore be harsh. The point of view of the journalists involved with Operation MOCKINGBIRD was that their actions were faithfully performed for a government intent on acting for the best interests of its citizenry. The flip side point of view is that Operation MOCKINGBIRD journalists were compliant pawns of a government hell bent on global dominance. Possibly the truth lies somewhere in the middle of the two opposing statements, but one has to come to their own conclusions. In the case of Steinbeck's "Secret Weapon," a fictional story is at question, but John's efforts in supporting American propaganda and intelligence networks had just begun with the September 1940 meeting with FDR.

For the next year, the uncertainty of the United States' entry into the Second World War mirrored ambiguities in Steinbeck's personal life. Steinbeck had sidestepped a world where counterfeit Deutsche Marks and Mexican politics would have been part of his daily agenda by turning down FDR's mysterious job offer. Given the context of FDR and Steinbeck's first meeting, the job was likely some post within what would become OCCRBAR overseeing Latin American propaganda or another post that would have made use of his creativity. Steinbeck, like many Americans during 1940 and '41, simply wanted to be left alone. The war in Europe was something Americans prayed could be avoided by sending ships full of supplies to Great Britain. Secretly Steinbeck shared a precognition with the rest of America; the day of resolve was coming.

John's personal Pearl Harbor was the realization that he had to make a choice between his first wife, Carol, and his companion, Gwyn Conger. Steinbeck's relationship with Carol was hopeful and light when they met in Lake Tahoe in 1928, where John was working as a tour guide and caretaker of a fish hatchery. Like many in their early- to mid-20s, John and Carol equated compatibility during good times and romantic interludes as the prerequisites for long-term happiness. At the time they married in January of 1930, John was trying to find his way in the world as a writer and Carol took odd jobs supporting the couple. Having moved back to Monterey, the couple would begin their married life at the height of the Great Depression. Amid the despair of the times, John and Carol found distractions at Ed Ricketts' Pacific Biological Laboratories. A marine biologist by trade, Ricketts would open his workplace up after hours to support Monterey's need for an intellectual nightlife. It was not uncommon to hear alcohol-induced philosophy being discussed to a

Gregorian chant soundtrack at Pacific Biological until the wee hours of the morning. Those taking a peek inside Ricketts' lab would see the likes of writers Henry Miller and Joseph Campbell, and composer John Cage swigging hooch alongside Steinbeck and his wife.[70]

It was through Pacific Biological that the first cracks would appear in John and Carol's marriage. John spent an increasing amount of time with Ricketts as the years went on, and Carol became overly fond of Joseph Campbell. The writer's wife and the mythologist would have an affair in 1932. John would forgive Carol's transgression, but the symptoms of discontent would grow into contempt after the publication of *The Grapes of Wrath*. Carol had been the long-suffering wife of a now-successful author and received none of her husband's accolades. Despite the notoriety from his literary successes, John battled bouts of depression that further hamstrung his relationship with his wife. The only thing that seemed to bring joy to John was to be found in a fiery singer, named Gwyn Conger.

Through the majority of 1940, Steinbeck had been secretly meeting with Conger to escape the turmoil in his home life. The love triangle between John, Carol, and Gwyn is well documented in the major Steinbeck biographies and there is little reason to rehash the particulars, but for the purposes of this text, it explains two points. First, it goes a long way to explain why John automatically refused FDR's job offer. Steinbeck was a man who accepted projects on his terms, but also had a sense of performing tasks when necessary. With the publication of *The Grapes of Wrath,* money was of no real consequence to Steinbeck and he could afford to be picky about how he spent his days. The major concern for Steinbeck at the time was to reduce friction with Carol. Even if John had wanted to take a full-time position with the government, it is unlikely that Carol would have been pleased with the decision. After separating from Carol in the spring of 1941, Steinbeck would, somewhat reluctantly, accept FDR's offer by working for various government agencies. Free from Carol's brand of psychosis, John's self-imposed limitations were gone.

The second barbed reason John's affair with Gwyn is important to our discussion is that this was the first time in Steinbeck's life he had colored outside of the lines. Aside from the social lubrication of alcohol, Steinbeck's personal demeanor was fairly traditionally conservative. John's sense of honor had kept him with Carol much longer than the marriage's sell-by date and it has been argued that Carol's nuttiness drove John into the arms of Gwyn. There has even been some conjecture that John's relationship with Gwyn did not have a sexual component until after John and Carol's separation in April of 1941. For the purposes of this discussion, these distinctions are not necessary. There is no doubt that Steinbeck was seeing Gwyn without Carol's knowledge and John's character had to change with the addition of Gwyn in his life. The nature of a "successful" emotional or physical affair necessitates a person compartmentalizing their lives. One must create a plausible fiction for one's significant other to create time for a paramour. The narrative has to be remembered and repeated in such a manner that one's spouse does not question the story. One also has to build up an attention to detail for physical evidence—the clichéd lipstick on a collar or the scent of perfume has to be expunged before returning home. The traits of a person who pulls off a long-term affair are also the mannerisms a spy needs to present a convincing cover story. In a strange way, John's affair with Gwyn was a personal dry run for work in espionage.

A common problem with cheating spouses and spies is that duplicity takes a toll on one's psyche. Living an invented story heaps culpability on all those without sociopathic tendencies. One either copes with the guilt and succeeds in their intended purpose, or one collapses under the weight of the lies. After Carol became aware of Gwyn's existence in John's life and Gwyn was pressuring John to leave Carol, Steinbeck chose not to live with the guilt or crumple under the moral pressures. Instead the story goes that John put both women in a room to decide which one he was to be with.[71] Gwyn would be victorious for Steinbeck's affections in the emotional steel-cage match, and the two were married in March of 1943. The solution shows a certain level of calculated pragmatism previously unseen in Steinbeck. Using an analogy of the Arthurian legends Steinbeck was so fond of, before the affair with Gwyn, Steinbeck could be viewed as taking the morally absolute role of the Fisher King. As the Fisher King had healed his flagging kingdom with the Holy Grail, John had attempted to right the ills of the dustbowl with *The Grapes of Wrath*. The entry of Gwyn into John's life reassigned Steinbeck to the position of the adulterous and flawed Lancelot. As Lancelot, Steinbeck was no longer in the iconoclastic position of honorable superiority and could no longer dictate the terms of his service to any metaphorical king.

This change in Steinbeck's character can be seen in his interactions with FDR in the fall of 1941. The notion that the United States could somehow escape entry into the conflicts across the Atlantic and Pacific oceans had become a pleasant fairy tale for Steinbeck and most Americans. The question was not of if the United States would enter the war, but when. To this end, FDR had begun to make subtle moves to prepare the nation for war. Steinbeck's part on FDR's chessboard would once again revolve around propaganda. Steinbeck's story gets somewhat muddled from the summer of the 1941 meeting until he becomes a war correspondent in 1943. By Steinbeck's own hesitant admission, he did work for the government in a number of capacities during this timeframe. The difficulty of pinning down John's early war activities from a historical standpoint is because John was never technically a government employee. He always operated in the capacity as an "unpaid consultant" and would not have the paper trail of a *bona fide* civil servant. John's status as a consultant, peculiarly enough, made the need for security checks unnecessary. As we will see a little later in this chapter, John's presumed connections with the Communist Party would have made the security clearance process difficult. It would seem that FDR felt Steinbeck was valuable enough an asset to bend the rules for the author.

Since there is a lack of official records, we must piece together Steinbeck's early wartime service from the scant information available. The *New York Herald Tribune* ran an article by Steinbeck called "Reflections of a Lunar Eclipse" in 1963, where Steinbeck spoke of his government work and the origins of his novel *The Moon Is Down*.[72] According to John, he worked for the Army Air Corps, Writer's Board, OWI, and OSS writing everything from speeches, plays, radio broadcasts, and essays.[73] Also Steinbeck states that he was interviewing refugees from Nazi-occupied countries for the OWI and that contact gave him the idea to write *The Moon Is Down*. Many of Steinbeck's biographers have pointed out that this would have been impossible since the OWI was not formed until three months after the publication of *The Moon Is Down* and Steinbeck's memory must have been muddled.[74] In Benson's biography, *The True Adventures of John Steinbeck, Writer*, the assertion is that John worked for Robert Sherwood's propaganda branch of the Foreign Information Service (FIS) beginning in October of 1941.[75] A close acquaintance of Steinbeck's, Lewis Gannett, recalls that *The Moon Is Down* was born out of a discussion between the future head of the OSS, William Donovan, and Steinbeck about how to aid European resistance groups.[76] Gannett's comments about *The Moon Is Down* were first published in the introduction to *A Portable Steinbeck*, but Gannett gives no citation. Finally, in the introduction of the 1995 edition of *The Moon Is Down*, Donald Coers states that Steinbeck was probably working for the proto-version of the OSS in mid-summer of 1941.[77]

Statue of William "Wild Bill" Donovan at CIA headquarters. Photo courtesy of the CIA.

Somewhere in the midst of all these accounts lies the truth about Steinbeck's government work between 1941 and 1943. The first concrete evidence of Steinbeck's involvement with a government agency was his October 7, 1941, attendance of an FIS conference.[78] The goal of the meeting was a brainstorming session on how best to dole out propaganda in a wartime setting. The FIS was the embodiment of the propaganda office that Steinbeck had presented to FDR the year before and was under the purview of Washington's Coordinator of Intelligence (COI), William Donovan. Carrying the nickname of "Wild Bill," Donovan was a former federal attorney and Medal of Honor winner during the First World War when he took the post of COI in July 1941. Donovan had traveled extensively in Europe, meeting with heads of state in the years leading up to the Second World War, and was often called on by FDR to give insight into Europe's political situation. Seeing the need for America's fragmented intelligence network to operate more cohesively, FDR created the COI as a clearinghouse for the nation's intelligence. After the United States entered the war, the office of the COI was turned into the OSS—the forerunner to today's CIA.[79]

With Steinbeck's officially unofficial status, the confusion about specifics surrounding Steinbeck's duties has not only been left as a historical question, but seems to have dazed John as well. In a number of his letters to friends and family during this time period, Steinbeck conveys a sense that no one was quite sure what to do with his talents, so he invented ways to assist in the propaganda war. John had little choice if he wished to be of some good. No one in Washington would technically hire John, nor would they release him to seek fulltime assignments from other agencies. Exactly which agency John was attached to has always been in question, but it was likely the FIS. At one point, Steinbeck was so frustrated with backroom politics he wrote FDR that he had already turned down one job offer from him, but that he now had a job—whether he wanted one or not.[80] Whatever role John was playing for the government, it was pressing enough by mid-November that he rented a two-bedroom apartment in a Manhattan residential hotel.[81] By the early spring of 1942, John would take up more permanent digs in the Palisades community outside of New York City. Basing himself in New York instead of Washington would seem to give credence that John was working with the FIS. Since New York was the country's media hub during the 1940s, John would need to be close to the country's largest radio and newspaper outlets.

Through most of November to mid-December, John worked on the manuscript for *The Moon Is Down*. It is also likely from the October to November time period that Steinbeck came into contact with the refugees from Nazi-occupied countries. The stories John heard from the refugees were the origin point for *The Moon Is Down*. Steinbeck downplayed the association with the refugees, making it sound as if the contact was that of casual acquaintances.[82] It is more likely that John was given the task of interviewing those who had escaped the Germans as a way to craft effective propaganda for the FIS. The byproduct of Steinbeck's interviews would have been sharing the information with Donovan to construct ways to bolster resistance groups. This explanation fits the conditions of both the Benson and Gannett assertions that Steinbeck was working for both the COI and FIS simultaneously. Anecdotes have floated around that Steinbeck and Donovan would come up with harebrained schemes to help

An example of propaganda produced by the OWI during the spring of 1942. Image from the NARA.

European resistance forces. One of the more colorful tales was that Steinbeck suggested to Donovan that tiny grenades be airdropped over Nazi-occupied nations so children could throw them on the roofs of German facilities.[83]

In mid-December of 1941, John turned in the first draft of *The Moon Is Down* to be reviewed by an unknown government agency. Steinbeck's first stab at *The Moon Is Down* was actually titled *The New Order* and had a different setting than the final version. *The Moon Is Down* chronicles the occupation and resistance in an unnamed country by an unnamed occupier. *The New Order* was set in a Pacific Coast town after a Japanese invasion. The powers that be, likely either the FIS or Office of Censorship, turned down *The New Order*. It was felt the novel would cause panic on the West Coast because the government was preparing the populace for a successful Japanese invasion that would never happen.[84] Steinbeck changed the title and setting to a cold-climate, unnamed European country that has always been identified as either Norway or Denmark, and the work was accepted. Since Steinbeck submitted the work for review, one can also assume that the novel was written at the behest of whatever government agency urged him to make the changes. Benson asserts that agency was the FIS, but given how *The Moon Is Down* was utilized, it is likely the book was written at the behest of William Donovon's office of the COI.

The failings of John's memory in the 1963 "Reflections of a Lunar Eclipse" were not the momentary lapses of an aging writer. Steinbeck was obfuscating the origins of *The Moon Is Down* intentionally. If we accept that Steinbeck was involved with the CIA until at least 1964, the reason for the ruse makes perfect sense. "Reflections of a Lunar Eclipse" was published immediately before John went on a goodwill trip to the Soviet Union with playwright Edward Albee. The piece could very well have been written to deflect the Soviets from connecting Steinbeck to any serious work with the COI/OSS during the Second World War. All fiction has to have some kernel of truth, so Steinbeck mentions that he did some civilian work for the OSS amongst all the other agencies he performed tasks for. The focus of the article is John's contact with the refugees being the prime mover for penning the novel. This fits with *The Grapes of Wrath* vision of Steinbeck being the champion of the oppressed, and not that of a man who would knowingly write propaganda for his government. Finally the article was published by the *New York Herald Tribune*, which has been shown to have been deeply involved with the CIA.

The pieces fit considering what was done with *The Moon Is Down* after its publication in March of 1942. Thousands of copies of *The Moon Is Down* were smuggled into Nazi-controlled countries and were distributed throughout resistance groups. The novel was so influential within the Norwegian resistance that King Haakon VII awarded Steinbeck the Norwegian Liberty Cross in November of 1946. The Italian resistance even mimeographed copies of the novel for distribution through their network.[85] DCI William Colby would also give a ringing endorsement of *The Moon Is Down,* having read the novel

Major William Colby and the Norwegian Special Operations Group parading in Trondheim at the end of World War II. Colby is at the front left. Photo provided by the Municipal Archives of Trondheim.

shortly after its publication. Colby would lead a sabotage mission into occupied Norway as an OSS agent late in the war. America's future top spy had a unique perspective on how the novel captured the disposition of Norwegians. With all of this, we are led to believe that the covert distribution of *The Moon Is Down* was thought of after its publication.

In reality, the distribution of *The Moon Is Down* had to be a calculated and thoughtful exercise to have achieved penetration deep into Nazi-occupied countries. After working for months with various government agencies, Steinbeck writes a novel on a whim that is designed to give hope to an oppressed European populace. It is far more likely that Steinbeck was given the assignment of writing such a book for distribution into Europe, rather than the powers in Washington thinking *The Moon Is Down* would be a nice bonus to regular weapons drops for resistance fighters. Going back to Steinbeck's submitting the manuscript for approval lends credence to this theory. *Cannery Row*, for example, was published in 1945 and was not submitted to anyone other than Viking for publication. Only materials that pertained to the war were reviewed by government offices, the Office of Censorship always having the final audit, during the Second World War.[86] Since it is likely *The Moon Is Down* made its way through the Office of Censorship, or whatever other government office it could have originally been submitted to, and not *Cannery Row*, *The Moon Is Down* was part of the war effort.

There are other indications that Steinbeck worked closely with the COI and other methods to bolster resistance movements in Europe. It is difficult to pin down exactly how much support the United States provided European resistance groups from October 1941 to May of 1942. Steinbeck felt that there was a significant amount of assistance that was given, in particular, to the Danish resistance. In a July 1962 letter to John F. Kennedy outlining a plan to diffuse the Berlin Wall Crisis, Steinbeck twice mentions his work to aid the Danish resistance.

> The Danes were masters of ridicule during the occupation of their
> country as I have good reason to know . . . (and later)
> I worked with the Danes against the Germans and I know.[87]

Exactly how Steinbeck worked with the Danes is not known. The British are credited with creating intelligence networks within Denmark as early as April of 1940, but there is little history of American involvement with the Danish resistance immediately before and after the United States entered the war.[88] Had Steinbeck been speaking of the effect of *The Moon Is Down*, it would stand to reason that he would have mentioned the Norwegian resistance to Kennedy. Having been awarded the Norwegian Liberty Cross would have been the perfect example of how Steinbeck's fruitful imagination had a real-world

A young boy is "tagged" for relocation to an internment camp in Salinas, California, May 1942. Image courtesy of the Library of Congress.

effect. By mentioning the Danish resistance to Kennedy, we can assume that Steinbeck was referring to something more meaningful than an award to sway Kennedy's opinion of his Berlin Wall proposal. Likely it was some hereto-classified work Steinbeck did for the COI/OSS that Kennedy could have verified.

It is also certain that Steinbeck was more than simply casually involved with Donovan's budding intelligence network. A week after Pearl Harbor, Steinbeck wrote a memo to Donovan outlining how Japanese-Americans should be treated and utilized in the war effort. Steinbeck's thought was to embrace the loyal Japanese-American community and let them ferret out real Japanese spies. This alternative was presented to FDR by Donovan on December 15, 1941.[89] FDR had no use for the idea and signed an executive order authorizing the internment of Americans with Japanese descent in late February of 1942. Steinbeck, in turn, had no use for FDR's policy of placing American citizens under what amounted to unlawful arrest and the subject rankled the author for the rest of the war. Regardless of the internal feelings about internment camps, the memo from Donovan and the publication of *The Moon Is Down* establishes more than a passing relationship between Steinbeck and Donovan.

There are other indications that Steinbeck was working on the more classified end of the pool during the last quarter of 1941 through the summer of 1942. The issue of security would become more than a passing interest to Steinbeck. While writing *The Moon Is Down*, Steinbeck hired a court reporter to transcribe portions of the novel as he dictated. John became suspicious of her competence when reading back one of the session's minutes and found entire scenes had been deleted or verbiage changed. Steinbeck would fire the court reporter only to learn later she was a member of the German-American Federation. The society was made up of German immigrants and those of

German-American heritage who were sympathetic to Hitler's regime. In the Federation's largest showing of force, in February of 1939, a rally of 20,000 Federation members was held at Madison Square Garden to malign FDR's New Deal policies.[90] A number of Federation officials were arrested by the FBI after the declaration of war against Germany on charges of violating the 1940 Selective Service Act.[91] One can then imagine that the matter of Steinbeck's stenographer was more than a fly in the ointment; she represented a potential security breach. It is likely Steinbeck mentioned the flakey stenographer he hired to someone at the COI or FIS. The incident was strange enough to conduct a background check on the unnamed stenographer and that is how Steinbeck found out about her involvement with the German-American Federation. Another possibility is that the stenographer in question applied for a job requiring a security clearance and the association with Steinbeck and the Federation was discovered that way.

In either of the stenographer scenarios, the fact Steinbeck could have been approached by a German spy would have been unnerving. With the United States officially at war in December of 1941, security measures were ratcheted up across all government agencies. This would have been especially true at the offices of the COI. A majority of the wartime intelligence was being collected and collated by this office. Any work Steinbeck subsequently did for the COI would fall into that mire of classified materials and there would have been checks into Steinbeck's background. Steinbeck certainly thought that someone was checking up on him. On May 11, 1942, Attorney General (AG) Francis Biddle received a terse letter from Steinbeck asking that the FBI surveillance teams "stop stepping on my heels" because the practice was "getting tiresome."[92] Biddle, in turn, sends a letter to J. Edgar Hoover simply stating, "Will you note this letter from John Steinbeck, playwright?"[93] Hoover replies to Biddle ten days later saying that the FBI is not now nor has ever investigated Steinbeck.

The above exchange has been laughed off over the years as quirky Steinbeck getting in a twist over imagining g-men following him about. Also Hoover's comments about the FBI never investigating Steinbeck have been called into doubt since Steinbeck has a 120-page FBI file. How could the Bureau not investigate someone and yet have such an extensive file on them? Anyone applying for a federal job or any level of security clearance has an FBI file. Even temporary Census Bureau employees have their fingerprints taken and filed with the FBI. An FBI investigation would denote that the Bureau was investigating a crime linked to a certain person. Under Hoover's watch of the FBI, it was common to amass information on famous or influential persons because of Hoover's own special brand of paranoia. However, sending agents out into the field to investigate a potential crime is another matter entirely.

Hoover then was likely telling a shaded truth that the Bureau had never investigated Steinbeck. Hoover's answer never sat well with Steinbeck and he believed Hoover was behind John's yearly IRS audits. Unfortunately, John was probably wrong about this as well. It is far more likely that the CIA was the cause of John's IRS woes. The Agency would have used the audits to ensure John's finances were on the level and that he had not been receiving unusual income, which might indicate he had been compromised by a competing spy agency. Examination of Steinbeck's financial records would also explain why the CIA requested information from the FBI about a check sent to Steinbeck from a Bulgarian bank account in 1959.[94]

If the FBI wasn't following Steinbeck, who was? Two events in May of 1942 could have precipitated a detailed look into Steinbeck's life from some government agency. A few weeks before John sent the letter to AG Biddle, he had been offered a paid full-time position at the OWI. Here is another situation where we do not exactly know what the position was or what duties Steinbeck would perform for the OWI. John did turn down the job offer in hopes of gaining an Army commission. Had John taken the job with the OWI, he would have been classified as being necessary for the war effort as a civilian with no hope of obtaining a commission. Also on May 5, 1942, John wrote to the Secretary of the Navy about the use of oceanographic charts that had been published prior to the war by Japanese marine biologists.[95] Ed Ricketts had floated the idea past Steinbeck after coming across detailed tide charts of Japanese-held Pacific Islands that were available in most universities with a marine biology department. The Navy didn't seem too interested in the suggestion, not because it wasn't a good idea, but because other academics had already brought it to the Navy's attention.[96] Ricketts was visited by an ONI officer later that summer as a follow-up to Steinbeck's letter who seemed less than impressed with Ricketts' findings.

Either of these two events could have triggered a detailed background check into Steinbeck's life. Steinbeck's FBI file references an ONI report that a confidential informant claimed Steinbeck had received literature from Russia via the offices of his literary agents Otis and McIntosh from 1942–44.[97] The report could have been a happenstance piece of information given to the ONI by one of their assets, but with Steinbeck's letter to Knox, it would seem more likely that the ONI took a long, hard look at Steinbeck. As for the job at the OWI, anyone from the OSS to the State Department could have been performing background checks on Steinbeck before the offer of a full-time position was made. Also dependent on Steinbeck's actual job role within the government machine from October 1942 to May 1943, Army Counterintelligence could have been performing routine checks to ensure Steinbeck wasn't either a target or security risk. There is also the possibility that Steinbeck wasn't the target at all. John had been sued for divorce by Carol in late March of 1942 and had brazenly taken up with Gwyn Conger shortly there after. A government agency could have been performing background checks on Gwyn to confirm John's new flame wasn't a security risk. If the FBI wasn't following Steinbeck, or Gwyn, it is likely that someone inside the government was.

Whoever was following Steinbeck around would take a psychological toll on the author. The brash letter to AG Biddle was followed up by another act of a man who feared for his personal safety. Through a bit of historical sleuthing, writer Steve Hauk discovered that Steinbeck had applied for a permit to carry two .38 Automatic Colt Pistols (ACP) in the state of New York.[98] The date of the application was May 12, 1942, the day after AG Biddle received Steinbeck's letter. The timing of the two events is likely not a fluke. One does not send a ranting letter to the Attorney General of the United States about being followed by secret agents and then apply for a carry permit if one does not feel some personal peril. The application for the permit also could have been filed because Steinbeck was hedging against members of a government agency trailing him. He might have considered that Axis agents were targeting him. No matter what the case, the letter to AG Biddle and the application of the pistol permit would denote that Steinbeck was pushed into a position of paranoia, in which he had to take action in securing his peace of mind.

May of 1942 would not be the first nor last time John Steinbeck would find it necessary to go armed. Shortly after the publication of *The Grapes of Wrath*, John was advised by a member of the Monterey County Sheriff's Office to carry a firearm. In John's pre-*Grapes of Wrath* Salinas, the concept of personal protection was unknown to Steinbeck. Having grown up in California's Fertile Crescent, John had found few menacing figures stalking the streets of Salinas. *The Grapes of Wrath* forever changed that landscape for John. Men John had known his entire life turned hostile toward the author because of his indictment of the sharecropping system. There were more than a few death threats sprinkled in the hate mail Steinbeck received after *The Grapes of Wrath* hit bookstore shelves, and John took the Sheriff's advice to heart. In a town where John freely tipped his hat to neighbors, he would now go everywhere assessing threats with the surety of an armed man.

One can understand the previous instances of Steinbeck carrying a firearm, given his perception of personal danger. The oddity is that John continued the practice for the rest of his life. According to Thomas Steinbeck, "My father was the best-armed man I knew, and went most places armed."[99] The arsenal of John's weapons Thomas knew of was quite a bit more exotic than the two .38 ACPs mentioned in the application for a New York pistol permit. Because of a hip injury sustained in a 1947 fall from a second-story balcony and a lifetime plagued with back problems, John always kept a cane close at hand. Thomas revealed that two of the canes John used were actually concealed weapons. One of the canes was a .410-bore shotgun that was always loaded out with a slug shell, and the other hid a nine-inch stiletto blade. As Thomas recalls, John obtained these canes from a dealer in Paris, sometime during the 1950s. (Interestingly enough, Childéric de Saone in *The Short Reign of Pippin IV* brandishes a sword concealed within a cane, as discussed in chapter 10 of this text.) Other canes owned by the elder Steinbeck were made from Irish Briarwood and sported a ball at the end of the cane's crook. John would have the ball hollowed out and filled with a couple of pounds of ball bearings. The extra weight at the end of the cane's crook was explained away by John to balance the cane on his arm when reaching in his pockets or opening doors. Thomas now believes the Briarwood canes were just another discreet weapon readily available to his father. Certainly a blow from a cane constructed in such a manner would discourage any would-be attackers.[100]

If the canes were not enough, John also commonly carried one of two .38 derringer-style pistols. These weapons are designed to be fired from a range of less than thirty feet and are used as a weapon of last resort. Before being deployed to Vietnam, John gave one of the derringers and the shotgun cane to Thomas. During his tour, Thomas kept the derringer in a jury-rigged interior boot holster that afforded Thomas more blisters than protection. The

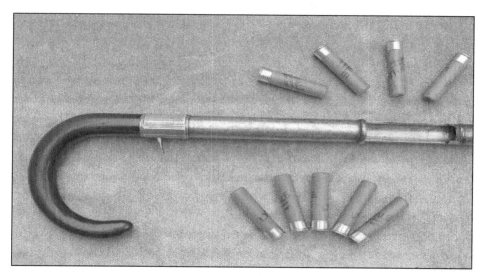

A Belgian cane concealing a .410-bore shotgun that would be similar in design to Steinbeck's cane-shotgun. The drop-down trigger is concealed near the horn of the cane.
Photo courtesy of Michael Shepherd of MicksGuns.com

shotgun cane was of more use to Thomas when on liberty in Saigon and other Vietnamese urban areas. Both the derringer and shotgun cane were given to different comrades at the end of Thom's tour. Thomas does still own a number of John's other firearms, including a ridiculously overpowered .44 magnum, made famous in Clint Eastwood's *Dirty Harry* movie franchise.[101]

It is difficult to imagine that Steinbeck felt a level of threat post-World War II that would have made it necessary to continually bear arms. After the war, there were no Nazi spies and the furor over *The Grapes of Wrath* was a distant memory. The explanation could be as simple as John being afraid of getting mugged, or being an easy payday for kidnappers looking for a prosperous target. It is equally as plausible that the Agency either outfitted John with these exotic weapons or advised Steinbeck to do so himself. In either case, John felt that his life could be in danger for the majority of his adult life, and his actions fit with a man conducting covert operations.

As quickly as the wave of 1942 paranoia seemed to sweep across Steinbeck's mind, a new job offer would give John hope that everything was about to change. In late May of 1942, John began research on what would become *Bombs Away: The Story of a Bomber Team*. The Army Air Corps had envisioned Steinbeck writing two books about Air Corp operations and sent Steinbeck on a whirlwind tour of the United States' aerial assets. During that summer, John would fly in most every aircraft the Army Air Corps had in service and visit a number of air bases throughout the Southern United States.[102] Officially John had become Special Consultant to the Secretary of War attached to the Army Air Corps, while also performing job duties as the foreign news editor for the OWI.[103] Once again, we are faced with John coming in contact with classified materials in both job roles. As the foreign news editor of the OWI, John would have made decisions about what press releases the government would make about events overseas. To place the proper spin and redact sensitive information, one must know a good helping of unabashed reality.

While on tour with the Army Air Corps, John would have gained some working knowledge of the Norden bombsight. The technology behind the bombsight was a few shades less classified than the Manhattan Project. The Norden bombsight was actually a primitive computer that calculated the optimal conditions in which a bomber's cargo would be released, greatly improving accuracy over bombsights previously used by the Army Air Corps. Bombardiers had to take an oath that they would never disclose the capabilities of the sight and should an aircraft go down in enemy territory, the number -one priority was to destroy the sight with a thermite grenade. Even stateside, an armed guard accompanied bombardiers to install or remove the bombsight before and after each flight.[104]

A carrot was dangled in front of Steinbeck with the assignment for the Army Air Corps. John had been promised a commission in the Army Air Corps as an intelligence officer. The unnamed promissory would grant the commission right after these two books were written. So confident was Steinbeck in this promise that he wrote longtime friend Toby Street on July 23rd that the commission would come through in the fall of 1942.[105] One of the most perplexing turn of events in Steinbeck's life was about to happen. We know that Steinbeck had worked with William Donovan, the OWI, and been given close access to the Norden bombsight, all of which would entail levels of classification much higher than the average solider. But John would be denied both a commission and entry into the Army as an enlisted man. The story of John's woes with the Salinas draft board, where legally his permanent residence was still located, are well documented within Steinbeck's major biographies and shows that the board basically turned him down because of the flap over *The Grapes of Wrath*. Officially, John's age and other bureaucratic factors made him ineligible for the draft. John had even received a letter from the head of the Army Air Corps, General Curtis LeMay recommending him for service. Still the old prejudices applied with the draft board and every avenue Steinbeck took to serving in uniform was denied.

From the July 1942 letter to Street until John applied to be a war correspondent in March of 1943, Steinbeck bounced from assignment to assignment as he had before the *Bombs Away* tour. The conventional theory is that John became sick of dealing with draft boards, promises of commissions, and unsteady government ground work in early 1943. The only way John felt that he would be a part of the war was to become a correspondent. Leaving his government jobs behind, John would strike out on his own.

There is a problem with this point of view. John was not denied an Army commission until July 27, 1943—nearly a full two months after John had been in Europe as a correspondent.[106] Steinbeck's FBI file shows that the Army Counterintelligence did not even begin its investigation on Steinbeck's suitability for a commission until February of 1943.[107] The recommendation by the investigation officer, Lt. Colonel T.H. Fairchild of the Army's Military Intelligence branch, was that Steinbeck be given a commission. When the findings of Steinbeck's background check were forwarded up the chain of command, John's commision went sideways. Lt. Colonel Boris Pash, of Army Counterintelligence, quashed Fairchild's initial review by stating:

> This office does not concur in the recommendations by the reporting agent in closing report (sic). In view of substantial doubt as to the Subject's loyalty and discretion, it is recommended that Subject (sic)

not be considered favorably for a commission in the Army of the United States.

Undeveloped leads will not be followed in the absence of request, and this case is considered closed in this office.[108]

Pash was quite the Army's counterintelligence guru whose story deserves a book of its own. Aside from his accomplishments in the intelligence community, Pash was credited with "discovering" Lana Turner at Schwan's Drugstore while working with the film industry before the war.[109] At the time of Steinbeck's commission investigation, Pash was serving as the head of security for the Manhattan Project, and by all accounts was hell on wheels investigating Robert Oppenheimer and his fellow scientists. In September of 1943, Pash was reassigned to Washington and developed Operation ALSOS (the Greek word for "grove") to gather intelligence on Germany's nuclear program. The members of ALSOS operated forward of Allied lines in Italy and France, searching for physicists who were working with the Nazis. Possibly Pash's biggest accomplishment during the war was liberating the Curie Institute in Paris where eighteen tons of uranium ore had been stockpiled by the Germans.[110] After the war, Pash was rolled up into the CIA blanket and ran a high-level counterintelligence group codenamed PB-7. The ominous-sounding group worked under the direction of DD/P Frank Wisner and was tasked with eliminating double agents and other low-level Soviet operatives. Pash was once interviewed about the activities of PB-7 and was asked if the group carried out assassinations; Pash would neither confirm nor deny the charges.[111]

We are left wondering why the head of security for the Manhattan Project had time on his hands to evaluate routine commissioning investigations. It is possible that Pash was also in charge of vetting public figures and celebrities for Army service, although it is difficult to believe the man guarding America's

Boris Pash (left) commanding an April 1945 ALSOS mission in Hechingen, Germany. Photo courtesy of the US Army.

nuclear program, a project so secret that it was kept from Vice-President Truman,[112] would have had routine background checks put on his plate as well. Steinbeck had to have been a unique case to have been placed on Pash's desk. It's also not difficult to ascertain why Pash blackballed Steinbeck from Army service. Pash was a rabid anti-Communist in the vein of J. Edgar Hoover and Ayn Rand. In 1954, Pash even testified against Robert Oppenheimer at the HUAC hearings that eventually blacklisted the man whose research delivered the atomic bomb to America. Oppenheimer was an unrepentant Communist, having written on his Los Almos security form he had been "a member of just about every Communist Front organization on the West Coast."[113] Steinbeck's tacit connections to Communists were probably enough to raise Pash's ire.

The conventional thinking also is that Steinbeck totally left government service when he became a war correspondent. Steinbeck was still working for the OWI and Army while he was a correspondent and was tasked with making a movie about the Army's Service of Supply (SOS) branch. The film sounds rather mundane but denotes that John's government service was not over. In fact, John seems to have gone about doing background research for the project with great zeal for someone who had fallen out of love with government projects. Literally the same week Steinbeck was given the boot by Pash, he was interviewing members of General John C.H. Lee's SOS staff. Lee was responsible for all the supplies in the European Theater and his staff obviously had better things to do than speak with Steinbeck. In a staff meeting in early August, a Colonel Pickens stated:

> Mr. John Steinbeck took up four days of good time of the best men I have on my staff during the past week.[114]

The situation truly makes little sense. If Steinbeck were so untrustworthy, as Pash recorded, why was he continually given access to personnel performing vital and sensitive work? As we will see in the next chapter, John was imbedded with a top-secret Naval commando unit. Could John's role within the wartime machine be more than we were led to believe? Unfortunately the documentation simply is not there to make that case. There is little doubt that John's contacts and job duties within the intelligence community during the war would have made him a more attractive candidate for working with the CIA in 1952. As we will see, it is also possible that John never fully left government service from 1940 until 1964.

As the PT boat sped toward the pocket-sized island floating in the Bay of Naples, John absently ran his hand over his upper arm and felt nothing but the rough material of his field jacket. The shoulder of the olive drab garb held no rank and the collar bore no branch insignia. Normally the only adornment on John's standard issue fatigues was a thin band of dark green wool with the words "War Correspondent" circling the letters "US." The armband was magically supposed to differentiate John from a combatant while he was embedded with a front-line unit. John had no illusions that the piece of wool would become a talisman against oncoming small arms rounds or artillery fire. The constriction of the armband against one's bicep was a comfort to many reporters in combat, but John felt all of the restraint and none of the calm the flimsy material supposedly provided.

At every opportunity John had over the past few weeks, he had retired the cursed armband to his belongings aboard the USS *Knight* when leaving for a mission and dutifully replaced the armband after an action was conducted. The destroyer was a platform for Douglas Fairbanks Jr.'s commando group and John took every chance he could to accompany his friend on missions. John would replace his green wool armband with a Tommy gun on each mission. One of the lads in Lieutenant Fairbanks' group would sneak an extra weapon onto the patrol boat that whisked the men to their mission site. The risks of stripping his status as a war reporter were not lost on John or Fairbanks. Fairbanks could have been severely reprimanded for issuing weapons to a civilian. For John, if he were captured, he would have no combatant status under the Geneva Convention and would be considered a spy. While the rulebook for warfare did call for those accused of espionage a trial, there was little doubt what would happen if John were captured. The only hearing he might receive was that of a torturous interrogation before receiving a lead medal for bravery in the back of his head.

The tiny plot of land jutting out of the Bay of Naples played host to a radar instillation garrisoned by both Germans and Italian forces. The *Knight* had been ordered to secure the island shortly after the news of the unconditional surrender of Italian forces was officially announced. The results of the surrender had been something of a mixed bag throughout Italy. Mussolini had been effectively deposed from power on July 25, 1943, by members of Italy's Grand Council on Fascism, and the new government had entered into secret negotiations to end hostilities soon afterward. The official announcement of Italy's capitulation to Allied forces did not happen until September 8, 1943. German forces had taken the intervening weeks to fortify their positions and to secure the loyalties of as many Italian hard-line Fascist troops as they could. Allied command was well aware that any contact with Italian troops after the armistice was signed could still result in bloodshed.

The USS *Knight* in New York Harbor, 1943. Photo courtesy of the US Navy.

The decision was made aboard the *Knight* to wait until darkness had fallen and bluff the Axis forces on Ventotene into a peaceful surrender. This was exactly the type of mission Fairbank's unit of commandos had been performing in the weeks leading up to the Italian armistice. Fairbanks had modeled his unit of "Beach Jumpers" on British special operations groups and employed weapons of deception rather than directly engaging the enemy. The mission of the "BJs," as Fairbanks' commandos would call themselves, was to fool enemy forces into thinking amphibious landings and naval operations were taking place far from actual targets. The nature of the BJs' work necessitated a high level of classification for the sailors and their methods. The security measures were to ensure enemy forces would not be alerted to the unit's elaborate ruses. To give one an idea of the secrecy surrounding the BJs, James Franklin spoke about his service with the Beach Jumpers during the Vietnam War:

> We were in country from '64 to '68 and it wasn't supposed to be known. I had to prove [to the Veterans Administration] that I was overseas because the military has no record of our activity.[1]

Secrecy was not the only tool the BJs used to engage the enemy. Fairbanks and the BJs literally created specialized equipment and tactics to achieve their goals. One common setup was to run a number of small patrol boats within range of an Axis radar station. The crews would deploy aluminum foil sails to increase their boat's radar signature and transmit previously recorded radio traffic between the small craft. The effect created a phantom fleet of ships much larger than the patrol boats. The BJs' methods were so successful that an entire German division was redeployed away from the Allied invasion site at Salerno.[2]

Fairbanks' BJs would have to employ all their tricks and specialized equipment to crack the resolve of the Italians and Germans on Ventotene. Naval intelligence estimated that there was a small force of Italian militia and German regulars guarding the island. There was little doubt that the Italians would surrender the island, but there was no knowledge of exactly how many troops were stationed on Ventotene. The *Knight* might have been only able to muster less than one hundred men for direct combat if the island's defenders did not surrender outright. To even the odds in their favor, the BJs did what they did best—deceive. As soon as the sun set on September 8th, the BJs deployed their patrol boats to run a radar hoax similar to the tactics previously described. The crews of the patrol boats also played recordings of airplanes in flight and noises from larger ships to create the illusion of a larger force bearing down on Ventotene. Now all the BJs had to do was to press the ruse to the coast of Ventotene.

A prerecorded message boomed from the *Knight's* loudspeakers that the island was surrounded and the Allied troops would accept the surrender of all Italian and German soldiers. The offer for clemency was good for ten minutes. If the offer was not accepted, the island would be considered belligerent and taken by the "overwhelming" Allied forces circling Ventotene. Many of those in the *Knight's* task force had not seen ground combat with enemy forces. The mission of the BJs was that of stealth and deception, not direct combat. The probability of storming the beaches of Ventotene expanded exponentially with each tick of the minute hand. At the ten-minute mark, there was no sign that Ventotene's defenders would go quietly and the *Knight's* crew began firing the ship's five-inch guns toward the shore. During a short break in the shelling, three white flares of truce lazily arched into the sky above Ventotene.

As the crew of the *Knight* began to cheer at their good fortune, Captain Andrews still had a problem. He wasn't directly concerned with the Italians on the island. Left to their own devices, Andrews felt most of the Italians would lay down their arms and surrender. The unknown factor on Ventotene was the Germans. There was always the chance that the Nazis would compel the Italians to defend the island and the white flares were simply a ruse. Andrews opened the floor to suggestions from his junior officers. Fairbanks began to pontificate about Navy procedures, which led Andrews to believe he was volunteering for a scouting mission. Before Fairbanks could clarify his position, Steinbeck excitedly chimed in, offering to accompany Fairbanks. Andrews thought the plan of sending a few men on a recon mission was an outstanding idea and ordered the men to get underway.[3]

Fairbank's crew would be backed up by an OSS contingent led by Henry Ringling North.[4] Fairbanks and the OSS men hit Ventotene's beach first and began taking fire. The goal of the BJs was to get in and out of their missions

Left and Below: 2005 pictures of Ventotene's old harbor area where Steinbeck and Fairbanks landed.*

without being detected. Fairbanks wasn't used to getting shot at and conjured up a mental image of what Gary Cooper would have done in a movie, given a similar situation. Emulating Cooper's actions, Fairbanks took cover behind the wall of a building and began to return fire. As the bullets flew between Fairbanks and the yet unknown shooters, Fairbanks thought, "None of my own old movies called for this sort of maneuver."[5] Circling back to a dock he had seen approaching the island, Fairbanks saw a group of Italians that looked like they wanted to surrender. As Fairbanks approached the group of Italians, the boat carrying Steinbeck and a few more BJs and OSS troopers landed. John had no idea what the situation was, having heard gunfire as his boat approached the dock. Upon seeing his friend faced with a group of Italian soldiers, he jumped out onto the beach ready for action.

John would have his chance to fight soon enough, and he was fully aware that he was violating War Department regulations regarding war correspondents in combat. In a letter to Gwyn on September 18th, Steinbeck states that in the last few weeks he'd, "broken all the rules."[6] There was no turning back for Steinbeck or for Fairbanks as he spoke to the surrendering Italian soldiers. A grim picture began to emerge of what lay ahead. The Italians were more than willing to surrender, but they reported there were still four hundred German troops buttoned down in their garrison. There were not nearly enough men aboard the *Knight* to take on a dug-in German stronghold of that size. After communicating the situation to Andrews, it was decided there was little other option than to keep up the fiction that the Allied force was considerably larger than it actually was. Andrews was also sending what reinforcements he could from the *Knight*. Fairbanks ordered the men at his disposal to patrol and then take defensive positions in and around the dockside buildings. The reinforcements would be easy targets if the Germans infiltrated Fairbanks' position and fired on the *Knight*'s troops as they disembarked their transports. The Germans continued to lob mortar rounds and harassing small-arms fire as Fairbanks' men took positions around the quay. German munitions cared little if Steinbeck was a correspondent or solider, but John took his place next to the BJs and OSS men as if he was one of their own.

The reinforcements from the *Knight* bolstered the Allied forces to less than forty men. Fairbanks had to occupy as many key positions around the Germans as possible. To maintain the illusion of a larger force, the lines of BJs, OSS troops, and sailors from the *Knight* stretched their frontage as far as tactically possible. Taking pot shots in the dark from a greater frontage would go a long way to buttress the grand bluff Fairbanks was trying to pull off. Steinbeck took up position alongside the others for a night of shrugging off the sporadic fire from the Germans. The *Knight* assisted Fairbanks' force by firing its five-inch

deck guns at the Germans' position. No one slept on Ventotene that night. German or American, the men locked in conflict for little more than a half square mile of land jutting from the Tyrrhenian Sea, murmured the prayer both warriors and mothers of sick children have said for millennia: "Please, God, let me just get through the night."

The sun did rise the morning of September 9th and there were no reported casualties in Fairbanks' ranks. With daylight also came the chance the Germans would see through Fairbanks' paper-thin scam. There is an old military

The unit patch for Fairbanks' Beach Jumper Unit 1.

adage that says, "Make a decision. Right or wrong just make a decision," and Henry Ringling North did just that. The OSS agent held a white towel above his head and marched straight toward the German garrison. Fairbanks and Steinbeck looked on with stunned silence. North's life depended on nothing less than honor between enemy soldiers. Three German soldiers took North into custody where he spoke to the garrison commander. The genetic memories of circus showmen showed through in North's assertion that hundreds of Allied troops were on the island and the German officer's situation was untenable. The ploy worked and the German garrison surrendered to North.

It turned out there were fewer Germans on Ventotene and not the four hundred that was reported to Fairbanks by the Italians. Steinbeck states the number at three hundred in a September 11, 1943, letter to Gwyn.[7] This is not the only incongruity that exists within the various accounts of the capture of Ventotene. After North had secured the German surrender, a scout company of the American 509th paratroopers landed on Ventotene to bolster the assault of the Germans' position. In the history listed by the official 509th Infantry Parachute Association, the paratroopers were briefed on the morning of the 9th by Fairbanks and the boys of the 509th were the heroes of the day.[8] The official Navy report filed by Vice-Admiral H.K. Hewitt contradicts this story. Hewitt states that the morning of the 9th, sixty-five reinforcements did arrive and were not needed.[9] Then there is the account in Fairbanks' autobiography, *A Hell of a War*, which mentions nothing of North bluffing the German commander. To make matters worse, the National Archives published an account in *The Secrets War: The Office of Strategic Services in World War II* that claims the OSS was in charge of the mission supported by the BJs, and elements of the 509th and 82nd Airborne Infantry Divisions. This account claims that Ventotene "surrendered to our numerically inferior OSS forces without firing a shot."[10] Finally we have Steinbeck's own dispatches that were written for publication. John had to change a number of facts within the account to get past military censors, so the account in *Once There Was a War* can only be taken as historically accurate in the most general of senses.

The broad strokes are there in all of the accounts, but as with many wartime stories, the fine points are lacking.[11] There are also no real mentions of Steinbeck's individual actions during the nights of September 8th and 9th. We simply know he was there and he was an integral part of the success of the operation. However Steinbeck distinguished himself on Ventotene, it was worthy of a recommendation for a Silver Star by either Fairbanks or Captain Andrews.[12] Fairbanks makes no bones about Steinbeck taking up arms during his time with the BJs saying that John "preferred a Tommy gun to his notebook, and in he went."[13] Although his actions on Ventotene may have warranted the medal for heroism, John would never receive the Silver Star. According to one biographer, Steinbeck was not considered for the award because "he was not a member of the armed services, [so] he was not eligible to receive it."[14] This might have been the reason that was furnished to Steinbeck, or the biographer for that matter, for not receiving the award. The problem with this explanation is that civilians can be awarded the Silver Star. The legislation that created the Silver Star award does not state the award is available only to members of the armed forces.

> The Silver Star may be awarded to *any person* [emphasis added] who, while serving in *any capacity* with the Armed Forces of the United States, is cited for gallantry in action:
>
> 1. Against an enemy of the United States;
>
> 2. While engaged in military operations involving conflict with an opposing foreign force; or
>
> 3. While serving with friendly foreign forces engaged in armed conflict against an opposing armed force in which the United States is not a belligerent party.[15]

Even today, Navy awards manuals address situations in which civilians can receive military decorations.[16] There are also precedents for civilians earning the Silver Star during the Italian Campaign of the Second World War. James Shaw was awarded the Silver Star while working as a field director for the American Red Cross. Shaw had landed with American soldiers near Licata, Sicily, on July 11, 1943. Shaw watched as waves of landing craft hit the shore disembarking additional troops. A flight of enemy bombers (the citation does not mention if the aircraft were German or Italian) began to strafe the defenseless American transports. Shaw waded out into surf pulling survivors back to shore as the bombing runs continued.[17] Another Silver Star recipient in the Sicilian operation was International News Service correspondent Michael Chinigo. A native Italian, Chinigo was one of the few men with that particular unit who spoke Italian and advanced under enemy fire to interrogate Italian prisoners. The plucky reporter also pulled wounded American soldiers under fire to medics during the action.[18]

Given the cases of Chinigo and Shaw, it would seem that Steinbeck was certainly eligible for a Silver Star. The question is why anyone would be told that Steinbeck was not eligible on the grounds he was a civilian? The most plausible explanation is that Steinbeck did not receive the Silver Star because he had crossed the line between reporter and combatant. The War Department specifically forbade war reporters from removing the correspondent's armband and taking up arms during combat.[19] A war correspondent was also "subject to military law from the time at which he commences to accompany troops or personnel who are on active service."[20] Steinbeck could have also faced charges on another infraction of the War Department's regulations for correspondents. In speaking with troops, correspondents "are requested and expected to refrain from conversing with troops at work or on guard, or from discussing subjects or soliciting answers to matters which are clearly secret."[21] Steinbeck was involved in a combat operation with a highly classified Naval commando unit and was privy to their activities and methods. Steinbeck had broken enough of the War Department regulations that the recommendation for a Silver Star could have easily resulted in a highly publicized court martial.

But if Steinbeck was tried for violating War Department regulations, the Navy and the Roosevelt administration would have taken a black eye from the press and the public. One can imagine how a headline of "Steinbeck Faces Court Martial for Fighting Germans" would have played with the American public. The War Department would face a similar dilemma with Ernest Hemingway in August of 1944. Hemingway had taken up with a group of French resistance fighters, known locally as the Maquis, a few weeks before the Allied push to liberate Paris. Hemingway and his guerillas had been conducting small-scale raids and created an intelligence network in the village of Rambouillet. Any information Hemingway gathered was then passed on to Colonel Charles "Buck" Lanham of the OSS. The Colonel was impressed with the quality of Hemingway's intelligence and unofficially supported Hemingway's efforts by making arms and explosives readily available to the irregular troops. Lanham also had another strong connection to the author. Hemingway's son Jack was a member of the OSS and Lanham viewed the elder Hemingway as an extended part of the OSS family.

Hemingway and the Maquis under his command had taken up residence in eight rooms of Rambouillet's only hotel. The same thirty-five-room hotel was besieged by forty other war correspondents hoping to be part of the liberation of Paris. In his usual flamboyant fashion, Hemingway took no steps to hide his command of the guerrilla force. Hemingway's room was full of weapons, maps, and explosives. The room's door was always left open for his fellow reporters to see the hardware. While wandering around Rambouillet, Hemingway would openly carry a rifle or sidearm while wearing his war correspondent credentials and the Maquis commonly would refer to Hemingway as "Colonel."

The situation came to a head as many of the reporters did not have a bed to sleep in and had to sleep on the floor of the hotel's bar. *Chicago Sun Times* editor Bruce Grant squared off with Hemingway demanding some of the rooms be released to the reporters. Hemingway squared his shoulders to Grant and told the Chicago newspaperman that fighting men deserved a bed much more than any of

Ernest Hemingway (left) and OSS Colonel Charles "Buck" Lanham pose for an Army photographer during the 1944 attack on Hürtgenwald, Germany. Photo courtesy of the US Army.

the correspondents. Grant barely had time to mentally process the retort before Hemingway's fist crossed Grant's jaw. The pair continued to brawl until Harry Harris of the Associated Press wriggled in between Hemingway and Grant to break up the fracas. Andy Rooney, later of *60 Minutes* fame, was then a reporter for *Stars and Stripes* and viewed the altercation. Rooney recalled that Hemingway stormed out of the bar only to return a few minutes later yelling at Grant, "Well are you coming out to fight?"[22] Grant didn't take Hemingway's bait and the Maquis kept their rooms.

If the dust-up in Rambouillet didn't put enough unwanted attention on Hemingway's "command," the liberation of Paris did. Stories of Hemingway's exploits filtered throughout the American 3rd Army like a combat fairy tale. The stories included Hemingway and his Maquis breaching the German defenses before Patton or Leclerc's armies reached Paris, and that Hemingway's troops had single-handedly secured the Ritz Hotel. The most colorful tale that emerged from the liberation was that Leclerc was about to take cover in a Paris church. Reaching the church's doorway, the French General was slightly taken aback when he saw a sign that read: "Property of Ernest Hemingway."[23] The veracity of these stories has been discounted by World War II historians, but the tales were repeated frequently among Allied troops. The stories of Hemingway's "conquests" in Paris eventually made their way back to the Inspector General (IG) of Patton's 3rd Army.

The IG held a semi-official inquest into Hemingway's activities in October of 1944. The investigation was more a matter of fulfilling the requirements of Army regulations than an actual attempt to stitch Hemingway up. Predictably, Hemingway denied any wrongdoing in his contact with the Maquis and the IG saw no reason to take the case any further. There is little doubt that not only had Hemingway perjured himself, but his testimony had been coached by Colonel Lanham.[24]

In 1952, Hemingway all but verified his testimony was a sham in a letter to *New York Times* editor C. L. Sulzberger. After making Sulzberger aware of the IG's charges, Hemingway stated in reference to his guerrilla activities:

> . . .I was willing and happy to work for or be of use to anybody who would give me anything to do within my capabilities.[25]

In 1944, no one in the 3rd Army seemed to care if Hemingway had lied or not. A potentially explosive public relations scandal had been averted for the 3rd Army and the capture of Berlin was just beyond the horizon.[26]

The similarities in Hemingway's situation and Steinbeck's are striking. Like Hemingway, Steinbeck had conducted combat operations in a pseudo-official capacity that threatened to become public knowledge. Steinbeck's saving grace was that his infraction of the War Department's regulations was only known about by the small group of commandos in a top-secret unit. If Fairbanks' crew was entrusted with keeping security protocol for their deception operations, keeping the secret of Steinbeck's combat heroics would not have come into question. The incident at Ventotene and the Silver Star were quashed for the very same reasons Hemingway had been given a pass by the 3rd Army.

The timing of events after Ventotene also seems to bear out a Hemingway-like scenario. John's gallantry on Ventotene would not have been written up in dispatches until a few days after the island was secured. We know that the *Knight* transferred German prisoners to the fleet on September 10th[27] and officers of the *Knight* met with Vice-Admiral Hewitt's command staff aboard the USS *Ancon* on September 12th.[28] At either one of these meetings, the action reports, intelligence gathered, and other paperwork related to Ventotene would have been handed over to the appropriate fleet officers. Sometime in the next few days, as the reports were being sorted, the citations from the *Knight* would be reviewed. One can almost hear the conversation between junior and senior staff officers.

"Sir, what do we do about this request for giving Steinbeck a Silver Star?"

"Well, what did he do? He's a journalist."

"I know, but he was with the *Knight* at Ventotene. You gotta read this."

"Sweet, greased up baby Jesus! He can't do that. I don't know what to do, but find out where Steinbeck is. And someone tell Fairbanks to keep his trap shut about this until we sort it out."

While these sentiments were being bandied about by the Navy's staff, John took another opportunity to assist the BJs. On the night of September 10th, John volunteered to accompany Lt. John Kramer on a diversion run through the Gulf of Gaeta. The pair sailed around in the middle of the night shooting signal flares, hoping to attract the attention of the German forces. September 11th was a bit of a rest day for John. As he wrote to his wife Gwyn:

I haven't slept in three days more than an hour at a time and I haven't had my clothes off in four days and I smell terrible.[29]

Steinbeck and the BJs participated in the "liberation" of the Isle of Capri on the evening of September 12th. The term liberation is something of a misnomer given the situation on Capri. When the Italians capitulated on September 8th, Pietro Badoglio officially replaced Mussolini as the Italian head of state. Badoglio ordered that the Italian armed forces would now take up arms against the Germans and be placed under Allied command. The story told on Capri today is that after the surrender, the island's Italian defenders were ordered to relocate to Palermo, Sicily. The garrison commander wished he could have obeyed the order, but there was not enough fuel on the island to transport the 2,500 troops under his command. Having no other option, the commander sent an officer in a motorboat to inform Allied command of their situation.[30] The Salerno invasion started the next day and apparently the word had not gotten out to the fleet of Capri's disposition.

On the afternoon of September 12th, an Italian torpedo boat flying a white flag sailed from the direction of Capri and intercepted the *Knight*. When the vessel got close to the *Knight*, the Italians called over their loudspeakers that they had a message for Fairbanks. The crew of the *Knight* allowed the Italians onboard and Fairbanks met with an Italian officer. The Duke of Acosta, nephew to Italy's deposed king Victor Emanuel III, wished to let the Lieutenant know that if he came to the Isle of Capri quickly, the island would be delivered to the Allies. The Duke also offered Fairbanks the use of a squadron of Italian torpedo boats to assist in the "capture" of Capri. Fairbanks had held covert communications with the Duke and members of the royal family for some time before the Italian armistice. Officially sanctioned by Allied Command, Fairbanks had convinced the royal family to support the use of Italian troops against the Germans after the armistice.[31] The royal family gambled that by throwing their support to the Allied forces, Italy would be handed back to the royal family after the Germans were kicked out of the country.

A view of Mount Soaro on the Isle of Capri, ca. 1900. Photo courtesy of the Library of Congress.

The Duke's offer of letting Fairbanks "capture" Capri was a way of personally thanking Fairbanks for opening lines of communications between them and Allied command. The Italian troops on Capri had technically already surrendered, but couldn't leave the island. Shortly after 6:30 p.m. on the 12th,[32] Fairbanks, Steinbeck, and elements of the BJs set off to "liberate" Capri. When they reached Capri, the residents had lined the beach cheering and waiving colored handkerchiefs at their liberators. The few Germans who were still on the island had been restricted to one side of the island before Fairbanks' force arrived and made no fuss over being captured.[33] In keeping with the theatrics of the liberation, a hastily drawn-up unconditional surrender document was signed by Capri's garrison commander.[34] The credit for the surrender would be chalked up to Fairbanks, and the Duke of Acosta won brownie points with the Allied command. The capture took less than four hours. Fairbanks and his BJs were back aboard the *Knight* by 10:30 p.m. the same evening.[35]

The event appears to have been staged to benefit Fairbanks' reputation with his commanders. Still the liberation of Capri made a grand impression on the island's residents. Steinbeck would return to Capri in January of 1962. The owners of the hotel Steinbeck was staying in rushed out to greet him shouting, "Liberator! Liberator!"[36] To Steinbeck, the capture of Capri would be a stark contrast to what he would experience next during the Salerno invasion. Capri and Ventotene had been captured with relative ease using politics and deception. Salerno would be purchased with every ounce of barbaric fury one human can inflict upon another.

Steinbeck's writings and the action reports of the USS *Knight* do not give a clear indication as to when John arrived on the Italian mainland. From September 13th to 20th, the *Knight* was patrolling the southwest Italian coast. Fairbanks and his BJs had set up bases of operation on the Islands of Capri and Ischia, at that time. From either island, the Italian mainland is less than seven miles and John could have easily been transported there by one of the BJs' attack crafts. For approximately the next week, John toured the Italian mainland in the wake of the Allied landing.

Allied forces had conducted a surprise amphibious landing on the shores of Italy's west coast on September 9th while Steinbeck was on Ventotene. There was no naval or aerial bombardment of the Salerno coast to alert German forces that an invasion was eminent. While this tactic did give the Allied forces an element of surprise, German coastal fortifications and emplacements were intact when the invasion began. For the first four days of the invasion, the Allies had fought just to maintain their beachhead. After the liberation of Capri, Steinbeck would have reached the invasion on September 13th or 14th, the Allies could easily have been pushed back into the sea.[37] The Germans were constantly bombing Allied positions by night and Steinbeck seems to have been caught in one of the raids on the night of September 14th. After jumping out of a landing craft onto the beach, John's foot hit the sand wrong and twisted his ankle. To make matters worse, the Germans began shelling the beach with Flak 88 guns. The weapon had been designed as an anti-aircraft artillery piece, but in the 1940 French invasion, the Germans found it was equally effective against ground targets. A short time after landing, a piece of shrapnel hit a stack of empty fifty-gallon fuel drums in Steinbeck's vicinity. One of the barrels arced through the air, hitting Steinbeck in the back.[38] The concussion from the blast also burst his eardrum and caused the author temporary blackouts and dizziness. The physical wounds of Salerno would plague Steinbeck for a number of years, as would the psychological scars of bearing witness to the human price of warfare.

There is a pain in Steinbeck's dispatches from Salerno that only comes from someone who has witnessed events that had been previously unimaginable. In John's dispatch "October 6, 1943—Mediterranean Theater," John writes of dead children, wounded soldiers, and the constant artillery barrages.[39] John can't bring himself to write this piece in the first person. There was an unconscious defense mechanism by speaking in the third person in this article. Steinbeck even admits that he wasn't sure why he wrote the October 6th piece in this manner:

> In describing a scene I invariably put it in the mouth of someone else. I forget why I did this. Perhaps I felt that it would be more believable if told by someone else.[40]

The Salerno invasion had a lasting impact on John, both physically and emotionally and the scenes at Salerno weighed more heavily on John than he wished to admit. Speaking in the third person was a way to place a barrier between him and the carnage. Upon coming back to the United States

An early assault on the Salerno beachhead by members of the US Army. Photo courtesy of the US Army.

from Europe, John exhibited classic signs of post-traumatic stress disorder.[41] Nervousness, memory loss, depression, disorientation, headaches, and excessive drinking (even for Steinbeck) were the order of the day for a number of months after returning home.[42]

By September 20th, the battle for a beachhead on Salerno had been won and the Allies were looking for opportunities to exploit their advances. Steinbeck had gathered enough material to post dispatches about the invasion and boarded a ship steaming toward an undisclosed rear area that day. John reached an unnamed base of operation (possibly Sicily) on the 22nd of September and took time to write to Gwyn. In this letter, John relays how his mail had finally caught up with him and how tired, dirty, and flea-bitten Salerno had left him. John is also showing the strains of being in a combat zone for extended periods of time by saying:

> . . . I have done the things I had to do. I do not think any inner compulsion will make me do them again.[43]

Steinbeck had tested himself in combat at Ventotene. There was no reason for him to further test himself in that manner. What this letter does not say is that John was leaving the Italian front, yet four days after this letter was written, John was in London. The omission is highly unusual for anyone who is planning to leave a combat zone.

In John's letters to Gwyn in August and September of 1943, he constantly reassures his wife he is well. John went to further lengths to maintain the illusion that nothing ill had happened to him as he wrote Gwyn on September 22nd that he didn't have a "scratch" from his experience in Salerno.[44] John has just written a boldfaced lie to his wife. A husband who colors the truth in order to reassure his wife is not a man who would fail to mention he was leaving the Italian Theater. The only published mention of Steinbeck returning to London was in a letter to Gwyn on August 13, 1943, that he would "probably" be returning to London "in three weeks."[45] John would take the time in London to write up his North African and Mediterranean escapades. The inclusion of his plans also means that John's travel to London was not an issue for censorship and therefore could have been included in the September 22nd letter. Why then would John not tell his wife he was going back to London on the 22nd? Perhaps John did not know he was going back to London at all.

The conventional theory is that John had seen enough of the war and the ordeal of conflict had been too much for him. That coupled with the concussion injury John sustained at Salerno definitely was a major factor in John's exit strategy from the Italian Theater. There is also the very real possibility that the recommendation for the Silver Star was an additional component to John's decision to return to New York. If John's mail had caught up with him by

September 22nd, the Navy certainly could have too. The implications of John taking up arms at Ventotene would have to be addressed by military officials just as Hemingway's activities in France were. Steinbeck had the distinct disadvantage, over Hemingway's situation, of having his combat activities written up in a Silver Star recommendation.

The 22nd or 23rd of September would have been the first time anyone in the Naval hierarchy would have had a chance to discuss Ventotene with Steinbeck. Taking the risk of sending someone to the Salerno front to find Steinbeck, and question him in a combat situation that could very easily have gone south, is unlikely. Any investigation is also likely to have been a more informal affair than that of Hemingway's official questioning. Not only had the legend of Hemingway's "conquests" in Paris been retold by countless GIs, other war correspondents were calling for Hemingway to be held accountable for his actions.[46] Knowledge of Steinbeck's actions on Ventotene was limited to the a handful of BJs, OSS agents, and sailors.

The conversation about Steinbeck taking up arms could have been anything from a slap on the wrist to a full-blown threat. On the minor end of the scale, Steinbeck might have been told that he shouldn't have acted as a combatant and to forget the whole incident. The worse end of the spectrum would have been a directive for Steinbeck to immediately return to London, finish up his work, and head home. In either situation, Steinbeck would have been told that the official story, if it ever came up, was that he was considered for the Silver Star and couldn't receive it because he was a civilian. Steinbeck would have also been forbidden to discuss taking up arms in anything he was to publish about his time with the BJs. The story would not be questioned because civilians receiving military heroism awards are a rare event. Certainly the story of "John Steinbeck and the Silver Star" has held by years of being repeated in various sources and little attention has been paid to its validity. We unfortunately have no records of the Navy discussing John moonlighting as a BJ, but the possibility has to be entertained as a factor in Steinbeck's decisions post-Salerno.

There is another lesson that Steinbeck would have learned contrasting his time in Salerno and with the BJs. Covert actions are equally as important as outright combat. Ventotene had been taken by subterfuge. Capri was "taken" by a political flanking maneuver. The actions he had been party to with the BJs had arguably pulled an entire German division away from the Salerno landing, contributing to the eventual success of the invasion.[47] John had participated in all these operations and seemed to thrive working in the shadows. It was when John was in the daylight things went sideways. The attention John could have received after being recommended for a Silver Star might not have gone well for the author. Being in the middle of a full-scale invasion had only served to break his body and spirit. But perhaps John could still make a contribution to the war effort that was just as important as being on the front lines.

Sixteen days after the capture of Ventotene, Steinbeck was back in London and portions of his communications hint at there being more to his departure from Europe than having his fill of the war. When John reached London on the 24th of September, he cabled the offices of the *New York Herald Tribune*. The telegram informed the editors that he was in London and floated the idea of leaving for America to write up the events of the Italian campaign. The reply to John's message was a "frantic cable"[48] from Steinbeck's boss at the *Herald Tribune*, George Cornish. John's request to leave Europe was news to the staff at the *Herald Tribune*. The newspaper had contracted Steinbeck to cover the war through December and Cornish pled with John to return to the front. To lose a correspondent of Steinbeck's caliber would have been a blow to the *Herald Tribune*'s reporting on the war and Cornish seemed determined to keep John in the field. In a September 25, 1943, letter to his wife Gwyn, John indicates regret about leaving the front lines and his plan while in London:

> I suppose he [Cornish] is right, but in answer to your other question, I SHALL be home by Christmas if I have to crawl home . . . I have a great number of stories to write and besides I have to finish the picture for SOS [Service of Supply] . . . I'm going to take a couple of weeks and just pound them out and try to get well ahead . . . As long as they do not want me to go home now, I will fill out the six months which will bring me home about the first of December.

Later, in the same letter, John speaks about how being in combat had shaken him:

> Well anyway your little friend here has seen enough war. Enough for him anyway . . . And the dark gentleman was very near. I think I wrote you about one particular night [September 14, 1943] when I felt his breath.[49]

There seem to be a number of issues facing John upon his return to London. The pressure of combat and John's obligation to complete the terms of the *Herald Tribune*'s contract are implicitly stated. The letter can also be interpreted that there is an unmentioned force at work on John's decision to leave Europe. "As long as *they* do not want me to go home now" would not seem to be related to the wishes of the *Herald Tribune*. John's frame of reference to the *Herald Tribune* is Cornish in this letter. Had John been speaking of the *Herald Tribune* removing him from Europe, the statement would be about "he" (Cornish) and not "they." The only conceivable circumstance where

Cornish would immediately recall John to the States, unless Cornish were particularly vindictive, would be to limit expenses incurred by Steinbeck while abroad. Had John wanted to stay in London a few more weeks, he certainly could have paid his way. The only other consideration that might have affected John was if the *Herald Tribune* discontinued their sponsorship of John's correspondent status. Had the *Herald Tribune* pulled this maneuver, John could have changed his status to that of a freelance journalist. *Time, Life,* and *Newsweek* commonly used freelance correspondents for content during the war and Steinbeck certainly could have found another media outlet to purchase his work.[50] It would seem that Steinbeck had no real concerns about the *Herald Tribune* influencing the timing of his departure from Europe.

Given the Silver Star situation, the "they" John spoke of in the September 25th letter could have been some other party that held the keys to whether or not he would remain in Europe. Aside from the sponsorship of the *Herald Tribune*, the only entity that could make decisions about John's status as a correspondent was the War Department. Had word of John participating in combat at Ventotene gotten back to Washington, their reaction would be a looming question in Steinbeck's mind. Had the reaction of the War Department been unfavorable, Steinbeck faced being shipped stateside on the next available transport. This was not to be and Steinbeck would remain in London until mid-October writing articles about his experiences on the Italian front. The author would return to New York on October 15th. John violating War Department regulations on correspondents acting as soldiers would have been a faint second-hand memory of Ventotene to anyone who had taken part in the action by then.

Fifty years after the capture of Ventotene, Douglas Fairbanks would give first-hand evidence that Steinbeck's involvement at Ventotene was to be forgotten. In his 1993 biography, *A Hell of a War*, Fairbanks barely mentions Steinbeck was on the island. The comments about John on Ventotene were limited to describing Steinbeck as "gutsy" and how John had volunteered to go ashore before any of the BJs had been assigned to the mission.[51] Six years after the publication of his biography, Fairbanks slightly amended his recollection of the Ventotene operation. In a 1999 interview with *World War II Magazine*, Fairbanks does not mention Steinbeck at all. Fairbanks' recollections of the Second World War are quite clear during the interview. Jon Guttman interviewed Fairbanks for the piece and confirmed that Fairbanks never mentioned Steinbeck on or off the record.[52] During the interview, Fairbanks stated: "[Captain] Andrews then assigned me and three other BJs to lead a landing party into the harbor to make sure it wasn't a trick or a trap."[53] While Fairbanks' statement is not inaccurate, it does shield Steinbeck's participation in the raid. The omission is odd because Fairbanks mentions brushes with George Patton, the Duke of Acosta, and Marshall Tito during the Guttman interview. Fairbanks obviously had no issue with namedropping, so why was Steinbeck not mentioned? Fairbanks could very well have been trying to keep with admonitions to limit discussions of his comrade-in-arms and friend John Steinbeck's actions with the BJs that were given fifty years ago.

The implication of a recommendation for the Silver Star creates a revisionist version of John's final days as a war correspondent. As with many of the topics in this text, the records simply either do not exist or are still classified that could prove this hypothesis to be accurate. If nothing else, John's service with Fairbanks' BJs gives yet another glimpse into the evolution of Steinbeck that culminated in John wishing to become an asset for the CIA. Information and deception are as powerful tools in warfare as are tanks and airplanes. Steinbeck was able to see the applications of the covert side of conflicts firsthand, and moreover excelled in playing his part *sub rosa*. The impression would not only give John a way to later contribute in the Second World War, but would lay the foundation for his eventual work with the CIA.

The step into individual covert work seems to have come after John returned to the United States. John and Gwyn vacationed in Mexico from mid-January to late March 1944. The trip was taken so John could recover from a back injury and burst eardrum sustained during the Salerno invasion. Another anomaly exists in Steinbeck's FBI file that is highly unusual for a fun-in-the-sun Mexico adventure. On March 22, 1944, a memo was sent to J. Edgar Hoover by a Mexican Embassy Civilian Attaché named Birch D. O'Neal with the subject line: "John Steinbeck, Mexico Latin American Matters." The body of the memo reads:

> Dear Sir: There are enclosed for the Bureau's information two copies of a memorandum for the Ambassador dated March 22, 1944 containing information relative to this individual and to Ernest Hemingway, well-known writer.[56]

The other two pages of the memo are redacted per exclusion b1 with the exception of a short sentence relaying Steinbeck is working in Mexico City as a correspondent for the *New York Herald Tribune*. The Bureau file also has a record of Steinbeck's reentry into the United States on March 15, 1944. The oddity is that the travel report is an FBI document, but was declassified by the Army in 1978. There are no other such border-crossing documents held within Steinbeck's FBI file.

Birch D. O'Neal was not only a Foreign Service employee, he was an FBI agent working in the SIS branch. (O'Neal would also be one of the many people in the fringes of Steinbeck's life who would eventually end up in the ranks of the CIA.[57]) The FBI's own *History of the SIS* chronicles that it was a common practice for SIS agents to obtain cover as Embassy employees.[58] In late February of 1944, O'Neal was tasked with keeping an eye on the Russian intelligence agents in Mexico City.[59] The FBI had a pipeline into Soviet communications that would have assisted O'Neal in his task. In 1943, the Army's Signal Intelligence Service had broken the ciphers used by Soviet embassies in North America. Dubbed Project VERONA, the code breakers deciphered over three thousand messages from the Soviets by 1947, and shared their findings with other government agencies including the FBI.[60]

O'Neal had been following the movements of Soviet agents embroiled in a plot to break Leon Trotsky's assassin, Ramón Mercader, out of a Mexican prison. On February 20th, Project VERONA intercepted a cable from the Russian Embassy in Mexico City that set up a meeting between a Spanish Communist politician, Jesus Hernandez Tomas, and KGB heavy hitter Leonid Kvasnikov, ostensibly to discuss Mercader's prison break. The cable also ordered an unidentified Soviet agent, Khoze, to relocate to Cuba.[61] O'Neal was also trailing another prison break conspirator named Jacob Epstein, who had been in the company of unknown Soviet agents on February 21st and 22nd. One of the stops Epstein's colleague made was to the Soviet Embassy in Mexico City, the day before Steinbeck attended a party commemorating the 26th anniversary of the Red Army's formation.[62]

The poor timing of Steinbeck visiting the Soviet Embassy in the middle of a spy hunt would be happenstance if it were not for O'Neal's March memo to J. Edgar Hoover. Because of the heavy redactions (all of the memo's text is blacked out, save the subject line and sender/recipient information), there is no way to ascertain exactly why Steinbeck was in O'Neal's crosshairs. One might think O'Neal was reporting on Steinbeck visiting the Soviet Embassy, but if that was the case, then why would Ernest Hemingway be mentioned in the memo's subject line? Obviously Steinbeck and Hemingway were somehow linked to a specific event or chain of events in Mexico during March of 1944. Other than being celebrity authors and having a mutual friendship with Robert Capa, Steinbeck and Hemingway had little in common. They would not meet until Capa arranged for both men to attend a party in the spring of 1944. The one and only recorded meeting between the two authors was a disaster, as Hemingway deliberately broke a walking stick Steinbeck had given fellow author John O'Hara over Hemingway's own head.[63] (For Hemingway's sake, we can hope the walking stick was not one containing a shotgun, sword, or any other hidden gear John would become fond of after 1947.) The churlish behavior could have come to blows had Steinbeck not removed himself from the situation.

Hemingway also did not have much of a connection to Mexico, other than a few trips to the country. The one place Hemingway was associated with, of interest to the FBI, was Cuba. In the fall of 1942, Hemingway ran a rather unsuccessful intelligence network for the United States Embassy in Havana.[64] During the 1940s, Cuba was something of an Amsterdam floating in the Gulf of Mexico. The Cuban government allowed a myriad of vices to fill tax coffers and took little notice of what nation's currency was collected. The island was a paradise for spies and gangsters who could ply their trade with a friendly bill-filled handshake to the right local official.

The influx of Germans into Cuba was distressing to Hemingway and he offered his unique knowledge of the island's underbelly to the American Embassy. Soon Hemingway was running an intelligence network of at least twenty agents, funded by the Embassy. J. Edgar Hoover was not as hopeful for Hemingway's spy craft and ordered the sixteen FBI agents stationed on the island to keep an eye on the group Hemingway liked to call "The Crook Factory."[65] Hemingway's foray into espionage for the FBI lasted less than a year, as the American Ambassador to Cuba found Hemingway had gathered no useful intelligence.

Being cut loose from the FBI did not totally end Hemingway's spying for the United States government. Two different June 1943 reports in Hemingway's FBI file describe his work with Naval Intelligence.

> It is learned that at the present time, Hemingway is continuing a project [One and a half lines have been redacted under exclusion b1.] involving a check of coastal waters off northern Cuba for possibility of enemy submarine or clandestine radio activity... The naval patrol war of Mr. Hemingway is regarded by him and the Naval Attaché as extremely confidential... [The remainder of paragraph has been redacted under exclusion b1.][66]

Hemingway's work with the Naval Attaché, and ostensibly with the ONI, continued at least until March of 1944. The JFK Library holds a typed letter by Hemingway to a "John" written on March 3, 1944. A staff member at the JFK Library was unable to provide the last name of "John" or any other potential clues as to his identity. This letter has been donated as part of a larger collection and no other information about the letter is in their catalog.[67] The letter asks if "John" has any information on a Spanish passenger liner that has "left its last port of call enroute to Havana" and should dock in Cuba's capital within the next three days, according to a representative of the shipping line. Hemingway is almost giddy about the prospect of what seems like either shadowing this ship on the high seas, or of being a passenger on this ship. He goes on to say that he "doesn't want to miss anything," and that he could be ready to "sail westward" on "a fishing trip" either the night of the 3rd or the next morning. The letter was returned to Hemingway with handwritten notes from the recipient stating that the ship will be in port on the 6th and there was no need to for Hemingway to leave on his "fishing trip" within the day.

The question of a Hemingway/Steinbeck connection could have been tied up neatly if the correspondence was between the two men. However, the March 3rd letter's context and seeming return to Hemingway the same day would preclude a transfer between Steinbeck in Mexico City and Hemingway in Cuba. The most likely recipient of Hemingway's letter was the Cuban Embassy's Naval Attaché, Marine Corps Lieutenant Colonel John N. Hart.[68] If this is the case, Steinbeck and Hemingway could have been working on the same problem from two different angles.

The February 20th VERONA decrypt refers to agent Khoze being moved from Mexico City to Havana. If Steinbeck had supplied information relevant to Khoze from Mexico, Hemingway could have been tasked with shadowing Khoze's ship from Mexico to Havana. The reason for monitoring the ship could have been anything from sniping radio transmissions to ensuring Khoze didn't drop a life raft to be picked up by another vessel in the Gulf of Mexico. A week's timeframe fits for Khoze leaving the country if he needed forged documents, needed to ditch FBI tails, or simply had to wait on a specific ship. The March 22nd report from O'Neil to J. Edgar Hoover would have represented an after-action review of Steinbeck and Hemingway's independent actions related to the same operation. Considering that the majority of the information in the O'Neal document was still classified when Steinbeck's FBI file was released to the public, there has to be more to the memo than routine reporting. Hemingway's FBI file holds nothing, that has been declassified to date, that would corroborate this hypothesis, other than the aforementioned connection with the Navy operations.

Was Steinbeck acting as an operative in Mexico during the 1944 trip? We will never know since the FBI has seen it fit to destroy the very documents that could shed light on the unusual O'Neal memo. Still, the O'Neil memo does seemingly link Hemingway and Steinbeck to a classified FBI operation in March of 1944. This completes a pattern of brushes with either the intelligence community or classified operations during Steinbeck's experiences before and after his war correspondent days in 1943. The conundrum of a man allowed access to the president and head of the OSS, but who cannot obtain entry into the United States Army as a private, is astonishing. While simple explanations of "questionable loyalties" and tacit links to the Communist Party could clarify Steinbeck being barred from a commission in the Army, the same simple account would have also kept Steinbeck from any jobs he performed for the government. Yet the same man whose loyalty and discretion was questioned by Boris Pash, was welcomed with open arms to work for the CIA a few years later.

It is difficult to tell if Steinbeck's World War II experiences were totally happenstance or if after showing his worth to FDR, via the "1940 Nazi propaganda in Mexico letter," there was a concerted effort by the government to channel Steinbeck into roles within the intelligence and propaganda arms of the United States wartime juggernaut. What can be said with a high degree of certainty is that Steinbeck did perform work for and had contacts in the intelligence community during the war years. The most likely scenario is that his work between 1940 to early 1943 left Steinbeck feeling that because he was not in any real danger stateside, his contributions to the war effort were nowhere near equal to those in combat. Steinbeck then makes his application to be a war correspondent to at least get into the thick of things. This idea is sold to those Steinbeck is beholden to in the halls of government with the idea of giving war reporting a slant that had rarely been seen in journalism to date. As the emanate war correspondent Ernie Pyle would later say, "Now that Steinbeck is here the war will finally have a heart."[69]

Even during the months in Europe and Africa in 1943, Steinbeck never fully left government service as evidenced with his work on the SOS film during that time. It is possible that the carrot of a commission in the Army was still being dangled to Steinbeck, given the timing of the Army's pre-commissioning investigations. Steinbeck might have returned from Europe with that commission had it not been for Boris Pash's decision to blackball the author from the Army. As Steinbeck returns home, wounded at Salerno and battered from the post-Ventotene debacle, he returns to what had originally started him down the path of the last three years—Mexico. This time, John takes an active role in gathering information for either Army Intelligence or the FBI during 1944. The operation John is involved in cements him as an operative in the intelligence services and will lead to other chances to serve in that capacity and provide him protection during the post-war Red Scare.

The hearings of the House Committee on Un-American Activities (HUAC) are possibly the best-documented assault on Constitutional freedom since the beginning of the Republic. While HUAC and the Red Scare were defining points of 1950's America, the history of HUAC itself goes back to the First World War. From 1918–19, the Overman Committee was originally set up to investigate pro-German influences in the liquor industry. The Russian Revolution in 1917 sparked America's first Red Scare and increasing fears of a Socialist uprising in the United States diverted the Overman Committee's focus to Bolshevik propaganda. The Fish Committee (1930) and the McCormack-Dickstein Committee (1934–1937) held hearings on groups with Communist and pro-Nazi (respectively) sympathies.

The immediate progenitor of the 1950's Red Scare HUAC was the Dies Commission (1938–1944). This incarnation of lawmakers exploring subversive Americans was named for its chairman, Texas Representative Martin Dies. Following themes of the previous committees, the Dies Commission's goal was "to investigate alleged disloyalty and subversive activities on the part of private citizens, public employees, and those organizations suspected of having communist or fascist ties."[1] The Dies Commission had planned a run at the Ku Klux Klan and German-Americans with Nazi sympathies. These groups were largely dropped from the Commission's agenda in favor of examining Communist Party infiltrations into FDR's New Deal programs. The move was likely politically motivated to discredit the policies of FDR by members of both Democratic and Republican Parties. Rumors of FDR running for a third term in 1940 rankled those with higher aspirations than their present political standing.

The paranoia the American people held that outside influences were undermining the foundations of the Republic was growing in direct proportion to the country's involvement with world affairs. The formula reached critical mass at the end of the Second World War. America was directly involved with the internal affairs of more nations than any time in the country's history. The Russians were the only stumbling block to what most Americans believed would be a difficult, but peaceful, rebuilding of Europe. General George S. Patton was one who believed otherwise. In 1945, Patton wrote in his diary:

> Russia knows what it wants. World domination. And she is laying her plans accordingly. We, on the other hand, and England, and France to a lesser extent, don't know what we want and get less than nothing as the result.[2]

Patton's diary was not published until 1974, but had this statement been known earlier in the Cold War, most Americans would have thought it was a divine prophesy. Every step the Russians took from 1945 to 1947 to consolidate their powerbase resulted in a response from the Americans. The reaction to Soviet policies often resulted in increased American contributions abroad. Keeping with the mathematics of paranoia, with each boost in foreign affairs, the paranoia of the Reds destroying us from within increased as well. Something had to be done.

The call to arms came in the form of the 1946 incarnation of HUAC. Before 1946, the previously mentioned committees had somewhat defined scopes that would limit the duration of that committee's hearings. HUAC version 1946 was a permanent fixture pursuant to Public Law 601. The law enabled a nine-person committee to investigate suspected threats of subversion or propaganda that attacked the form of government guaranteed by our Constitution.[3] The great irony is that HUAC represented a greater attack on the Constitution than internal Communist sympathies ever could. HUAC found its first crusade in the spring of 1947 as Steinbeck was planning his second trip to the Soviet Union. According to the official 1947 HUAC records:

> Responding to the demand of the people, the present Committee on Un-American Activities made a preliminary investigation which produced ample evidence that a full-scale investigation was in order of the extent of Communist infiltration in Hollywood.[4]

HUAC was operating under the theory that if Communists had infiltrated the motion picture industry, the Reds were surreptitiously planting propaganda in the content of films. The fear of covert propaganda would have been a natural assumption to the members of HUAC. The United States government nudged Hollywood into producing anti-Axis propaganda just a few years earlier. The very same persons who worked on films used to inspire a victory against the Axis in World War II could be sleeping Communist agents waiting to spring on a complacent American populace.

Congressional subpoenas had gone out to a number of people employed by the film industry literally as John would have been unpacking from the Soviet trip. HUAC did what Congress does best. The august body held hearings, investigated, and summarily cast aspersions on Hollywood's elite in late October of 1947. Walt Disney, Gary Cooper, Jack Warner, Louis B. Mayer, Ronald Reagan, and dozens of others were questioned:

> Have you ever observed any efforts on behalf of the Communist Party to suppress a picture?
>
> Have you ever noticed any effort on the part of Communist individuals to gain influence in the Screen Actors Guild?

Have you ever participated in any picture as an actor which you considered contained Communist propaganda?[5]

While these are just sampling of questions asked to a number of those testifying, it exemplifies the timbre of the proceedings.

Author Ayn Rand was called before the committee on the first day of hearings seemingly as an expert on the Soviet Union. Rand had emigrated from the Soviet Union to the United States in 1928 and proceeded to make a writing career based on anti-Communist themes. By comparison, Rand's stance on Communism made Joe McCarthy look like a liberal. The early questions posed to Rand were to compare her experiences in Russia with the 1944 film *Song of Russia*. The film was a maudlin love story set in the Soviet Union shortly before the German invasion. The film starred Robert Taylor and Susan Peters in the lead roles. Also featured in the film was Robert Benchley, the father of Steinbeck's close friend Nathan Benchley. *Song of Russia* was tagged as being pro-Communist for its portrayal of life under Soviet rule.

Rand testified, in a near scene-by-scene dissection of the film, that the inaccuracies portrayed in *Song of Russia* were obviously a work of Communist propaganda. Rand stated:

> Now, I use the term to mean that Communist propaganda is anything which gives a good impression of communism as a way of life. Anything that sells people the idea that life in Russia is good and that people are free and happy would be Communist propaganda.[6]

Rand had given HUAC a definition of Communist propaganda that would stand until the committee's dissolution in 1961. It did not seem to matter to the members of HUAC that Rand had not seen conditions within the Soviet Union in nearly twenty years. Her testimony verified the committee's theory that Communist propaganda was alive and well in Hollywood.

In a rather bizarre twist during Rand's testimony, Georgia Congressman John S. Wood began to treat Rand as a hostile witness. Wood began a hypothetical line of questions to Rand based on if she thought Allied countries during the First and Second World Wars would have been better off without the assistance of the Soviet Union. Wood was of the opinion that financial aid and the Second World War lend-lease program strengthened the Soviet Union to the point of challenging the United States after the Axis powers were defeated. Rand's answers were fairly neutral during Wood's questions, but she was obviously taken aback by the theoretical rhetoric. Wood's questions appear to have been designed to make Rand "slip up" by taking a sympathetic bearing toward the Soviets. While the thought is preposterous to anyone who has read Rand's works, Wood's interrogation of Rand sent a message. Even one of the country's most ardent anti-Communists was not above being tested by the mighty HUAC.

The crowning achievement of the October 1947 HUAC hearings was bringing to light the "Communist machinations" of ten writers and a director who were called as witnesses. The other witnesses called before the 1947 HUAC hearings were considered "friendly witnesses" whose loyalties were not in any serious question. As with the case of Ayn Rand, HUAC was prepared to explore any unknown factors that came out during testimony. The eleven other witnesses to appear before the committee were considered as the tribunal's hostile witnesses who had been suspected of Communist ties before the hearings began. German-born screenwriter Bertolt Brecht was the only one of the eleven to cooperate and answer HUAC's questions. Shortly after his appearance before the committee, Brecht fled back to East Germany. The other nine writers—Herbert Biberman, Lester Cole, Albert Maltz, Adrian Scott, Samuel Ornitz, Dalton Trumbo, Ring Lardner Jr., John Howard Lawson, and Alvah Bessie along with director Edward Dmytryk—refused to answer any questions related to their political affiliations based on the Fifth Amendment's right to not self-incriminate. Little did this group, who would popularly become known as the Hollywood Ten, know that the Fifth Amendment was not a shield in the court of HUAC.

The greatest irony of the HUAC hearings was that legally there was very little the members could do to someone proudly brandishing a Communist Party membership card. The Department of Justice (DOJ) could and did prosecute members of the Communist Party who were conspiring to forcibly overthrow the United States government under the Smith Act. If there was no evidence of this type of conspiracy, there were no laws that stated someone could not be a member of the Communist, Socialist, or American Vegetarian Party.[7] There was one side-step around the spirit of the Fifth Amendment that HUAC used to ensnare witnesses. HUAC did not actually have to do anything more than pose questions in which the answers could not result in prosecution. Are you now or have you ever been a member of the Communist party? Do you know any Communists? If a HUAC witness did not answer or refused to answer questions under the provisions of the Fifth Amendment, HUAC would charge the witness with contempt of Congress. Those being convicted of this offense faced a penalty of not less than one month or more than twelve months in jail and a fine of not less than $100 or more than $1,000.[8] The members of the Hollywood Ten would be charged on such a legal technicality.

Aside from the contempt of Congress charge, privately owned businesses were the real sword of HUAC. Not wishing to raise the ire of customers or the government, companies would not employ known or suspected Communists. In response to the Hollywood Ten's refusal to testify, the Motion Picture Association of America (MPAA) met in a closed-door session at New York's Waldorf-Astoria

Hotel. Their stance on the Hollywood Ten was issued in a December 3, 1948, press release that would become known as the Waldorf Statement.

> Members of the Association of Motion Picture Producers deplore the action of the 10 Hollywood men who have been cited for contempt by the House of Representatives. We do not desire to prejudge their legal rights, but their actions have been a disservice to their employers and have impaired their usefulness to the industry.

And later in the press release:

> We will forthwith discharge or suspend without compensation those in our employ, and we will not re-employ any of the 10 until such time as he is acquitted or has purged himself of contempt and declares under oath that he is not a Communist.[9]

The Waldorf Statement was the beginning of the infamous blacklist. Being on an officially unofficial list of those deemed by the powers that be that one was a Communist meant no one in Hollywood would hire you. Each of the Hollywood Ten was eventually convicted of contempt of Congress and not only endured jail time, but faced an unemployable future.

Today being terminated for one's political beliefs would be followed by a multi-million dollar discrimination lawsuit against the company. In the 1950s, the laws were not sufficient to dissuade companies from discrimination based on political affiliation.[10] The few lawsuits that were filed in relation to HUAC proceedings were generally for libel against informants. Two lawsuits were filed against a publication that started the practice of "greylisting." Actor Joe Julian filed a lawsuit against *Counterattack Magazine* on the basis of libel. The lawsuit was decided in favor of the publication based on a disclaimer buried within the text. CBS radio personality John Henry Faulk would successfully sue one of the authors of a *Counterattack* publication in 1962, long after the Red Scare was over.

Counterattack Magazine was one of the first private anti-Communist publications to appear during the period. The magazine was founded by three ex-FBI agents and a former ONI officer who operated under the parent company of ABC Business Consulting. In later June of 1950, *Counterattack* published *Red Channels: The Report of Communist Influence in Radio and Television*. The pamphlet reported on 151 persons within the entertainment community who had questionable political beliefs. In order to avoid being outright libelous, *Red Channels* placed listings of persons along with documented sources of political groups that person belonged to. The reader was to make an informed decision about each of the persons profiled with this quote from FBI Director J. Edgar Hoover:

The [Communist] Party has departed from depending on the written word as its medium of propaganda and has taken to the air. Its members and sympathizers have not only infiltrated the airways but they are now persistently seeking radio channels.[11]

Steinbeck's close friend, actor Burgess Meredith, was one of the individuals under fire by *Red Channels*. As proof of Meredith's Communist leanings, their listing on the actor was the following:

American Committee for Yugoslav Relief. Reported as: Signer of letter. Letter, 10/23/45. Chairman, Winter Clothing Campaign. Letterhead. 10/23/45.

Committee for First Amendment. Signer. Advertisement in protest of Washington hearings. *Hollywood Reporter,* 10/24/47, p. 5. *Un-Am. Act. in California, 1948*, p. 210.

Coordinating Committee to Lift the Embargo Against Spanish Loyalist Government. Representative individual: *House Un-Am. Act. Com., Appendix 9*, p. 670.[12]

As far as *Red Channels* was concerned, being involved with a humanitarian effort to provide clothing to the people of Yugoslavia was tantamount to being in contact with the Kremlin on a daily basis. Meredith had been in twenty-one films before the publication of *Red Channels*, including acting in the film adaptation of Steinbeck's *Of Mice and Men* and narrating *The Forgotten Village*.[13] After the listing in *Red Channels*, Meredith was reduced to minor TV roles during the majority of the 1950s. He would return to the silver screen taking a bit part in the Audie Murphy picture *Joe Butterfly* (1957), but the damage to Meredith's role as a leading man was nearly irredeemable. Ironically, Meredith would not achieve critical success until a 1977 Emmy for his role in the TV bio-pic of Joseph McCarthy, *Tail Gunner Joe*. The other 150 listed within *Red Channel's* pages would suffer similar fates as Meredith.

The front cover of *Red Channels* featured a bright red hand prepared to clutch a microphone.

In another slight irony of the anti-Communism fervor of the time, the man who has become synonymous with the Red Scare had nothing to do with the October 1947 HUAC hearings. The crusade of cleansing the airwaves of Communists was taken up by Senator Joe McCarthy in February of 1950. In a speech on Lincoln's Day, McCarthy claimed to hold a list of 205 members of the United States State Department who were in league with the Reds. This propelled McCarthy and his chief prosecutor Roy Cohn into the driver's seat of the anti-Communist hearings. The pair would continue on with the HUAC hearings until public support and legal challenges effectively ended the hunt for Communist Party sympathizers and members during the years 1957–58.

The effects of the McCarthy hearings, based on the 1947 HUAC template, are difficult to judge on an overall scale. There were hundreds of names on the black and grey lists drawn up at the time. Informants, FBI files, political associations, personal links, and outright gossip were the fuel in which HUAC ground up the lives of entertainers. It is curious that in slightly over ten years of HUAC hearings, John Steinbeck's loyalties were never investigated by either the official or unofficial Communist hunters. At the very least, Steinbeck should have been on the HUAC's radar. By the time of the October 1947 HUAC hearings, there was ample evidence, by HUAC standards, that John either was a Communist or he knew names of Communist party members. But John was never called to testify. Consider the following evidence that was at HUAC's disposal:

1. John had traveled to the Soviet Union in 1937 and had just returned from the Soviet Union in October of 1947.
2. John's first wife Carol registered with the Communist Party in 1938.[14]
3. John attended the Western Writer's Conference in November of 1938 with known Communists.[15]
4. Steinbeck's article, "The Blood Is Strong," was published by the Simon L. Lubin Society in April of 1938. The Lubin Society was acknowledged as being a Communist front organization during Congressional hearings in 1938.[16]
5. Harper Knowles, an investigator of radicals and subversives for the American Legion, testified to the Dies Commission in 1938 that John had Communist ties and sympathies.[17]
6. John was not recommended for a commission in the United States Army in July of 1943 due to "substantial doubt as to the Subject's [Steinbeck] loyalty and discretion" by Army Counterintelligence Lieutenant Colonel Boris Pash.[18]
7. Steinbeck attended a function at the Soviet embassy in Mexico City in February 1944.[19]
8. Steinbeck is listed in the articles of incorporation for Associated Magazine

Contributors INC in February 1946. The California version of HUAC would list Associated Magazine Contributors as a "completely Communist controlled and dominated publication."[20]

The listing is by no means exhaustive. Steinbeck's FBI file contains examples of what the FBI sources believed to be Communist-leaning organizations that recommended Steinbeck's work. If one adds in the furor over *The Grapes of Wrath*, his personal associations, and work supporting "Communist infiltrated" WPA programs, there was more than enough cause to target Steinbeck for the 1947 hearings.

While John was never called during the 1947 session of HUAC, he was not left unscathed by the session either. John is mentioned by name in two separate instances during this HUAC investigation. First, John is brought to HUAC's attention in a 1946 article entitled "What Shall We Ask of Writers?" by Albert Maltz. This article was read into the official Congressional record as evidence that Maltz was a Communist.

> For instance, in sections of *Grapes of Wrath* John Steinbeck writes a veritable poem to revolution. Yet we would be making an error to draw conclusions from this about Steinbeck's personal philosophy or to be surprised when he writes *Cannery Row* with its mystic paean to Bohemianism . . . the critics on the left will not be able to deal with the literary work of their time. Writers must be judged by their work and not by the committees they join. [And keeping in the same vein later in the article, Maltz continues]But they don't always have to do with it (Marquand—Steinbeck), and any assumption that as a writer's polities do, so inevitably does his art go—forward or backward—is the assumption of naiveté.[21]

In Steinbeck's case, Maltz's statements were accurate in that an author's works are not always indicative of their politics. However, Maltz's views on the nature of writers would not have held sway with the members of HUAC. As part of the Hollywood Ten, Maltz even writing about Steinbeck could have been viewed as one Commie covering for another. The next reference to Steinbeck during the proceedings did link Steinbeck to authors whose loyalties to the United States would come into question in the next few years.

HUAC's head of research, Benjamin Mandel, gave testimony on the investigative team's findings on Alvah Bessie. In this section, Mandel reviews Bessie's teaching a class at the Communist Party USA's training facility, the New York Workers School, in 1942. The school opened in 1923 with the objective of presenting classes to educate new party members on Marxist doctrines. Each term the Communist Party USA's publication *The Daily Worker* presented a class schedule and an overview of the Workers School goals. In announcing the Workers School's second term in 1924, *The Daily Worker* said this about the role of education in the Communist Party:

> Education has so far been monopolized by the master class to maintain the working class in subjection. It is the duty of the Working Class to break the wall of darkness with which the capitalist class has surrounded them. WE MUST USE THE WEAPON OF EDUCATION TO HELP US ACHIEVE THE LIBERATION OF THE WORKING CLASS.[22] [Emphasis in original copy]

With such a mission statement, it's easy to understand why Mandel would use Bessie teaching a class at the Workers School as evidence of Communist affiliation. Mandel states that the September 27, 1942, edition of *The Daily Worker* listed the annual Workers School class schedule, which included this description of Bessie's class "Literature and the World We Live In":

> The announcement states that leading dramatic writers (Steinbeck, Smolokov (sic), Richard Wright, Lillian Hellman, Clifford Odets, and others) will be used as a point of departure for discussions of the history of social institutions as they have been reflected by the writers of all times.[23]

Bessie's curriculum proved to be detrimental to Wright, Hellman, and Odets. Wright and Hellman were eventually blacklisted. Wright's blacklisting was largely symbolic as the American-born author had become a French citizen in 1947. Smolokov is a poor transcription of the Russian author of *And Quiet Flows the Don*, Mikhail Sholokhov. Being a citizen of the Soviet Union and Party member, Sholokov's writings had no need to be vetted by HUAC.

Of those discussed in Bessie's course, only Steinbeck and Odets were not blacklisted. Odets barely escaped being blacklisted in May of 1952 by giving HUAC names of others who he knew to belong to the Communist Party. (Odets' testimony will be discussed later in this chapter.) As with Maltz's mention of Steinbeck, Odets didn't do John any favors by bringing his name to the attention of HUAC. All of these references simply put Steinbeck's works in a tacit association with advancing the goals of Communism within earshot of HUAC members. Had these mentions of Steinbeck been the only outstanding "evidence" HUAC might have been privy to about the author, one might understand why he was never called to testify before any of the committee meetings in 1947. There was more than enough evidence to question Steinbeck's political leanings.

Is it feasible that since the focus of the 1947 HUAC hearings was specifically based on Communist influences in Hollywood, Steinbeck simply escaped the noose? That could be a possibility, but by 1947, John had been a writer or held adaptation credits in eight films that were released to the general public. This count does not include the films John worked on for the government during the Second World War. When comparing Steinbeck's movie writing and adaptation to those of the Hollywood Ten, we see that Steinbeck was involved with more movie projects than six of the Hollywood Ten. The following are the credited writing and adaptation credits of these six Hollywood Ten members before the 1947 HUAC hearings:

Alvah Bessie: 4	Albert Maltz: 7
Herbert Biberman: 5	Adrian Scott: 5
Bertolt Brecht: 8	(with 6 production credits)[24]
Ring Lardner Jr.: 9	

The other members of the Hollywood Ten were more prolific in their writing credits. Since Edward Dmytryk was a director, his credits cannot be compared accurately in this light. The point being that Steinbeck had an equal or greater amount of influence and/or exposure to Hollywood than over half of HUAC's original eleven hostile witnesses. Still Steinbeck was not called before HUAC.

Steinbeck would also metaphorically poke the bear in 1948 by being the first known person to offer a job to a member of the Hollywood Ten. *The Los Angeles Examiner* reported on June 11, 1948, that Ring Lardner Jr. had signed a contract with Steinbeck. Lardner was to write a screenplay for an adaptation of John's collection of short stories *Pastures of Heaven*. At the time of the press release, Lardner and the other members of the Hollywood Ten were on bail and were vigorously appealing their contempt of Congress convictions. The MPAA fired back at Steinbeck's offer based on the 1947 Waldorf Statement reaffirming that unless the convictions against the Hollywood Ten were reversed on appeal, MPAA members would be barred from working on any film written by any of the Hollywood Ten.[25] The event has been largely overlooked by Steinbeck biographers, but was a more powerful statement about Steinbeck's feelings toward the HUAC hearings than his 1957 defense of Arthur Miller.

Miller's case represents a full-out government assault on an individual's First Amendment rights. HUAC's gaze turned to Miller with the 1953 opening of his most remembered play, *The Crucible*. While the play was considered a moderate commercial success, the play used a thinly veiled 1692 Salem witch trial setting to question the validity of HUAC's tactics. HUAC was understandably not pleased with Miller's open defiance and he was denied a passport in 1954 to travel to the London opening of *The Crucible*. Miller again applied for a passport in 1956 and HUAC used this as an excuse to call him before the committee for questioning. Miller appeared as subpoenaed and supposedly made a side deal with the hearing's chairman Francis Walter. The playwright would openly discuss his political history if the committee did not ask him to name others he believed to be Communists. Walter agreed and promptly the pact slipped his mind as Miller was questioned. Miller refused to answer the questions on the basis that the First Amendment implies that silence is a form of free speech.[26] The tactic failed and Miller was cited for contempt of Congress. He would later be convicted of that charge and in 1958, the conviction was overturned on appeal. Steinbeck wrote an impassioned article in defense of his friend, "The Trial of Arthur Miller," for the July 1957 edition of *Esquire Magazine*. The piece unabashedly takes HUAC to task by asking if Congress had the right take advantage of their position to ask questions of one's political beliefs.[27] "The Trial of Arthur Miller" has been used as a high-water mark for Steinbeck's activism and the growing public opposition to the HUAC proceedings, but surely the action of signing a member of the Hollywood Ten sent a much stronger and earlier message about Steinbeck's feelings toward the committee.

Even before the defense of Miller, John's friendship and work relationship with Elia Kazan would inadvertently swing the crosshairs of HUAC dangerously close to Steinbeck. Kazan had collaborated with Steinbeck on a bio-film with an anti-Communist tinge, *Viva Zapata!* Kazan had worked sporadically with Steinbeck on the script since 1949 and would direct the film. Steinbeck had been ardent in presenting a script that depicted a historically accurate story of Mexican revolutionary Emiliano Zapata. That turned into a problem for the film's studio, 20th Century Fox. Studio executive Darryl Zanuck was concerned that a film about a popular uprising in Mexico would come across with Communist undertones and constantly tinkered with the film's script and direction. Any thought of presenting an objective view of Zapata was quickly quashed and Steinbeck abandoned his historical idealism in favor of presenting a more democratic revolutionary. The film turned out to be problematic enough on an ideological level coupled with issues with filming in Mexico that Zanuck considered scrapping the project entirely.[28]

With all the background drama surrounding *Viva Zapata!*, the film was completed a few months before Kazan was called before HUAC on January 14, 1952. Even with Kazan's complicity in altering the presentation of Zapata's story, Kazan was in trouble before the proceedings began. The man who would go on to direct *On the Waterfront*, had been a member of the Communist Party from 1934–36. Kazan's membership in the Communist Party was no secret and there was little reason to hide the fact to the committee. The question of Kazan's recollections of other Party members met with resistance from the film director. At the time, Kazan was one of Hollywood's most respected directors and his refusal to name names could very well have been the resistance Hollywood needed to break the spell of HUAC's blacklists.[29]

HUAC recognized the sway Kazan had in Hollywood circles and offered him a chance to appear before the committee a second time to reconsider his position. HUAC members feared that if Kazan defied HUAC again, the film director's example would give other actors and filmmakers the strength to do the same. Kazan appeared before the committee for a second time in April of 1952. This go around, Kazan feared he would be imprisoned for contempt of Congress and read a prepared statement in which he recanted his previous silence and gave the names of eight persons who were in the Communist Party. The move to save his own neck at the demise of others prompted a wave of outrage through the Hollywood community. The stigma still hung over Kazan when winning a 1999 Lifetime Achievement Oscar. During the award presentation, actors Nick Nolte, Ed Harris, and Amy Madigan stayed in their seats and did not applaud for Kazan.[30]

Steinbeck was somewhat more kind to his friend. John received word of Kazan's April 1952 testimony to HUAC while in Madrid and wrote to Pat Covici on April 18th. In Steinbeck's mind, Kazan's decision to testify must have been a difficult one to make and Steinbeck stood behind Kazan for foul or fair.[31] John had not heard from Kazan by mid-May and wrote back to Covici, speaking of Kazan's statement to HUAC:

> One can never know what one could do until it happens. I wonder what I would do. *I'll never know.* Isn't that strange?[32] [Emphasis added]

Given what we know of John's involvement with the CIA, Steinbeck's statement has just betrayed the secret that had kept him out of a HUAC witness stand. Unless John was psychic, there is no conceivable way he would know in 1952 that he would never appear before HUAC. "I'll never know." The missive would mean very little to Covici, but the slip of the pen indicates that John felt certain he would never be called before HUAC.

The subject of HUAC also touched a nerve with Steinbeck's third wife, Elaine. While gathering information for his biography on Steinbeck, Jackson Benson asked Elaine about John's opposition to HUAC and Kazan's testimony. Elaine was happy to discuss John's opposition, but on Kazan, she simply told Benson that she preferred not to discuss the subject.[33] Was it Elaine's preference not to further discuss HUAC or was there a reason she could not further discuss HUAC with Benson? The Kazan issue did come up while John was gathering information for the CIA. Why would he believe that he was safe from HUAC's scrutiny? Any questions posed to John during a HUAC hearing would have been uncomfortable for John at best. At worst, a stray question to Steinbeck could have compromised his position as an asset.

The relationship between the CIA and HUAC was complicated before the summer of 1952 and swiftly went downhill from there. The CIA had always taken a dim view of what HUAC was trying to accomplish. There was a real Communist threat to combat in Europe and Asia, and hunting down actors and screenwriters was not high on the CIA's priority list. The feeling among those in CIA operations was that HUAC's methods were heavy-handed and did nothing to produce any intelligence of value. Intelligence officers tried to stay far away from HUAC. Most Agency people thought HUAC was obsessed to the point of unreality and tried not to get involved with that particular mess.[34]

Another reason the CIA would have distanced their agents and assets from HUAC was that the provision of the 1947 National Security Act specifically forbids the Agency to conduct covert or intelligence gathering operations within the borders of the United States. The function of the CIA was to gather information on foreign powers and the Agency was never intended to use its resources to investigate and perform surveillance on American citizens within the country's borders. Legally any criminal investigation into United States citizens within the borders is the purview of local/state law enforcement and the FBI. The delineation of the CIA's "foreign operations only" mandate has been blurred since the passing of the Patriot Act in 2001, but in the 1950s, there was no real legal reason for the CIA to operate at home. If a link between the fledgling CIA and HUAC became public, there would be consequences in both the political and public arenas. The trouble that supporting HUAC would have caused the CIA was simply not worth the Agency's resources. The entire Agency did have a real Communist threat to contain in Europe and chasing the likes of Elia Kazan was not high on their list of priorities.

None of this meant very much to Senator McCarthy who set his sights on Communists within the CIA. The play by McCarthy had a dual purpose. First, there was a concern that those with Communist sympathies were brought into the Agency on the merits of their service with the OSS. William Donovan was not as concerned with the political ideology of the members of the OSS as he was with their performance in their job roles.[35] Second, McCarthy and J. Edgar Hoover wanted information held within CIA files to expand HUAC's net. Actual records of CIA and HUAC interaction are in short supply either through classification or non-existence.[36] We do know that Smith testified in open and closed hearings of HUAC in October of 1952.[37] Smith did admit the CIA had a few alleged Communists in its ranks; he said none were Americans "within the scope or interest of this committee."[38] It can never be said that those at HUAC's helm always made the best decisions about who was called to testify. Testing the loyalty of a man like Walter Bedell Smith would seem to be a monumental waste of time. A man who served as Dwight Eisenhower's right-hand man during the Second World War had to be above reproach. Considering Eisenhower was predicted to win the 1952 presidential election by a landslide, Smith might not have been the most politically expedient person to have investigated.

HUAC left the Agency alone until Allen Dulles replaced Smith as DCI in 1953. This time HUAC subpoenaed William Bundy, an assistant to the DDI. Bundy had terse connections to suspected Soviet agent Alger Hiss. At one time, Bundy had been a law partner with Hiss's brother and this was the extent of HUAC's evidence against Bundy. Dulles felt the implications absurd and stalled the proceedings by sending Bundy on mandatory annual leave. In the interim, Dulles made a polite phone call to Vice-President Richard Nixon for assistance. After face-saving posturing from McCarthy, the need for Bundy to testify evaporated.[39] The Bundy incident simply goes to show that the CIA did have the clout to quash HUAC subpoenas when necessary.

There was one possible unsanctioned link between HUAC and the CIA. If there was any support for HUAC's cause within the CIA, it would have come from the Director of Counterintelligence, James Jesus Angleton. The ultra-paranoid Angleton was also a far right anti-Communist. He also played in a running Tuesday night poker game with fellow fanatical anti-Communist, FBI Director J. Edgar Hoover.[40] The FBI, under Hoover's direction, provided a majority of the information used in HUAC investigations.[41] It is difficult to believe that Angleton and Hoover did not pass along some shop talk during their poker games. The professional courtesy of Angleton giving Hoover leads could also have been reciprocated. A word from Hoover would have also diverted HUAC's eyes away from any CIA asset the committee was getting too close to.

Moving past the spring of 1952 for Steinbeck, there were a number of close calls in the HUAC universe that, once again, did not lead to John being subpoenaed by HUAC. John often associated with the blacklisted. Margo Albert, Leonard Bernstein, Charlie Chaplin, Howard Fast, José Ferrer, and Burl Ives were just a handful of blacklisters, besides the previously mentioned Meredith and Miller, who were known to have been linked with John. Any one of these person's name in union with Steinbeck could have triggered a HUAC investigation. The domino effect of associations can be seen in Kazan's own testimony about playwright Clifford Odets belonging to the Communist Party. Odets and Kazan had worked out a scheme in which they would name each other as members of the Communist Party if they were ever called before HUAC.[42] During his testimony, Odets had only named members of the Party who had previously been named. Odets felt that by not giving HUAC any new information, he would be safe from the stigma of being a complicit witness. The plan backfired in the court of public opinion and Odets was publicly shunned as a fink. In addition to his failed plan, Odets made mention of Steinbeck during his May 1952 testimony:

I remember telling you that when my plays came out one after another, they received fantastically bad notices, although a play like *Waiting for Lefty* was widely used not only by the Communists but by all liberal organizations and trade-union movements. I not only disagreed with their critical statements of my work, but I disagreed with their critical estimates of anybody's work, writers that I didn't know, as I mentioned, like Steinbeck and Hemingway. I had a great number of fights about that.[43]

Odets statement is nowhere damning to Steinbeck, but it does once again remind HUAC that Steinbeck's work is being bandied about by members of the Communist Party.

HUAC did take notice of the way Steinbeck's work seemed important to the Communists. In the spring of 1953, Roy Cohn and G. David Schine, chief aides to Senator Joseph McCarthy, conducted an investigation of USIS and State Department posts in Europe for evidence of Communist influences. The pair removed an estimated 30,000 books from USIS libraries that they felt had pro-Communist influences. These works included books written by Steinbeck, Melville, Thoreau, and the blacklisted Dashiell Hammett.[44] The father of hard-boiled detective fiction, Hammett had been called before HUAC in late March of 1953 and was blacklisted for not cooperating. Cohn and Schine returned from their tour in Europe in late April of 1953. While Hammett was fresh on their minds, it must have slipped Cohn and Schine's minds to have Steinbeck appear before HUAC when they returned home.

The move to remove Steinbeck's books from European government facilities was actually a positive event for Steinbeck as a CIA asset. Wittingly or unwittingly, Cohn and Schine had reinforced the thought that Steinbeck's writings were detrimental to government employees abroad. After the publication of anti-Communist propaganda pieces for *Harper's Magazine* in 1952, Cohn and Schine's cleansing the temples of government would

Joseph McCarthy (left) and Roy Cohn confer during a March 12, 1954, hearing in Washington. Photo courtesy of the Library of Congress.

have made it seem there was tension between Steinbeck and the United States government. Steinbeck's cover as a shunned left-leaning writer was somewhat strengthened, making him more approachable to those with similar sympathies.

Oddly enough, a month after Cohn and Schine had removed Steinbeck's Red influences in European government offices, there was a positive testimony given to HUAC on Steinbeck's behalf. Roland William Kibbee, a Hollywood scriptwriter, went before HUAC on June 2, 1953, of his own free will. Kibbee's claim to fame to date was writing the screenplay for the Marx Brothers' 1946, movie, *A Night in Casablanca*. He was also a member of the Communist Party from 1937–39. Evidently Kibbee felt that it was his civic duty to testify before HUAC. It's possible that Kibbee was trying to get ahead of the HUAC eight ball and volunteered his insights into 1930's Communism in Hollywood.

After naming a number of those who were in the Party with Kibbee, HUAC investigator William Wheeler asked, "What caused your disillusionment with the Communist Party?" As part of his answer, Kibbee contributed:

> I remember John Steinbeck who wrote, I thought, a most effective novel about the agricultural workers in the San Joaquin Valley, or, take it a step further, that the man did more for them than anyone else. A motion picture was made of the very sorry situation that existed there. I recall that John Steinbeck was at odds with the Communist Party. I can't say just how. It was a question of hearing them attacked and the work deplored and too bad he doesn't see the light, and so forth, and these things troubled me a good deal.[45]

The timing of Kibbee's testimony was *surreptitious* good luck for Steinbeck given the pasting Cohn and Schine had just given the author. Kibbee would go on to work on a number of TV and film projects including writing for *The Bob Newhart Show* and production credits for *Barney Miller*.[46]

From 1952 onward, it appears that the CIA let it be known to HUAC that John was off limits. But the true danger of Steinbeck being called before HUAC was before 1952. Did Steinbeck's Irish heritage give the author that bit of luck from 1947 to 1952 to avoid being subpoenaed? That's certainly the simplest answer given what we know. HUAC also may just not have gotten around to speaking with Steinbeck before 1952. Given the evidence in John's FBI file of "Communist connections" and his celebrity status, it is difficult to believe luck was the only factor in the equation.

A shield from the intelligence community usually comes with a price tag. It would seem that from 1947 to 1952, Steinbeck had paid the admission price, not only with his work during the Second World War, but by performing a bit of work in the one place HUAC feared the most—the Soviet Union.

The best ideas for trips are generally born out of alcohol and boredom. Steinbeck would say as much when discussing the genesis for a 1947 journalistic adventure in Russia. One night in late March of 1947, Robert Capa had joined Steinbeck at the Bedford Hotel bar for a drink where the men ruminated over finishing their current work projects. Talk of endings generally leads to hope for new beginnings and the alcohol-fueled men began to discuss "what there was left in the world than an honest and liberal man could do."[1] In a world full of possibilities, Capa and Steinbeck set their sights on Russia. Aside from the discussions of Soviet political and military intentions in the post-World War II Europe, the pair agreed that the world knew nothing of what life was really like in the Soviet Union. The banalities of everyday life for the common Soviet citizen were bandied about like a discussion of extraterrestrial civilizations. There was no press coverage of how the men and women under Stalin's rule shopped, worked, or relaxed. Capa and Steinbeck devised a plan to bring parity to the social divide. They would travel to Russia and see for themselves what life was like beyond the Iron Curtain.

The next morning brought an unusual result of resolve to the previous night's scheme sketched out on bar napkins. Steinbeck contacted his old friend George Cornish at the *New York Herald Tribune* and set up a time for the sales pitch. After hearing Steinbeck out, Cornish was hooked on the idea and set about lining up the paperwork necessary to insert two journalists in Stalin's police state. Steinbeck and Cornish also were in lock step on the manner of reporting that would be done during the trip. The goal for Steinbeck was to provide accurate reporting of life and conditions within the Soviet Union without the baggage of current political tensions between the United States and Russia. Agreed on the purpose, Steinbeck spent the next few months in preparation for the trip. Visas at the Russian Embassy, photo equipment for Capa, travel arrangements, and a thousand fine details were ironed out for a mid-May departure. Any excursion born in the confines of a bar is bound to have unforeseen complications and the Soviet trip was no exception. Steinbeck had broken his kneecap after an accident at his home. While leaning over a second-story balcony to see if a houseguest had arrived, the railing had given way, dropping Steinbeck to the pavement below. The injury delayed the trip until July when Steinbeck and Capa finally made their way to Europe. After extended stays in Paris and Stockholm, the pair reached Moscow on the night of July 31st.[2]

Steinbeck and Capa's arrival in Moscow was more of a *Seinfeld* episode than the well-planned entrance the pair expected. After passing through the necessary checkpoints, there was no one to meet the travelers. Both the United States Embassy and their contact from the *New York Herald Tribune* were nowhere to be seen. Steinbeck and Capa were standing in the heart of the enemy's camp with no money or an inkling of how to proceed without raising the ire of the Soviets. Fortunately for Steinbeck and Capa, a group of French journalists took their American counterparts under their wing and provided the unlucky duo with a hotel room and meals until they could sort out their arrangements. The light of the next day would show that both the Embassy and the *New York Herald Tribune* had forsaken Steinbeck and Capa. The Embassy staff claimed they had no clue Steinbeck and Capa were supposed to be in the country. The *Herald Tribune* had assigned their Russian beat reporter, Joe Newman, to babysit Steinbeck and Capa during their first few days in-country. Unfortunately for our new arrivals to Russia, Joe had been cleared to cover a fur auction in Leningrad and wasn't available upon Steinbeck and Capa's entry into the country. With the assistance of other American journalists, Steinbeck and Capa took over Newman's apartment and proceeded to drain their absentee host's liquor supply.

For a few days, Steinbeck and Capa explored Moscow with a factual derivation of Hunter S. Thompson's gonzo approach to journalism. The two journalists' tribulations became the story and the backdrop coincided with being in the Soviet Union. Russian officials were perplexed by their presence since they had no official sponsorship by any Soviet organizations. To travel outside of Moscow, some Soviet institution, such as the Writers' Union, had to vouch for visitors. The United States Embassy was no assistance because the staff was not sure why Steinbeck and Capa were even in-country. Stuck in Moscow, Steinbeck and Capa attempted to keep their journalistic integrity, but quickly became the topic of their own story. The men without official

The Kremlin as seen from across the Moscow River, 2012.*

standing lived off the donations of ration tickets, Rubles, and liquor from American newspapermen while attempting to find some official standing with the Soviet government. Horatio Alger and Hunter S. Thompson would have been proud of the pair for finally getting the recognition by the American Embassy in the form of a dinner invitation. Ambassador Walter Bedell Smith, the same man Steinbeck would write in 1952 after Smith had moved on as head of the CIA, had been indisposed for the first few days Steinbeck and Capa were in Moscow and apparently wished to make some amends by hosting an intimate dinner party.

If the United States State Department truly did not know about Steinbeck and Capa's field trip, Smith was presented with a truly unique opportunity. In a time before U-2 spy planes, satellites, and electronic listening posts, intelligence was primarily gathered by an on-the-ground observer. The Soviet police state and the fruit basket turnover of American intelligence had made it impossible to gather any useful information from the interior of the country. But now, sitting across the dinner table from Smith was the world's best wartime photo-correspondent and a Pulitzer Prize–winning author who had relatively unrestricted travel throughout the Soviet Union. In the years since the end of the Second World War, Steinbeck and Capa were possibly the first Americans to have been granted this privilege.

As dinner drew to a close, Smith was faced with two choices. The Ambassador could wish the pair safe travels or he could pigeonhole Steinbeck to solicit a trivial favor. Of the two, Steinbeck was the more attractive option for Smith. Steinbeck's service with the OWI, OSS, and BJs during the Second World War would not have gone unnoticed by Smith. Capa, on the other hand, was an impulsive playboy given to risk taking. The weight of Smith's favor would have necessitated a light touch that Capa was not suited for. The photographer was a miniature force of nature behind a camera who would stop at nothing to obtain the perfect shot. Chances were that Capa's photography might push Soviet censorship envelope too far and accidentally show the journalists were digging for more than human interest pieces. If Smith were bold enough to ask for an informant, the candidate was Steinbeck.

Taking Steinbeck aside, Smith could have asked, "Would you be interested in sharing your experiences with some folks at the State Department before you go back to the home?"

The question now becomes why would Smith *not* ask for Steinbeck's assistance? Smith was not the type of person to let such an opportunity pass. The General would not have been foolish enough to ask the author to do anything that would get either of them in Dutch with the Soviets. Simple honest reporting and a debriefing after the pair left the Soviet Union would be enough to advance intelligence efforts of the Russian interior by light years. All Steinbeck had to do was complete his avowed purpose and accurately report on conditions they observed during their travels. There may have been specific things Smith instructed Steinbeck to look for, but the cloak and dagger work would be limited to paying attention.

An alternate theory of espionage and *A Russian Journal* trip exists in which Steinbeck was approached in Paris before reaching the Soviet Union. Steinbeck's second wife, Gwyn, was not looking forward to the prospect of her husband leaving the country for a couple of months. By way of extending an olive branch to his less-than-thrilled wife, Steinbeck proposed a week in Paris as the first leg of the Soviet trip. A week in Paris was an agreeable buyoff for John's shrewish wife and would give the author additional time for his knee injury to heal.

One morning Gwyn and Capa had agreed to explore Paris while John attended a series of media events. Before setting out, the hotel's front desk rang to tell the party that Steinbeck had an unusual guest waiting in the lobby. A rural vintner had shown up at Steinbeck's hotel with his best stock in hand, hoping to share a bottle with the author. John agreed to meet the winemaker in his room and Steinbeck greeted his guest still donning a bathrobe and slippers. Steinbeck quickly discovered that his unexpected guest spoke as much English as he spoke French, which was none. Fluent in several languages, Capa acted as translator for the Frenchman and discovered the visit was prompted by Steinbeck's own winemaking efforts. The quartet broke out a corkscrew and drank until it was time for Capa and Gwyn to leave the hotel. They left Steinbeck and the vintner sipping on merlot and having a silently animated conversation due to the language barrier. Upon returning to the hotel, Capa and Gwyn were stunned to find John and the Frenchman had formed a fermented friendship. Steinbeck's morning interviews had been forgotten in the name of international relations.[3]

The story of the French winemaker is as quaint as it is anomalous. Steinbeck was never one to have shied away from an adoring public, or fire water for that matter, but Steinbeck was also a man who kept appointments. Another oddity of the story is how did the Frenchman know what hotel Steinbeck was staying in? Certainly there could have been mention of Steinbeck's Paris arrival in newspapers, the Frenchman's cousin could have worked in the hotel, or any of another dozen possibilities that would have flagged Steinbeck's location to a rural Frenchman. It is equally as likely that the hotel meeting was contrived by the Central Intelligence Group (CIG) to recruit Steinbeck. (It's worthy to note that the CIA did not exist until later in 1947. The CIG operated from 1946–47 and handled America's intelligence needs during the period.) This would be ample reason for Steinbeck missing his interviews that morning. A Paris recruitment also could explain the shoddy reception Steinbeck and Capa received in Moscow. If Russian counterintelligence believed United States Embassy staff cared so little for Steinbeck as to botch a proper airport reception, chances are Steinbeck would be perceived by the Soviets as a low risk individual. Steinbeck was just another journalist who deserved the same level of scrutiny as any other visiting Western journalist. As far flung as the theory might seem, an American intelligence officer posing as a French vintner and airport pickup misdirection are the type of tools employed by intelligence agencies.

Had Steinbeck been recruited by the Frenchman or Smith, a number of our other questions are immediately answered. The familiar tone Steinbeck takes with Smith in the 1952 letter is instantly explained; 1952 would not have been the first time Smith and Steinbeck had worked together covertly. Even if Steinbeck had been recruited in Paris, as the American ambassador to Russia, Smith would have been notified of the operation. Successfully passing along information after the 1947 trip would have assured Smith that Steinbeck could be trusted to perform similar work in 1952. Conversely, Steinbeck would have felt confident enough to approach Smith with a further offer of intelligence assistance. Being a passive spy during the 1947 trip might also have kept HUAC off Steinbeck's back. It would be difficult to question the loyalty of an American who has given the United States government detailed information about the Soviet Union. The potential embarrassment of Steinbeck admitting he had "spied" on the Soviet Union would have been enough to keep him out of HUAC's witness stand.

Steinbeck's FBI file may give a hint that supports the theory of Smith asking Steinbeck for information. On April 12, 1957, the FBI sent a summary of information the Bureau held on Steinbeck to the CIA's Office of Security. The information on page eight of this report begins with the California Committee of Un-American Activities condemnation of Steinbeck's business interests in Associated Magazine Contributors and moves on to reactions to *A Russian Journal*.[4] The paragraph that separates the two topics has been redacted by the FBI under exemption b1 (national security issues). While there is no way to discern what the paragraph holds, it would be reasonable to assume the redacted paragraph is the beginning of the FBI's findings on *A Russian Journal*. Certainly any report of Steinbeck cooperating with the American Embassy during the 1947 trip would have been classified as a matter of national security or foreign policy as the b1 redaction notes. Since the FBI has been less than forthcoming on an MDR (Mandatory Declassification Review) for Steinbeck's file, we may never know if the redacted text supports Steinbeck sharing information with the Embassy or not. The only trail left is to look at *A Russian Journal*'s text for answers.

If one gets past Steinbeck's kitschy descriptions of Capa's bathroom habits and kleptomaniacal obsession with books, *A Russian Journal* contains a surprising amount of information useful for intelligence purposes. Food rationing, the exchange rate of Rubles in gray markets, agricultural output and methods, and the status of commercial aviation are a few examples of intelligence topics covered within the first forty pages of the text. As one would also expect, Steinbeck reported about the daily life of the Soviet people. After all, that was the purpose of the expedition. The subject matter also betrays the overall condition of the Soviet state, which would be of prime interest to American diplomats and intelligence officers. Rationing could indicate stockpiling of foodstuffs for military use in an offensive, as easily as it could mean the Soviet infrastructure had not been repaired from the ravages of the Wehrmacht. Even the types of prosthetics used by those wounded during the Second World War, or lack thereof, speaks to the level of Russian medical care and technology. Taken on the whole, Steinbeck's observations of day-to-day life in the Soviet Union would have given intelligence analysts a perspective they had never had before. The closed Soviet society of a postwar Russia made any information useful, no matter how inconsequential it may seem.

Steinbeck even fibs a little about his capability as an observer within *A Russian Journal*. In attending an air show in Moscow, Steinbeck mentions that it was ridiculous that Capa wasn't allowed to take pictures of military aircraft. Military attachés from any Embassy could attend, seeing the military hardware firsthand. Steinbeck goes on to say that he and Capa "didn't know an airplane from a hole in the ground."[5]

But Steinbeck did know quite a bit more about airplanes than a "hole in the ground." In mid-August of 1940, John had taken flying lessons at the Palo Alto airport.[6] More importantly, Steinbeck spent May and June of 1942 with a B-17 aircrew gathering materials for the book *Bombs Away*. Steinbeck knew more about aircraft than the average civilian spectator. Even within *A Russian Journal*, Steinbeck makes knowledgeable observations on the poor state of the Soviet's aging lend-lease era C-47 cargo aircraft. Steinbeck might not have been that familiar with Soviet aircraft types, but the gaffe is reminiscent of John's writing for the *New York Herald Tribune*. During the war, John had to either change or omit facts about troop strengths, locations, and dates to pass military censors. There's little use in keeping operational security if all the pertinent details of an action are printed in this week's Sunday Edition. Steinbeck's articles would usually rely on recounting quirky stories that had little to do with military hardware or operations. The notable exceptions to

Steinbeck's pattern are his articles about the BJs and Salerno. In these pieces, actual events were slightly distorted to pass the censor's desk. For example, larger-than-life Douglas Fairbanks is split into two different characters in Steinbeck's articles.[7] It would appear that when writing up the events of the Soviet air show, Steinbeck fell back into old habits. The difference in 1947 was that if Steinbeck was passing information back to the American Embassy, John was shielding his own abilities.

The balance of *A Russian Journal* can be interpreted with the same eye toward espionage. Possibly the strongest case for Steinbeck's eye toward intelligence data can be found in the section on Stalingrad's tractor factory. The industrial facility was used to produce T-34 tanks during the Second World War and was the center of some of the most fierce fighting during the August 1942 to February 1943 German offensive. During Steinbeck's visit to the facility, the author notes the factory had reverted to producing agricultural equipment. In the description of the factory, Steinbeck makes mention of production estimates, factory conditions, types of machinery used in the production process, and a heavy dependence on recycling German tanks for metal. In estimating the factory's output, Steinbeck actually laments not getting better figures.[8] All of the information gathered by Steinbeck would be advantageous to intelligence services ascertaining the capabilities of a facility that could produce tanks as easily as tractors.

The usefulness of *A Russian Journal* in intelligence work was hinted at by ex-CIA officer TC. He recalls reading the book before his employment with the Agency. In prep school, TC had already decided he wanted to work in intelligence and read as much as he could on Communism and the Soviet Union. A number of senior field operatives had read *A Russian Journal* in the 1950s at the behest of senior Agency officials.[9] TC would not say specifically, or did not know, how else *A Russian Journal* might have been used within the

German soliders prepare to assault Stalingrad's tractor factory, late 1942.

Agency. The impression was that *A Russian Journal* was on a spook's version of a summer reading list. It's reasonable to say that if *A Russian Journal* was being passed around by field officers, an in-depth analysis of the book was done elsewhere in the Agency. Even if the theory that Steinbeck was recruited by Ambassador Smith or the Frenchman is incorrect, the publication of *A Russian Journal* did put Steinbeck on the Agency's crosshairs at a time when Soviet intelligence was at a premium.

While Steinbeck and Capa toured the Soviet Union, the United States government birthed a brand new intelligence agency. With the signing of the National Security Act in 1947, President Truman introduced a philosophical change in the way American policymakers viewed the need for both intelligence and defense. Prior to World War II, the United States had operated with a nineteenth-century concept of warfare. Nations on a peaceable footing generally did not have a default position of defense and usually only raised armies only when an external threat was recognized. The rapid mobility of both troops and communications seen during the Second World War meant that threats could crop up in a few hours instead of weeks or months. To keep up with the new speed of combat, America's intelligence services had to evolve the ability to become not only timely but predictive as well. Foreseeing a crisis gave policy makers and military leaders the luxury of additional reaction time.

The realities of security in the twentieth century were not lost on President Truman. The signing of the 1947 National Security Act created a military and intelligence topography that mirrored the newly emerging philosophy of combat. The Department of War changed names to the Department of Defense (DoD) signaling that the DoD's mission was ongoing even during peacetime. The CIA came into existence through the parentage of the OSS and interim Central Intelligence Group (CIG). The sad truth is that America's intelligence capabilities were in a shambles after the end of World War II. Prior to the Second World War, intelligence gathering and analysis was fragmented by the efforts of diplomatic corps, Army Intelligence, and Naval Intelligence. Communication between these groups was near non-existent and the country's overall intelligence capabilities suffered. During World War II, the OSS was the first step at a unified analytical and covert operational group. The OSS had the ability to filter information from all available government sources into a cohesive picture. This mission was passed along to the CIG in the fall of 1945, but many of the responsibilities of the OSS were parsed throughout various government departments. The need for an independent and relatively inclusive intelligence organization was answered by the formation of the CIA.[10]

As a newly formed Agency, CIA leadership had to invent methods of gathering/analyzing intelligence and covert operations on a global scale. In a climate of Cold War escalation, the CIA had to adopt a mantra of creativity over convention to fulfill their daunting mission. One of the first standing operations adopted by the Agency was the previously mentioned MOCKINGBIRD. The invention of Frank Wisner began sometime between the years of 1947–50. The exact dates are still classified, but most authoritative works place MOCKINGBIRD's inception closer to the birth of the Agency than later dates. Wisner's scheme to utilize journalists as assets instantly increased the Agency's gathering capabilities where setting up assets on foreign soil could take months or years to enact. Dependent on the journalist, Wisner had a fair amount of control over news content. At the Agency's behest, a "friendly" journalist could drop or add details to a story to fit the CIA's agenda. According to Carl Bernstein in a 1977 article for *Rolling Stone* magazine, at least four hundred journalists were on the Agency's payroll during MOCKINGBIRD's twenty-five-year run.[11] *The New York Times*, CBS, *Saturday Evening Post*, and the *New York Herald Tribune* are just a few of the news agencies that were named by Bernstein as being friendly to the needs of the CIA.

The breadth of how individual journalists and news sources served CIA requests ranged from passive intelligence gathering to actually inserting CIA agents within newsrooms as a cover story. In some cases, journalists were used as go betweens, or "cut outs" in Agency parlance, to foreign officials and the Agency. Operational details of MOCKINGBIRD are difficult to come by, but Bernstein did get *New York Herald Tribune* syndicated columnist Joseph Alsop to go on record about his work with the Agency. Joseph was asked by Frank Wisner to go to Laos in 1952 to monitor a popular uprising, and in 1953, Joseph was sent to the Philippines in an effort to influence the country's elections. Working with the CIA was a family affair for the Alsops as Joseph's brother Stewart also had a relationship with the Agency. Stewart was a first-class newspaperman in his own right and served as the *New York Herald Tribune*'s international bureau chief. Bernstein had discussed Stewart with one CIA officer who went as far as to say Stewart was a CIA agent.[12]

The more conspiratorial of views on Operation MOCKINGBIRD have suggested that the CIA controlled the media to the point of large swaths of news content originating within the Agency. It is difficult to believe that the CIA has had this level of power. Would the *Pentagon Papers* ever have seen the light of day had the CIA been able to flick a switch to turn off the presses?[13] The same could be said for any news story that was embarrassing to the government from 1947–74; My Lai, Watergate, the Bay of Pigs, etc. Given that the downfall of MOCKINGBIRD, and other domestic CIA projects, was instigated by *New York Times* reporter Seymour Hersh, the total control of the media at the hands of the CIA seems unlikely. By the same token, it is tricky to ascertain where journalistic integrity stopped and loyalty to the Agency kicked in with MOCKINGBIRD. Joseph Alsop maintained that no matter how much work he did for the Agency, it did not affect his writing.[14] If accurate, it can be hoped that all journalists acted with similar integrity.

While Steinbeck's name has never before been directly associated with Operation MOCKINGBIRD, it is likely his service to the CIA fell under MOCKINGBIRD's operational umbrella. If we apply Joseph Alsop's known activities with the Agency as a model for how Steinbeck could have been utilized, the possibilities of Steinbeck's CIA service would seem infinite. Without additional documentation from the CIA, every contact and anomalous behavior exhibited in Steinbeck's life from 1952 onward is suspect of being part of his service to the Agency. One has to access the anecdotal evidence with the probability that Steinbeck's actions were coupled with Agency goals. For example, there is a very low probability that the *Travels with Charley* road trip was made to further the Agency's domestic spying program. In order to weed out the more fantastical theories of Steinbeck's CIA service, one had to look for the lightning strike points in John's life. First, this lightning is the "dots" in Steinbeck's life that cross paths with known CIA activity. Second, we must examine decisions in Steinbeck's life that seem to have no explanation. Steinbeck was not an overly eccentric man, but he was given to fits of tilting at windmills. For example, doggedly supporting Adlai Stevenson's two runs at the White House could be seen as idealism in the service to a lost cause. Even with this Quixotic behavior, some decisions in Steinbeck's life simply do not track.

One of the instances of Steinbeck's unexplained behavior would happen two months after his return from the Soviet Union. Uncharacteristically, Steinbeck decided to start a television production company with Robert Capa. The idea of the company that would become known as World Video Inc. was pitched to Steinbeck by ex-radio executive Harry S. White. White had left radio with the vision of a world in which television made print and radio media obsolete. According to White's paradigm, television content would outstrip radio at the same level film content exceeded that of radio during the 1930s and '40s. Eager to cash in on his media contacts, White presented the idea of World Video to Steinbeck before the Russia trip. Steinbeck had a fair amount of experience with the film industry by 1947. Having been involved with all the production aspects of *The Forgotten Village* and having given direct input on the film versions of *The Grapes of Wrath* and *Of Mice and Men*, Steinbeck knew his way around a soundstage better than most of his contemporary authors. White's offer would roll around Steinbeck's mind during months of the Soviet trip and he would further explore the option after returning home.

The grand apparition of television's future and Steinbeck's involvement was not shared by those closest to him. Gwyn thought the move was a terrible idea and that John's talent would be squandered on cranking out subpar material. Longtime friend and confidante Ed Rickett's ex-girlfriend, Toni Jackson, was hired by Steinbeck as World Video's office manager. After learning the ropes of the television business, Jackson also tried to get John to back away from the deal. Even if the recommendations of two amateur television outsiders was not enough, Steinbeck's film and television agent, Anne Laurie, tried to wave John off entering into the television business. The advice would go unheeded and John would launch headlong into the new venture. To act this impulsively was highly unusual for John. In Jay Parini's biography of Steinbeck, the plunge into television is described as a move "out of nowhere."[15]

John signed World Video's articles on incorporation on December 18, 1947.[16] The articles stated that John was the corporation's president. Robert Capa and RKO vice president Phil Reisman were to serve as World Video's vice presidents. The choice of Capa as vice president makes perfect sense. Capa's eye for dramatic photography would be useful in the endeavor. Reisman had an impressive resume that made him an attractive, if not a cryptic choice, as a vice president. At the time of the incorporation of World Video, Reisman was RKO Pictures' vice president of foreign sales. Reisman had a reputation for understanding how American-produced films needed to be presented successfully in foreign markets. His expertise and connections were called upon by the OIAA in 1941. The quasi industrial/intelligence/propaganda agency was interested in developing strategies to make Hollywood films pass strict Brazilian censorship policies. Reisman, John Hay Whitney (director of the OIAA's film division), and Walt Disney traveled to Rio de Janeiro on the fact-finding junket. The OIAA was eager to sanitize pro-American films for distribution. In return for the assistance of the Brazilian government, Hollywood would produce films that highlighted Brazil's history and culture to the world.[17] Orson Welles' over-budget debacle *It's All True* was one of the byproducts of Reisman's negotiations with the Brazilian government. A year later, at RKO's behest, Reisman would again return to Rio to pull the plug on Welles' artistic vision.[18] Reisman gave Welles a chance to complete the film under strict time and budgetary constraints, ostensibly to fulfill Reisman's end of bargains made with the Brazilian government in 1941. Containing a project by Orson Welles was much like training blind cats to fetch and Resiman's mediation with Welles failed miserably. *It's All True* would never be completed and languished as a mess of unedited footage until a 1993 documentary chronicled the project.

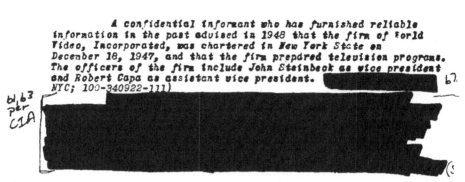

A confidential informant who has furnished reliable
information in the past advised in 1948 that the firm of World
Video, Incorporated, was chartered in New York State on
December 18, 1947, and that the firm prepared television programs.
The officers of the firm include John Steinbeck as vice president
and Robert Capa as assistant vice president.
NYC; 100-340922-111)

The entry of World Video and subsequent CIA redaction in Steinbeck's
FBI file. The full document can be seen in the Appendix of this text.

What is unknown about Reisman's involvement with World Video is why the film executive would bother with a start-up television production company while still employed by RKO. The film company was purchased on a whim by aviation tycoon Howard Hughes in the summer of 1948. Reisman could have been looking for a professional exit strategy should RKO's sale turn south. But Reisman's talents lay in the distribution end of the film business, not the behind the lens activities of a budding television industry. To that end, Reisman's role in World Video appears to have been a token position. Trade journals of the day barely mention Reisman in connection with World Video and his role in the venture is not well chronicled in the scant accounts of World Video's operations. Any mention of World Video and the initial board members is passed off as a cautionary tale of how very talented persons should not stray far from their bailiwick.

One source that did take notice of World Video's incorporation was the FBI. Information about the company's incorporation was part of the April 12, 1957, summary on Steinbeck sent from the FBI to the CIA's Office of Security. An unnamed informant relayed the formation of World Video to the Bureau. The name of the informant has been redacted from the file under FOIA exemption b7 (law enforcement records), and the document makes no mention of Harry White or Paul Reisman. The very next paragraph has been redacted by the CIA under exemptions b1 (national security matters) and b3 (information exempt under miscellaneous other laws).[19] This section of Steinbeck's FBI file follows a rough chronological order and the next visible entry summarizes a May 18, 1948, *New York Herald Tribune* article that mentions Steinbeck. One can make the reasonable assumption that the redacted material chronicles an event that happened between the incorporation of World Video on December 18, 1947, and May 18, 1948. During this period, Steinbeck was writing copy for World Video's first project, *Paris: Cavalcade of Fashions*. The short series gave World Video a glamorous opening salvo into the TV scene and a free trip to Paris for Capa who was the series' director and creator.[20] The only other noteworthy event in Steinbeck's life between December 1947 and May 1948 was the publication of *A Russian Journal.*

The quandary with this redacted text is the same as the previously mentioned sections referring to *A Russian Journal.* The difference is that with the redaction around the World Video text, we know the text was specifically redacted by the CIA. For the CIA to have performed a redaction, the information had to be related to a CIA asset, agent, or classified operation. Since the previous pages of the FBI report deal specifically with redactions to *A Russian Journal,* we can suppose that there would be no need for further references to the book. From the information at hand, it would appear that the redacted text relates to the operations of World Video. The question now becomes why would the CIA have any interest in a start-up television production company? One explanation is that World Video acted as a front for the Agency or a prototype for Operation MOCKINGBIRD. The hand of the Agency in World Video would explain Steinbeck's dogged loyalty to the venture and other questions that crop up around the company.

The concept behind using a newly formed television production company as an Agency cover follows with the CIA's formula of setting up front companies; find a willing private citizen and fund their endeavor. Either Steinbeck or Reisman would have been the willing citizen in the World Video front hypothesis. Steinbeck's supposed deal with Ambassador Smith would have put Steinbeck squarely on the CIA's radar as an approachable target. Reisman's work with the OIAA during the Second World War placed Reisman directly in line with America's wartime intelligence machine. The players in World View were right for cultivating a front and World Video's business model fit the Agency's needs as well. The span of locations, coupled with the need for onsite crews, would have afforded intelligence officers latitude in developing believable cover stories. A prime example of how media fronts were developed and used by the Agency is chronicled in the 2012 film *Argo*. The movie loosely recounts the extraction of six American Embassy employees caught up in the 1979 Iranian hostage crisis by using a fictitious film company as a cover.[21]

The Agency was in the driver's seat in terms of content CIA-funded media companies produced. *Paris: Cavalcade of Fashions* can be viewed as not only an escapism documentary produced for the stereotypical postwar housewife, but the short series also held a healthy dose of propaganda. Six months prior to the formation of World Video, Secretary of State George Marshall presented a reconstruction plan for Europe. The appropriately tagged "Marshall Plan" required an expenditure of 13 billion dollars (almost 20 percent of the 1948

Ads and articles were "placed" in *Variety* to enhance the CIA's cover for *Argo*. The ads trumpeted *Argo* being a "cosmic conflagration" written by Teresa Harris (an alias selected for one of the Americans awaiting rescue). Photo from the CIA.

U.S.'s gross domestic product) by the United States over a four-year period beginning in April of 1948. The funds did not include the estimated 13 billion dollars the United States had already spent on European reconstruction from the end of the war to June 1947.[22] The Marshall Plan was a polarizing topic for a country that had paid the price of Western Europe's freedom with the blood of their sons and daughters. *Paris: Cavalcade of Fashions* was a visualization of how Europe could return to its prewar glory. Images of stunning models in chic clothing were a concrete example of the return on American investment in Europe.

One also has to consider that *Paris: Cavalcade of Fashions* was a rather ambitious project for an infant company. Orchestrating the filming of eight one-hour episodes 3,600 miles away from the company's base in New York would be a daunting project for a veteran production company, let alone an untested venture. Capa found the setting almost impossible to film and could not complete the project without going far above the show's budget. Capa, acting as the documentary's director, was forced to pay expenses out of his own pocket. Some of these expenses were disputed as being Capa's own personal extravagance by World Video's board and were never reimbursed. Capa left the company over the issue after returning stateside.[23] The lessons of *Paris: Cavalcade of Fashions* were not taken to heart by the board of World Video and their next project was to film a French fishing competition for the newly created *Field and Stream* TV program.[24] After the financial fiasco and internal strife *Paris: Cavalcade of Fashions* had created, one would have thought that filming closer to home would be appropriate. The histories of defunct businesses are littered with poor decisions and World Video's projects may have been another journal entry. However, if the programming decisions of World Video were made for covert reasons, European filming makes sense.

Lightning continues to strike around a connection between World Video and intelligence agencies in the form of degrees of separation. In March of 1950, World Video had a shakeup in leadership. Harry White took a job with CBS as an associate director of programming and Richard H. Gordon Jr. took over as the company's vice-president.[25] White did not have what anyone would call a resume builder in World Video. The company had a number of projects on paper, but had produced little more than *Paris: Cavalcade of Fashions* by 1950.[26] Either Harry White was a PT Barnum-like self-promoter or the job at CBS was arranged by the Agency. As we have seen earlier, CBS had close ties with the Agency and White's new position with the network cannot be ignored in light of Richard Gordon's replacement of White at World Video.

Professionally, Richard Gordon did not leave many tracks within the entertainment industry. It appears that Gordon held bit parts in three Broadway shows in the 1940s.[27] As for Gordon's television credits as of 1950, there were none. Gordon does have production credits for six episodes of the science fiction anthology series, *Tales for Tomorrow*, from 1951–53.[28] On the surface, Gordon does not seem to have the pedigree to be named a vice-president of a TV production company in 1950. There is another explanation for Gordon's orbit of World Video; Gordon was a member of New York's Union Club. As New York's second oldest "gentleman's club," the Union Club has taken members such as Dwight Eisenhower, Averell Harriman, and Harold Vanderbilt. The Union Club has also been accused of having been frequented by CIA operatives and leadership.[29] Gordon could simply have been a trust-fund baby whose connections and capital made him vice-president material for World Video. It is equally possible Gordon had Agency connections via the Union Club that made him attractive for the vice-president slot.

One other initiative of World Video could fit into the Operation MOCKINGBIRD mold. A month before the leadership changes at World Video, CBS partnered with the production company to hold a scriptwriting contest. The contest, dubbed "CBS Awards," was:

> . . . open to college students all over the country, giving aspiring young "soap opera" writers a chance to enter into the field of video.[30]

Steinbeck, CBS program director Charles Underhill, and playwright Donald Davis were listed as judges for the contest. CBS had the possibility of airing new programming and World Video would likely handle the production. Holding contests of this type are not uncommon for any media outlet looking for fresh material. If World Video operated as a front for the Agency, the contest could have been used for Agency recruiting purposes as well. Operation MOCKINGBIRD was gearing up in 1950, and the CIA was on the hunt for recruitable writers.

While oblique links such as club connections to the Agency and writing contests are not proof, CIA lightning keeps striking around World Video's players. Phil Reisman's son had an undeniable link to the Agency. The younger Reisman joined RKO Pictures after attending Brown University a couple of years ahead of Watergate conspirator E. Howard Hunt. In his early years at RKO, Reisman was tasked with writing the narration for newsreels and documentaries. Possibly seeing the handwriting on the wall for the flagging RKO, Reisman struck out as an independent scriptwriter and producer in 1952.[31] Among numerous television projects, Reisman was credited as a writer and creator of the 1955 TV series *I Spy* starring Raymond Massey and Frank Sutton. *I Spy* presented viewers with an anthology of espionage tales introduced by Raymond Massey as Anton the "Spy Master." Unbeknownst to the cast and crew of *I Spy*, Reisman had a unique doorway into the intelligence world. Phil Reisman Jr. was recruited by the CIA in 1955 to write pro-American film scripts for the Central American market.[32] According to Phil Jr.'s son, his father was given a cover name of Lewis Allmine and issued a weapon for personal protection by the Agency.[33]

The crossover with World Video and *A Russian Journal* with John's 1952 letter to the CIA gives ample possibilities for the author to have had a connection with the Agency before 1952. While the arguments are anecdotal, the submissions demonstrate "means, motive, and opportunity" for a Steinbeck/CIA relationship before 1952. Any of the events discussed in this chapter could have been a bridge for Steinbeck rekindling his connections to the United States intelligence formed during the Second World War. Too often prewar Steinbeck, World War II Steinbeck, and postwar Steinbeck are compartmentalized in respect to his writing, and therefore the man's life is viewed in a similar fashion. To take this view would be a mistake because the same person who worked for the OSS and wrote propaganda during the Second World War is the same person who volunteered for service with the CIA. There is no reason to believe that Steinbeck would not have looked for ways to serve his country in the interim.

What we can say with a high degree of certainty is that Steinbeck was active with the Agency during his 1952 European trip.

In November of 1951, Steinbeck had finished his most ambitious work-to-date, *East of Eden*. The lives of most authors are defined by periods before, during, or after writing a specific book. *East of Eden*'s "before" period was possibly one of the darkest in John's life. His marriage to Gwyn had seen the birth of two children and a rapid descent into chaos. The pressures of new motherhood and the inability to create a meaningful singing career had taken a toll on Gwyn. The once affable and passionate woman Steinbeck had married had been replaced by a person seeking the comfort of a bottle. The disintegration of Steinbeck's second marriage was not a one-sided affair. At times, John was no peach to live with. His usual periods of depression were compounded by both mental and physical problems related to covering the Salerno invasion.

Misery loves company, as the old saying goes, and in the late 1940s, Steinbeck was a magnet for suffering. In early May of 1948, John was to go on another marine expedition with longtime friend Ed Ricketts to British Columbia. A week before the pair were to begin their grand adventure, Ed was crossing a railroad track in Monterey and was hit by a train. The trauma sustained in the accident was not immediately fatal and Ricketts survived three days in a coma before dying on May 11th. Unable to get to Monterey before Ed's passing, Steinbeck would forever feel that he failed a friend in need. John would stay in Monterey until after Ed's funeral and take it upon himself to go through Ed's journals and correspondence at Pacific Biological Laboratories. A fair percentage of the material Steinbeck found in Ed's office was burned. Letters, pages of Ed's personal and professional journals, and any other objectionable writings were grist for the fiery mill. One can only assume that in their nearly twenty-year friendship, the two men had written each other about matters that were not for public consumption and therefore had to be disposed of.[1] Whatever Steinbeck's reasons for the purge, it would be an act that should have brought a modicum of closure to Steinbeck over Ed's death.

Upon returning to New York, it was evident that John's burn party at Pacific Biological did not achieve this end. Increasingly despondent, John retreated behind the curtain of drink and depression. This would be the final straw for Gwyn and the second Mrs. Steinbeck asked for a divorce in August of 1948. John would try to ease the passing of both Ed and Gwyn out of his life by throwing himself into his work and moving back to Monterey to recapture the comforts of home. Neither tactic worked and John languished in his own personal brand

Ed Ricketts' Pacific Biological Laboratories on Monterey's famous Cannery Row, 2007. Photo by author.

of grief for the next year. Then over the Memorial Day weekend in 1949, John would meet the third and final Mrs. Steinbeck, Elaine Scott.

Born into the Anderson Texas oil family, Elaine grew up enjoying the perks that come from new money and high Texan society. One of her good friends growing up was Claudia Alta Taylor whom the world would later know as Lady Bird Johnson. Her early love affair with the theater resulted in pursuing a theater degree at the University of Austin where she met her first husband Zachary Scott. The two would marry in 1934 and move to New York where both attempted to make a go of stage acting. Zachary was the most successful at the acting game of the two and would go on to be a Hollywood leading man. Elaine had found a different niche in stage production and gained some notoriety as being the stage manager for the original production of *Oklahoma!* As often happens in the married lives of creative folk, Elaine and Zachary grew apart as their careers blossomed. By 1949, the couple was spending more time apart than together and their marriage was more business arrangement than a union based on love.

Over the Memorial Day weekend of 1949, Elaine decided to have a girls' weekend in California with her close friend, actress Ann Sothern. The same weekend, John had gotten roped into escorting the same Ann to a dinner party thrown by Ava Gardner. When Steinbeck arrived at Sothern's place, she politely informed him that she had other plans for the evening. Not wanting to see John attend the party alone or her friend spend a night washing her hair, Ann suggested Elaine accompany John to the party. There was an instant attraction between Elaine and John that night and the couple would embark on a year-and-a-half love affair. Elaine would end up seeking a divorce from Zachary and married John a week after the legalities were final in December of 1950.

Being no stranger to fame or fortune, being "Mrs. Steinbeck" was a role Elaine easily fit into and relished her husband's accomplishments. This is not to say that Elaine turned herself into a dinner party accessory for John. For the first time in his life, John had found a true partner in marriage who accepted John's faults, charms, and acclaim equally, while keeping her own sense of self. Elaine had the advantage of being at a different place in her life than the previous Mrs. Steinbecks when she met John. She had come to the point in life where one becomes comfortable in one's own skin. All of Elaine's strengths and weaknesses were her old friends long before Steinbeck ever came into the frame.

The newlyweds moved back to New York in early 1951 and John began working on *East of Eden*. The influence of Elaine in John's life was another turning point in Steinbeck's life. The depression that plagued the author during the late 1940s was all but gone and he was once again focused on his work. Throughout 1951, John ground out the manuscript for *East of Eden* and Elaine made a home in a 72nd Street brownstone. The "during" phase of *East of Eden* gave John the chance to rewrite the narrative of his personal life. It is not surprising then that John would see fit to take on larger challenges in the "after" *East of Eden* period, and readdress his old friendships within the intelligence community, which would begin with his January 28, 1952, letter to Walter Bedell Smith.

The untailored tone of Steinbeck's 1952 letter to Smith would make it seem that Steinbeck got out of bed on January 28, 1952, and decided to take a four-month jaunt to Europe. The trip had actually been pitched to Steinbeck by the editors of *Collier's Weekly* in April of 1951.[2] The editors of *Collier's* really had no expectations as to Steinbeck's content; only that he produce five general interest articles about his experiences in Europe. Steinbeck saw this opportunity to pay for an extended second honeymoon with Elaine, and agreed to *Collier's* open-ended terms. Tiny glimpses into the journal Steinbeck kept while writing *East of Eden* in 1951 show that even while working on the manuscript, the *Collier's* trip was never far from his mind. For example, in late October of 1951, Steinbeck mentions purchasing a raincoat for the trip. With Steinbeck parsing out details such as raincoats three months before the departure to Europe, we can assume that few elements of the trip were left up to chance.

As further evidence of Steinbeck's trip planning, on January 21, 1952, John wrote Bo Beskow about the trip's itinerary. The adventure was to begin in late February with a thirty-one-day cruise from New York to Alexandria. Steinbeck specifically mentions that they have already booked passage on a ship and the basic itinerary of the trip had been set. John was intent on seeing the Giza pyramid complex before moving on to Cyprus and obtaining visas for Israel. John's great-grandfather, Johann Grossteinbeck, had gone to present-day Israel on an extended missionary trip a hundred years before. The expedition would turn out to be a pivotal point in the heritage of the Steinbeck family. Johann would meet and marry John's great-grandmother during the expedition and after a tragic Muslim raid on their missionary colony, the couple moved to America under the name Steinbeck. John had been furiously putting the finishing touches on the semi-genealogical *East of Eden* while planning his own voyage to retrace his family's history during the Israel leg of the tour. From Israel, John and Elaine planned on seeing the Greek islands and then Rome. From the eternal city, Steinbeck states there were no specific travel plans.[3]

The timing of events surrounding the planning for the 1952 European trip would seem to indicate that the CIA did not play a part in the early stages of the trip. *Collier's Weekly* had approached Steinbeck the year before and the itinerary had been set prior to John sending his letter to Smith. Since Steinbeck offered his services to the CIA, it is unlikely that there was some collusion between the CIA and *Collier's Weekly* to recruit Steinbeck. This does not mean that John had not considered the possibility of turning the trip into a venture for the Agency long before sending the letter to Smith. On Halloween of 1951, Steinbeck writes in his *East of Eden* journal that he was, "beginning to have some plan of action which I must think out very carefully."[4] In the published version of Steinbeck's *East of Eden* journal, the section following the previous quote has been redacted from the text and we are left wondering if John could have been considering expanding his role within the intelligence community. No matter what forethought John had placed in the European trip and the CIA, there is evidence that the Agency radically altered John's original plans for the trip.

The trip John and Elaine took was very different than the one outlined to Beskow on January 21st. The couple would leave New York a month later than they originally planned on an unnamed ship bound for the Greek Islands via Genoa, Italy, but they would never reach their original destination of Alexandria.[5] Cutting the Egyptian portion of the voyage was a reasonable choice for the couple, given the country's political climate. Five days after Steinbeck sent the outline for the trip to Beskow, tensions over the British

The port of Algiers, 1980.*

occupation of Egypt had reached a boiling point. A skirmish between Egyptian police and the British army regulars erupted in the Suez Canal zone that left fifty Egyptians dead. The next afternoon Egyptian rioters tore through Cairo burning 750 buildings in a wave of anti-Western sentiment.[6] The political situation in Egypt was fluid enough that the threat of a British invasion of the country persisted until the summer.

The Steinbecks changing their travel plans not to include Egypt are perfectly understandable, but the alterations to the rest of their expedition are more puzzling. After leaving New York in late March 1952, John and Elaine's ship sailed across the Atlantic and made an unscheduled stop in Casablanca, and another unscheduled layover in Algiers two days later. There is no way to pin down what ship the Steinbecks boarded in New York. Not knowing the exact dates of travel, and just looking at New York Port records for late March 1952 cannot produce a precise match. On a daily basis, there were fifteen to twenty ships leaving New York, and Genoa was a popular port of call for ships sailing in the Mediterranean. Without knowing the name of the ship, it is difficult to say why the ship added two ports of call. The reason for the impromptu stops could have been mechanical issues or a medical emergency aboard the ship. The weather was not a factor as there were no tropical storms or hurricanes in the Atlantic during March or April of 1952.[7]

In Algiers, the Steinbecks inexplicably attended an all-night party hosted by a French Air Force General.[8] The party would be the first time in the 1952 trip that John would be able to gather information for the CIA. Loose talk at a high-powered French dinner party had the potential to be intelligence gold for the Agency. France had been a growing concern for other NATO countries in recent months. The French were already embroiled in the fight for their holdings in Indochina and Algeria had been a crisis away from revolting since the end of World War II. France itself did not have the most stable government and at any given time during the Cold War was one election away from adopting Communism. From the perspective of the French, NATO wasn't doing the country any favors. The "Schuman Plan" called for the first steps in a unified European steel industry that would give large concessions to Germany on top of NATO plans to rearm the country that had devastated France twice by the midpoint of the twentieth century.

From Algiers, the couple decided to book passage on a ship to Marseille where they would hire an American driver to chauffeur them down the southern coast of France into Spain. The route would take a winding path along the eastern edge of Spain via Valencia and Grenada for an extended stay in Seville. The exact dates for this portion of the trip are not precise, but John's letters from Europe give us a fairly good timeline for the rest of the voyage. The only portion of the Steinbecks' original travel plans that held was visiting Rome. Israel and the Greek Islands had somehow been forgotten and the omissions of those destinations have no real reasoning. In March and April of 1952, the political situation in Israel was as stable as it ever has been in the last sixty years. The Greek Civil War had ended three years prior and there was no overt reason for the couple not to conduct a tour of the islands. The deviation in the couple's itinerary has never been questioned and has been attributed to the open-ended nature of the vacation. Now knowing that John was working with the CIA, the travel changes could have been at the behest of the Agency.

While writing his literary agent Elizabeth Otis in May, John alludes to unseen forces altering the original intent of the trip:

> It is certain that we have changed our plans. We changed them to match conditions we didn't know about in advance . . . Manning [*Collier's Weekly* editor Gordon Manning] thinks I should go to Slovak. I am going to Jura. If they think I'm hanging around Paris too long—let them.[9]

It would be natural to think that the editors of *Collier's* were the source of the trip's alteration; however, John makes it clear that the wishes of *Collier's* editors had no bearing. Since there were no other forces to bear, we can only assume that something happened in Algiers that radically altered the couple's travel plans. Another indication that an invisible hand was at work is that John and Elaine were originally slated to leave Europe on June 25th[10] but would not leave the continent until August 31st.[11] The couple had reservations on the *Queen Mary* bound from London to New York, but never utilized the tickets. One can suppose that these reservations were made some time before leaving for Europe in March. Cruise lines are notorious for not giving refunds and the frugal Steinbeck would have had to have a good reason for not only extending the trip, but eating the cost of passage back to the United States.

Had the Steinbecks known from their March departure from New York that they would be going to Spain, the unexpected layover in Casablanca would have been the perfect point of departure. Casablanca is only 220 miles from the Spanish port of Cadiz and booking passage on a ship or plane bound for Spain would not have been an issue. A short hour-and-a-half drive from Cadiz would be the Steinbecks' first extended point of stay at Seville. Instead the couple takes the long way around to Seville via a boat ride to Marseille and then hires a driver to take them a little over a thousand miles to Seville.

Vacations are often devoid of logic, but the Marseille to Seville side trip and giving up on Israel and Greece seems excessive on a whim. Another incongruity in the Marseille adventure was that of renting a car and hiring a driver. Steinbeck was notoriously worried about money and renting a car was an expense he wished to eliminate from this trip. In the same January 1952 letter to Beskow, Steinbeck already has a mind to purchase a car to drive the couple around Europe.[12] In May, the couple would purchase a used Citron they dubbed *Aux Armes O Citroën* ("To arms, oh Citron" and a play on words off the French national anthem) to drive from Paris to Italy.[13] After the trip was completed, Steinbeck would sell the vehicle and recoup a good portion of his investment. Why then would Steinbeck not purchase a car a few weeks earlier in Marseille? John was not averse to driving in Europe, so why incur the extra expense of hiring a driver on top of renting a car? The behavior is unusual on the surface and we are left with two conclusions. The Steinbecks either acted impulsively or John's mission for the CIA came into play.

With the Steinbecks' radical change in travel plans, it is possible that whatever information he had gathered from the Algerian party necessitated contacting the Agency. Instead of continuing on to the Greek Islands, Steinbeck could have been ordered to Marseille for a debriefing and been issued a CIA driver and car for the next portion of their trip. The CIA had maintained a heavy presence in Marseille since 1950. In protest over French military action in Indochina, Marseille's dock workers paralyzed France's largest Mediterranean commercial port for sixty days. The CIA maintained elevated operations in Marseille during the early 1950s, ensuring that the flow of Indochina-bound war materials was not hindered again.[14] Marseille would have been the closest, most secure, and least innocuous place for the Agency to debrief Steinbeck. From Marseille, the Steinbecks could easily have found a ship or airplane to any point in the Mediterranean they wished, but they took a chauffeured overland route to Spain instead.

At this point, one has to wonder if Elaine was aware of her husband moonlighting as a spy. Of Steinbeck's three wives, Elaine would have been the one privy to this side of John. Given John and Elaine's equal partnership in John's public and private life, it would be difficult to believe that Elaine didn't know about John's CIA connections. If John had not told her before leaving for Europe, she would have figured out, at the very least, something was amiss during the trip. Radical changes in travel plans are not the sort of thing Elaine would have gone along with unquestioningly. Although not a very academic argument, one gets the feeling in reading accounts of John and Elaine together that John would not have wanted to hide anything from her or unwittingly bring her in harm's way. John might even have shared part of his secret, telling Elaine that he was working with the CIA but could not discuss specifics about his activities. Warm fuzzies are no better proof of Elaine's knowledge of John's covert work than information gleaned from a séance. Other than Elaine's reluctance to speak with Jackson Benson about Steinbeck's feelings about HUAC, there is one piece of evidence that indicates she knew.

John's alma mater, Stanford University, holds the original July 20, 1957, letter written by Steinbeck to Thomas Malory scholar Eugene Vinaver that has been reprinted in *Steinbeck: A Life in Letters*. The letter was written during John's 1957 trip to England and is a thank-you note for Vinaver agreeing to meet Steinbeck for the first time. The body of the text reads like a teenager writing their favorite rock star. Steinbeck gushes about basking in Vinaver's sunlight and ends the letter with a postscript that conveys a totally different tone. John suggests to Vinaver that they meet at Winchester College in London on a specific day the next week to view a manuscript of *Le Morte d'Arthur* with Winchester's librarian J.M.S. Blakiston. Steinbeck has picked that day because, in his own words, they would be "relatively secure." The choice of wording is unusual and very specific. Why anyone would need to be "secure" in viewing a medieval manuscript is open to debate. Steinbeck did feel that his research flew in the face of traditional academic research into both Malory's work and the search for a historic King Arthur. John could have been concerned that any assistance Vinaver gave Steinbeck might have tarnished Vinaver's standing in the academic community and wanted to keep the meeting secret. It is also not known if that meeting ever took place. The Winchester's assistant librarian in 1957, Michael Tweedy, didn't recall Steinbeck ever visiting the library.[15] Then again, if the meeting was on the down low, no one would have known about it other than Steinbeck, Vinaver, and Blakiston.

The reasons why John would seek security at Winchester College is not as curious as why the July 20, 1957, letter's postscript was left out of *Steinbeck: A Life in Letters*.[16] Publishing a volume of Steinbeck's letters was Elaine's brainchild and in the early 1970s, she began to ask John's friends for copies of any correspondence they had with John to be published. Assisting Elaine in the monumental effort of selecting and editing John's letters was Steinbeck's longtime friend Robert Wallsten. Both Elaine and Wallsten received editorial credit for *Steinbeck: A Life in Letters* and controlled the material that was published. This means that Elaine had full knowledge the postscript of this letter was excluded. The exclusion could have been an editorially based layout decision, since the body of the letter takes most of a full page and is at the end of the book's section. However, it is equally as likely that Elaine saw the phrase "relatively secure" and thought the meeting at Winchester College had relevance with John's work with the Agency. Not wishing to betray a meeting that could have been part of a CIA operation, Elaine cut the postscript.

With or without Elaine's deeper knowledge during the 1952 trip, John and Elaine would spend mid-April through mid-May of that year bouncing around

General Ridgway (second from the left) during the breakout from Normandy in 1944. Photo courtesy of the US Army.

from city to city in Spain. In the early 1950s, Spain was a wildcard for NATO nations. The country had been shunned by the rest of Europe for its fascist government, but pragmatically Spain could be a useful ally in the fight against Communism. In 1955, Spain was welcomed back into the European fold after decades of trade and diplomatic isolation. Other than a few anecdotes, Steinbeck's time in Spain is not very well documented. There is certainly nothing unusual about anything we know about the month the Steinbecks were in the country. If Spain had been part of Steinbeck's assignment for the CIA, it was likely to gather general information about how Spaniards felt about participation in the Cold War.

On May 11th, John and Elaine left Spain for Paris. The timing couldn't have been better for any covert purposes John had. General Matthew Ridgway had replaced Eisenhower as the supreme NATO commander and would make Paris the first stop in a tour of Europe. Ridgway should have been a popular choice as NATO commander with the French. As the commander of the 82nd Airborne Division, Ridgway had planned airborne operations for the Normandy invasion and actually jumped into the combat zone along with his troops. Airborne troopers are known for brutal strikes behind enemy lines and efficiently breaking things. Not surprisingly, tact is not a skill taught at Fort Benning's airborne school. Ridgway would find himself offending the French by disparaging the efficacy of French troops early in the Korean War. Although Ridgway would go on to praise the actions of French troops who turned the tide at Hamburger Hill, the damage to French pride was done. To seal his public opinion fate with the French, and other member NATO countries, Ridgway filled the upper echelons of NATO command with American officers. Not having a voice in military affairs tends to not go well with allied nations and Ridgway became the brunt of any anti-Americanism that had been building in Western Europe since the end of the Second World War.

Steinbeck got to Paris at the same time Ridgway detractors were starting to come out of the woodwork. Whipped into a frenzy by the French Communist party, sporadic riots occurred in the week before Ridgway's arrival in Paris.

The largest of the demonstrations happened on May 27th and resulted in the Secretary of the French Communist Party, Jacques Duclos, being arrested after a pistol, a club, a notebook, and two pigeons were found in his car. The French authorities claimed that the pigeons were used for communications between Duclos and his Soviet connections.[17] In the midst of the Parisian chaos, Steinbeck allowed the leftist publication *Combat* an interview. One would think that after finding out about Elia Kazan's testimony before HUAC the month before, Steinbeck would have stayed as far away from anything hinting of Communism. Steinbeck had other goals than shameless self-promotion for the interview.

Writing to Elizabeth Otis about the *Combat* interview, John states:

> . . . being interviewed is the best way of getting information. The very nature of the question can tell you a great deal.[18]

The seemingly innocuous statement by Steinbeck takes on a different meaning when read with CIA-colored glasses. If the interview was part of Steinbeck's CIA assignment, the interview's timing would mean that John was directed to gather information about the French Communist Party's intentions for Ridgway's visit.

The wake of Ridgway's command of NATO would become an undercurrent for the rest of Steinbeck's European trip. A debate about the General and American foreign policy would turn into "The Soul and Guts of France" a few weeks later. It was not unusual for John to receive a steady stream of invitations to social gatherings in the City of Lights. Dinners with John Houston, José Ferrer, Robert Capa, Suzanne Flon, and the cast of *Moulin Rouge* at the Eiffel Tower Restaurant were a staple of John's Parisian hobnobbing.[19] Still John was very much the same man of the people who wrote *The Grapes of Wrath* and accepted an invitation from English teacher Louis Gibry, to visit his hometown of Poligny. Gibry was an admirer of Steinbeck's works and wanted to show John what life in rural France was like. Either on May 28th or 29th, John and Elaine packed up *Aux Armes O Citroën* and headed for the French-style *Green Acres*. After a leisurely three-day drive into Western France's wine country, the Steinbecks arrived at their destination for a three-day stay.

The experience in Poligny would form the basis of Steinbeck's first article *Collier's Weekly* accepted for publication. Steinbeck had submitted a piece on Spanish bullfighting that Collier's had turned down and the magazine's editor suggested a number of more suitable topics for Steinbeck's next attempt. Rejection for one's writing is a constant no matter how famous one might be . . . The quaint and rustic aspects of Poligny were sure to be a hit with the editors at *Collier's*, not that Steinbeck really cared. John had already made the decision to chuck out *Collier's* advice on topics and write about what he wanted to write about. Certainly most of Steinbeck's critical reviews and biographers have winked at "The Soul and Guts of France" as a piece worthy of a *Town and Country* exposé on bedskirts of the Hamptons. The four-page article in *Collier's Weekly* is neither picturesque nor heartwarming and "The Soul and Guts of France" is little more than pro-United States/NATO propaganda. *Collier's* tag line for the article leaves little doubt as to the piece's intention.

> What can we expect of our French allies? Here's an illuminating answer—not from the mouths of politicians, but from the tough, individualistic farmers who once terrorized the Germans.[20]

Steinbeck sets the overt political tone from the get-go by stating that intelligent Americans wishing to take a true political pulse of the country go out and talk to farmers. The allusion quickly turns to reading Paris newspapers gets in the way of good ol' country wisdom and Steinbeck has found truth in French politics in Poligny. The platitudes swiftly end as Steinbeck descends into describing rural France in terms one might reserve for the poorest part of Appalachia. The shoeless children of Poligny had no reason to go shod before Steinbeck's visit, but with the arrival of the famous American, the money was somehow scraped up to shoe the little ones. Hunting hounds traverse Poligny's kitchens unfettered by their master's displeasure and a stitch of plumbing or running water is nowhere to be seen in the home of Louis Gibry. Rounding out the verbal assault are pictures of some of Poligny's residents. One poor soul pictured is wearing a Jed Clampett–style hat and missing his two front teeth. Elaine had taken all the photos for the *Collier's* articles, so the addition of the dentally challenged Frenchman was intentionally taken to punctuate Steinbeck's thoughts. The caption above the picture reads:

> We do not want to do anything that will lead to war. We have peace now and we want to keep it.[21]

The inference completes the tone of the article's tagline that Americans can expect toothless pacifist yokels in a fight against the Communists. The editors of *Collier's* have only reinforced Steinbeck's subtext that these insolvent, out-of-sorts Frenchmen need the type of help only American ingenuity can provide.

From the physical needs of Poligny's denizens, which John actually uses the term "peasant" in a number of places, John jumps into a political discussion with the locals. The conversation ranges from rumors that the United States was using biological agents against Chinese troops in Korea, to why the French should love Ridgway. In discussing the charges of biological weapons, the vice president of the local wine collective recounts a North Korean claim that leaflets and insects tainted with biological agents were dropped by American aicraft all over the country.[22] The use of the term "wine collective" in describing the place this person uses is a subtle read that he is involved in a Communistic endeavor. No one in the heartland of America would have batted an eyelash at this gentleman working at the local co-op, but the word "collective" distances this farmer from his American counterparts. Steinbeck counters the claim and comments that he could "believe a half literate completely dominated people" could believe the North Korean's claim, but the author can't believe that a "modern Frenchman" could stomach such guff.[23]

All the debates Steinbeck engages with Frenchmen in "The Soul and Guts of France" are little more than brow-beating jingoism. There is little in this article to suggest that Steinbeck is trying to understand the rural Frenchmen from their frame of reference and is possibly one of the most un-Steinbeck pieces Steinbeck ever wrote. One might expect that the author of "The Soul and Guts of France" would have written *The Grapes of Wrath* from the perspective that the Joads deserved their plight because they should have kept up with their loan payments. One can only wonder if "The Soul and Guts of France" was written to spec as a part of John's CIA assignment. The article was the first written by Steinbeck for *Collier's* but was actually published after "A Duel without Pistols" which would be written in Rome a few weeks later.

Collier's ran "The Soul and Guts of France" in their August 30, 1952, edition just ahead of the first meeting of the European Parliament, a precursor to the European Union, on September 10th. There was a growing sentiment both in the United States and Europe that with Marshall Plan funds ending at the end of 1952, and the beginning of a more unified Europe, that America should get out of European politics. "The Soul and Guts of France," if not specifically written for this purpose, clearly conveys that Europe still needed the guiding hand of Americans.

The French reaction to "The Soul and Guts of France" was not favorable in many quarters. Rita Reil of the International Press Alliance Corporation (IPAC) wrote Elizabeth Otis on September 25th,

One of a number of posters created by the US Economic Cooperation Administration, to "sell" Europeans the Marshall Plan, 1950.

1952, of a disturbing development in France. The French news publication *Samedi Soir* had purchased publishing rights for "The Soul and Guts of France" from *Collier's Weekly* and had run the article shortly after it appeared in *Collier's Weekly*. Not everyone in France was taken with the romantic notion of John and Elaine roving the French countryside in an unreliable Citron. The same week "The Soul and Guts of France" appeared in *Samedi Soir*, rival tabloid *France Dimanche* printed a reaction piece. *France Dimanche*, the equivalent of America's *US Weekly* or *People Magazine*, had blasted Steinbeck's take on Poligny. Reil describes the article in her letter to Otis:

> In this article it is demonstrated that Steinbeck either spoke the untruth (sic) or made very grave errors; that the conclusions which he reached were most certainly false and everybody from the mayor to the smallest street urchins are interviewed to prove Mr. Steinbeck is at fault.[24]

The problem with these accusations lay not only at Steinbeck's feet, but that of International Press Alliance Corporation's Paul Winkler as well. The letter obliquely indicates that *Samedi Soir* had purchased rights to syndicate "The Blood and Guts of France" from either IPAC or its French parent company, Opera Mundi. Winkler had started Opera Mundi in the mid-1920s as a press Agency that sold news articles throughout Europe. By 1930, Winkler made a deal with Walt Disney's American publisher, King Features, to syndicate Mickey Mouse comic strips throughout Europe. A few years later, Winkler's Opera Mundi published the first European Mickey Mouse comic books. At the height of distribution, Mickey was selling 400,000 issues weekly.[25] In 1938, Winkler expanded Opera Mundi's reach again by opening offices in America under the name Press Alliance Incorporated. The success of Opera Mundi's diverse operations came to a sudden halt as the Germans invaded France in 1940. Winkler and his family stayed in France until it was obvious the country was lost to the Germans and escaped to America in early June of that year. The Winklers settled in New York and resumed the syndication business with Press Alliance Incorporated.

Winkler's organization was a sizable enough media outlet that one would think a literary agent of Otis's caliber would not want to alienate. However there is no indication that Steinbeck ever officially responded to the allegations in *France Dimanche*. Bernard Cabiron, the author of *Steinbeck et les Résistants du Jura* (Steinbeck and the Resistance at Jura), took an in-depth look at the effects of "The Soul and Guts of France" from both the Parisian press and by interviewing residents of Poligny who were present during Steinbeck's visit. According to Cabiron, the flap over "The Soul and Guts of France" died in both Paris and Poligny as quickly as it erupted.[26] This is likely the reason that Steinbeck did not respond as robustly as he would a few weeks later in response to similar claims in Rome as chronicled in "A Duel without Pistols."

After leaving the backwoods of France, John and Elaine wound up the rubber bands in the capricious *Aux Armes O Citroën* for the road trip to Rome via Geneva. Oddly enough, the Steinbecks arrived in Rome the same day as Ridgway on June 16th.[27] The first few days in Rome are described by Steinbeck in "A Duel without Pistols" in terms of how the Italian demonstrations against Ridgway's visit had caused the couple issues in moving about Rome and at their hotel. Another coincidence in the bag is that Steinbeck stayed at the same hotel as Ridgway. Undoubtedly there would also be a contingent of CIA officers staying in the same hotel to provide security for the new NATO commander, making any contact with Steinbeck's handlers easier. One of these intelligence agents could very well have been the person that Steinbeck refers to as "a friend" who informed John that the Communist paper, *L'Unita*, had published "An Open Letter to John Steinbeck."[28] The article trashes Steinbeck's character, but in "A Duel without Pistols" Steinbeck takes the opportunity to outline how Ridgway's character is maligned by using Steinbeck's perceived flaws as a vehicle. John's response to the allegations can be summed up, once again, in *Collier's* tagline:

> How does it feel to be used as a Red propaganda weapon? "At first, I was amused," says the author. "Then I got mad." Here's his own story of a now-famous exchange of letters in Rome.[29]

Steinbeck chronicles how he tried to get *L'Unita* to publish a response letter and when they did, Steinbeck's words were cut and pasted together in such a way as to make the author look ridiculous for retorting. The tone of "A Duel without Pistols" is totally different than that of "The Soul and Guts of France." With a dry wit, Steinbeck is recounting events as they unfolded. The actions of the staff of *L'Unita* were damaging enough to the publication that John did not have to craftily spin the information. The intriguing part of "A Duel without Pistols" is that *Collier's* published this piece before "The Soul and Guts of France." Magazines generally publish serial travelogues in chronological order to give readers a perception of taking part in the trip. *Collier's* purposely circumvented this convention for the sake of leading with the more sensation headline. The events described in "A Duel without Pistols" paint Steinbeck in the sympathetic light of the prey of propaganda. The technique of self-defense after a sneak attack is a common practice to rouse public support for politically unpopular marches to war. One simply has to look at the conflicts America has been involved in for the last one hundred years. Remembering the *Maine*, the Zimmermann Telegram, and the Gulf of Tonkin episode have all given the United States a victim status in which to morally justify going on the offensive. "A Duel without Pistols" is a "weapons of mass destruction" justification for Steinbeck to bite back in next week's *Collier's Weekly* with "The Soul and Guts of France."

The earlier-made allusion to Steinbeck utilizing his writing and service with the Agency as warfare against Communism seems to be an accurate metaphor when examining both "The Soul and Guts of France" and "A Duel without Pistols." As Steinbeck saw on the beaches of Salerno, war is a brutal affair in which there are few rules. "The Soul and Guts of France" is an unabashed propaganda piece in which Steinbeck comes to blows with his words as his time with Fairbanks' BJs had taught him—fight dirty and smart. Why shouldn't John use the skills he honed while cranking out propaganda during the early part of World War II in the battle against Communism? The commanders in Korea were utilizing the same skill set they learned on the battlefields of Europe and the Pacific. Right, wrong, or indifferent, Steinbeck would have felt that using such measures was equal to the threat of Communism and therefore a just and proportional Cold War response.

We will never know if the CIA directly utilized John's writing talents as part of his service with the Agency. It would seem unlikely that either party would not have taken advantage of John's words as well as any loose talk he might have picked up during the 1952 trip. The next article that *Collier's Weekly* ran as part of their five-article deal with Steinbeck was "The Secret Weapon We Were Afraid to Use" in the January 10, 1953, edition.[30] The original agreement was that Steinbeck was to write about his observations in Europe and "The Secret Weapon" has nothing to do with jaunting about Europe. The article was run ten days before Eisenhower's inauguration. The Soviets were as nervous about the Normandy Invasion mastermind sitting in the Oval Office, as the Iranians were skittish about Reagan taking office at the tail end of the 1979–81 Hostage Crisis. In a speech delivered to the Commonwealth Club on October 10, 1952, Eisenhower made his views on Communism clear:

> Communism and freedom signify two titanic ideas; two ways of life, two totally irreconcilable beliefs about the nature and destiny of man. The one, freedom, knows man as a creature of God blessed with a free and individual destiny, governed by eternal, moral, and natural laws. The second, communism, claims man to be an animal creature of the State, curses him for his stubborn instinct for independence, governs him with a tyranny that makes its subjects wither away.[31]

While Steinbeck had no particular love for Eisenhower who "only read Westerns," the goal of the Cold War was to make the Soviets back down from the perceived position of requiring world dominance to achieve their goals. Coupling the warrior's rise to the presidency with a dose of how we can hit the Reds without nukes presents the country with a hopeful and winnable outcome to the Cold War. Like the chronological publishing flip-flop of "A Duel without Pistols" and "The Soul and Guts of France," the timing of publishing "The Secret Weapon" seems circumspect. It could be that the editors of *Collier's Weekly* were savvy enough to present the articles for maximum effect or the magazine's staff was also being guided by Frank Wisner's Operation MOCKINGBIRD.

The events of the remainder of Steinbeck's 1952 trip do not seem suspect for having links to any CIA-related duties. Then again, the documentation does not exist to ascertain exactly what those duties were. John could have been doing anything from setting meetings between intelligence officers with people he had come in contact with, to just reporting on the odd bits of party gossip that might interest the Agency. The best connection we are left with is to probe Steinbeck's writing after the trip and see if there is a pattern of behavior that lends itself to John actually being a part of Operation MOCKINGBIRD.

In the next chapter, we will see that while the pieces John wrote for *Collier's Weekly* certainly fit the MOCKINGBIRD mold, other media outlets Steinbeck had connections with had direct ties to the Agency.

Locked away within the Special Collections Department of the New York Public Library are a series of notebooks kept by Steinbeck's research assistant Chase Horton. Within the story of Steinbeck's life, Horton appears as a footnote compared to the supporting cast members with the status of Elizabeth Otis or Pat Covici. The tidy and always immaculately dressed Horton came into Steinbeck's life at the insistence of Elizabeth Otis. Steinbeck's literary agent suggested that Horton aid the author in researching what would become *The Acts of King Arthur and His Noble Knights*. If we view John as an author-knight searching for the Holy Grail in the form of writing *The Acts of King Arthur and His Noble Knights*, Chase played the part of John's dutiful researcher-squire. As John chased words around a page, Horton did a majority of the heavy lifting, tracking down obscure references to support the modernization of *Le Morte d'Arthur*. The two men's association was not limited to simply that of employer and employee. Horton was a true believer in Steinbeck's Malory-driven odyssey when others in Steinbeck's life merely gave the project lip-service support. Because of Steinbeck's enduring love for the works of Malory, the project was more than writing a novel. Steinbeck wished to honor the spirit of Malory's early work in *The Acts of King Arthur and His Noble Knights*. The gravity of responsibility Steinbeck felt for "getting Malory right" was as weighty as Tolkien's Frodo taking the One Ring to Mount Doom. In this respect, Chase Horton was Steinbeck's Samwise Gamgee. Supportive in most areas to a fault, Horton's character in Steinbeck's tale is as understated as Tolkien's second-fiddle hobbit.

A native of Cleveland, Ohio, Chase Horton was born in 1897 to a prominent family of dentists. Chase's grandfather, William Perry Horton, was a founding member of the Ohio State Dental Society and was the Society's first president.[1] Continuing in his father's footsteps, Chase's father, William Perry Horton Jr., also became a dentist in Cleveland. Dentistry did not appeal to the bookish Chase and he took steps during the First World War to escape the confines of Ohio. Volunteering for the Naval Auxiliary Reserve in April of 1918, Chase was trained as a Quartermaster. Reaching the rank of Seaman, Second Class, Chase mustered out of the Naval Reserves in May of 1919.[2] Sometime between 1920 and 1923, Horton made the decision to leave the industrial trappings of Cleveland for New York City. The reason for the move and its timing is not known. One can only guess that given Horton's interests in literature and history,

Cleveland was not the place to fulfill his needs. No matter what the young man's intentions were, Chase would find himself literally thrust in the middle of New York's Greenwich Village Bohemian culture via Josephine Bell Arens.

The woman who would become Chase's wife in 1923, was described by her nephew, as "something of a wild child."[3] A native of Topeka, Kansas, Josephine studied at the Chicago Institute of Art and later taught at the Parsons School of Design.[4] New York's magnetism for artistic souls claimed Josephine in the middle of the First World War. Her political idealism ran toward the Marxist end of the spectrum and Josephine fell in with Max Eastman. If Communism had an epicenter in New York during this time, it would be Greenwich Village and Eastman was its bright shining star. Eastman published the left-leaning journal, *The Masses*, which was surprisingly forward-thinking for the period. Supporting free love, birth control, and women's suffrage, *The Masses* was a perennial target for conservatives. Josephine would periodically write for *The Masses* and one of her poems landed her in jail.

Josephine's poem, "A Tribute,"[5] protested the arrest of anti-war anarchists Emma Goldman and Alexander Berkman. The pair had been imprisoned under the Espionage Act of 1917 for "conspiracy to induce persons not to register [for military service]."[6] *The Masses* had planned to run Josephine's poem in the August 1917 edition, but the Postmaster General refused to allow the publication to be sent through the mail. Josephine, Eastman, and six other employees of *The Masses* were arrested as part of the Goldman and Berkman conspiracy. Luckily Josephine's lawyer was better than her poetry. After Josephine's lawyer read "A Tribute" to the court, the judge asked, "You call that a poem?" The barrister replied, "Your honor, it is so called in the indictment." The judge immediately dismissed Josephine's charges and called the next case.[7]

Josephine's arrest would cement her as a fixture in the Greenwich Village community for the rest of her life. By all accounts she was a free spirit who easily hobnobbed with the true and pseudo intellectuals who flocked to the Village. At one time, she had an affair with *Nero Wolfe Mysteries* author Rex Stout and nearly captured his heart.[8] But it

> **Josephine Bell's poem "A Tribute."**
> Emma Goldman and Alexander Berkman.
> Are in prison.
> Although the night is tremblingly beautiful.
> And the sound of water climbs down the rocks.
> And the breath of the night air moves through.
> multitudes and multitudes of leaves.
> That love to waste themselves for the sake of the summer.
> Emma Goldman and Alexander Berkman.
> Are in prison tonight,
> But they have made themselves elemental forces,
> Like the water that climbs down the rocks.
> Like the wind in the leaves.
> Like the gentle night that holds us.
> They are working on our destinies.
> They are forging the love of the nations.
> Tonight they lie in prison.

was to be the dashing Egmont Arens who would try to forge a life with the willful Josephine. The two were married in 1917 and purchased Frank Shay's Washington Square Bookshop. Arens continued Shay's practice of using the shop as a short-run publishing house and started a series called the "Flying Stag Plays." Under the Flying Stag Press imprint, Arens and Josephine also published *Playboy: A Portfolio of Art and Satire* (which had no links to Hugh Hefner's publication) and the guidebook, *The Little Book of Greenwich Village*.[9] Arens' efforts did not go unnoticed in the literary community and from 1922–23, he was an editor for *Vanity Fair*.[10] As Arens' star was on the rise, Josephine was stuck running a bookstore. Even with New York's literary elite as regular customers, running a business with a half partner was too much for Josephine and the couple divorced in 1923.

Shortly after Josephine and Arens' breakup, Chase Horton entered Josephine's life. There are no records to attest to how the two met, but it is apt to have been through the bookstore. The charismatic Ohioan's interests in history and literature would naturally have been drawn to Greenwich Village and the exotic Josephine. The two were married the same year of Josephine's divorce and Chase took over Arens' role as co-owner of the Washington Square Bookshop. The bookstore was something of a surrogate child for the couple, as they never had children. The store gained popularity within the Village because of Chase's discretion about his customers. Over the years, James Baldwin, e. e. cummings, Dashiell Hammett, Lillian Hellman, and Eleanor Roosevelt were just a few of the famous who stepped over Washington Square Bookshop's threshold. Horton would never idly speak of who had been in the store or what their purchases had been.[11] Everyone was treated with the same respect and Horton's growing knowledge of books made him an embodiment of a Village card catalog. To their customers, Chase and Josephine had found what few couples ever do—an alignment of passions.

The original location of the Washington Square Bookstore in New York City's Greenwich Village, 2007. Photo by author.

New York is a city where illusion and reality coalesce into the viscous paste, holding larger-than-life souls together. By the late 1930s, the false impressions customers had of Chase and Josephine began to become apparent to them. Both of the Hortons were given to the bottle and all the entrapments alcohol abuse plays within a relationship. Chase sought help within the ranks of Alcoholics Anonymous (AA) and slowly began the process of dealing with his addiction. Within the circle of those drawing strength on each other to break the grips of liquid compulsions, Chase met a kindred spirit in Steinbeck's agent Elizabeth Otis. One can imagine the two discussing books at meetings and developing a commonality aside from the avowed purpose of the AA meetings. Otis and Horton would eventually become lovers and Chase was faced with what to do about Josephine. Not wishing to damage Josephine's reputation, or that of the bookstore, Chase told Josephine about his infidelity and proposed a unique solution. Chase would remain legally married to Josephine and assist her in running the bookstore, but the two would never live together again as man and wife. Chase would also ensure that Josephine was taken care of financially and assist her any way he could. The secret would be maintained in such a way that overtly no one would know the couple had broken up and Chase would move in with Elizabeth.[12]

Josephine was distraught by the revelation and relayed the news to her sister Sue. If Josephine was the "wild child" of the Bell family, Sue was the "good girl." In 1920, Sue had married diplomat Donald R. Heath. The consummate envoy, Heath had been posted in a number of European countries before the Second World War. From 1937 to 1941, Heath served in the American Embassy in Berlin and smuggled intelligence on the Nazis out of the country on a regular basis with the assistance of his son's academic tutors. After the war, Heath would go on to ambassadorial posts in Saudi Arabia, South Vietnam, and Cambodia. Heath also contributed to the development of the "Domino Theory" of the spread of Communism during the Cold War. Needless to say, Josephine had no wish for a scandal about her arrangement with Chase to blow back on Sue and Donald. The family decided the best course of action was to inform their children of what had happened between their aunt and uncle. "After my parents told us about Chase and Josephine, we were never to speak of it again," said Josephine's nephew about the situation.[13]

Josephine's nephew recalls visiting New York as a teenager and having a good relationship with Chase despite the situation with Josephine. While in prep school, he independently visited both Josephine and Chase. Josephine seemed worse for the wear and developed eccentricities later in life. She kept the room in the Hotel Earle on Waverly Place that she and Chase had lived in until she died in 1967, but refused to set foot north of 14th Street. Chase fared much better after the breakup. The bookseller always gave the air of being connected to virtually anyone in New York and could always get tickets to any event Josephine's nephew wished to see in the city. In keeping with Chase's familial obligations, he was quick to give advice to the young nephew when needed. Chase never made a secret about his relationship with Otis to Josephine's nephew, but never discussed the matter unless he was asked. Occasionally Chase would mention to Josephine's nephew reading manuscripts for Elizabeth and that she valued his input. According to Josephine's nephew, Chase had called him a few years before his death in 1985 to catch up. Chase had sold the bookstore after Josephine's death and worked since then in a semi-official capacity for Otis. Elizabeth had set Chase up with a bank of phones in their apartment to do fact checking and bird-dog manuscripts her agency received. Sadly the next time the nephew tried to contact Chase, he was informed his uncle had died a few months before. Chase's death had been such a private affair, the nephew even had difficulty ascertaining his final resting place.[14]

The revelation of Horton and Otis's intimate relationship has either been a well-kept secret in the literary world, or it was well kept enough that no one knew of it. It is understandable that the major biographers of Steinbeck's life could have kept Horton and Otis's relationship out of the public eye. The stigma that would have been attached to Otis and Horton would have been crippling to their reputations in the past. The time of Ward and June Cleaver has long passed and Otis and Horton can now be judged on their merits rather than their personal life. But this raises the question of how influential Chase Horton was in Steinbeck's works prior to 1956. If Chase was given manuscripts to read by Elizabeth, certainly her biggest client's work would have been passed along to Chase. It is doubtful we will ever know how much Chase may, or may not, have shaped Elizabeth's take on Steinbeck's works during this period.

What can be charted is the relationship and influence Chase had directly on Steinbeck from 1956–59. In the summer of 1956, Elizabeth had written John with the suggestion he take on Chase as his research assistant for the Malory project. Otis had done this to keep Chase busy in the summer months. Chase had a problem dealing with hot New York summers and the temptation to drink was greater for Chase during these months.[15] Aligning Chase and Steinbeck would take care of two problems for the literary agent. Steinbeck would receive a much-needed assistant and Chase would throw himself into a venture that reduced his temptations. Otis's plan worked even better than she had initially envisioned. In reading letters between Steinbeck and Horton, one begins to see Horton as a terrier tracking a prize fox. Aside from rare texts, Steinbeck often requested very specific items for his research. Before going to Somerset in 1958, Steinbeck expressed a need for aerial photographs and topographical maps of the area.[16] Steinbeck wanted to find actual places Malory might have been describing in *Le Morte d'Arthur* to make a physical connection with the tales of Arthur. Horton dutifully filled this singularly odd request and any others Steinbeck threw his way. Nothing seemed out of Horton's grasp during the Malory project.

More importantly than playing "my man Friday" to Steinbeck, Horton was a cheerleader for Steinbeck. The self-deprecating author often doubted the wisdom of tackling the Malory project. The amount of research both Steinbeck and Horton put into the rewrite was staggering. At one point, in the 1959 portion of Horton's journal, the total hours Horton had working on the Malory project was 2,526.[17] For purposes of comparison, that is a little over 105 days if one worked twenty-four hours straight. The frustration Steinbeck experienced with his obsession with Malory was based on his lack of confidence that he could actually produce a tome worthy of Malory. Throughout the process, Horton's letters express a gentle encouragement that in many cases talked John off his own psychological ledge.

As is often the case with those who we have deep personal relationships with, their opinions can be as hurtful as they are helpful. Horton and Otis would nearly become the undoing of Steinbeck's foray into Malory after reading a rough draft in 1959. Otis was highly critical of what Steinbeck was trying to achieve and Horton remained circumspectly silent. One can imagine that Horton did not want to go against the opinion of his life partner Otis and held his tongue in deference toward a man he had come to regard as a friend. Steinbeck viewed the review as a personal affront to his talent and work on the Malory project stalled until the mid-1960s.[18] From that point, a rift existed between Steinbeck and Horton; the two stayed in touch and Horton would do some minor work for Steinbeck in 1965.

John would never see the publication of *The Acts of King Arthur and His Noble Knights*. The manuscript never achieved the greatness Steinbeck wanted to pass along to Malory's previous work and it would take Horton to resurrect John's vision. In the early 1970s, Horton began pushing Elaine and Elizabeth to dust off the manuscript for publication. Chase's diligence and loyalty to Steinbeck paid off and *The Acts of King Arthur* was published in 1976, eight years after Steinbeck's death.

Chase Horton also had a part to play in the connection with Steinbeck and the CIA. On a lone page of Chase Horton's 1958 journal is an entry with three names and their respective addresses. Entries for "Griscomb," "Mary Morgan," and "Praeger" are found before any other journal entry that year. The first two names make sense as being included in Horton's research journal. Griscomb refers to the offices of Griscomb Photography. The company produced photographic equipment including microfilm cameras and readers. At one time, the Pierpont Morgan Library furnished Steinbeck with a microfilmed copy of the Winchester Manuscript for the author's private use. Steinbeck had been interested in purchasing a microfilm reader for his home use and Horton had been able to secure the perfect machine for Steinbeck's personal use.[19]

The second name that appeared on the list was of Steinbeck's typist, Mary Morgan. Most everything Steinbeck wrote, including manuscripts, was written in notoriously awful longhand. It follows that Horton would need to get in contact with Morgan for clerical parts of the project. Horton may even have needed help deciphering the letters he received from John.[20]

The final name in the list is the one that raises questions. The address for "Praeger" matches up with the 1958 New York Telephone Directory listing for Frederick A. Praeger of Praeger Publishing. One would think that a rare book dealer having the name of a book publisher in his journal wouldn't be unusual. Truthfully, if the listing was for any of the other throngs of publishers in New York, the name wouldn't have been unusual. But Frederick A. Praeger was not an average publisher. A number of books in Praeger's catalog would end up becoming manuals for the CIA.

Praeger is another character who deserves a text devoted solely to his story. Born in Austria in 1915, Praeger's parents owned a publishing company in Vienna. His studies at the University of Austria were cut short in 1938 by the forced consolidation of Germany and Austria. Preager's parents made

Memorial statue at Buchenwald, 2012*

arrangements for the college student to flee the country while they stayed behind, hoping the situation for Jews would improve. Being publishers and of Jewish descent, the members of the Praeger family would have been a high-priority target for Austria's new Nazi regime. Frederick himself had evaded arrest from the Nazis on three occasions before finally leaving Austria. The rest of the Praeger family was not so fortunate. In the autumn of 1939, Frederick's father was arrested and sent to the concentration camp at Buchenwald.

After leaving Austria, Frederick found his way to Paris. The momentum of the Nazis' campaign soon left little doubt in Praeger's mind that Paris would soon fall to the Germans. America presented the best bolt hole for the college student–turned refugee and he sailed to New York ahead of the Germans crossing the border into France. By the time Praeger reached the States, he would have been emotionally and financially drained. In order to make a living, he took a number of menial hourly jobs. As the war in Europe escalated, Praeger joined the United States Army in November of 1942.[21] The Army had been in the process of reinventing its intelligence branch since the spring and intelligence officers were now being embedded within combat units. Given Praeger's level of education, fluency in German, and firsthand knowledge of the terrain in Austria, the immigrant was a perfect fit for this type of intelligence assignment. After training, Praeger would be assigned to the 6th Armor Division of Patton's 3rd Army.[22]

Praeger describes a heartbreaking scene of the 3rd Army's liberation of Buchenwald in the foreword of *The Buchenwald Report*. Praeger had been a part of Patton's westward push to Germany, knowing that his father had been taken to Buchenwald. For Praeger, each offensive was another step closer from freeing his father from the horrors of the concentration camp. In early April of 1945, Praeger received word that Buchenwald had been reached by a reconnaissance battalion of the 6th Armor Division. Praeger raced to the scene hoping to find his father. On the road to Buchenwald, Praeger encountered a group of refugees leaving the camp and asked if they knew his father. One of the men had been in the same logging group as Max Praeger and had grim news for his son. Two weeks before Buchenwald's liberation, an altercation with an inmate trustee had left Max with an infected eye. Like thousands of others injured prisoners, Max Praeger was loaded onto a boxcar bound for Auschwitz's gas chambers.[23]

Shortly after the liberation of Buchenwald, Praeger was reassigned to run General Lucius Clay's intelligence staff in Wiesbaden. The central German city would turn into the American logistical and intelligence center for the occupied country. The OSS had taken up headquarters in Wiesbaden and Praeger would have had close contact with the organization. Frank Wisner, for example, was stationed in Wiesbaden running a network of ex-Nazi intelligence officers spying on the Russians.[24] Unlike many of those who worked in intelligence during the Second World War, Praeger did not take a job with the CIA. The publisher's son took out a $4,000 loan to follow in his father's footsteps and opened Praeger Publishing in 1949. Praeger's original intent was to secure American publishing rights for European titles. In a number of cases, Praeger was able to obtain the rights to works published behind the Iron Curtain. Most notably, Praeger was somehow able to obtain the manuscript for Aleksandr Solzhenitsyn's *One Day in the Life of Ivan Denisovich* less than a year after its publication in the Soviet Union.[25]

Praeger Publishing found its true niche in the publication of books that would interest the intelligence community. The ex-Army intelligence officer was able to leverage the contacts made in the Second World War to supply government agencies with relevant titles during the 1950s. The publishing house's books were often used as reference materials by CIA officers throughout the Cold War.[26] When Chase Horton had made his notion of "Praeger" in his research notebook, books like *Suspect Documents: Their Scientific Examination*, *The Communist's New Weapon: Germ Warfare*, *Communism in Guatemala*, and *The American Communist Party: A Critical History* were the staples of the Praeger catalog. Praeger did publish historical and art texts in the 1950s, but books on these subjects were few and far between. Of these books published by Praeger, few would have been of benefit to Steinbeck's Malory research.

After an extensive search through Praeger's publications, *Wessex before the Celts* by J.F.S. Stone stands out as a single corollary source for Steinbeck's work.[27] Praeger Publishing would hold the American rights for Arthurian cultural historian Geoffrey Ashe during the 1970s. Unfortunately for Ashe, Steinbeck and Horton were familiar with his work and held the author's theories in distain.[28] Also Robert DeMott compiled an inventory of the books Steinbeck owned or referenced in *Steinbeck's Reading: A Catalogue of Books Owned and Borrowed*. While DeMott admits that the list cannot be taken as an exhaustive one, his work shows only two books by Praeger Publishing: R.E. Oakeshott's *The Archaeology of Weapons*, and *The Sword in the Age of Chivalry* published in 1960 and 1964 respectively; these were far outside of the early 1958 Praeger notation by Horton.[29]

There are a number of specific texts mentioned in letters between Steinbeck and Horton in which none appear to be published by Praeger.[30] The probability that Horton had made a note of Praeger for obtaining a catalog now seems quite low. Had Horton needed a title in the Praeger catalog, being the owner of a bookstore, Horton would have ordered the book from a distributor. Had Horton needed a catalog, he would have called Praeger and a phone number would have been listed rather than an address. By listing Praeger's address, we can assume that Horton needed to visit the publisher's offices. Griscomb Photography and Mary Morgan definitely represented places Horton felt he would have to visit over the coming year. Manuscripts to Morgan and supplies from Griscomb would be the type of errands Horton was often asked by John to perform. If this was a list of recurring tasks for Horton, what was to be done at Praeger Publishing?

The loyal-to-a-fault Horton could have been an unwitting courier for Steinbeck's CIA sideline. Praeger Publishing was a perfect fit for the Agency to perform a number of tasks. Praeger did have a reputation for publishing books from authors living in Soviet Bloc countries. Travel to Iron Curtain countries therefore would have been a necessity to find new authors and close deals. Intelligence officers with the cover of Praeger Publishing literary agents would be believable and innocuous enough to hold up under scrutiny. Praeger would benefit from having a unique source of information for their publications. The Agency had the advantage of using a company being run by a former Army intelligence officer who was familiar with the ins and outs of espionage.

The connection with Steinbeck and Praeger could have been as simple as the Agency seeking John's opinion on books Praeger was publishing at their behest. One of the niggling accusations that has surrounded Praeger Publishing is that the company printed propaganda at the CIA's bidding. On December 18, 1974, the infamous Watergate burglar E. Howard Hunt testified before the Senate Watergate Committee that the CIA had funded Praeger's publishing operations.[31] Praeger admitted his company had published twenty to twenty-five books at the CIA's insistence during the 1950s, but when pressed by a reporter, he would not comment on the CIA funding allegations.[32] If Hunt's testimony is accurate, that association between Praeger Publishing and the CIA went far beyond vendor/client. Since Steinbeck was already a CIA asset, best-selling author, and produced propaganda pieces for the OWI during the Second World War, it would follow that the Agency would seek his advice on materials they had printed. The use of Horton as a go-between would have put distance between Steinbeck and both the Agency's operations and Praeger. Materials that were going to be published for public consumption would not have required a courier to hold a security clearance. Also had John's regular publishers, Viking, caught wind that he was regularly visiting a rival publisher's office, the appointments might have led someone to ask uncomfortable questions.

The links between CIA interests and Praeger do not end with Hunt's testimony. Praeger appears to have had a business relationship with Allen Dulles after Dulles stepped down as DCI. Dulles had caught the brunt of

President Kennedy's wrath over the failed 1961 Bay of Pigs invasion and was forced out of the DCI's office in October of the same year. Outside of Langley, Dulles wielded an unprecedented amount of influence to those who had served under him. Dulles' correspondence and day planners have been archived by Princeton University and show frequent meetings with Frank Wisner, Cord Meyer, and James Jesus Angleton.[33] The contents of the meetings are not recorded by the archives, but it is difficult to believe these men wanted to trade recipes with their former boss. Interestingly enough, there are a number of redactions in the archives for meetings after Dulles left the CIA. This would seem to indicate that Dulles still had some hand in classified matters. Likely the core of Dulles' lieutenants were seeking advice from the ousted spymaster. Praeger also seems to have looked to Dulles for guidance in a January 14, 1964, letter as he relays his views on competitors. Praeger writes of another publishing house:

> …their edition is "authorized" and otherwise quite bad. The translation is particularly lousy. Furthermore, they are doing a good job of acting as a propaganda conveyor belt for the Soviet Embassy.[34]

The letter bitterly continues to discuss an Army contract that Praeger has lost to another publisher. Apparently there was some question with staff members of the USIA about Praeger publishing works from Soviet authors without contracts. The inference could be that there would be no contracts if permissions were gained from these authors by the use of covert methods and the USIA was afraid of a blowback from the Soviet propaganda machine.

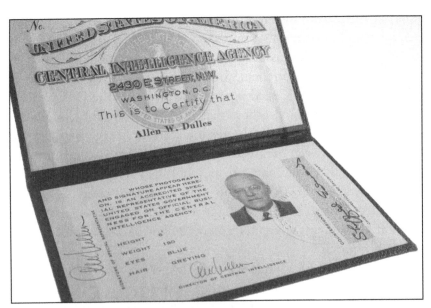

DCI Allen Dulles's CIA identity card. Image courtesy of the CIA.

Praeger's letter would also seem to discuss the early stages of Dulles' book *The Secret Surrender*. The volume published in 1966 by Harper and Row chronicled Dulles' involvement in Operation SUNRISE, which resulted in the unconditional surrender of a million German troops a week before VE day. The German force had dug-in positions in Northern Italy and Western Austria and represented the most cohesive contingent of Wehrmacht in the European Theater. Praeger's letter indicates that the two men were in discussions of a version of *The Secret Surrender*, which would never come to pass. Praeger speaks of "the Italian surrender volume" in his letter to Dulles:

> Your dream of a female paragon of virtues who speaks Italian and can write is a noble dream, but it will not be easy to find her.[35]

It would seem that Dulles was considering using a ghostwriter for a fictionalized version of *The Secret Surrender*. Dulles was likely concerned that some of the materials regarding Operation SUNRISE were still classified and the book could not be published as non-fiction. The two men had obviously discussed the book at length and Dulles had no problem entrusting Praeger to find a suitable shill for writing the piece. Praeger was not directly involved with the publication of a very different *The Secret Surrender* in 1966. Dulles would be credited with writing the text himself and any guise of the pretext of a ghostwriter was forgotten.

Still, 1967 would prove to be a year of dramatic change in Praeger's life. The company that Praeger had nursed into life in 1949 would be sold off to CBS.[36] Through a number of sell-offs over the years, Praeger Publishing is still an imprint of ABC-CLIO publishing house. The timing of the sale coincided with the first cracks appearing in the public shell of Operation MOCKINGBIRD. The editorial staff at *Ramparts* magazine had discovered the CIA had funded the National Student Association from the early 1950s. The publication in *Ramparts'* of these findings in March of 1967 would lead the way for others to delve into questionable CIA projects. By 1975, the lid was off on not only Operation MOCKINGBIRD, but a half-dozen other Agency operations that ranged from domestic spying to plots to assassinate foreign government officials.

The situation between Praeger and the CIA was likely complex at best. No matter what artistic ideas we ascribe to those in the book business, publishers produce books to create a profit. Praeger producing books that filled the needs of the CIA only implies that Praeger was an adept businessman. Had Praeger taken funds from the CIA to publish books at the Agency's behest for propaganda purposes, it holds the connotations of selling out the integrity of Praeger Publishing. How far Praeger went with his relationship with the CIA is destined to be yet another classified conundrum which the public may never sort out. What the theoretical Praeger/CIA connection serves is to show how some aspects of Operation MOCKINGBIRD worked.

Praeger Publishing is not the only media outlet with Operation MOCKINGBIRD connections Steinbeck had ties to. Steinbeck's freelance journalism may have been directed to CIA-sympathetic media outlets. Of the media outlets Steinbeck wrote for from 1948 to 1964, the *New York Herald Tribune, Saturday Evening Post, Louisville Courier-Journal,* and *The Saturday Review* are known to have been part of Operation MOCKINGBIRD. The *New York Herald Tribune's* association with the Agency was mentioned earlier, but bears a mention here as well. Aside from the Alsop brothers working closely with the Agency, the *New York Herald Tribune* is also reputed to have provided cover stories and other resources to Agency officers. The activity was also seen by the *Saturday Evening Post* and *Saturday Review*.[37] The information on specific acts these media outlets performed on behalf of the CIA are still classified and only exist in the public record, thanks to Carl Bernstein's confidential Senate and CIA sources.

The *Louisville Courier-Journal* has the best-documented case of any of the publications Steinbeck wrote for during the time period. In an outlandish twist, the CIA/*Courier-Journal* connection was first reported by *Courier-Journal* reporter James R. Herzog in 1976.[38] Written at the height of the Church Commission, Herzog relays that the *Courier-Journal* hired CIA agent Robert Campbell in 1964 to get experience in newsrooms, presumably to enhance a future cover story. The leadership at Langley could have come up with a better candidate for a journalistic cover as Campbell couldn't type and had horrid writing skills. One assignment given to Campbell by the city editor was to complete a fluff piece on the history of wooden Indians. The article was such a shambles it was never published. Any other reporter who couldn't blow the lid off wooden Indians would have been immediately dismissed from the three-time Pulitzer Prize–winning paper.[39]

A quick look at Campbell's employee file would have given anyone pause to send the cub reporter a pink slip. The underqualified spook was hired by the *Courier-Journal's* executive editor Norman Isaacs with the blessing of owner Barry Bingham. Both Isaacs and Bingham denied they knew Campbell worked for the intelligence agency, but the default setting in any intelligence matter brought to light is denial. According to Bernstein's sources, Bingham and Isaacs would have been well versed in cooperation with the CIA. The *Louisville Courier-Journal* had been taking on assignments for the CIA throughout the 1950s and '60s.

Steinbeck's freelance work for the *Courier-Journal* began after meeting the newspaper's publisher, Mark Ethridge, aboard the *Andrea Doria* when returning from a 1954 European trip.[40] Coupling the *Louisville Courier-Journal*'s complicity with the CIA and Ethridge's background, one can easily make the leap of logic that Ethridge was likely entrenched with the Agency. Ethridge acted as the *Courier-Journal*'s publisher from 1936 to 1963. Taking a hiatus from 1945–48, Ethridge acted as a representative of the State Department on a special mission to investigate the Communist influences in Balkan nations. As part of his duties, Ethridge was the State Department's representative for the United Nations Security Council Commission of Investigation for border crossing violations into Greece from Soviet Bloc Balkan nations supporting pro-Communist forces in the Greek Civil War.[41] The Greek Civil War was a hot-button issue for the Truman administration that resulted in Truman's doctrine of financial and military assistance to any country besieged by Communism. It would be quite unlikely that the Greek situation would not have necessitated Ethridge having extensive contact with the intelligence community to complete his investigations. The contacts Ethridge made with his State Department stint might also explain why he was named as a trustee to the Ford Foundation from 1954–67. We have already seen a number of examples in which the Ford Foundation was linked to funding CIA front organizations.

John would write primarily travelogues and political commentary for the *Courier-Journal* from the mid- to late-1950s. The vast majority of Steinbeck's frequent contributions to the *Courier-Journal*, and most of Steinbeck's journalism from 1952–1959, have been forgotten, due to the unremarkable nature of John's copy. Steinbeck scholar Robert DeMott even goes as far as to say the body of work was "generally uninspired" and "pedestrian."[42] The two most memorable contributions Steinbeck made for the *Courier-Journal* were covering the Kentucky Derby and both Republican and Democratic Conventions of 1956. To ascertain if the associations with the *Courier-Journal*, *New York Herald Tribune*, and *Saturday Review* to MOCKINGBIRD would require further documentation from the CIA, which may never be

DCI George H. W. Bush at a meeting following the assassinations in Beirut of Ambassador to Lebanon Francis E. Meloy Jr. and Economic Counselor Robert O. Waring, June 17, 1976.
Photo from the Gerald Ford Presidential Library.

forthcoming. It does suffice to say that there are "chancery" lightning strikes around John, the CIA, and these media outlets.

It is worth mentioning that the ghosts of Operation MOCKINGBIRD still haunt American journalism. MOCKINGBIRD was officially terminated by the newly installed DCI George H.W. Bush, who made it very clear in February 1976 that:

> Effective immediately, the CIA will not enter into any paid or contract relationship with any full-time or part-time news correspondent accredited by any U.S. news service, newspaper, periodical, radio or television network or station.[43]

The caveat to this policy was that the DCI could make the call if there were American journalists who *volunteered* their services to the CIA and Bush's policy did not include foreign journalists on the Agency's payroll. At Langley, agents who were running American journalists were told under no uncertain terms they would be clearing out their desks if contact was made with an American journalist asset. For the American journalists in service to the CIA, there would be no pink slips, severance packages, or even a thankful farewell.

One would like to believe that collusion between the intelligence and journalism worlds parted ways in 1976. But in late August 2012, the *Guardian* (UK) reported on an email exchange between the *New York Times* national security and intelligence reporter, Mark Mazzetti, and CIA spokeswoman Marie Harf. In August of 2011, the Agency had caught wind that Maureen Dowd was writing a piece on the CIA's role in pumping the filmmakers with information about the raid on Osama bin Laden's compound. Harf was worried about how Dowd's column would reflect on the CIA. The article alleges that Mazzetti sent Dowd's piece to Harf prior to publication with the message:

> This didn't come from me . . . and please delete after you read. See, nothing to worry about.[44]

The *New York Times* public editor took the hit for Mazzetti's actions and described the email exchange as a "clear boundary violation."[45] The Mazzetti/ Harf email exchange seems to fall in line with the Agency's post-Church Commission policy on journalists, but does not make this instance of swapping information close to ethical.

It is difficult to demonize all of the journalists who were assets for the Agency using Mazzetti and Harf as a singular gauge. The majority of journalists who were, and possibly still are, CIA assets were in the same category as Steinbeck, as mainly passive intelligence gatherers. Furthermore, we should expect that journalists with information about life or death situations should come forward to the proper authorities. For example, if a journalist had caught wind of the plot to bomb the USS *Cole* in 2000, and not reported their findings to the proper authorities, that journalist would have been morally responsible for the seventeen sailors who died that day. The Mazzetti/Harf affair places the CIA/journalist relationship in an area of political gain and is an unacceptable use of both parties' positions. The gray area exists when, and if, the CIA utilizes any journalist to write a specific article. The information given to the journalist might very well be truthful, but ultimately serves the Agency's goals. Let's say a headline of "US Military Closing in on Bin Laden's Pakistani Hideout" was part of a larger operation to force the terrorist leader to change locations. Would the CIA using a journalist in this way violate the journalist's ethical obligation to the public? The slippery slope spirals downward from there to propaganda, planting false stories for operational purposes, and outright abuses of position as the Mazzetti/Harf exchange signifies.

For those journalists who have done work for intelligence agencies, one must reconcile their patriotic duties with their obligation to their readers on a case-by-case basis. To say that all journalists who do, or did, hold standing as CIA assets would paint the issue with too broad a brush. We have seen examples of articles Steinbeck wrote that appear to be Cold War propaganda and the articles written for *Courier-Journal*, *New York Herald Tribune*, and *Saturday Review* should be reviewed with an eye critical of the timing and content to detect the hints of CIA direction. The scope of such an analysis is outside of this text, but raises a worthy project for the proper venue.

In the next chapter, one of the least known of all Steinbeck novels raises another question: Could John have ever used anything from his connections at the Agency for material in one of his books?

The focus thus far in finding links between Steinbeck and the CIA has been to explore where anomalies in Steinbeck's life exist and discern if any Agency activity dovetails with those experiences. Possibly one of the most uncharacteristic moves of Steinbeck's life was the publication of the little known book, *The Short Reign of Pippin IV: A Fabrication*, in April of 1957. Set in an undetermined year in the late 1950s, Steinbeck takes his first, and only, stab at political satire. The novel tells the story of amateur astronomer Pippin Héristal and his unlikely ascension to the throne of France.

The thought of the French people returning to a monarchy is as absurd as French post–World War Two politics. After the war, the French had something of a political identity crisis. Charles de Gaul had created a parliamentary government controlled by a series of coalitions under the moniker of the Fourth Republic. The constitution drafted in October of 1946 was more an appeasement to wildly differing French political parties than a form of effective government. The result was an ineffectual rule by political mobs who constantly tinkered with the government to the extent that between 1946 and 1958, the French changed their government twenty-four times and had seventeen prime ministers.[1] By 1958, the French people were at the point of a civil war when the Fourth Republic was abandoned and a new constitution was penned.

The situation in *The Short Reign* opens with France struggling to find its political voice once again. The power brokers of various political factions cannot agree upon what form their government will take. The only thing they are sure of is that it is time for change to sweep across France. In the incessant bickering of political parties, it is suggested that the monarchy be readopted. The idea takes hold with each of the groups knowing that a monarchy is destined to fail and revolting against a despotic king will make all the parties look like a good alternative to the French people. The only question that remains is which royal bloodline will take the throne. During the fray, the Merovingian representative, Childéric de Saone speaks his mind. The sly Childéric has hung back through the proceedings and has waited for his rivals to come to a stalemate before making his pitch. Theatrically Childéric takes a sip of brandy and brandishes a dagger hidden within his cane. With a bit of a preamble, Childéric advocates the holy blood of Charlemagne should grace the throne.[2] The assembly acquiesces to Childéric, and Pippin Héristal, being one of the last of the Merovingian line, is tapped to be king. The rest of the book deals with Pippin coming to grips with being a king and eventually he is deposed for actually trying to implement change within the country.

No one in Steinbeck's professional circles wanted the book published.[3] Both Pat Covici and Elizabeth Otis thought the novel was not what the public wanted out of Steinbeck and advised he drop the project. Critically speaking, Covici and Otis were right about *The Short Reign of Pippin IV* as the novel was generally panned in the United States. Critic Howard Levant said of the book:

> Pippin's will to institute the good life is a more serious matter than the bulk of the novel's comic dance can sustain. The work has remained a minor one.[4]

Steinbeck was usually quite sensitive to criticism, but shrugged off the warnings of Covici and Otis. In 1959, Elizabeth Otis and Chase Horton's disapproval of his rewrite of Mallory's *Le Morte d'Arthur* would stymie any meaningful work on the project until 1964, but the criticism of *The Short Reign of Pippin* was laughingly brushed aside by Steinbeck. In a letter to Covici, Steinbeck simply states that he's having too much fun writing *Pippin* to stop.[5]

A bizarre convergent evolution was happening in France as Steinbeck was penning *The Short Reign of Pippin IV* in the summer and fall of 1956. An organization registered with French authorities on June 25, 1956, that would advocate the return of a Merovingian king to the throne of France. The organization would grow into one of the most famous and debated secret societies of all time—the Priory of Sion. Considering that there could be some link between John Steinbeck and the Priory of Sion sounds as insane as a connection between Steinbeck and the CIA, were it not for a comment by Steinbeck's son, Thomas. In 2008, Thomas consented to be interviewed by me and we discussed Steinbeck's affinity for the works of Thomas Malory. Offhandedly, I mentioned how the field of study into the Holy Grail and Arthurian legends had exploded with the publication of Dan Brown's *The Da Vinci Code*. Thom mentioned that his father, "never believed in the Priory of Sion."[6] Slightly shaken by the statement, I asked Thomas how John even knew of the Priory's existence. According to Thom, the elder Steinbeck had "connections with scholars all throughout Europe" and "[John] must have heard about the Priory from one of them."[7] Thom also was emphatic that John had spoken to him of the Priory, but he could not exactly remember when.

Steinbeck certainly did not have knowledge of the Priory of Sion in 1956 through any sources made available to the general public. The Priory of Sion was first mentioned in print with Gérard de Sède's publication of an obscure 1962 French book, *Les Templiers sont parmi nous, ou, L'Enigme de Gisors* (*The Templars are Amongst Us, or The Enigma of Gisors*). In that text, there were only passing references to the Priory of Sion. In 1967, Gérard de Sède would publish another text, *L'Or de Rennes, ou La Vie insolite de Bérenger Saunière, curé de Rennes-le-Château* (*The Gold of Rennes, or The Strange Life of Bérenger Saunière, Priest of Rennes-le-Château*) that would outline the Priory of Sion as the secret society written about in *The Da Vinci Code*. Furthermore, *L'Or de Rennes, ou La Vie insolite de Bérenger Saunière, curé de Rennes-le-Château* did not initially sell very well until the paperback edition came out in 1968, the same year Steinbeck died.

The questions now become when did Steinbeck find out about the existence of the Priory of Sion and did knowledge of their goals influence *The Short Reign of Pippin IV*? Conversely, could Steinbeck have given the members of the Priory of Sion the idea of returning a Merovingian to the throne of France? To come to a meaningful hypothesis to these questions, one must overlay the Priory's history with that of Steinbeck and any clues found within the text of *The Short Reign of Pippin IV*. The debate has raged for years that the Priory of Sion was the sole invention of a convicted fraudster—a Frenchman named Pierre Plantard—or a real secret society with roots in the Middle Ages. One must also realize that for the purposes of this discussion, it is irrelevant if the Priory of Sion is a real or a fraudulent organization. In order for Steinbeck's writings to have been influenced by the mythos surrounding the Priory, it does not necessitate validating the claims of the Priory. Steinbeck makes a reference to the mythological story of Leda and the swan in *The Short Reign of Pippin IV*. We do not scramble to see if it is possible that a swan could impregnate a woman, but we do recognize that Steinbeck was versed in mythology in order to make such a reference. The same holds true for the Priory's influence in *The Short Reign of Pippin IV*. One does not have to believe that the Priory has a one-thousand-year-old pedigree in order to explore a link to Steinbeck's writing.

The public history of the Priory of Sion begins on May 7, 1956, when the Priory wrote up registration papers to file with the French government. Since 1901, by law all organizations have to file paperwork with the French government. The process is similar to corporations in the United States filing their articles of incorporation with a state official. The Priory of Sion stated their headquarters was at the residence of Pierre Plantard, who was also the Priory's Secretary General, and the Priory published a newsletter called CIRCUIT.[8] Once the Priory's paperwork was filed on June 25, 1956, the Priory was free to openly congregate and go about their avowed purpose of carrying out "good deeds, to help the Roman Catholic Church, teach the truth, defend the weak and the oppressed." The Priory of Sion, in this form would, be dissolved in October of 1956 only to be reregistered via the French government again by Plantard at seemingly random times until the 1990s.

The spartan title page of the Priory of Sion's *Dossiers Secrets*. Image courtesy Rene Barnett.

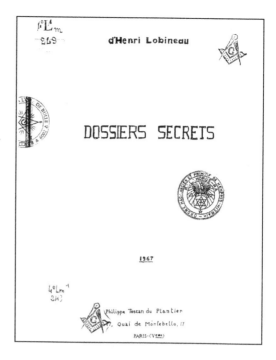

No one might have known about Plantard or the Priory of Sion had it not been for an eclectic collection of documents the Priory produced between 1956 and 1964, mysteriously called *Dossiers Secrets*. These documents were anonymously deposited in the Bibliothèque Nationale de Paris (analogous to the United States' Library of Congress) between 1956 and 1967. Many sources put the date of deposit between 1960 and 1964, however rumors persist in the community of Priory of Sion researchers that the date is as early as 1956. *Dossiers Secrets* is a mishmash of seemingly unconnected genealogy of the Merovingian Kings, newspaper clippings, maps, and a listing of Grand Masters of the Priory of Sion reaching back to the Crusades. Plantard supposedly used these documents to gain the confidence of French author Gérard de Sède. Within the pages of *Les Templiers sont parmi nous, ou, L'Enigme de Gisors* and *L'Or de Rennes, ou La Vie insolite de Bérenger Saunière, curé de Rennes-le-Château,* both texts speculate on the fabulous wealth hidden by the Knights Templar (mentioned earlier in this text) after their arrest in 1307. Plantard insinuated to de Sède that the Priory of Sion was a secret society that had existed since the Crusades. The Priory was also somehow involved with not only the Knights Templar but the mysterious wealth of Rennes-le-Château priest, Bérenger Saunière. Located in the Pyrenees Mountain range, Rennes-le-Château is little more than a hilltop village. Saunière was Rennes-le-Château's priest from 1885 to 1917 and inexplicably was able to spend a fortune in francs improving Rennes-le-Château's infrastructure.

Gérard de Sède's writings caught the attention of BBC writer and presenter Henry Lincoln in 1969 who produced a number of BBC documentaries on Rennes-le-Château and the Priory. Lincoln's take on the affair was that the Priory of Sion actually held information about a supposedly dead line of Merovingian King Dagobert II and Rennes-le-Château was a nexus point in the centuries-old conspiracy. In 1982, Lincoln, along with co-authors Michael Baigent and Richard Leigh, published the controversial book *Holy Blood, Holy Grail*. There the trio of authors speculated that the Merovingian Kings were descendents of the union between Jesus and Mary Magdalene. The Priory's ultimate goal was to place the rightful Merovingian King on the throne of France and announce this King was Jesus' heir. The trio of authors also holds the distinction of discovering the *Dossier Secrets* in Bibliothèque Nationale while doing research for *Holy Blood, Holy Grail* sometime in 1980–81. Dan Brown used Lincoln, Baigent, and Leigh's research as the backdrop for *The Da Vinci Code*, propelling the Priory of Sion into millions of households across the world.

This is a truncated version of the history of the Priory of Sion and the details of the organization are far more convoluted than this abridged history permits. Since the publication of *Holy Blood, Holy Grail*, there have been many who have dismissed the Priory of Sion as a hoax perpetrated by Plantard. Things do look bad for the validity of the Priory considering Plantard was caught up in a fraud investigation in 1993. The subject of the investigation was Roger-Patrice Pelat who had been named by Plantard as a Priory of Sion Grand Master in 1989. A French judge issued a search warrant for Plantard's home to search for evidence related to Pelat's insider-trading indictment. While the French police did not find any evidence related to Pelat, they did find a cache of forged historical documents Plantard supposedly had created as further evidence of the Priory's rightful place as a historical secret society. Plantard was forced to testify about the documents and admitted, under oath, that the Priory was nothing more than a forty-year-old long hoax. Those who believe that the Priory of Sion is a legitimate one-thousand-year-old organization, counter that Plantard's testimony was an effort to keep the intrusion of the government at bay by falling on his sword.

As previously stated, for purposes of this discussion, it does not matter if the Priory of Sion is a fraud or a real secret society. As pointed out by *Inside the Priory of Sion* author Robert Howells, the Priory is real in the sense that there are people who claim to be Priory members and there are documents produced by the Priory. Whether the Priory of Sion existed during the Crusades is open to debate, but from the twentieth century onward, there certainly exists a Priory of Sion. Today the Priory even has an "ambassador" to the world in an Englishman named Nicholas Haywood. His assertion is that the Priory's purpose is to nudge world events in a direction that would bring about the next step in humanity's spiritual evolution.[9]

I contacted Mr. Haywood in November of 2011 to see if the Priory had a known connection with Steinbeck. In the query letter, the theory of Steinbeck having used the Priory as a basis for *The Short Reign of Pippin IV* was presented, as well as Thom's statements about John not believing in the Priory. Haywood's verbatim replay was:

> You've certainly done your homework in respect of Steinbeck. Having contact with, and "believing in" are two entirely different scenario (sic) are they not? I am NOT, at this moment in time, affirming J.Ss involvement with the order, but nor am I denying it. His son, may be correct, but this does not necessarily mean that Steinbeck didn't have contact with Sion, merely that he, perhaps, did not or could not reconcile their methods or modus operandi. I can only make some discreet enquiries on your behalf if that is what you wish (?)(sic)[10]

Since Mr. Haywood claims to be the ambassador of the Priory of Sion, one would think obtaining this information would be in his grasp. The discreet inquiries have been going on for more than a year and Mr. Haywood has never presented any further information about Steinbeck and the Priory.

The "official" story behind the genesis of *The Short Reign of Pippin IV* is that John came up with the idea on Elaine's birthday, August 14, 1952. For the occasion, John rented a château outside of Paris as a birthday party venue. The château's waitstaff was dressed in period costumes and the idea behind Pippin hit Steinbeck while driving back from the dinner party.[11] Steinbeck was ruminating over the party's anachronistic setting and wondered how that would play out in the chaotic modern French political scene. The idea would take a backseat with Steinbeck until he returned to France from May to September 1954.

In addition to being good for generating ideas for a novel, the 1954 European trip also appears to have been taken with the Agency in mind. On March 10, 1954, the FBI would generate a fact sheet on Steinbeck to an unknown recipient. This eight-page document contains three paragraphs redacted "per CIA" under FOIA exclusions b1 (national security reasons) and b3 (information exempt under other laws).[12] Furthermore the reference slips following the March 10th document include file reference numbers with prefixes for espionage and treason. The timing of the report, redactions, and reference files gives a strong indication that the Agency was performing a routine check on Steinbeck before he ventured out into the field once again. The Steinbecks' 1954 trip was quite similar to the 1952 trip, in that their goal was to ramble around Europe finding whatever adventure came their way.

Other bits of intrigue are afoot during the Steinbecks' 1954 Paris stay. Thomas and John IV Steinbeck were living with John during this trip and clearly recalls that every few days, someone from the United States Embassy would drop off an attaché case for John. This case was then picked up a day or so later by a member of the Embassy's staff. This practice was kept up throughout their Parisian adventure of 1954. A young Thomas was not privy to what these communications were, but the transactions are suspicious. At the time, the only previously known tie to the government John had was being infrequently interviewed by the USIA for Radio Free Europe broadcasts. One might expect a list of interview questions to be dropped off at the Steinbeck residence, but not a constant stream of communications with the Embassy during a four-month period. Presented with the theory that John was in the service of the CIA, Thomas indicated that it was entirely possible the document swaps were of a clandestine purpose.[13]

Thomas also recalled that it was not the best of times for anyone to be in Paris. The summer of 1954 saw the fall of France's colony in Vietnam, and tensions in Algeria were rising. Protests in Paris turned violent that summer and there were a number of bombings against American- and British-owned businesses. Thomas recollects a heavy French military presence in Paris during their 1954 stay with machine gunners guarding key intersections in the city. Even with an unstable political situation, the Steinbecks not only stayed in Paris that summer, but John devised a weekly outing with his young sons. Each Thursday the Steinbecks' housekeeper would pack a picnic basket and John loaded Thomas and John IV into the Jaguar John had acquired for the summer. The outing would soon turn into a game of "let's get lost in and around Paris." John and his sons would seemingly randomly drive around the area and stop somewhere interesting looking to have lunch. Commonly, John would run into someone he knew when they stopped for lunch. John's friend would usually stay for lunch and would sometimes show John and the boys around their "lost" destination.[14]

Unfortunately, Thomas could not bring to mind the names of anyone they met during the Thursday outings. "I was just discovering girls and you expect me to remember names?" Thomas responded when asked for specifics. Thomas did think that the trips were odd and now feels that John could have used Thomas and his brother as cover for a covert agenda. "Who would suspect that a guy with two kids was a spy?" Thomas said. Also during that summer, according to Thomas, his father "would just disappear" from their Number 1 Avenue de Marigny home, at random intervals. "There were always reasonable explanations for my father's absences," said Thomas, but he would not discount that John could have been stepping out for Agency business. Part of that business could have been gathering information for *The Short Reign of Pippin IV*. Thomas now believes that this is a reasonable explanation for the genesis of *Pippin* and that his father would have had no issue with writing such a book at the suggestion of the CIA. The notion holds with the unlikely publication of a book that was "wrong" in so many ways.[15]

In the backdrop of French châteaus and constant communications with the American Embassy, the muses would fully speak and *The Short Reign of Pippin IV* would take life in Steinbeck's mind. Steinbeck would write his friend Toby Street that nothing was commercially viable about the novel. The subject matter down to the novel's length would make *Pippin* unattractive to everyone from readers to his publishers, but Steinbeck was so enamored by the idea he had to write the book.[16] In a letter to his editor Pat Covici, John would admit that *Pippin* was a self-indulgence that was more than a missive. "I find myself almost completely believing in it," commented John.[17]

There was no reason that John could not believe in *The Short Reign of Pippin IV*, as a number of the book's elements came from John's life. Steinbeck owned a sword/cane made in Paris much like Childéric. The protagonist Pippin Héristal lives in a building at Number 1 Avenue de Marigny, the same address of Steinbeck's rented house during the 1954 trip. The house is in a rather swanky neighborhood off the Champs-Élysées across the president's residence and next door to the Rothschild's Paris home. Steinbeck also describes the house as being part of the Knights Hospitilar Parisian headquarters in the opening paragraph of Pippin.[18] (Interestingly enough, the Knights Hospitilars were rivals of the Templars and were given a majority of their holdings after the Templars fell in 1307.) Pippin's wife and daughter are very similar to Elaine and her daughter Waverly. Marie, Pippin's wife, is a grounded woman who very much believes in Pippin. Their daughter Clotilde is a precocious girl of twenty who wrote a best-selling novel at fifteen and is currently enamored of an American egg farmer's heir. While Waverly Scott was not a novelist, she was a bright, handsome young lady who was once wooed by a young Robert Redford. In his biography, Redford claims to have visited Waverly once and accidentally walked into a bedroom where John and Elaine were . . . "fluffing the pillows."[19]

Steinbeck was notorious for placing little bits of his personal experiences in his novels. Doc of *Cannery Row* and *Sweet Thursday* is a version of his friend Ed Ricketts; *East of Eden* is semi-genealogical; *The Winter of Our Discontent* shows New England through Steinbeck's eyes. So are there any clues within the text of *The Short Reign of Pippin IV* that may indicate knowledge of the Priory? Other than the storyline mimics one of the avowed goals of the Priory, the Merovingian representative Childéric reads as a mysterious figure that could represent the Priory. Also in Clotilde's romance with the "Egg King" Tod Johnson, we see the ancient fertility symbol that is often associated with Mary Magdalene. In one of *Pippin*'s oddest chapters, Pippin takes his scooter out into the French countryside and finds himself at Château de Neuville. This château is supposedly the same one Steinbeck rented for Elaine's birthday in 1954. Around the château's moat are two statues local hooligans keep pushing into the water. Pippin befriends the château's groundskeeper and they sit drinking wine and admiring the statues. The studies in stone depict the mythological Leda and the swan aside a statue of Pan. Leda and the Swan are closely associated with the alchemical process of distillation and the Priory supposedly still practices the ancient art of alchemy.[20] The pipe-playing rogue Pan is generally associated with being the patron of shepherds in his homeland in the Arcadian woods of Greece.[21] Plantard indicated that a painting by Nicholas Poussin, *Shepherds of Arcadia*, was important to the Priory and the Rennes-le-Château mysteries. The previous assertions could be straight out of *The Da Vinci Code*, but the additions of the statues at Château de Neuville seem to be Steinbeck's invention. The moat around Château de Neuville is a functional and not a decorative feature of the estate and there is nothing to indicate that any such statues were ever on the grounds.[22] One can then assume that Steinbeck had some reason for those two mythological references.

So how do secret societies, the CIA, and John Steinbeck fit together in the backdrop of *The Short Reign of Pippin IV*? The simplest explanation is that if knowledge of the Priory of Sion did factor into *The Short Reign of Pippin IV*, it was through the Agency. Plantard could have been on the American intelligence community's radar since the Second World War. Accounts vary on Plantard's activities during the war from being a Vichy collaborator to operating with the French resistance.[23] Also before the official birth of the Priory of Sion in 1956, Plantard distributed an anti-Semitic, anti-Masonic, and pro-European Union newsletter called *Alpha Galates*. The chance that the Agency became aware of Plantard and his political leanings through either of these venues is quite likely. Given the unstable political situation in France after the Second World War, the Agency would have taken an interest in any organization that might become a player in the unstable government. The inclusion of Plantard and any of the organizations he was behind could easily have made their way into the Agency's briefing of Steinbeck as early as 1952. This would explain how Steinbeck was aware of an organization that was not mentioned to the public until de Sède's works were published. The limited release of *Les Templiers sont parmi nous, ou, L'Enigme de Gisors* and *L'Or de Rennes, ou La Vie insolite de Bérenger Saunière, curé de Rennes-le-Château* in France would have made it unlikely that John heard about the Priory post–1962. There is also an outside chance that French Malory scholar Eugene Vinaver had read de Sède's works and mentioned them to Steinbeck. Vinaver was as hardcore an academic as they come and probably would have discounted de Sède's books even if they did cross into his field of vision.

If one believes that the Priory of Sion was a hoax perpetrated by Plantard, another possibility is that Steinbeck inadvertently created an important part of Plantard's fiction. Those who discount Plantard as a fraudulent hack point to a 1960 magazine *Les Cahiers de l'Histoire* that inspired the genealogical claims of the Priory and Merovingian Kings. *The Short Reign of Pippin IV* was a best-seller in France and was taken well by the French people. As a publicity stunt for the book's release, John's French publishers held a party aboard a boat that trawled up and down the Seine. Flying high above the boat flew a Merovingian flag.[24] It would have been difficult for Plantard to not have known about *The Short Reign of Pippin IV*, especially given his penchant for the line of French Kings. Steinbeck's story could have given Plantard a blueprint in which to create the most enduring portion of the Priory of Sion's myth.

Along the same vein, *The Short Reign of Pippin IV* could have been born out of a need to show the French people how ridiculous their government was. Since the early days of NATO, France was always a wildcard in the treaty organization and would eventually begin breaking ties with NATO in 1959.[25] The Agency could have thought a satirical look at the French government by Steinbeck could have the same rallying effect that *The Moon Is Down* had within World War II resistance groups. John would have been free to write whatever he wished, but the theme had to be couched in terms of the need for France to stabilize its governmental system. If *The Short Reign of Pippin IV* swayed the opinions of the French, it would be difficult to ascertain, but the Fourth Republic did fall a year after the publication of *Pippin*.

Had Steinbeck written *Pippin* at the loose behest of the Agency, this would also explain why John was so vehement about having the book published in light of his advisors warning against the project. If Steinbeck was willing to write "The Soul and Guts of France" as Agency-driven propaganda, it holds that writing a full novel as a reverse psychology type of propaganda would not be out of bounds. Certainly if *The Short Reign of Pippin IV* and "The Soul and Guts of France" were Steinbeck's first forays into international politics with the Agency, they would not be his last.

According to the locals, early May is one of the best times of the year to visit Washington, D.C., Tourists from the Cherry Blossom festival have shipped out and the summer vacation crowds are still a few weeks off. Washington, D.C., isn't a town that ever fully empties of visitors and early May of 1963 was no exception. The majority of those visiting the capital city that year had the single-minded objective of manufacturing memories to impress the folks back home. The quality of hotels or quantity of monuments D.C.'s guests experienced was not part of the equation. Whether they consciously understood it or not, D.C.'s pilgrims of the past two years wanted to recount the feeling of Kennedy's Camelot.

However, there was little feeling of Camelot in the State Department offices when John Steinbeck and Edward Albee visited that May. The pair had been summoned to attend a number of classes that were designed to keep them safe during a Russian goodwill tour in October. As part of a State Department cultural exchange program that had its roots in Nelson Rockefeller's OIAA, the program had taken on a different face during the Cold War. In 1955, President Eisenhower and Russian Premier Nikita Khrushchev met in Geneva, taking the first steps of hammering out the differences between the two countries. One of the elements that precipitated from the summit was a need to build mutual understanding by having those without government ties visit the other's country. Scientists, artists, and those in various business concerns would make the trek across either side of the Iron Curtain to build the metaphorical bridges today's workshop facilitators are so fond of.[1]

For any journey, there must be preparation, and for Steinbeck and Albee, the stakes were slightly higher than leaving one's deodorant on the bathroom vanity. While not officially part of a diplomatic mission, both men would represent the United States to the Soviet people and that posed inherent risks. The two men would be briefed on everything from local customs to what type of food they could expect to eat. After the talks on borsht and Soviet taxi services, the real education began. Steinbeck and Albee were taught how to avoid being used as Soviet propaganda. There was a very real threat that the Soviet intelligence services would try to snare the men with everything from their own words to sex. The classes were enough to put anyone off from taking the trip. Steinbeck was an old hand at the Soviet gambits, but Albee had never been to Russia and still the discussions of bugged hotel rooms did nothing to affect his resolve.

The Berlin Wall Monument at CIA Headquarters in Langley, Virginia taken in 2009. The components of the monument are actual items preserved from the Berlin Wall. Image courtesy of the CIA.

"I thought we were doing important work then and the risks didn't bother me," said Albee about the cultural exchange program nearly fifty years after the fact.[2]

For Edward Albee, the chance to accompany Steinbeck to Russia was "one of his life's greatest accomplishments."[3] The playwright of *Who's Afraid of Virginia Woolf* and a lifetime Tony Award winner making such a statement tells one how significant the trip's purpose was. Albee and Steinbeck would be in Russia for the first anniversary of the Cuban Missile Crisis. To have gone from the brink of nuclear war to standing in Moscow in the space of a year was a surreal turn of events. In speaking with Albee about the voyage, there was a hint of remorse in his voice. In Albee's mind, the cultural exchange program contributed to the end of the Cold War, but no one seems to have taken notice. When the Berlin Wall fell in November of 1989, the Soviet Union's decision-makers were made up of college students Albee and Steinbeck spoke to in 1963. The Cold War is analogous to Albee's *A Zoo Story* taken on a global level. Two countries with preconceived notions, struggling to stave off a predestine violent solution to their problems, is not far from the experience of Peter and Jerry in *A Zoo Story*.

Albee's chance to be part of the cultural exchange program might not have happened for either of the men had it not been for a change of heart in Steinbeck. During the 1960 election cycle, Steinbeck was less than captivated with Kennedy. Steinbeck's loyalties had lain with Adlai Stevenson during the last two presidential campaigns where Steinbeck had actively campaigned and wrote speeches for the underdog candidate. It was evident from the 1960 primary results that Stevenson's ship had sailed after losing 1956's presidential race against Eisenhower. Steinbeck didn't buy into the cult of Kennedy that had popped up during the democratic primaries. Many of Kennedy's more colorful detractors took exception to his Catholic faith, fearing Kennedy would turn the United States into a Catholic theocracy. Lurid witticisms like, "Do you know why Catholic churches are built on hills? Because hills make good gun emplacements," were bandied about by the theocracy conspiracy mongers.[4] Steinbeck's concerns were far from pedestrian apprehension over religion and reached into the realm of family history. To Steinbeck, the Kennedy family patriarch Joseph was a crooked banker whose sons couldn't be much different. The rather harsh evaluation of the Kennedys left little room for Steinbeck to wish JFK a successful presidential bid.

The usually stubborn Steinbeck would eventually change his preconceived notions of JFK during his campaign and early days in office. The campaign promises of rum runner Joe's progeny imparted a sincerity Steinbeck had never expected from the younger Kennedy. The highest regard for Kennedy was shown by Steinbeck when he offered his thoughts on the young president's first international crisis as the Berlin Wall was constructed. As previously mentioned, Steinbeck wrote a monograph on how the Berlin Wall's construction could be made to look ridiculous by having West Berliners hang laundry on barbed wire and paint murals on their side of the fence.[5] Unknown to Steinbeck was that if anyone got too close to the wall, even on the West Berlin side, the East Berlin guards were likely to open fire on the intruders. While "The Wall" letter to Kennedy might be tallied as yet another harebrained scheme of Steinbeck's to a president, the effect on Kennedy was that of fondness for the author's considerations. "The Wall" was likely one of the reasons Kennedy extended the invitation to Steinbeck for Soviet cultural exchange. Steinbeck, in turn, suggested that Albee, twenty years Steinbeck's junior, be invited along to represent the next generation of American writers. Also at John's instance, Elaine would also be part of the junket. Everything was as it should be, including the fact that John was still working with the CIA.

Going back to the evidence in John's FBI file, there are indications of CIA fingers in the 1963 Russian trip. A copy of an October 29, 1963, article "Steinbeck in Moscow Impressed by Progress" that appeared in *The Worker* made its way into the FBI file. The page subsequent the clipping has been fully redacted by the CIA under our old friends FOIA exceptions b1 and b3. After the redacted page, there is a reference sheet that is linked to a summary report of FBI files that have been sent to the Agency. The reference sheet lists two files that are marked "CIA Info" with the prefixes for espionage and foreign counterintelligence. The redacted page could very well have been an after-action report on John's findings during the 1963 trip. Certainly the redactions and reference sheet file prefixes give us a signal that there was a component to Steinbeck's activities that were of importance to the Agency. If John was willing to become a CIA asset in 1952, it is likely that nothing had changed nine years later. One specific element of the 1963 trip fits in with the conclusion that John was still working for the CIA.

Steinbeck in Sweden during his trip to accept the Nobel Prize for Literature, 1962.

Though much of the two months Albee and Steinbeck spent behind the Iron Curtain was what one might expect out of a cultural exchange, the pair was constantly talking to student groups, attending dinners in their honor, and otherwise being the American role models the State Department expected them to be. Albee remembers that when attending functions involving university students, one could always pick out the KGB agents. "They were the forty-year-old students with full beards."[6] The predictions of their State Department mentors were spot on as well. Soviet intelligence tried every covert method at their disposal to discredit the two men. Albee was approached on more than one occasion with dangerous liaisons he turned down. To prove the rooms were bugged, Steinbeck spoke into the light fixture of his and Elaine's hotel room that he really wished he had a bottle of champagne. Like magic, a few minutes later a bellhop dutifully knocked at the door bearing the bubbly. There were also tense moments in which neither man could keep their composure. At one student meeting, the KGB officer in the lot asked Steinbeck why he once told the truth about America in his novels, but his recent efforts were all lies. Albee recalled that Steinbeck's eyes flashed as he jumped out of his chair and started the retort with, "You motherfucker if you think my books are lies . . ." It was difficult for anyone to tell what the rest of Steinbeck's statement was as both the hosts and Steinbeck's State Department handlers jumped in to diffuse the situation.[7]

The official meetings with students led to unofficial late-night meetings with the more rebellious students. Steinbeck would sometimes sneak out of his hotel room at night to ostensibly speak with the more rebellious youths about their writing.[8] Whipping up the imaginations of young dissident writers could have been the entire intent of Steinbeck's assignment during the 1963 trip. Certainly the gambit would be a relatively low-risk proposition for both the CIA and for Steinbeck. A sixty-year-old Nobel Prize–winning author taking a little extra time out with a Russian youth in love with the written word could be explained away even to most hardcore KGB agents. Since we do not know exactly what was discussed in these late-night forays, Steinbeck could have been doing anything from inspiring the young Soviet writers to feeling out assets for the Agency. One thing is for sure, if Steinbeck had to meet with student groups on the sly, his American handlers would have been in full cooperation. Both Albee and Steinbeck were assigned a specific translator/guide from the State Department that accompanied each man wherever they went. For the majority of the trip, the American Embassy officer was the same, but at different points their guide either changed or other Embassy personnel showed up at an event. Albee felt that at any given time, there were even odds one of the State Department fellows was a CIA agent and also claims that the Agency never approached him for intelligence work on the trip.[9]

Albee viewed any intelligence work during the 1963 trip as somehow sullying the trip's pure intent and denies that either he or Steinbeck was involved with the CIA.[10] However for much of the Soviet tour, Albee and Steinbeck had different appearance schedules and did not always travel together. From Albee's perspective, there would have been no evidence of Steinbeck's *sub rosa* agenda. Upon returning to the United States in mid-December 1963, both Steinbeck and Albee were debriefed by the State Department. Steinbeck's debriefing lasted three days.[11] Albee couldn't exactly recall how long his debriefing was, but he does remember that it was nowhere in the neighborhood of three days. The best Albee could estimate was the chat with State Department officials took the better part of a day. One has to wonder why John was given the third degree for two extra days. Either Steinbeck was long winded or there was much more the elder author had to report than his younger companion.

In attendance at both men's debriefing was Assistant Secretary of State for Education and Culture Lucius D. Battle.[12] The long-standing diplomat was no stranger to espionage. While holding the post of First Secretary at the United States Embassy in Copenhagen during the mid-1950s, Battle was the primary point of contact for the legendary CIA operative Dorothy Bauman.[13] Battle would later have an association with Frank Wisner's lieutenant, Cord Meyer, as they co-chaired the CIA-driven Inter-Agency Youth Committee in April of 1962.[14] During Steinbeck and Albee's 1963 Soviet trek, Battle was attached to the State Department's Bureau of Education and Cultural Affairs, which oversaw projects like the cultural exchange program. Among the Bureau of Education's staff was at least one ex-CIA agent, Guy Coriden, and a former Ford Foundation employee Phil Coombs.[15] If the Bureau of Education and Cultural Affairs didn't operate with an association with the CIA, the branch of the State Department was missing a fine opportunity.

One of the connections Steinbeck made in Russia that would have been of interest to Battle and the Agency was in the editors of the dissident *Novy Mir*

(*New World*) magazine. Published in Moscow since 1925, *Novy Mir* was a run-of-the-mill literary publication. In the early 1960s, the editors changed the magazine's focus from featuring mainstream Soviet authors to publishing the works of the dissent fringe. In November of 1962, *Novy Mir* printed Aleksandr Solzhenitsyn's novella *One Day in the Life of Ivan Denisovich* about life in the Gulag. Steinbeck would also write for *Novy Mir* and receive payment for his work in April of 1964.[16] In early 1964, there was some connection between John and the pro-Communist Russky Golos Publishing Company. Steinbeck's FBI file indicates that the report of the Steinbeck/Russky Golos connection was sent to the CIA in March of 1964.[17] One would expect Steinbeck to prop up rebellious Soviet magazines, but having dealings with Russky Golos is further confounded considering Russky Golos' president Theodore Bayer was thought to be a high–level Soviet GRU agent.[18] Espionage does make strange bedfellows and one can only assume that any dealings Steinbeck had with Russky Golos were at the Agency's behest.

Taunting us all the way, Steinbeck made a remark in an August 1964 letter to his personal assistant Nancy Pearson. John had just sent out a preprinted letter as an expanded thank-you note to those he had contact with during the 1963 trip. Steinbeck realized that he had made a huge mistake by sending a form letter and a number of the recipients were less than impressed by not getting a personal letter from Steinbeck. At the end of the letter to Pearson, Steinbeck relays that:

> I am engaged in urgent work which is only slightly less top secret than atomic weapons, and I hope is more destructive.[19]

While the statement to Pearson is meant to be a witticism, one can imagine the twinkle in Steinbeck's eye as he penned the words.

Transworld Airlines (TWA) Flight 514 took off for a quick hop between Indianapolis and Washington, D.C.'s, Dulles International on the morning of December 1, 1974. Nothing seemed out of the ordinary to the seven crewmembers and eighty-five passengers aboard the Boeing 747 as the plane made a routine flight. That condition would change while flying over Virginia's Blue Ridge Mountains. At 11:01 a.m., the aircraft's crew received flight path instructions from Dulles' control tower and the flight rapidly deteriorated in eight minutes. At 11:09 a.m., Flight 514 slammed into the west slope of Weather Mountain. The events of a mere eight minutes turned a normal flight into a tragic accident. The National Transportation Safety Board (NTSB) had a laundry list of reasons those ninety-three people lost their lives that December morning. Micro-airbursts, poor visibility, bad communication between Dulles' tower and the flight crew, and misinterpretation of instrument data were all found to be contributing factors to the accident.[1]

As tragic as the human cost of misjudgment was in the case of Flight 514, an airplane accident would not normally be the type of news that would raise many eyebrows in Washington's power elite. However, this tragedy did ruin the lunch plans of a number of government officials. The concern from Washington was not because of the accident itself, but of where the accident happened. Flight 514 had gone down within a mile of a secret bunker complex buried hundreds of feet below the top of Weather Mountain. In the event of nuclear war or natural catastrophe, elements of the government would be whisked to the safety of Weather Mountain's grotto. As far as the American public was concerned, Weather Mountain's name derived from a 1907 atmospheric observatory and the National Weather Service still used the desolate mountaintop for research purposes.[2] Now within hours of Flight 514's crash, hundreds of first responders, NTSB accident investigators, media, and civilian onlookers would be on top of one of America's best-kept secrets.

After arriving on the Blue Ridge Mountain's site, it didn't take long for *Washington Post* reporter Ken Ringle to start asking questions. The only official comment Ringle could get was from a spokesman for the DoD saying he was not allowed "to comment on what Mount Weather was used for . . . or how long it has been in its current use."[3] Ringle was able to work out the true purpose of Weather Mountain and published an article in the *Washington Post* the next day entitled "Hush-Hush Mt. Weather Is a Crisis Facility."

DCI William Colby would have been one of those persons in Washington who had to rearrange their calendars on December 1st. Had William Colby been a spymaster in ancient Greece or Rome, the crash of Flight 514 might have been recognized as an omen foreshadowing the tenor of the rest of December. The ancient counterpart of William Colby would have called upon his soothsayers to examine the entrails of a chicken, or some other beast, to obtain a glimpse at what the next thirty days would hold. Pattern recognition and predicative algorithms have replaced the superstitions of omens and the old ways have been shuttled away as a literary device. So the modern-day William Colby would have seen the crash of Flight 514 as a random event with no more meaning than a turn of bad luck. In this case, Colby would have been better served listening to the genetic memories of his ancestors. Had he listened to the omen of Flight 514, he would have heard, "Nothing stays secret forever."

Along with working stiffs everywhere, the Director of the CIA has the right to hope for an easy week before Christmas. Colby's last hurdle before the holidays was a meeting with CIA counterintelligence Chief James Jesus Angleton scheduled for December 17th. The famously paranoid Angleton's antics had become a liability to the CIA's counterintelligence efforts and therefore a threat to the entire Agency. Colby had little choice but to issue an ultimatum to Angleton to either retire or accept a "consultant" position within the Agency.[4] Angleton, who had been hunting unseen Soviet moles within the CIA for years, would have undoubtedly seen Colby's move as another conspiratorial step in Moscow's slow takeover of the United States. For Colby, the meeting with Angleton was another stride in clearing a longstanding problem. Barring any international crisis, the meeting with Angleton should have been "it" before Christmas. "It" wasn't. The omen of Flight 514 was about to show itself.

The premonition appeared the next day in the form of a phone call from *New York Times* reporter Seymour Hersh. The journalist had been following the trail of a huge story that involved illegal activities by the CIA and wanted a sit down to discuss the allegations with the DCI. In Colby's words, the call would "not only ruin the Christmas season for me, but nearly all of the rest of the next year as well."[5] Colby set a meeting with Hersh for December 20th knowing, as any spy does, the only way you can combat a threat is to find out what that threat is capable of.

The CIA had been involved with many questionable activities since its inception in 1947, and Colby was well aware of most of them. In 1973, while the CIA's operations chief and director-designate, Colby had helped compile a listing of the Agency's "questionable practices" at the behest of DCI

James Schlesinger.[6] The list was racked up amidst allegations the CIA was involved in the Watergate scandal. Schlesinger wanted to ensure that, *sans* any other sins, the CIA had nothing directly to do with Nixon's Watergate folly. The result of this effort was 693 pages of documents that would become known as the "Family Jewels." While the document was far from 693 pages of explosively damning indictments of CIA activities, the Jewels held enough transgressions to have worried Colby. There was no way for Colby to know exactly what Hersh had on the Agency until their meeting. Spies never like operating from a position of weakness, but there was little Colby could do to improve his situation.

Colby and Hersh did have a past history that would likely fall in favor of the journalist. The dogged reporter had won a Pulitzer Prize for uncovering the My Lai massacre and earlier in 1974, Hersh had come to Colby with a story that seemed more science fiction than CIA operations. Hersh had confronted Colby about the *Glomar Explorer*'s mission while the ship was performing salvage operations.[7] Colby had asked Hersh to hold off on publishing the story until the salvage operation was complete. Hersh was a reasonable man who didn't want to spark an international incident and held the article until the *Glomar Explorer*'s mission was completed. For Hersh's silence in the *Glomar Explorer* matter, Colby owed Hersh a debt. Wittingly or not, William Colby would pay his debt to Hersh with interest on December 20th.

Hersh would have wasted little time with pleasantries during his meeting with Colby. If Colby confirmed Hersh's suspicions, the time he had spent developing his information since August was set to be the biggest find of Hersh's career. The CIA had conducted surveillance of American citizens on American soil. Specifically, the CIA was interested in those whipping up protests against the war in Vietnam. The National Security Act of 1947 specifically forbids the CIA from conducting any operations within the borders of the United States. If Hersh's accusations were confirmed, the legal implications for members of the CIA participating in illegal surveillance could be staggering. There was a real danger of CIA agents being prosecuted for their actions. Falling on the heels of a country poised to prosecute President Nixon for obstruction of justice, any notions of public servants being above the law had dissolved.

Colby was well familiar with a number of domestic operations the Agency was conducting, but had no idea how much Hersh knew or could prove. Hersh opened up with questions about Operation CHAOS. The late 1960's CIA action was designed to conduct domestic surveillance of Vietnam war protestors. The next statement from Colby would prove to be a pivotal point in the spymaster's life. "A few incidents of the Agency straying off the straight

President Gerald Ford meeting with the National Security Council in the Cabinet Room of the White House, 1976. William Colby is seated at the far left. Photo courtesy of the Library of Congress.

and narrow," would be Colby's response to the reporter.[8] Hersh took Colby's statement as an implicit confirmation of the accusations and the front page of the *New York Times* ran the headline: "Huge CIA Operation Reported in US Against Antiwar Forces, Other Dissidents in Nixon Years," on December 22, 1974. The article triggered outrage in an American public that was already reeling from the implications of Watergate. The Senate had never extracted their pound of flesh from the Agency over Watergate, finding no credible direct link between the break-ins and the CIA, and now took another stab at the Agency's leadership.

In early January of 1975, President Ford called for a full Legislative branch investigation into the supposed misdeeds of the CIA. This call to action by the president would be known commonly as the Church Committee and politically Ford hoped the hearings would quell the growing calls for CIA blood within the Legislature and media. In reality, Ford had no intentions of allowing Hersh's accusations to be fully investigated. At a January 16, 1975, luncheon for the publishers and editors of the *New York Times*, Ford announced that the contents of the "Family Jewels" files mentioned in Hersh's article were matters of national security and therefore off limits to the media and public hearings. Without the ability to access the entirety of the "Family Jewels," Ford's tactic would have limited the scope of questions the Church Committee could pose to the CIA. In Ford's grand announcement on the matter, the president went one step too far in commenting that the "Family Jewels" would "blacken the reputation of every President since Truman." Upon hearing this, a *New York Times* editor perked up and asked, "Like what?" Ford clumsily answered, "Like assassinations . . . but that's off the record."[9]

There would be no shielding of the "Family Jewels" now and Ford's "off the record" comment turned Colby into a convenient scapegoat for the damning documents. The President's blooper would cause Colby to be at the beck and call of the Church Committee for most of 1975. There was a quandary at the very core of Colby's patriotism during the proceedings. As an American citizen, he felt that all government agencies should be accountable to the duly elected representatives of the people. On the other hand, there is a level of secrecy that exists within the covert world that is necessary for the transaction of normal business. In May, Colby testified before the Church Committee:

> These last two months have placed American intelligence in danger. The almost hysterical excitement surrounding any news story mentioning CIA or referring even to a perfectly legitimate activity of CIA has raised a question whether secret intelligence operations can be conducted by the United States.[10]

Trying to find the line of parity between secrecy and accountability, during the course of the Senate hearings, Colby would end up speaking about a number of those "straying off the straight and narrow" CIA operations. From allegations of assignation plots of the Vietnam war's PHOENIX Program to experimenting with LSD-based mind control in MK-ULTRA, Colby opened up more about CIA operations than all other DCIs combined. Within the ranks of the Agency, Colby was equally lauded and vilified. Some at the Agency felt that Colby's remarks had been tantamount to treason and needlessly exposed assets. Certainly Colby outing MOCKINGBIRD did put every American journalist on foreign soil in danger of overzealous intelligence services leveling charges of espionage against even the most innocent among them. Conversely there were those in Langley's ranks who agreed with Colby's openness and understood the DCI's moral dilemma.[11] Can a spy agency, whose success or failure is directly proportional to the level of secrecy that organization can achieve, ever truly have public oversight?[12]

Colby's crusade during the Church Commission would become a Pyrrhic victory for the spymaster. On the recommendation of the Church Commission, a number of laws were enacted to redress the sins of the "Family Jewels" and force the CIA to become more forthcoming about operations to the Legislative Branches.[13] By letting idealism overcome political expediency, Colby would pay a personal price for Agency activities he was never in charge of. A man who had begun his service as an OSS agent three-and-a-half decades before would be run out of the DCI's office by President Ford. Colby was obviously a man who "would go with the program" and he cleared out his desk for his replacement, George H.W. Bush, in late 1975.[14]

As egregious as some of the operations Colby, and other CIA operatives, testified about to the Church Committee, Operations HTLINGUAL and MOCKINGBIRD fall within the scope of our discussion on Steinbeck. Within the testimony about HTLINGUAL, we find the final implications of Steinbeck performing long-term service with the CIA. In the summary of the Church Committee findings, Steinbeck's name once again comes up in association with an Agency operation:

> While Bureau requirements clearly augmented the emerging "domestic intelligence" nature of the Watch List, CIA components also contributed generously to this trend. Among the individuals and organizations who came to be placed on the Watch List by the CIA were numerous domestic peace organizations, such as the American Friends Service Committee; political activists, scientists and scientific organizations, such as the Federation of American Scientists; academics with a special interest in the Soviet Union; authors, such as Edward Albee and John Steinbeck; businesses, such as Fred A. Praeger Publishers; and Americans who frequently travelled to or corresponded with the Soviet Union, including one member of the Rockefeller family.[15]

Why would the CIA mention that these people were targets of an illegal mail-opening program?

Steinbeck could have been a target of HTLINGUAL, not because he had correspondence with persons in the Soviet Union, but because the CIA's counterintelligence branch was doing their job to assess the purity of assets and intelligence officers. As painful as it is to set aside the civil rights

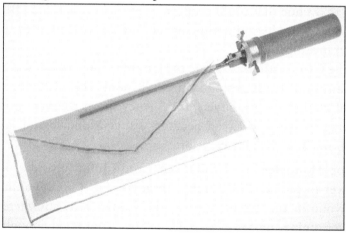

A World War II–era device used to extract a letter from an envelope without breaking the envelope's seal. A similar device would have been used to open mail during Operation HTLINGUAL. Photo from the CIA.

implications of HTLINGUAL, counterintelligence is not purely about finding foreign agents working within one's country. The addition of Steinbeck and Praeger Publishing to the list of HTLINGUAL's targets, if one accepts both had a high level of involvement with the Agency, opens the door into the counterintelligence world. Spies spy on spies. It is a common practice within any intelligence Agency to monitor the activities of their employees for vulnerabilities. The counterintelligence process begins during the application process where candidates are given a thorough background check, polygraph tests, psychological evaluations, and drug tests. After one sets foot in the intelligence world, these activities do not cease and the Agency reminds applicants that:

> Your responsibility to adhere to high standards of personal conduct does not end on the first day of employment. CIA employees undergo regular reinvestigations, including periodic polygraph examinations.[16]

Today, mail opening, phone taps, credit checks, and social media monitoring all are practical methods of the ongoing counterintelligence process. Since we are not privy to what rights an agent, or asset, signs away before working for the Agency, one can only imagine the level of scrutiny faced by intelligence officers. During the writing of this book, the downfall of DCI David Petraeus made headlines across the country. A personal email account of Petraeus was examined by the FBI and led to the discovery of an extramarital affair Petraeus was having with his biographer Paula Broadwell. As the story unfolded, difficulties arose about how and under what legal authority the FBI had to search Petraeus's personal email account. Since extramarital affairs are considered an avenue that could result in a security breach, the FBI may very well have been within its counterintelligence purview to follow the email-trail as part of an investigation.

Any of the CIA's testimony before the Church Commission was a carefully crafted quantum of truth posing as the full monty. By including Steinbeck in the list of HTLINGUAL targets, the Agency shows a clever sight of hand. The following exchange between Senator Walter Mondale and James Jesus Angleton shows how the ploy came off:

> **Senator Mondale:** . . . I think our Constitution provides plenty of power to protect this country. In any event, I see no authority for anyone in the executive or in the Congress or anywhere else for determining, on his own, that the law is not good enough and therefore taking it into his own hands. I see no way of conducting a civilized, democratic society with those kinds of rules.

Now in your system for covert [mail] openings, there was prepared a watch list which set forth certain names of organizations and purposes and those names were the trigger for opening mail to or from them which was sent internationally.

Mr. Angleton: To the Soviet Union.

Senator Mondale: To the Soviet Union. The list included Linus Pauling, John Steinbeck, the author, and Victor Reuther of the Auto Workers. What counterintelligence objective was it you thought you at a bar association convention, that certain individual rights have to be sacrificed for the national security.

Mr. Angleton: Sir, I would prefer, if possible, to respond to that question in executive session.

Senator Mondale: Do you believe that national security cannot be protected except through the sacrifice of these rights?

Mr. Angleton: I believe that all matters dealing with counter-espionage require very sophisticated handling and require considerable latitude.[17]

Angleton deflects Mondale's questions by proposing testimony continue in a closed-door executive session. If pressed, Angleton, or any other representative of the CIA, could explain away the opening of Steinbeck's mail as a matter of ensuring the reliability of an asset. The public reaction to the CIA targeting Steinbeck would still be of outrage, but not unexpected. Just as child actors are always associated with their youthful roles, the perception of Steinbeck as forever the liberal who wrote *The Grapes of Wrath* and visited the Soviet Union three times eternally lives in the public's collective consciousness. Finding out that the CIA targeted a "liberal" author would not be an unexpected move for the Agency and therefore the public impact is somewhat lessened.

Just as Steinbeck's name had been carefully chosen to be offered up to the Church Commission as an example of HTLINGUAL's reach, so were the other persons. Praeger Publishing and Victor Reuther would have been mentioned for reasons similar to Steinbeck. The potential links between Praeger Publishing and the CIA has been discussed previously in this text. Victor Reuther also had ties to the Agency. The United Auto Workers (UAW) labor leader had gained considerable influence in European administrative circles during the early days of the Marshall Plan. Communist infiltration of labor unions had always been a concern of the CIA in the 1950s and '60s and made steps to ally the Agency with the UAW for both intelligence and organizing front companies. Reuther personally oversaw Agency subsidies during the 1950s to various labor groups.[18] The identity of "one member of the Rockefeller family" is anyone's guess. The Rockefeller name and fortune have been associated with the intelligence community since Nelson Rockefeller headed the OIAA. Post–World War II, the Rockefeller family has been linked to the Agency by setting up front foundations.[19] By using persons with CIA links in the HTLINGUAL testimony mix, the Agency created an effective firewall against further legislative scrutiny into the program.

The only two names in the seemingly random HTLINGUAL Church Commission proffer that did not have CIA links were Edward Albee and Linus Pauling. Edward Albee was a safe option because he is a true believer in the American government and was linked to Steinbeck by way of their 1963 Soviet trek. The playwright, by his own admission, couldn't have cared less if the CIA opened his mail. Given the context of the Cold War, Albee believes it was reasonable that his mail was opened and has never attempted to find out why he was targeted.[20] Linus Pauling was another "usual suspect" for the mail-opening program. The Nobel Peace Prize–winning quantum chemist had worked on government-funded weapons projects during the Second World War and could have been classified as a security risk. Unlike Albee, Linus Pauling was outraged that any government Agency had been keeping tabs on his mail and attempted to investigate what mail of his the CIA had opened. Through strongly worded FOIA requests, Pauling took on a twelve-year campaign to have the information released.[21] Out of the persons mentioned in the previous two sections of the Church Commission reports, Pauling was the most vocal against the program.

The CIA has denied my request that any of Steinbeck's letters that were examined as a part of HTLINGUAL be released to the public. The original FOIA request I sent to the Agency very specifically mentioned materials gathered by HTLINGUAL. At the time, I had a secondary objective for the request. Even if Steinbeck was not working with the CIA, there was the chance that the Agency had made copies of unpublished Steinbeck letters during HTLINGUAL. The Agency could be sitting on a treasure trove of previously unknown letters by the author. Secrecy outweighs historical merit and we are left wondering what the basement of Langley may hold.

In this way, John Steinbeck's service to the CIA concluded six and a half years after his death in 1968. One of America's greatest authors metaphorically pulled one more covert maneuver by having his name invoked during the Church Committee hearings. It's not the Hollywood ending of a typical espionage movie, but for Steinbeck, the extreme irony might have brought a smile to his face. Steinbeck joined the brotherhood of those who have wrapped themselves in a cloak, armed only with a dagger, out of the same unselfish motivation that caused him to write *The Grapes of Wrath*—service to one's country. As maudlin and trite as concepts of loyalty to one's country are in a conspiratorial post-September 11th world, in 1952, the landscape was viewed in terms of white and black hats. Through the revisionist lens, we now know that was never the case. The United States of America has not always acted on the side of righteousness, altruism, or even divinely inspired wisdom for that matter. On the morning of January 28, 1952, when Steinbeck wrote to DCI Smith, the reality of America was different because "we the people" willed it so. The strength of that resolve came from the conviction that if, as a country, our actions were not pure of heart, at the very least, our motivations were.

An examination of motivations has always held sway with Americans. In looking at the HTLINGUAL or MOCKINGBIRD operations, we question not the actions of the CIA so much as what their motivation behind performing these actions was. Did the CIA illegally open citizens' mail and use journalists as assets for the best interest of the citizens of this country, or was the CIA acting as a despotic force attempting to leverage their powerbase for the good of the Agency? Did the United States invade Iraq and Afghanistan over actionable intelligence gathered from the September 11th attacks or was the move into both countries driven by resource-demented colonialism? One could almost forgive an oversight of the law if the result was successful and had a reasonable motivation. If that sounds outlandish, consider a pop culture example from the Cold War.

In a two-part episode of CBS's *Magnum PI*, "Did You See the Sun Rise?" (1982), the paragon of virtue, Thomas Magnum, shoots a KGB Colonel who had once tortured Magnum in a Vietnam prisioner of war (POW) camp. The outcome of the episode would not have been that shocking, as Magnum shot one or two folks an episode, had it not been for the circumstances around the shooting. In the final confrontation, Magnum catches the Colonel unarmed and far away from any witnesses. Our Hawaiian-shirt clad sleuth has found out the Colonel has become an assassin whose resume would have shamed Carlos the Jackal, and is planning a hit on Ronald Reagan or Margret Thatcher. The Colonel reminds Magnum that his code of ethics would never allow him to shoot an unarmed man and confidently turns to walk away. After a moment's hesitation, Magnum asks the Colonel, "Did you see the sun rise this morning?"[22] As the Colonel turns and answers that he did, Magnum promptly shoots the Russian in cold blood.

"Did You See the Sun Rise?" quickly became one of the most controversial two hours of television during the 1982 season. Luckily for Magnum, the show's writers gave the character a high ground on which to stand. Magnum's unlawful killing had the long-term result of saving lives. The public might not have been so willing to give Magnum a pass had he shot the KGB agent in a revengeful fit over atrocities in Vietnam. The difference between congratulations and condemnations are shades of the perception of motivation. Such is the case with Steinbeck.

It is easy, given the distrusting climate of the American populace, to condemn Steinbeck as nothing more than a puppet of the CIA. When speaking with Edward Albee about the 1963 trip to Russia, I directly asked him if he thought Steinbeck had been working with the CIA. Albee's response was, "If anyone ever thought John Steinbeck was a lackey for the CIA, they didn't know John."[23] That conversation happened before I had obtained Steinbeck's 1952 letter to Smith and I have considered Albee's statement ever since. I have no doubt that Edward Albee did not know that Steinbeck had even offered to work with the CIA, let alone that the possibility exists that Steinbeck was still working for the Agency in 1963. I also believe that Albee's statement is accurate after a fashion. John Steinbeck's work with the CIA was on John's ethical terms. The moral compass of a man like John Steinbeck may slightly waver off true north, but the compass always stayed in John's hand. I do not believe that anyone could have forced Steinbeck to put his compass away in his jacket pocket, never to be looked at again.

"What if," "assume," "could be," "likely," and "possibly" are over-used words in this text. We can thank the FBI and CIA for these words' heavy use. Had these agencies either not destroyed documents or declassified more of their holdings, there would be no need to speculate. While not an exhaustive examination into the questionable and synchronistic areas of Steinbeck's association with the CIA, there is enough smoke to draw a conclusion a fire exists. Whether that fire is for a weenie roast or bonfire, has still yet to be seen. Absent from these pages are mentions of John's friendship with United Nations Secretary General Dag Hammarskjöld, Steinbeck's days as a war correspondent in Vietnam, a curious 1966 invitation to the conspiracy-laden Bohemian Club, and detailed looks at the majority of Steinbeck's overseas travel, post-1952. (Dag Hammarskjöld would have made the perfect target for Steinbeck to glean information . . . I also have it on good authority that some of these topics could be covered in Thomas Steinbeck's upcoming memoirs.) Perhaps the time and tide of additional information will give evidence to dismiss or conclude CIA links to all of those events.

My arguments also show my own personal bias toward John. I have no doubt that I have heard hoof beats and presented zebras where horses were closer to the mark. The effort has been to present areas of Steinbeck's life that could fit a connection with the CIA. The motivation has not been to sensationalize the life of an already complex man, but to start the dialogue about what we don't know yet know about Steinbeck. Call this book a rallying cry rather than a work of absolutes. As such, I know there will be counterarguments and flaming hot posts on Internet forums citing dozens of sources that might have not been known to me while writing this text. As stated earlier in this text, valid arguments are one step closer to the truth. I stand with Thomas Steinbeck's feelings that the truth is far more important than personal egos or reputations built on the bones of John Steinbeck's life and works.

At the time of the printing of this book, there are unresolved FOIA requests and appeals I have made to a number of government agencies. These could take years to resolve and I am not planning on publishing this text just to move on to another project. There are those out there who will cry, "But why publish without exhausting every avenue?" The answer is simply that the story is too important not to "give it the old college try." Also if there is anything to the theories I have presented, public pressure is the only way the FBI, CIA, State Department, or any other government agency will release documents. Hopefully the awareness of the questions raised in this text hold the key to the release of other documents that will prove, or disprove, the contents here within.

Aside from the documents, letters, and circumstantial evidence left in Steinbeck's wake, we are left with the photograph featured on the front cover of this text. The image was taken in 1959 shortly after Steinbeck arrived in the United Kingdom on the SS *Liberte*. The ship had been pressed into service by the Germans during the Second World War and had been handed back to a French shipping line after the conflict as part of a war reparations deal.[24] Steinbeck could empathize with the ship's history, having been somewhat edged into service himself during the war.

Putting on a trench coat to stave off the ever-present threat of rain in the UK, Steinbeck is confronted with a photographer sometime after disembarking the ship. John politely tries to force a smile, because that is what he is supposed to do as a public figure, which comes across as a smirk for the photographer. The expression on John's face betrays a thought of, "Alright, you son of a bitch! Take my picture." Over five decades later, that photo of Steinbeck takes on a different meaning as Steinbeck fully clichéd as the spy in the trench coat. While we're a few steps closer in understanding Steinbeck's trench-coated life, the puzzle is not complete. Until then, there will be that damnable photo of John spurring us on.

Behind the scenes, during the creation of any book, there are those who silently give their support to authors. That support can come in the form of a word of encouragement or at the right time to cracking a key puzzle facing an author. I am truly fortunate to have many such supporters in my life and the word gratitude does not begin to convey my appreciation for these folks.

Laura, Robert, John, and Barbara Kannard—To my wife, son, and parents for never doubting I was on to something.

Thomas Steinbeck and Gail Knight—For text permissions, their support, and assuring me that this project was not tin-foil hat worthy.

Craig Bryant and Cheryl Reels—My alpha read team who were always quick to ask, "What the hell are you talking about here?"

Alice Sullivan—For her superb editorial services and tasty bars of soap.

Barry Edwards—For the cover, contacting Dr. Wendel J. Flanche, and cracking the "Lou for 52" code.

Dave Allen, Tim Avers, Rene Barnett, Dr. Tod Bushman, Jeremy Gossett, Charlie Millson, Susan Scott, Leesa Smith, Brent Swanson, and Gerald Swick—These fine folks know how to keep a secret and allowed me to rant and rave about Steinbeck after receiving the 1952 letters from the CIA.

Kristen Carter of the FDR Library, SGM (retired) Herb Freeman at Psywarrior.org, Eve Berliner of the Society of Silurians, the Stanford University Special Collections staff, the Beach Jumpers Association, the John F. Kennedy Presidential Library, and the New York Public Library Special Collections staff—For their assistance in obtaining research materials for this text that would have otherwise been unavailable.

Dee, Robert, Ahmed, and Kevin—Who made the decision to leave behind a previous life so much easier.

Thank you all!

After pursuing a degree in Finance and Economics at David Lipscomb University, Brian ran small business concerns for three years and entered the world of corporate management in 1998 for an eleven-year tour. In 2009, Brian left his management career to finish his first book, *Skullduggery: 45 True Tales of Disturbing the Dead*, and in early 2010, opened the independent publishing house Grave Distractions Publications. In the last three years, Grave Distractions has published over fifty books for nineteen different authors, including the works of Dead Sea Scrolls scholar Dr. Robert Eisenman of the University of California, Long Beach and American History Professor Dr. James T. Baker of Western Kentucky University. Brian also does freelance writing and his articles have been featured in such places as: *Armchair General Magazine*, CNN, Coast to Coast AM, *Psychic Oracle Magazine*, Red Ice Creations, Yahoo News, and Unexplained Mysteries. Brian is also a 32nd Degree Scottish Rite Freemason and writes the esoteric themed blog, *Grail Seekers*. Assisting Brian in his work is his lovely wife Laura, son Robert, and unholy black cats Preacher and Mercado. Currently, Brian is considering a number of projects delving into Cold War mysteries.

The author standing on the deck of USS *LST 325*. This Navy transport ship landed troops and equipment at the 1943 Salerno invasion.

Follow developments in the Steinbeck story and find out how you can help get more Steinbeck documents released from the CIA and FBI at www.SteinbeckCitizenSpy.com

The following pages are copies of some of the FBI documents and letters referenced in this text. For those wishing to peruse the entirety of Steinbeck's FBI file, the 120-page document can be found at www.SteinbeckCitizenSpy.com. The quality of these documents presented in this section are faithful reproductions of the document set the FBI has made available to the public, warts and all. One must remember that these pages are scans of documents originally duplicated by a mimeograph or early photocopiers and then digitally scanned by the FBI. Hopefully these documents are a visual reference for the type of information held within Steinbeck's FBI file and examples of places the CIA has redacted information.

Contents

Document Appendix

IX-0/S-14305c   27 July 1943

SUBJECT: John E. STEINBECK, 15041 De Gado Drive, Sherman Oaks, California

TO   : Chief, MIS, War Department, Washington, D. C.

1. Attention is invited to our CI-R1 report dated 27 January 1943, Subject as above, representing investigation conducted in the vicinity of Los Angeles, California, and memorandum report dated 25 April 1943, Subject as above, covering investigation conducted in the Second Service Command previously forwarded your office.

2. Inclosed find CI-R1 report dated 13 July 1943 representing investigation conducted in the vicinity of San Francisco, California.

3. This office does not concur in the recommendations by the reporting agent in closing report. In view of substantial doubt as to Subject's loyalty and discretion, it is recommended that Subject not be considered favorably for a commission in the Army of the United States.

4. Undeveloped leads will not be followed in the absence of request, and this case is considered closed in this office.

For the AC of S, G-2:

                                     BORIS T. PASH
                                     Lt. Col., M.I.
                                     Chief, Counter Intelligence Branch

1 Incl: (in trip)
CI-R1 dtd 7-13-43

KLARIN

February 25, 1944

DBC-41036

Mr. Birch D. O'Neal
The American Embassy
Mexico, D. F.

Re: Alto Case

Dear Sir:

Please refer to your cable of February 23, 1944, advising that Jacob Epstein, who has been identified as one of the writers of the secret writing letters emanating from Mexico in this case, met an unidentified individual at a restaurant and conferred with him on the night of February 21, 1944, for forty minutes. This unidentified individual then went to the Russian Embassy and the next day this same individual appeared at the airport in Mexico City in company with Alexei Prokhorov, Russian diplomatic courier who went to Mexico from the United States by plane on January 28, 1944, and was returning to the United States. The unidentified individual then went to the Geneva Hotel, and it was determined that one Paul Klarine was registered at the hotel from 7 East 62nd Street, New York City (the 62 was obtained from a garble and this could be 61), nationality Russian, registered at the Hotel Geneve since November 23, 1943.

Your office stated that it was believed this individual was identical with Pavel P. Klarin, a Vice Consul of the Russian Consulate-General in New York City, and a suspected Russian agent who had left the United States for Mexico in November 1943, but has not been located. You were advised by Bureau cable dated February 24, 1944 that the Russian Consulate General in New York City is located at 7 East 61st Street, and were requested to effect a discreet surveillance of Klarin and to forward a picture taken of him and Prokhorov at the Mexican airport.

Attached for your use are three photographs of Klarin together with his signature. You should advise the Bureau as soon as possible whether Klarin is identical with the unidentified individual mentioned above.

For your information and the information of the offices receiving copies of this letter, the following is set forth. This should be maintained in a strictly confidential manner. You are aware numerous secret writing letters in this case were intercepted up until November 1943, at which time it appears that the subjects became apprehensive of the security of their method of communication. They indicated that couriers were to be used in the future for their communications, and we know that an attempt was actually made to use Mrs. Anna Colloms, New York City, as a courier.

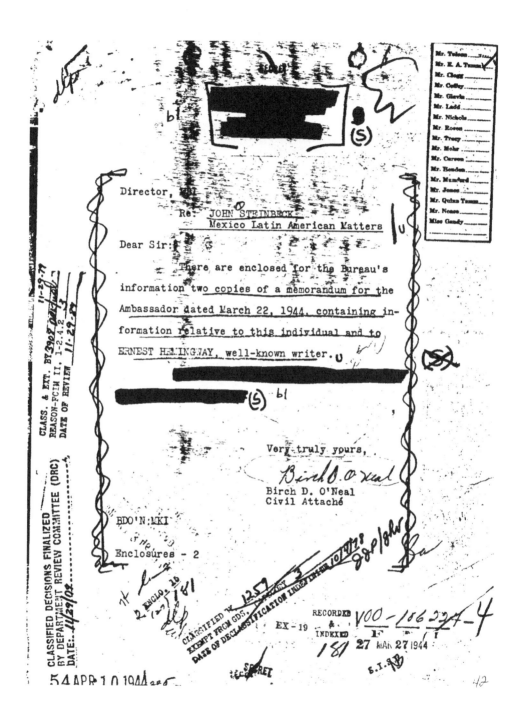

Director,

Re: JOHN STEINBECK
Mexico Latin American Matters

Dear Sir:

There are enclosed for the Bureau's information two copies of a memorandum for the Ambassador dated March 22, 1944, containing information relative to this individual and to ERNEST HEMINGWAY, well-known writer.

Very truly yours,

Birch D. O'Neal

Birch D. O'Neal
Civil Attaché

BDO'N:MKI

Enclosures - 2

EX-19   RECORDED
               & INDEXED

27 MAR 27 1944

S.I.S.

Re: JOHN STEINBECK   Page Two

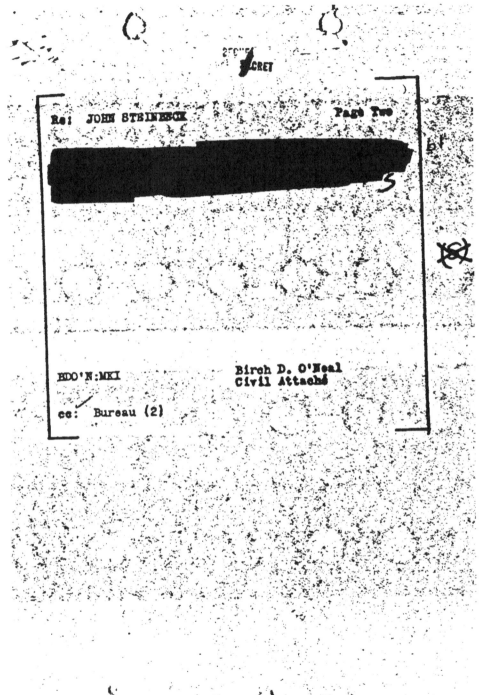

b7

HDO'N:MKI   Birch D. O'Neal
                                   Civil Attaché

cc: Bureau (2)

Steinbeck: Citizen Spy • Page 232

SECRET
Secret

March 22, 1944

MEMORANDUM FOR THE AMBASSADOR:

Re: JOHN STEINBECK
─────────────

As you know, John Steinbeck is a well-known writer who is presently working in Mexico City as a correspondent for the "New York Tribune". U

SECRET   ENCLOSURE

100-106224-7

STANDARD FORM NO. 64

Office Memorandum • UNITED STATES GOVERNMENT

TO : Director, FBI   DATE: April 8, 1944

FROM : SAC, San Antonio

SUBJECT: JOHN ERNST STEINBECK
Incoming Passenger, Brownsville, Texas
3/15/44
FOREIGN TRAVEL CONTROL

ALL INFORMATION CONTAINED
HEREIN IS UNCLASSIFIED
EXCEPT WHERE SHOWN
OTHERWISE

Reference is made to Bureau memorandum to San Antonio dated March 21, 1944, in the above-captioned matter. For the information of the New York City Office, reference memorandum advised that an investigation was conducted by Military Intelligence Division concerning the above-captioned individual to determine his loyalty and suitability to hold a commission in the Army of the United States, and that information had been received by the Bureau indicating that in view of substantial doubt as to the loyalty and discretion of the subject, a recommendation was made that he should not be considered favorably for a Commission in the U. S. Army.

This is to advise that on March 15, 1944, the subject, accompanied by his wife, GWYN CONGER STEINBECK, entered Brownsville, Texas, via Pan American Clipper enroute from the Reforma Hotel, Mexico, D. F. to their residence at 330 E. 51st Street, New York City. At the time of their entry, it was ascertained that the subject was an American citizen born at Salinas, California, on February 27, 1902, and that his wife was also an American citizen, having been born in Chicago, Illinois, October 25, 1918. It was also learned that the subject is presently employed as a writer by the New York Herald Tribune and that in 1943 he had been on a six-months assignment to England, Africa, and Sicily as a war correspondent.

The subject advised that on that assignment he had been slightly wounded and that the purpose of his present two-months trip to Mexico City had been to regain his health before resuming his work for the above-mentioned newspaper.

The above is being submitted for the information of the Bureau and a copy of this letter has been designated for the information of the New York City Office. No further action in this matter is presently contemplated by this Office.

DECLASSIFIED BY 2333 Pem   Army Letter dtd 8-2-78
ON 1-22-79

ERM:dmm   Gaalb;a

CC New York City   CLASSIFIED BY 1259
EXEMPT FROM GDS CATEGORY
DATE OF DECLASSIFICATION INDEFINITE 10/4/78

100-106224 - 4X

RECORDED & INDEXED

APPROPRIATE AGENCIES
AND FIELD OFFICES
ADVISED BY ROUTING
SLIP(S) OF
DATE

EX-2   157

100-166455-3
F   B   I
19 APR 15 1944

01 APR 24 1944

CONFIDENTIAL

March 18, 1952

46576

JOHN ERNEST STEINBECK

Reference is made to your request for information subsequent to February 13, 1948, concerning John Ernest Steinbeck, the writer. The FBI has not conducted an investigation on this individual.

A review of the files however, revealed newspaper reviews from the "Daily Worker" dated April 16, 1948, and the "New Leader" dated August 21, 1948, of John Steinbeck's book, "A Russian Journal". This book was published in April, 1948, by the Viking Press in New York and contained pictures by Robert Capa. The publication was based on experiences which the two "self-styled cold war team" had on a three weeks visit to Soviet Russia during the summer of 1947.

The writers of the reviews both seemed to doubt Mr. Steinbeck's ability to portray life in Soviet Russia authoritatively since he was there for such a short period of time.

(100-106224)

The foregoing information is furnished to you as a result of a request for an FBI file check only and is not to be considered as a clearance or nonclearance of the individual involved. It is for your confidential use only and is not to be disseminated outside of your agency.

Original to State Department

S. H. Rogers:jar

SHR

Mr. Tolson
Mr. Ladd
Mr. Clegg
Mr. Glavin
Mr. Nichols
Mr. Rosen
Mr. Tracy
Harbo
Belmont
Mohr
Room
Gandy

100-166188

100-106224-6

100-166188-4

RECORDED - 120
SE 39
INDEXED - 120

MAR 21 1952

61 APR 3 1952

FBI

RECEIVED

4-750 (Rev. 4-17-85)

FEDERAL BUREAU OF INVESTIGATION
FOIPA DELETED PAGE INFORMATION SHEET

_1_ Page(s) withheld entirely at this location in the file. One or more of the following statements, where indicated, explain this deletion.

☑ Deleted under exemption(s) _b1 , b3 per CIA_ _____ with no segregable material available for release to you.

☐ Information pertained only to a third party with no reference to you or the subject of your request.

☐ Information pertained only to a third party. Your name is listed in the title only.

☐ Documents originated with another Government agency(ies). These documents were referred to that agency(ies) for review and direct response to you.

_____ Pages contain information furnished by another Government agency(ies). You will be advised by the FBI as to the releasability of this information following our consultation with the other agency(ies).

_____ Page(s) withheld for the following reason(s):

_____

_____

☐ For your information: _____

_____

☑ The following number is to be used for reference regarding these pages:
_100- 106224 -9_

FBI/DOJ

2 - o y 1
1 - yellow
1 - Section
1 -

108-106224-9

X-120

April 12, 1957

JOHN ERNST STEINBECK

ALL INFORMATION CONTAINED
HEREIN IS UNCLASSIFIED
EXCEPT WHERE SHOWN

Steinbeck has never been investigated by
this Bureau, however, the files of this Bureau contain the
following information:

Steinbeck was born at Salinas, California,
February 27, 1902. He graduated from Salinas High School in
1918 and was a student at Stanford University for five years
but did not graduate. He married Carol Henning in 1930 and
was divorced from her in March, 1943. He married Gwyn Conger
on March 29, 1943, and Elaine Scott on December 28, 1950.
He has been the author of a number of books and was awarded
the Pulitzer prize in 1940. Among the books for which he is
most noted are "Tortilla Flat," 1935; "Of Mice and Men," 1937;
"Grapes of Wrath," 1939; "The Moon Is Down," 1942; "Cannery
Row," 1945; "The Wayward Bus," 1947; and "A Russian Journal,"
1948. He was also employed as a war correspondent and as a
writer for the "New York Herald-Tribune" during 1943, 1944, 1947
and 1948. (100-106224-7)

A Special Committee on Un-American Activities of the
United States House of Representatives, 75th Congress, published
a report in 1939 captioned "Investigation of Un-American
Propaganda Activities in the United States." On Page 1996 under
the heading of Western Writers Congress, information was set out
that during the Fall of 1936 a group of liberal and communistic
writers issued a call for a conference to be held in San Francisco,
California, on November 13, 1936, which conference continued
throughout the following day. This report indicated that one of
the sponsors of this Congress was John Steinbeck.

A confidential informant who has furnished reliable
information in the past advised in 1948 that John Steinbeck was
one of the writers who attended the Western Writers Congress in
1936. (Former

b2,b7d

CLASSIFIED BY 1259
EXEMPT FROM GDS CATEGORY 2,3
DATE OF DECLASSIFICATION INDEFINITE

WFS:vep
(S)

Orig & dupl to CIA

SEE NOTE ON YELLOW PAGE 12

BY DEPARTMENT REVIEW COMMITTEE (D)
DATE:

CONFIDENTIAL

JOHN ERNST STEINBECK

The Western Writers Congress was described as a
communist front by the Special Committee on Un-American Activities
in its report dated March 29, 1944.

A confidential informant who has furnished reliable
information in the past advised in 1944 that Sam Darcy was in
Russia in 1937 and that Darcy had corresponded with Ella Winter.
The informant stated that a letter from Darcy in March, 1937,
indicated he was pleased to hear about "Steinbeck's new book."
The informant stated Darcy commented that Steinbeck could write
and with the education "I am told you and our friends have been
giving him, he ought to make the grade better than he did in his
early book." The informant furnished no additional information
to identify the Steinbeck mentioned and it is not known if this
person is identical with the subject of your inquiry.
(highly confidential source; 100-18610-56 - pg 29)
        The "Times-Herald," a daily newspaper published in
Washington, D. C., on May 9, 1953, contained an article reflecting
that Herbert A. Philbrick before a United States Senate
Investigation Committee had named Ella Winter, the Australian
born wife of Donald Ogden Stewart, as one of twenty-three men
and women communists in Massachusetts. Additional information
concerning Ella Winter Stewart was forwarded to you on June 4,
1952, in the report of Special Agent ███████████ which b7c
was dated February 18, 1952. (100-18610-A & 222)

        A confidential informant who has furnished reliable
information in the past advised in 1941 that Samuel Adams Darcy
had stated in 1941 that he had traveled abroad in 1935 as he had
been elected by the Communist Party in the United States as a
representative to the Congress of the Communist International
held in Moscow, Russia. Informant advised that Darcy had also
returned to the United States in approximately May, 1937.
b7c   San Francisco,*
b7d   The Committee on Un-American Activities of the United
States House of Representatives, 83rd Congress, in a report
captioned "Investigation of Communist Activities in the Los Angeles
Area - Part 6" contains a statement of Roland William Kibbee,
which he furnished to a staff member of the Committee on June 2,
1953. On Page 2329 and 2330 of the above-described report appears
information which Kibbee furnished in answer to the question,
"What caused your disillusionment with the Communist Party?"
Kibbee stated "I can remember in my own case it even was involved
more or less with the theory of the Communist Party and not outside working in organizations. . . Several of the contradictions
that arose troubled me a great deal. . .

*California; 61-6593-209)

- 2 -

JOHN ERNST STEINBECK

"I remember John Steinbeck who wrote, I thought, a
most effective novel about the agricultural workers in the
San Joaquin Valley, or, take it a step further, that the man did
more for them than anyone else. A motion picture was made of
the very sorry situation that existed there. I recall that
John Steinbeck was at odds with the Communist Party. I can't
say just how. It was a question of hearing them attacked into
work deplored and too bad he doesn't see the light, and so forth,
and these things troubled me a great deal. . ." In this statement Kibbee admitted membership in the Communist Party for
approximately two years beginning in approximately 1937.
(61-7582-1975)

A pamphlet entitled "Their Blood Is Strong" by John
Steinbeck was published in April, 1938, by the Simon J. Lubin
Society of California, Incorporated. The Simon J. Lubin Society
was "deeply appreciative of the cooperation received from the
San Francisco news, who in October of 1936 published the seven
chapters that form the bulk of this pamphlet; and especially
grateful to John Steinbeck for his permission to use this
material." (61-7559-2-999)

The California Committee on Un-American Activities
in its report published in 1943 described the Simon J. Lubin
Society, Incorporated, as a communist front for California
Agrarian penetration, which was organized in the Fall of 1936
by Unit 104 of the Professional Section of the Communist Party.
(California Committee 1942 report - pg 86)

On Page 148 of the same California Committee report
appears information furnished by Rena M. Vale. Vale advised that
the Southwest Unit of the Federal Theaters, which was composed of
communists, had corresponded with the Simon J. Lubin Society in
San Francisco, California, to obtain research material which that
organization had turned over to John Steinbeck for his book (then
unnamed) "Grapes of Wrath" and which Steinbeck had returned.
She advised that when the material arrived she had examined it
carefully and found notes in handwriting signed by John Steinbeck,
which appeared to be field notes on migratory workers.
(California Committee Report, 1943, pg. 148)

A pamphlet captioned "Writers Take Sides" was published
by the League of American Writers, 381 4th Avenue, New York,
New York, in May, 1938, and was described as being letters about
the war in Spain from 418 American authors. On Page 56 of this
pamphlet appeared a letter from John Steinbeck, the author of
"Of Mice and Men" and "Tortilla Flat." (61-7561-2-87)

The "Daily Worker," an east coast communist newspaper,
on April 25, 1939, contained an article captioned "Noted Writers
Back Fight for Art Projects." The article reflected that 38
prominent writers, including John Steinbeck, had made public a
letter urging support of the Federal Arts Project and indicated

that the individuals were acting on their behalf as well as on
behalf of the League of American Writers. (61-7551-183 X 10)

The "Daily Worker" of September 7, 1939, contained an
article captioned "U.S. Writers League Ends Summer Session in
South." The article reflected that a two-week session for student
writers, which was held under the auspices of the League of
American Writers had just concluded. The article described the
League of American Writers as a cultural nonpartisan organization
and indicated that one of the vice presidents of the organization
was John Steinbeck.

The League of American Writers has been designated by
the Attorney General of the United States pursuant to Executive
Order 10450. (61-7559-6678X2)

The records of the Department of State, State of
New York, in 1941 reflected a certificate of incorporation was
filed in 1939 for the League of American Writers, Incorporated.
John Steinbeck, Route 1, Box 95D, Los Angeles, California, was one
of the directors who was appointed to act until the first annual
meeting of the corporation. (100-7322-8)

The "Los Angeles Times," a daily newspaper published
in Los Angeles, California, on January 23, 1941, contained an
article which reflected that John Steinbeck of Los Gratos,
California, was one of the California directors of the League of
American Writers, which organization was dedicated to the advance-
ment of peace and democracy as against fascism and reaction.
(100-7322-16)

The report of the hearings before a Subcommittee of the
Committee on Foreign Relations of the United States Senate, 81st
Congress, on Page 1504 contained information attributed to "The
New York Times" of January 31, 1939. The material was an open
letter to the Government and people of the United States which
urged that the embargo against the Spanish Republic be lifted.
John Steinbeck appeared as one of the persons urging that the
Spanish embargo be lifted. The article ended with a coupon which
urged that all individuals fill out the coupon and forward it
to the Washington Committee to Lift Spanish Embargo, Room 100,
1410 M Street, Northwest, Washington, D. C. (121-23278-267X12)

The Washington Committee to Lift Spanish Embargo was cited
as a communist front in the 1948 report of the California
Committee on Un-American Activities.

JOHN ERNST STEINBECK

In 1950 a confidential informant who has furnished
reliable information in the past and who was an admitted member
of the Communist Party until 1945 advised that Carey McWilliams
was the author of the book "Factories in the Field" published in
1939, which book was the foundation of John Steinbeck's book
captioned "Grapes of Wrath." The informant advised that when
this book was published he had received information from t
Communist Party leaders that McWilliams was under communist
discipline. The informant stated that this information had a
great deal to do with the way the book was handled as well as
Steinbeck's book, because McWilliams at that time was supposedly
making a communist of Steinbeck. (Louis Budenz, concealed 400;
100-998-77)

A confidential informant who has furnished reliable
information in the past advised in 1940 that the Committee to
Aid Agricultural Workers was organized under the leadership of
John Steinbeck, the author of "Grapes of Wrath," and that
Steinbeck was chairman of the Committee. The informant stated
that the Committee had the support of many prominent people in
California and that in the informant's opinion, they were all
people who had been active in behalf of communist united front
organizations.   ███████████ 100-3-23-X6)

A confidential informant who has furnished reliable
information in the past advised in 1941 that the name of John
Steinbeck, Route 1, Box 95D, Los Gatos, California, appeared in
the active indices of the National Federation for Constitutional
Liberties. ██████████████ 100-1170-49)

A representative of another Government agency advised in
1944 that various pieces of literature published in Russia,
including daily newspapers from Moscow, Russia, had arrived in the
United States during 1942 and part of 1943. The informant advised
that some of this material was addressed to John Steinbeck in care
of Elizabeth R. Otis, 18 East 41st Street, New York, New York.
██████████ of ONI; 65-1674-809)

The United States Office of Censorship advised by
letter dated July 4, 1944, that John Steinbeck, 18 East 41st
Street, New York City, had received the February 12, year not
given, issue of the "Moscow News," a newspaper published in
Russia. (65-49005-81)

The report of the Special Committee on Un-American
Activities of the United States House of Representatives,

- 5 -

CONFIDENTIAL

published on March 29, 1944, and captioned "Investigation of Un-American Propaganda Activities in the United States" on Page 101 contained the following: "The National Maritime Union of America, . . . has toed the Communist Party line through all its changes in recent years. (57-407-424)

"These ships of the American Merchant Marine are being supplied with libraries for the seamen to read while at sea . . . John Steinbeck's "Grapes of Wrath" is naturally present, as it would be in any Communists' selection. . ."

b1

(S)

(S)

(S)

- 6 -

CONFIDENTIAL

JOHN ERNST STEINBECK

b1

(S) A confidential informant who has furnished reliable
information in the past advised in May, 1945, that the American
Youth for Democracy in a list captioned "Recommended Reading
List for A.Y.D." contained the book entitled "The Moon is Down"
by John Steinbeck. ████████ 786 Broad Street, Newark, N.J.; 61-777-
3-60) b7E

The American Youth for Democracy has been designated
by the Attorney General of the United States pursuant to
Executive Order 10450.

A confidential informant who has furnished reliable
information in the past advised in 1945 that letters had been
prepared to be sent to John Steinbeck, among others, requesting
that he prepare a testimonial to the valiant Spanish exiles and
the work of the Joint Anti-Fascist Refugee Committee. The letter
requested a 75-word statement be prepared to be made a part of a
leaflet and with an attached photograph it was hoped that such
statements would enlist the widest possible mass support for the
campaign. (Highly confidential source; 100-7061-923)

The Joint Anti-Fascist Refugee Committee has been
designated by the Attorney General of the United States pursuant
to Executive Order 10450.

A confidential informant who has furnished reliable
information in the past advised in April, 1946, that the National
Council of American-Soviet Friendship was planning to give a
reception on May 5, 1946, in New York City in honor of three
visiting Soviet literary figures. The informant advised that one
of the persons indicated to receive an invitation to the reception
was John Steinbeck, the novelist. ████████ 100-146964-796)
b2,b7d

The National Council of American-Soviet Friendship has
been designated by the Attorney General of the United States
pursuant to Executive Order 10450.

"The New York Times" on February 21, 1946, contained an
article reflecting the formation of a cooperative publishing concern under the name of the Associated Magazine Contributors,

- 7 -

Incorporated. The article set forth the initial list of owner-contributors, which included the name of John Steinbeck. (123-11674-13)

The 1948 report of the California Committee on Un-American Activities reflected that in addition to completely communist-controlled and dominated publications there was also a long list of Trade Union, racial, minority, liberal and special interests publications into which communists had infiltrated. The report reflected that the communist influence was established through such news services as the Associated Magazine Contributors, Incorporated, and others. (100-15252-39 - pg 39)

[redacted]

(S)

The October 24, 1947, "Daily Worker," an east coast communist newspaper, published an article captioned "Found Soviets Eager for Peace, Capa, Steinbeck Tell Trib Forum." This article indicated that Capa read a joint report by himself and John Steinbeck at the Herald Tribune Forum. This report purportedly stated that the Russian people were destroyed and hurt much more than any others that they, Capa and Steinbeck, had seen during their many years on the battle fields. The report further indicated that the Russian masses would strongly approve the halt of the "vicious and insane games" of recrimination between Russia and the U.S. It was indicated that the Russians were particularly interested in hearing about "the persecution of liberals" in America. (100-106224)

The "Daily Worker" on April 16, 1948, contained a book review of John Steinbeck's "A Russian Journal," which was described as being a book containing photographs by Robert Capa, which had been published by the Viking Press in New York, New York. The article reflected "John Steinbeck's warm sympathy for people, as evidenced in his 'A Russian Journal,' (published today) is the one positive feature of an account of a visit to the Soviet Union which is otherwise overrun with frivolous provincialism and a coy disinclination to face political realities. . .

- 8 -
CONFIDENTIAL

JOHN ERNST STEINBECK

"What is one to say of a writer to whom the distinctive characteristic of American capitalist society is that it provides a government of 'checks and balances'? Or of the naivete which has it that 'our government is designed to keep anyone from getting too much power or, having got it, from keeping it'? And, 'we agreed,' Steinbeck writes solemnly, 'that this makes our country function more slowly, but that it certainly makes it function more surely...'

"One could go on quoting Steinbeck, but what for? A Russian Journal is much more enlightening about the kind of culture which develops such intellectual Sad Sackery than about the Soviet Union..."

The "New Leader," a weekly magazine, on August 21, 1948, contained an article captioned "Steinbeck Sans Wrath," which was a book review of "A Russian Journal" which was written by Steinbeck and contained pictures by Robert Capa. The article reflected that "Mr. Steinbeck has joined the fraternity of vodka visitors. For three weeks he toured the Soviet Union under the subtle guidance of VOKS, the government agency for 'cultural liaison,'..." The article reflected he had attended the "celebration of the 800th anniversary of Moscow with Louis Aragon, the French Stalinist writer" and had visited the country home of "such Soviet millionaires as Alexander Korneichuk – and concludes that the Russians have plenty to eat; he even states that the quality of Russian clothing improved during the few weeks he spent in Russia..."

The article further reflected "most startling, perhaps, is Steinbeck's own attitude toward the Soviet Union. His book is full of what Koestler would call false equations. When Capa is stopped from taking pictures at a lend-leased tractor plant in Stalingrad, Steinbeck reminds us that foreigners may not photograph Oak Ridge either. In his mind 'Moscowitis' and 'Washingtonitis' cancel each other out. When he admits that the collective farm he was shown put on a big show for him, he insists that 'any Kansas farmer' would do the same for his guests...

"Steinbeck used to be known as a man with a strong social conscience. The Grapes of Wrath 'and Tortilla Flat 'were full of righteous moral indignation about social and economic injustice. In 'The Moon is Down 'Steinbeck made a heated if somewhat pedestrian

- 9 -

CONFIDENTIAL

Document Appendix • Page 245

JOHN ERNST STEINBECK

attack on totalitarian aggression and conquest. Those were the
days when Steinbeck could be counted upon to stand up and wield
his pen in behalf of democracy and freedom. Even today had he
gone to Spain or China, he would surely not have come back to
write a book in order to demonstrate that the 'Chinese people
want good lives and comfort' or that 'the Spaniards like peace.' "

A confidential informant who has furnished reliable
information in the past advised in 1948 that the firm of World
Video, Incorporated, was chartered in New York State on
December 18, 1947, and that the firm prepared television programs.
The officers of the firm include John Steinbeck as vice president
and Robert Capa as assistant vice president.
NYC; 100-340922-111)

The "New York Herald-Tribune" of May 18, 1948, contained an article captioned "Women's Rally in Rome Hears Russia
Praised." The article, which was datelined Rome, May 17,
reflected that the meeting was that of the Democratic Women's
International Federation, whose aim was to fight "American,
British and French imperialists and warmongers." The article
reflected that the chief American delegate, Mrs. Muriel Draper,
chairman of the women's section of the American National
Committee for American-Soviet Friendship mentioned several persons converted to "the camp of war and anti-Sovietism," which
included John Steinbeck.

The "Los Angeles Examiner," a daily newspaper published
in Los Angeles, California, on June 11, 1948, contained an
article reflecting that Ring Lardner, Jr., had signed a contract
with John Steinbeck and others to write a film version of
Steinbeck's story "Pastures of Heaven." The article reflected
this was the first Hollywood employment given "any of the
'un-friendly ten' since their refusal to answer the Communist
question in Washington last fall." (100-295885-11)

The "Daily Worker" on April 1, 1955, contained an
article captioned "John Steinbeck Takes a Look at Matusow and

- 10 -
CONFIDENTIAL

Steinbeck: Citizen Spy • Page 246

'Death of a Racket.' " The article was a review of an article
by Steinbeck which appeared in the April 2, 1955, issue of
"Saturday Review." The article reflected that Steinbeck's
article captioned "Death of a Racket" was based on the book
"False Witness" written by Harvey Matusow. Steinback's article
reportedly stated:

"The Matusow testimony to anyone who will listen places
a bouquet of forget-me-nots on the grave of McCarthy. The
ridiculousness of the whole series of investigations now becomes
apparent, even to what a friend of mine used to call peanut-
munchers. Matusow will have a much greater effect than he knows.
What follows cannot be worse and may be better. It will surely
be funny."

The "Daily Worker" article continues, "It is impossible
not to be moved by this kind of statement of an angered scorn
which, if the record is to be kept straight, itself participated
in, and helped to create, that very climate, those same 'winds
of the time' as Steinbeck puts it, 'when certain basic nonsense
was allowed to pass unnoticed.' For Steinbeck was taken in tow
by the Cold War leadership to such an extent that he did not
scruple even to lend the authority of his literary achievement to
State Department broadcasts in fascist Spain, Italy, Vienna, etc."

The article continued "Steinbeck's contempt for the
'certain basic nonsense' which was believed under the influence
of the Cold War hysteria does not lead him to a rejection of the
Big Lie about the working-class Communist Party. He still says
that the Communists approve of 'the climate of disunity and suspicion which has haunted us for the last few years,' and that
Communists 'would much rather keep the investigations going with
their harvest of fear and disruption.' . . . It suffices that
John Steinbeck has expressed sentiments which a literary artist
with a sense of responsibility for his nation cannot long silence
without crushing his talent. . ."   (100-374988-A)

For additional information concerning Steinbeck you
may desire to contact the Assistant Chief of Staff, Intelligence,
of the United States Army and the Department of State.

The above information is furnished to you as a result
of your request for a name check and should not be construed as a
clearance or nonclearance of captioned individual. The information
is furnished for your use and should not be disseminated outside
of your agency.

- 11 -
CONFIDENTIAL

JOHN ERNST STEINBECK

NOTE:

Steinbeck never investigated by Bureau. Steinbeck sent letter to Attorney General Biddle in 1942 which contained "Do you suppose you could ask Edgar's boys to stop stepping on my heels? They think I'm an enemy alien. Its getting tiresome." The AG was advised on 5/21/42 that Steinbeck was not being and had never been investigated.

The Attorney General's office telephonically requested the Bureau's file on Steinbeck on 10/27/42 and was advised only information available was two pamphlets. G-2 investigated Steinbeck in 1943 and it was recommended Steinbeck not be given Army Commission. (100-106224) Per Army Letter dtd 8-2-78 ONI-22-79 2333 GAO/6, in

REC 19

100-106224-12

EX-115

March 4, 1964

JOHN ERNST STEINBECK Summary
Born: February 27, 1902
Salinas, California

A review of FBI files reveals the following information which may pertain to captioned individual.

Enclosed is a copy of an article appearing on page five of the "Worker" midweek edition dated October 29, 1963, captioned "Steinbeck in Moscow Impressed by Progress."

The "Worker" is an East Coast communist publication.

Your attention is directed to the following reports and memoranda which have been sent to your agency:

1. Memorandum dated April 12, 1957, captioned "John Ernst Steinbeck" sent April 15, 1957.

2. Report dated August 24, 1959, by SAA ███████ at New York captioned "Bulgarian Funds, New York Division" sent August 31, 1959.

b7c

3. Memorandum dated May 26, 1960, Chicago, Illinois, captioned ███████████, Internal Security-PO" sent June 8, 1960.

4. Report dated February 14, 1964, at New York, by SA ████████████ captioned "Russky Golos Publishing Company."

(100-106224-10, 65-34794-239, 105-81470-7, 100-39588-276)

Enclosure

Original & 1-CIA
Request Received-2-27-64

JSP:bss

(4)

6 4 MAR 12 1964

108

U.S. Department of Justice

Federal Bureau of Investigation

Washington, D.C. 20535

May 1, 2012

MR. BRIAN KANNARD

FOIPA Request No.: 1189085- 000
Subject: STEINBECK, JOHN ERNST (MDR)

Dear Mr. Kannard:

This is in response to your Freedom of Information/Privacy Acts (FOIPA) request.

In order to respond to our many requests in a timely manner, our focus is to identify responsive records in the automated and manual indices that are indexed as main files. A main index record carries the names of subjects of FBI investigations. Records which may be responsive to your FOIPA request were destroyed February 15, 2005. Since this material could not be reviewed, it is not known if it was responsive to your request. The retention and disposal of records is governed by statute and regulation under the supervision of the National Archives and Records Administration (NARA), Title 44, United States Code, Section 3301 and Title 36, Code of Federal Regulations, Chapter 12, Sub-chapter B, Part 1228. The FBI Records Retention Plan and Disposition Schedules have been approved by the United States District Court for the District of Columbia and are monitored by NARA.

Additionally, a search of the Central Records System maintained at FBI Headquarters indicated that potentially responsive records have been sent to NARA. If you wish to review these potentially responsive records, send your request to NARA at the following address using file number 100-HQ-145 as a reference:

> National Archives and Records Administration
> 8601 Adelphi Road
> College Park, MD 20740-6001

You may file an appeal by writing to the Director, Office of Information Policy (OIP), U.S. Department of Justice, 1425 New York Ave., NW, Suite 11050, Washington, D.C. 20530-0001. Your appeal must be received by OIP within sixty (60) days from the date of this letter in order to be considered timely. The envelope and the letter should be clearly marked "Freedom of Information Appeal." Please cite the FOIPA Request Number assigned to your request so that it may be identified easily.

Enclosed for your information is a copy of the FBI File Fact Sheet.

Very truly yours,

David M. Hardy
Section Chief,
Record/Information
  Dissemination Section
Records Management Division

U.S. Department of Justice

Department Review Committee
Suite 11050
1425 New York Avenue, NW
Washington, DC 20530-0001

Telephone: (202) 514-3642   **AUG 0 9 2012**

Mr. Brian Kannard   Re: MDRA 2012-00009
██████████████████   Request No. 1189085
                                            KWC:SKV

Dear Mr. Kannard:

You appealed from the action of the Federal Bureau of Investigation on your Mandatory Declassification Review (MDR) request for certain records concerning John Steinbeck.

By letter dated May 4, 2012, the FBI informed you that records which may have been responsive to your request were destroyed on February 15, 2005, and that further potentially responsive records are maintained by the National Archives and Records Administration. Because the FBI did not withhold any classified information, there is no action for the Department Review Committee (DRC) to consider on appeal.

If you construe this response as a denial of your request, you may appeal to the Interagency Security Classification Appeals Panel pursuant to Section 5.3 of Executive Order 13526.

Sincerely,

Mark H. Bradly

Mark A. Bradley
DRC Chairman

cc: Federal Bureau of Investigation

NATIONAL
ARCHIVES

November 6, 2012

Brian Kannard

Dear Mr. Kannard:

This is in response to your Freedom of Information Act (FOIA) request of August 30, 2012, which was received in this office on September 29, 2012. Your request has been assigned case number **NW 38734**. You requested access to Federal Bureau of Investigation (FBI) Headquarters Case Files 9-4583 and 100-106224 regarding John Ernst Steinbeck. These files are part of Record Group 65, Records of the Federal Bureau of Investigation.

We conducted a search for the files but could not locate them among our holdings. After contacting the FBI to request additional information, we learned that file 100-106224 was listed as "destroyed" on February 15, 2005. File 9-4583 was microfilmed, but we believe that the microfilm is still in the custody of the FBI. For your information, we noticed that the FBI has digitized these two files and made them available on their website. You may view the files at http://vault.fbi.gov/John%20Steinbeck.

If you consider this an adverse response, you may appeal, in writing, within 35 days of the date of this letter. Address your appeal to the Deputy Archivist of the United States, National Archives and Records Administration, 8601 Adelphi Road, College Park, MD 20740-6001. Please indicate that your correspondence is a FOIA appeal on both the envelope and the letter.

This concludes the processing of your FOIA request.

Sincerely,

MARTHA WAGNER MURPHY
Chief
Special Access and FOIA

NATIONAL
ARCHIVES

November 6, 2012

Brian Kannard

Dear Mr. Kannard:

This is in further response to your Freedom of Information Act (FOIA) request of August 30, 2012 (our case number **NW 38734**) for access to Federal Bureau of Investigation (FBI) Headquarters Case Files 9-4583 and 100-106224 regarding John Ernst Steinbeck.

In our previous letter dated November 6, 2012, we stated that file 9-4583 was microfilmed, but we believed that the microfilm was still in the FBI's custody. Today the FBI informed us, after checking thoroughly, that the file is **not** included on their microfilm.

Sincerely,

Mary Kay Schmidt

MARY KAY SCHMIDT
Archivist
Special Access and FOIA Staff

In doing research for this book, it became quickly apparent that comparing Steinbeck's travels and associations with government documentation might help me decipher Steinbeck's dual life. I did not know what tidbits would be pertinent as I came across events in John's life, so I compiled as detailed a timeline as possible. The majority of entries have a corresponding reference to aid in returning to material that seemed promising. Unreferenced events are sourced via major biographies and are generally accepted as accurate.

The main source for referenced events in this timeline is *Steinbeck: A Life in Letters*. One has to assume that Steinbeck's own record is the most accurate available. Where an exact date for an event is in question, I have attempted to note the estimation and why the estimation was made. I've also taken the liberty of including major world events into this timeline to place Steinbeck's life in proper historical context. For convenience's sake, references and citations for the timeline have been included at the end of the section.

1902

February 27: John Ernst Steinbeck was born in Salinas, California. He was the third of four children and the only son of John Ernst II and Olive Hamilton Steinbeck.

1915–19

Steinbeck attends Salinas High School.

1919

Summer: Steinbeck works at the Post Ranch and tracks the Big Sur Bear.[1]

1919–25: Attends classes at Stanford University, leaving without a degree. During these years, Steinbeck drops out for several months, and is employed intermittently as a sales clerk, farm laborer, ranch hand, and factory worker.

1921

Steinbeck joins the Order of DeMolay.

1925

November: Steinbeck travels by freighter from Los Angeles to New York City.

December: Steinbeck arrives in New York and gets a job on a Madison Square Garden construction crew. The job lasts six weeks and he quits after a nearby worker is killed falling off a scaffolding.

1926

January: Steinbeck gets a job as a reporter for the *New York American*.[2]

Summer to Winter: Lives in Lake Tahoe, California, and works as a caretaker for a summer home.

1929

January 18: Steinbeck applies for admission to Salinas Masonic Lodge #204.[3]

May 24: Steinbeck achieves the degree of Master Mason at Salinas Lodge.[4]

August: John's first novel, *Cup of Gold*, is published.[5]

October 29: Wall Street's "Black Tuesday" crash signals the beginning of the Great Depression.

1930

January 14: John marries Carol Henning.

October: Steinbeck meets Edward F. Ricketts.

1931

Mythologist and author Joseph Campbell comes to Monterey and meets Steinbeck and Ed Ricketts.

1932

March: Carol gets a job working at Ed Ricketts' lab.

June: Carol Steinbeck and Joseph Campbell have an affair that is broken off by mutual consent. Campbell and Ed Ricketts also go to Alaska for a specimen-hunting trip.[6]

October: *The Pastures of Heaven* is published.[7]

1933

February 11: Steinbeck sends *To a God Unknown* to his literary agents.

September: *To a God Unknown* is published.[8]

1934

February 19: Steinbeck's mother dies.

March: Steinbeck accompanies Ed Ricketts on a specimen-hunting trip at Laguna Beach.

May: Steinbeck starts gathering information on farm labor unions in the Salinas area.

1935

February 5: Steinbeck completes the manuscript for *In Dubious Battle*.

May: Steinbeck's father dies.

May 28: *Tortilla Flat* is published.[9]

September: John and Carol travel to Mexico for a vacation and to escape the media attention *Tortilla Flat* has generated.

October: Still in Mexico, John receives a telegram that Paramount Pictures has purchased the film rights to *Tortilla Flat*.

1936

January (Early): John and Carol travel from Mexico to New York to sign the *Tortilla Flat* film deal and then return to California.

April (Mid): Steinbeck begins work on *Of Mice and Men* (originally titled *Something That Happened*).

May 11: Steinbeck purchases land in Los Gatos, California.

June 11: The California Literature Gold Medal is awarded to Steinbeck for *Tortilla Flat*.

October: *In Dubious Battle* is published.[10]

October 5–12: John's series of articles about the migrant worker problem are published in the *San Francisco News*.

November 13: John attends the Western Writer's Conference in San Francisco.[11]

November 25: Ed Rickett's lab in Cannery Row burns to the ground.

December: *Saint Katy the Virgin* is published.

1937

February 6: *Of Mice and Men* is published.

March 23: Steinbeck and Carol set sail for Philadelphia from California.[12]

April 15: Steinbeck and Carol arrive in Philadelphia and later take a train to New York. There they attend a dinner honoring Thomas Mann.[13]

May (Late): The Steinbecks sail from New York to Sweden.

July: John and Carol travel from Sweden to Finland and then to the Russia.

August 13: The Steinbecks arrive in New York from Sandviken on the *Toledo*.[14]

September: *The Red Pony* is published.

October: "The Chrysanthemums" is published in *Harper's Magazine*.

October (Mid): Steinbeck visits the migrant worker camps in Los Gatos.

November 23: The stage version of *Of Mice and Men* opens in New York's Music Box Theater. The play runs through May 1938 (207 performances).[15]

1938

January 12: The stage version of *Tortilla Flat* opens at New York's Henry Miller's Theatre for five performances.[16]

February (Mid): Steinbeck spends ten days at migrant worker camps in Visalia with Tom Collins.

April: "Their Blood Is Strong," a nonfiction account of the migrant labor problem in California, is published by the Simon J. Lubin Society.[17]

April 15: "Starvation under the Orange Trees," is published by the *Monterey Trader.*

May: Steinbeck receives the New York Drama Critics Circle Award for the play *Of Mice and Men.*[18]

June 14: Steinbeck telegrams Eleanor Roosevelt that the Congressional Appropriations Committee failed to provide funds for the US Film Service. The lack of funding halted the efforts of Pare Lorentz and other filmmakers.[19]

September: The short-story collection, *The Long Valley,* is published. This edition includes the story "The Red Pony."[20]

October (Late): Steinbeck finishes *The Grapes of Wrath* manuscript.

October 25: American Legion investigator Harper Knowles testifies before the Dies Commission that Steinbeck has Communist ties.[21]

November 8: John's wife Carol registers with the Communist Party in Santa Clara County.[22]

1939

February 2: Steinbeck telegrams the Committee to Aid Agricultural Organizations to "portest (sic) any curtailment of the FSA Camp and relief program."[23]

February 9: Steinbeck sends a telegram to President Roosevelt urging the passage of a bill to extend the LaFollette Civil Liberties Committee.[24]

April 5: Steinbeck's editor, Pat Covici, sends a copy of *The Grapes of Wrath* to President Roosevelt.[25]

April 14: *The Grapes of Wrath* is published.[26]

Summer: John and Carol tour the Pacific Northwest.[27]

September (Mid): John and Carol travel to Chicago to visit Joe Hamilton, Pare Lorentz, and Paul de Kruief.[28]

December 15: Steinbeck travels to Los Angeles to view the screener copies of *The Grapes of Wrath* and *Of Mice and Men.*

December (Late): John urges Carol to get an abortion after finding out she is pregnant. Carol does and develops an infection that leads to a hysterectomy.

December 30: Film *Of Mice and Men* is released in the United States.[29]

1940

January 24: Film version of *The Grapes of Wrath* premiers in New York.[30]

March 11–April 20: John conducts a marine expedition in the Gulf of California with Ed Ricketts.[31]

March 15: Film version of *The Grapes of Wrath* opens in the United States.[32]

March 22: Steinbeck is in La Paz, Mexico.[33]

March 27: Steinbeck is in Loreto, Mexico.[34]

April 5: Steinbeck is in Guaymas, Mexico.[35]

April 22: Steinbeck returns home to Los Gatos. (Date estimated by Steinbeck in an April 6th letter to the staff at McIntosh-Otis).[36]

May: *The Grapes of Wrath* receives the National Book Award.

May 6: *The Grapes of Wrath* wins the Pulitzer Prize.

May 22: John and Carol attend a party in Hollywood thrown by Lewis Milestone. Known to have attended the party are Gwyndolyn Conger, Charlie Chaplin, Vladimir Horowitz, and Max Wagner.[37]

May 23: Steinbeck travels to Mexico City to work on the film script for *The Forgotten Village*.[38]

May 24: An assassination attempt is made on Leon Trotsky in Mexico City.

June (Early): Ed Ricketts joins Steinbeck in Mexico City.[39]

June 14 or June 22: Steinbeck sends a report of his findings in Mexico to his uncle Joe Hamilton. (See chapter 4 for explination of date discrepancy.)[40]

June 22: Steinbeck travels to Washington, D.C.[41]

June 24: Steinbeck's letter about an Axis threat in Mexico is received by President Roosevelt.[42] Also the same day, an FBI memo was issued to create the FBI's Special Intelligence Service to operate in Latin America.

June 26: Steinbeck meets with FDR and presents a plan of print and radio propaganda in Latin America.[43]

July–August: John takes sporadic flying lessons at the Palo Alto airport.[44]

August 13: John writes to FDR about flooding Germany with counterfeit Deutsche Marks in an effort to collapse the Nazis' economy.[45]

August 16: The Office for Coordination of Commercial and Cultural Relations between the American Republics was started by FDR with Nelson Rockefeller at the helm. The Agency would formally be chartered and renamed as the Office of Coordinator of Inter-American Affairs in July 1941.[46]

September 12: Steinbeck meets once again with FDR to discuss Steinbeck's plan to sabotage the German economy.[47]

September 14–27: John leaves Washington for New York and returns to California on the 27th.[48]

October (Mid): Steinbeck returns to Mexico to continue work on *The Forgotten Village*.[49]

November (Third week): John returns to the USA and meets Gwyn Conger in Hollywood.[50]

December 13: Steinbeck writes a letter to the Mexican Ambassador, Josephus Daniels, giving Daniels praise. The letter is forwarded to Archibald MacLeish of the Library of Congress and then to FDR.[51]

1941

January 1: Steinbeck and Carol have the flu at the Los Gatos ranch house.[52]

February 7: Carol leaves for a vacation to Hawaii.

March: Mavis McIntosh visits Steinbeck in California.

April (Late): Steinbeck separates from Carol.

May: The book version of *The Forgotten Village* is published.

July 11: Colonel William Donovan's "Memorandum of Establishment of Service of Strategic Information" results in President Roosevelt establishing the Office of the Coordinator of Information. Donovan is assigned as the "Coordinator of Information" of the intelligence agency.

July 30: Office of Coordinator of Inter-American Affairs is officially sanctioned by Executive Order 8840.[53]

September (Early): Steinbeck works on the script for the film version of *The Red Pony* in California.[54]

September (Late): John moves to New York City with singer Gwyn Conger.

October 7–8: Steinbeck goes to Washington, D.C., to attend a conference with the Foreign Information Service (FIS), after which, John begins writing material for the FIS.

November: Steinbeck begins work on *The Moon Is Down*.

November (Mid): John rents a two-bedroom apartment in a residential hotel in Manhattan.[55]

November 18: *The Forgotten Village* documentary is released in the USA.[56]

November 25: Steinbeck mentions in a letter to Toby Street that he "may have to go to Washington to do some work in about a week." (A citation with this letter in *Steinbeck: A Life in Letters* mentions John was already writing broadcasts for what would become the War Information Office.)[57]

December 5: *Sea of Cortez*, written with Edward Ricketts, is published.

December 7: Pearl Harbor is bombed by a surprise Japanese raid. The United

States responds by declaring war on the Japanese on December 8, 1941. A war declaration is issued for Germany on December 11, 1941.

December (Mid): John submits the manuscript for *The Moon Is Down* to Viking Press for publication.[58]

December 15: Steinbeck makes suggestions to COI William Donovan about cooperation with Japanese-American organizations.[59]

December (Late): John and Gwyn spend Christmas and New Year's holidays in New Orleans at Roark Bradford.

1942

January 7: John returns to New York to work on a stage version of *The Moon Is Down.*

February 24: Voice of America (VOA) conducts its first broadcast.[60]

February 27: Steinbeck's 40th birthday.

March: John is sued for divorce by first wife Carol.

March 6: *The Moon Is Down* is published.[61]

April (Early): John is offered a full-time position at the OWI.[62]

April 7: The stage version of *The Moon Is Down* opens in New York's Martin Beck Theater. The production runs through May 6, 1942 (71 performances).[63]

May (Mid): Steinbeck is offered a temporary assignment to write two books for the Army Air Corps.

May 5: Steinbeck writes the Secretary of the Navy, Frank Knox, about using Japanese oceanographic studies for intelligence purposes. Two months later, a Naval Intelligence Officer visits Ed Ricketts for a follow-up to Steinbeck's suggestion.[64]

May 11: Attorney General Francis Biddle forwards Steinbeck's "ask Edgar's boys to stop stepping on my heels" letter to J. Edgar Hoover.[65]

May 12: Steinbeck applies for a pistol permit in Rockland County, NY.[66]

May 21: Film version of *Tortilla Flat* released.[67] Also the FBI sends a letter to Attorney General Francis Biddle reporting that the FBI has never investigated Steinbeck.[68]

May (Late)–June: Steinbeck travels with photographer John Swope on board Army Air Corps flights gathering material for *Bombs Away.*

June 13: The Office of Strategic Services is officially established along with the Office of War Information.[69]

July 23: Steinbeck writes Toby Street that his official job title is now Special Consultant to the Secretary of War attached to the Army Air Corps and is also performing the job duties as the foreign news editor for the Office of War Information. John is also convinced that he will receive an Army commission as an intelligence officer "in the fall."[70]

September: John and Gwyn return to California ostensibly so John can work on a film for the Army Air Corps.[71]

October 27: Attorney General's office calls the FBI with a request to see the FBI's file on Steinbeck.[72]

November 27: *Bombs Away: The Story of a Bomber Team* is published.[73]

December: John begins a script for an Army Air Corps training film.

December 3: An unknown person reports to the FBI that Steinbeck is at Japanese internment camps dressed in an Army uniform agitating internees.[74]

1943

January: Steinbeck writes the screenplay for Hitchcock's movie *Lifeboat*.

January (Mid): John and Gywn move into a New York City apartment.

February 23: US Army Counter Intelligence does a background check on Steinbeck with the Office of Naval Intelligence, San Francisco Police Department, San Francisco FBI Field Office, and the American Legion Radical Research Bureau.[75]

March: John applies to be a war correspondent with *The New York Herald Tribune*.

March 14: Film of *The Moon Is Down* released in the United States.[76]

March 27: Steinbeck flies to New Orleans to get married to Gwyn.

March 29: Steinbeck marries Gwyn Conger in New Orleans at the home of Lyle Saxon.[77]

April 5: The War Department approves John's credentials as a war correspondent and Steinbeck notifies Toby Street by telegram.[78]

May: Steinbeck spends the month preparing to go overseas.

May (Late) to June (Mid): US Army Counter Intelligence agents conduct acquaintance check on Steinbeck in California.[79]

June 3: John leaves New York aboard a troop ship for London.

June 8: Steinbeck arrives in London.

July 25–31: Steinbeck spends four days with staff officers from General Lee's SOS.[80]

July 26: General Weaver is briefed that Steinbeck has "started his movie."[81]

July 27: Army Counter Intelligence Chief Boris Pash generates a report consolidating the military's investigation into Steinbeck's character. Pash does not agree with the reporting officer's recommendation that Steinbeck is loyal and declines John's commission in the US Army.[82]

August 13: John writes Gwyn that he is in Northern Africa (probably Algiers).[83]

August 19: Steinbeck writes to Gwyn that he has been traveling throughout the countryside with a cameraman and an enlisted man "taking some pictures."[84]

August 25: In another letter to Gywn, Steinbeck says that he is with a group of naval officers at a Gregorian monastery that is an *ad hoc* hospital. All indications in the letter are that Steinbeck is still in Algeria.[85]

September 8–9: Steinbeck participates in the capture of Ventotene with Douglas Fairbanks Jr.'s unit of Beach Jumpers and OSS operatives.[86]

September 9: The Allies begin Operation AVALANCHE to take Salerno.

September 10: John accompanies Beach Jumper Lt. John Kramer on a diversion mission in the Gulf of Gaeta.[87]

September 12: Still attached to the Beach Jumpers, Steinbeck participates in the liberation of the Isle of Capri.[88]

September 13 or 14: John reaches the Italian mainland to cover Salerno invasion.

September 14: Steinbeck mentions in a letter to Gwyn (dated September 23, 1943) that he had a particularly "rough night" referring to Salerno.[89]

September 20: Steinbeck is aboard a transport ship after Salerno.[90]

September 22: Steinbeck reaches an undisclosed military base in the Mediterranean.[91]

September 24: Steinbeck returns to London.[92]

October 15: Steinbeck returns to the USA from London.[93]

November: Steinbeck begins work on *Cannery Row.*

1944

January (Mid): Steinbeck travels to Mexico with Gwyn.

January 10: Steinbeck has seen an advance copy of *Lifeboat* and writes to 20th Century Fox. John is disappointed with script changes that depict the African-American seaman as "half-comic and half-pathetic."[94]

January 28: *Lifeboat* opens to film audiences in the United States.[95]

February 21: *The New York Times* reports that Steinbeck is an owner/contributor of Associated Magazine Contributors INC.[96]

February 22: An unknown associate of Jacob Epstein enters the Soviet Embassy in Mexico City.[97]

February 23: Steinbeck attends a reception at the Soviet Embassy in Mexico City.[98]

March 15: Steinbeck returns to the United States via Brownsville, TX.[99]

March 22: The United States Ambassador to Mexico sends a secret memo to J. Edgar Hoover related to Steinbeck and Ernest Hemingway in affairs in Mexico.[100]

Spring: Steinbeck meets Ernest Hemingway for the first, and only time, at Tim Costello's bar in Manhattan.[101]

April 8: The San Antonio FBI field office sends a report to J. Edgar Hoover regarding Steinbeck's entry into Mexico on March 15th.[102]

April 12: Steinbeck writes to Carlton Sheffield about the injuries he sustained during the Salerno invasion. John also speaks of his feelings about being blacklisted from the Army.[103]

June 24 and 29: Steinbeck's suggestions for a statement and a platform for the Democratic National Convention are forwarded to President Roosevelt on these dates.[104]

July 7: Steinbeck attends author Lion Feuchtwanger's 60th birthday party in New York. Steinbeck has planned the event with publisher B. W. Huebsch and screenwriter/director Berthold Vierte.[105]

August 2: Steinbeck's first son, Thomas, is born.[106]

August 8: President Roosevelt sends a letter to John congratulating him on the birth of Thom.[107]

October (Early): Steinbeck moves back to California with his family.[108]

November 23: A film version of *The Moon Is Down* opens in Sweden.[109]

October 15–January (late) 1945: Steinbeck works on *The Pearl*.[110]

1945

January 2: *Cannery Row* is published.[111]

February 9: John and Gwyn travel to Mexico City to assist in the filming of *The Pearl*.

February 4–11: President Roosevelt, Joseph Stalin, and Winston Churchill attend the Yalta conference to discuss the world's reorganization after the end of World War II.

April 5: Steinbeck and Jack Wagner take a train from Los Angeles to Mexico City.

April 12: President Roosevelt dies from a stroke.

April 16: *A Medal for Benny* is released in the USA.[112]

May 3–July 12: Steinbeck is in Cuernavaca, Mexico. (Dates of travel are unknown, but letters denote Steinbeck was here during this period.)[113]

May 8: Germany surrenders, effectively ending hostilities in Europe.

August: John works on the screenplay for *The Pearl*.

August 14: Japan surrenders to Allied forces, effectively ending the Second World War.

September 5: Igor Gouzenko, a clerk working in the Soviet embassy in Ottawa, defects and provides proof to the Royal Canadian Mounted Police of a Soviet spy ring operating in Canada and other western countries.

October 1: The OSS is officially dissolved by Executive Order 9162.[114]

November: John travels from New York to Mexico for filming of *The Pearl*.

December 15: Steinbeck returns to New York from Mexico.[115]

1946

January–May: Steinbeck works on *The Wayward Bus*.

March 5: Winston Churchill gives the "Iron Curtain" speech at Westminster College.

March 12: President Truman announces the "Truman Doctrine" and proposes giving aid to Greece and Turkey to fend off Communist aggression.

June 12: Steinbeck's second son, John IV, is born.[116]

July: Steinbeck returns to Mexico for post-production work on *The Pearl*.

October 18: John and Gwyn sail for Sweden aboard the SS *Drottningholm*.[117]

October 30: Steinbeck attends a legation luncheon in Copenhagen.[118]

November 15: John receives the Norwegian King Haakon Liberty Cross.

November 18–19: John and Gwyn fly from Stockholm to New York on Swedish Airlines flight 1039.[119]

1947

January 18: An undisclosed source in San Simeon, California, writes J. Edgar Hoover to tell him of Steinbeck's Communist tendencies. The source possibly works with or is related to the Hearst Media Empire.[120]

February: *The Wayward Bus* is published.[121]

March (Late): Steinbeck discusses a trip to Russia with Robert Capa at the Bedford Hotel bar.[122] *The New York Herald Tribune* is interested in publishing articles from Steinbeck and pictures by Capa of the trip.

May 14: John injures his knee after a fall from a second-story window. The trip to Russia with Capa is postponed.

June (Early): John, Gwyn, and Robert Capa travel to Paris.

June 5: Secretary of State George Marshall outlines a plan for reconstructing a war-ravaged Europe, that will become known as the "Marshall Plan."

July 18: Gwyn returns to New York from Paris.

July 21: Steinbeck and Capa fly from Paris to Stockholm.[123]

July 31–August 1: Steinbeck and Capa land in Moscow.[124]

August 4–19: Steinbeck is in Kiev. (Dates estimated from a letter to Pat Covici.)[125]

August 20: Steinbeck arrives in Stalingrad.[126]

October: House Committee on Un-American Activities begins hearings in Washington.

October 4–5: Steinbeck and Capa fly from Paris to New York on an Air France.[127]

November: *The Pearl* is published.[128]

November 24: The Hollywood Ten are cited with contempt of Congress and are "blacklisted" from working in Hollywood the next day.

December 18: Steinbeck incorporates World Video Inc. as president with Robert Capa and Phil Reisman as vice presidents.[129]

1948

January (Early): Steinbeck flies to California for research and to spend time with Ed Ricketts.

April: *A Russian Journal* is published by Viking Press.

April 20–27: John has a procedure to remove varicose veins in his legs and is hospitalized for a week. (Hospital indate is estimated from a previous letter to Ed Ricketts. Steinbeck's outdate is confirmed by a letter to Bo Beskow.)[130]

May 8: Ed Ricketts crosses a railroad track when his truck was hit by the Del Monte Express train at the Drake Avenue crossing off Cannery Row.[131]

May 11: Ed Ricketts dies in injuries sustained in the May 8th automobile accident; Steinbeck cannot get to California in time to see his friend before he passes.[132]

May (Mid): After Ed Ricketts' funeral, Steinbeck and George Robinson visit Rickett's lab on Cannery Row. The pair burns many of Ricketts' journals and Steinbeck's letters to Ed.[133]

May 20: Steinbeck returns to New York by this date.[134]

June (Early): Steinbeck returns to Mexico and is back in New York by June 19th.[135]

June 11: *The Los Angles Examiner* announces that Ring Laudner Jr., a member of the "Hollywood Ten," would write the screenplay for Steinbeck's *Pastures of Heaven.* This was the first time employment of a member of the Hollywood Ten had ever been considered. The movie was never made.[136]

June 24: Soviet Premier Joseph Stalin blocks all land routes into West Berlin through East Germany. The action will result in Western powers beginning the use of the Berlin Airlift to send supplies into West Berlin.

June–August: Steinbeck spends much of these months in Mexico working on the film *Viva Zapata!*

August (Mid): Gwyn tells Steinbeck she wishes to divorce him.[137]

September (Early): Steinbeck moves to Pacific Grove. John takes along former Navy steward James Neale as a domestic servant.

September 18: Ritch and Tal Lovejoy join John for coffee this morning.[138]

November 2: Steinbeck rendezvouses with Elia Kazan in Los Angeles.[139]

November 5: Steinbeck and Kazan fly to Mexico City to assist in the filming of *Viva Zapata!*[140]

November 14: John returns to California from Mexico.[141]

November 23: Steinbeck is elected to the American Academy of Arts and Letters.

December 25: "The Miracle of Tepayac" is published by *Collier's Weekly*.[142]

December (Late): Steinbeck spends New Year's in Los Angeles.[143]

1949

March 28: The film version of *The Red Pony* is released in the United States after a seven-year delay.[144]

March: Writers meeting at New York's Waldorf Astoria calls for the end of hostilities between the Soviets and Americans.

April 4: NATO is founded.

May: Steinbeck goes to Monterey's Del Monte Aviation to discuss flight lessons for his domestic servant John Neale and the possibility of purchasing an aircraft.[145]

May 27–30: John spends the weekend in Pacific Grove with Ann Southern and Elaine Scott. This is the first time he meets his future wife Elaine.[146]

June (Late)–August (Late): John spends the summer with his sons in Pacific Grove.[147]

August 29: The Soviet Union tests their first atomic bomb.

October 14: Toby Street visits John in Pacific Grove.[148]

November 1: Jules Buck works with Steinbeck in Pacific Grove for early script work on *Viva Zapata!*

November (Early)–November 14: Jack Wagner is a houseguest of John in Pacific Grove.[149]

December (Late): John is back in New York in time for the holidays.[150]

1950

January 28: John attends a party for Ethyl Barrymore. In attendance are Margo Albert, Bernard Mannes Baruch, Leonard Bernstein, Ray Bolger, Abe Burrows, Lillian Gish, Frank Loesser, John Ringling North, and William Saroyan.[151]

February 4: John sees *Caesar and Cleo* at New York's National Theater.[152]

June (Late)–September (Early): John and Elaine spend the summer with John's sons in Rockland County. The budding family rents a house that belonged to artist Henry Varnum Poor.[153]

June 22: *Red Channels* is published, effectively blacklisting over 150 actors, authors, composers, musicians, and broadcasters.

June 25: North Korea invades South Korea, beginning the Korean War.

October: Novella *Burning Bright* is published.

October 5: John is in Boston for rehearsals and last-minute rewrites of *Burning Bright*.[154]

October 18: The stage version of *Burning Bright* opens at New York's Broadherst Theater. The play runs until October 28, 1950 (13 performances).[155]

November 2: Steinbeck's interview with Eleanor Roosevelt on *The Eleanor Roosevelt Show* (NBC Radio) is broadcast. During the interview, the former First Lady asks John about his new play, *Burning Bright*.[156]

December 7: John and Elaine attend a performance of Clifford Odets' *The Country Girl* at the Lyceum Theatre.[157]

December 28: Steinbeck marries third wife, Elaine Anderson Scott.

1951

January (Early)–January 8: John and Elaine travel to Somerset, Bahamas, and leave for New York on the 8th, aboard Pan American flight 133.[158]

January 31: John and Elaine move into a house on New York's 72nd St.[159]

February 12: Steinbeck begins work on *East of Eden*.[160]

February 21: Steinbeck tapes an interview for VOA on art under dictatorship.[161]

February 24: Steinbeck attends a party; no other details are available.[162]

February 28: Steinbeck attends a World Video stockholder's meeting.[163]

March 9–11: Steinbeck and Elaine spend the weekend at Burgess Meredith's house.[164]

March 16: Steinbeck and Elaine see *The Rose Tattoo*.[165]

March 21: In his journal, Steinbeck predicts that the Soviet Union will break up under its own weight. He also believes the United States should reach out to dissidents to hasten Communism's end. John also prognosticates that a one-world government is in the works.[166]

March 24: During the Easter weekend, Steinbeck spends the night in Long Island for an unknown reason.[167]

March 29: Julius and Ethyl Rosenberg are convicted of espionage for passing nuclear secrets to the Soviet Union. Steinbeck and Elaine attend the opening of *The King and I* and have dinner afterward with John O'Hara at Sardi's.[168]

April 7: Steinbeck and Elaine attend a party for the musical *South Pacific* in New York.[169]

April 13: Steinbeck writes in his journal that *Collier's* wants him to "make the big trip" in January of 1952.[170]

April 17: Steinbeck spends the evening with Clifford Odets and Juan Negrin.[171]

April 29: Steinbeck and Elaine attend two separate parties. One party is at Faye Emerson's and another is for Joan Crawford at the Stork Club.[172]

May 1: The Steinbecks host a dinner party for Frank and Lynn Looser and Fred and Portland Allen.[173]

May 10: The Steinbecks have dinner with a distant relative of Elaine's, oil baron Lawrence Hagy.[174]

May 25: John is scheduled to attend the National Book Award (Poetry) nomination of Archie MacLeish.[175]

May 29: John and Elaine attend the second opening of *Oklahoma*.[176]

June (Mid) to September (Mid): John and Elaine spend the summer with John's sons in Nantucket. John continues to work on *East of Eden*.[177]

July 19: Elizabeth Otis visits Steinbeck and Elaine for several days.[178]

July 4: American journalist William N. Oatis receives a ten-year sentence in Czechoslovakia on an espionage charge.

August 8: Ballerina Tamera Geva visits John and Elaine.[179]

August 10: Geva and Kent Smith visit the Steinbecks. Kent appeared in Steinbeck's play *Burning Bright*.[180]

September: *The Log from the Sea of Cortez*, the narrative part of the *Sea of Cortez* (1941), is published by Viking Press. This edition includes an original essay *About Ed Ricketts*.[181]

September 26: Steinbeck attends a production of *Burning Bright*.[182]

October 16: John and Elaine go to a production of *A Streetcar Named Desire* with Elia Kazan.[183]

October 23: Steinbeck buys a raincoat for the 1952 European trip.[184]

October 24: Steinbeck tapes an interview for VOA.[185]

November (Early): John finishes the manuscript for *East of Eden*.[186]

1952

January 14: Steinbeck's friend and co-writer of *Viva Zapata!* Elia Kazan testifies before an executive committee meeting of HUAC. Kazan admits he was a member of the Communist Party in 1936, but is hesitant to name other members.[187]

January 28: Steinbeck writes CIA Director Walter Bedell "Beetle" Smith offering his assistance to the CIA during John's upcoming trip to Europe.[188]

January 31: A USIA interview with Steinbeck is broadcast on VOA.[189]

February 6: Walter Bedell Smith replies to Steinbeck's letter that the Agency would be interested in his help and instructs Steinbeck to visit him before leaving for Europe.[190]

February 7: *Viva Zapata!* is released in the United States.[191]

February 11: A USIA interview with Steinbeck is broadcast on VOA.[192]

February 26: A USIA interview with Steinbeck is broadcast on VOA.[193]

February 27: Steinbeck celebrates his 50th birthday.

March 11: Dwight Eisenhower wins New Hampshire's Republican primary.

March 18: The State Department is sent a report by the FBI fulfilling a request on any information the FBI holds on Steinbeck after February 13, 1948.[194]

March (Late): Steinbeck and Elaine leave New York bound for Genoa, Italy. The ship changes course and lands in Casablanca and then Algiers. While in Algiers, the Steinbecks attend a party thrown by a French Air Force General.[195] The couple takes a ship from Algiers to Marcelles and then drives to Spain.[196]

April 10: Elia Kazan testifies before HUAC for a second time. Kazan amends his January testimony and names persons he knew were in the Communist Party in the 1930s.[197]

April 11: Steinbeck and Elaine arrive in Madrid. (Date is estimated based on the source letter.)[198]

April 21: Steinbeck and Elaine travel to Seville.[199]

April 28: General Matthew Ridgway is named as NATO commander.[200]

May 11: Steinbeck and Elaine arrive in Paris via a train from Madrid.[201]

May 27: Steinbeck writes to Elizabeth Otis that he has been interviewed by the Communist publication *Combat*.[202]

May (Late)–July (Mid): Steinbeck and Elaine take a driving tour from Paris to Milan, Venice, Florence, and Rome.

May 28 or 29: Steinbeck and Elaine leave Paris and travel by car to Dijon.[203]

May 29 or 30: Steinbeck and Elaine travel by car from Dijon to Poligny.[204]

June 1: Steinbeck and Elaine travel from Poligny to Geneva.[205]

June 16: Steinbeck and Elaine arrive in Rome.[206]

June 23: Steinbeck's Italian literary agent throws a reception in John's honor.[207]

June 25: John and Elaine have reservations to depart South Hampton, UK, on the *Queen Elizabeth* bound for New York but do not board.[208]

July 13: John and Elaine arrive back in Paris.[209]

July 14: Steinbeck and Elaine have dinner with John Houston, José Ferrer, Robert Capa, Suzanne Flon, and the cast of *Moulin Rouge* at the Eifel Tower Restaurant.[210]

July 24: Steinbeck and Elaine leave Paris for London.[211]

July 25–August 16: Steinbeck and Elaine travel throughout England and Scotland.[212]

August 17: John and Elaine arrive in Londonderry, Ireland.[213]

August 23: "A Duel without Pistols" is published in *Collier's Weekly*.[214]

August 30: "The Soul and Guts of France" is published by *Collier's Weekly*.[215]

August 31: John and Elaine fly from Orly Airport in Paris to New York on Air France flight 037.[216]

September: *East of Eden* is published.

September 10: Steinbeck finishes reading Hemingway's *Old Man and the Sea*.[217]

September 25: Rita Reil of the International Press Alliance Corporation writes Elizabeth Otis about the French newspaper *France Dimanche* refuting facts in "The Soul and Guts of France."[218]

Fall: Steinbeck becomes involved with Adali Stevenson's campaign for president and writes speeches for Stevenson rallies throughout the East Coast. At this point, Steinbeck and Stevenson have never met.[219]

1953

January: Steinbeck and Elaine go to the Virgin Islands for a vacation.

January 10: *Collier's Weekly* publishes "The Secret Weapon We Were Afraid to Use."[220]

January 20: Dwight D. Eisenhower becomes President of the United States.

January 31: "I Go Back to Ireland" is published in *Collier's Weekly*.[221]

March 24–27: Steinbeck takes his sons to Nantucket for a brief vacation while Elaine visits family in Texas.[222]

April 23: Roy Cohn and G. David Schine, chief aides to Senator Joseph McCarthy, return from an investigatory trip to USIS posts in Europe. The pair removed 30,000 books from USIS libraries that included works from Steinbeck, Herman Melville, and Henry David Thoreau.

June 2: Roland William Kibbee testifies to HUAC that while Steinbeck's novels did more for agricultural workers than "anyone else in the Communist Party," Steinbeck was at odds with the Communists. The sources could not present any proof of the claim.[223]

July 27: An armistice is signed, effectively ending the Korean War.

September: Steinbeck rents a cottage in Sag Harbor to be closer to the producers of the musical version of *Cannery Row*.[224]

1954

January: John and Elaine vacation in Saint John and meet John Kenneth Galbraith and his wife.[225]

March 1: FBI sends a summary file check report on Steinbeck to the USIA.[226]

March 10: FBI generates a summary of findings on Steinbeck for an unknown reason, but could possibly be related to the USIA request.[227]

March 19: John and Elaine board the Italian Lines ship *Saturina* bound for Lisbon.[228]

March 26: Steinbeck and Elaine land in Lisbon for an extended tour of Europe.

April 21: Steinbeck and Elaine are in Seville.[229]

April 22: Steinbeck visits the Seville's Archives of the Indies to view original documents from Christopher Columbus.[230]

May 7: French forces fall to the Viet Minh at Dien Bien Phu.

May 14: Steinbeck and Elaine arrive in Paris after a six-day road trip. One of the stops along the way was an overnight at Blois.[231]

May 21: Steinbeck's French literary agent holds a reception in John's honor.[232]

May 25: Steinbeck moves into their rented house at Number 1 Avenue de Marginy.[233]

May 27: Steinbeck receives word that Robert Capa has been killed by a landmine in French-Indochina.[234]

June: *Sweet Thursday* is published.[235]

June 13: Steinbeck agrees to be part of a charity event for the children of soldiers who died under General Leclerc's liberation army. The event is held at the Tuileries Garden.[236]

July: "Jalopies I Cursed and Loved" is published in *Holiday Magazine's* July issue.[237]

July (Early): Steinbeck travels to Munich at the request of the USIA to record personal statements about the situation in East Germany. These comments will be broadcast on Radio Free Europe.[238]

August 14: John holds a birthday party for Elaine at a chateau outside of Paris. The party and its trappings are said to have been the genesis for *The Short Reign of Pippin IV*.[239]

August 25: "Fishing in Paris" is published by *Punch Magazine*.[240]

September 8: Elaine and Steinbeck leave Paris for London.[241]

September 29: Steinbeck is in Saint Paul de Venice, France, and notes in a letter to Elizabeth Otis that he has shaved his thirty-year-old moustache off.[242]

October 28 or 29: The United States Embassy in Rome holds a reception for Steinbeck. Steinbeck also mentions in an October 29th letter to Elizabeth Otis that "Italy is full of flying saucers" and that "Clare Luce says she saw something [UFO]."[243]

October (Late): Steinbeck leaves Rome with Elaine to take a tour with the Greek Islands with John McKnight (head of USIS in Rome) and his wife.

November 29: John and Elaine are in Sicily.

December 2: Steinbeck and Elaine travel from Positano, Italy, to Naples.[244]

December (Late): Steinbeck and Elaine return to New York aboard the *Andrea Doria* and land just in time to celebrate Christmas. During the trip, John meets Mark Ethridge of the *Louisville Courier-Journal*.[245]

1955

January: William Faulkner and Steinbeck meet for the first time.[246] The January edition of *Reader's Digest* runs "How to Fish in French."[247]

March: John purchases a summer home in Sag Harbor, New York.

March 9: John attends the premier of the stage version of *East of Eden* at the Astor Theater. In attendance are Raymond Massey, Elia Kazan, and Jack Warner.[248]

April 2: John begins writing editorials and articles for *The Saturday Review*. His first piece, "Death of a Racket," is published in the April 2nd edition.[249]

April 4: Steinbeck has lunch with Dag Hammarskjöld.[250]

April 10: The film version of *East of Eden* opens in the United States.[251]

May 28: "Some Thoughts on Juvenile Delinquency" is published by the *Saturday Review.*[252]

June: "Always Something to Do in Salinas" is published in the June edition of *Holiday Magazine.*[253]

July 5: Steinbeck takes his boat from Sag Harbor to fish off Montauk Point.[254]

September 26: John has lunch with *Pipe Dream* star Helen Traumbel.[255]

October (unknown date): Steinbeck travels to Boston for performances of *Pipe Dream.*[256]

November 30: New York City opening of *Pipe Dream* at the Schubert Theater. The production is a Richard Rogers and Oscar Hammerstein musical based on *Sweet Thursday* and runs for 256 performances ending on June 30, 1956.[257]

December: "What Is the Real Paris?" is published by *Holiday Magazine's* December issue.[258]

December (Late): John and Elaine travel to Trinidad for the New Year's holiday with Rogers and Hammerstein staffer John Fearnley. After New Year's, the trio sails around the Windward and Leeward Islands.[259]

1956

January: "The Yank in Europe" is published in *Holiday Magazine's* January issue.[260]

February: "Miracle Island of Paris" is published in *Holiday Magazine's* February issue.[261]

April 13: Steinbeck goes to Washington for an unknown purpose. He mentions in a letter to Pat Covici that he "haven't (sic) been there since the war. I hope they've cleared the rubble."[262]

May 5: Steinbeck covers the Kentucky Derby for the *Louisville Courier-Journal* and meets Harry Guggenheim and wife Alicia Patterson. The meeting will lead to John writing for the Guggenheim-owned *Newsday*.

July 1: Chase Horton talks to J.M.S. Blakiston at Winchester College at 9:25 a.m. and has lunch with Robert Payne at Winchester later that day. Horton takes a taxi to the Duke of Norfolk's Castle in Asundel.[263]

July 2: Chase Horton notes Steinbeck leaves London on this day.[264]

August: "Discovering the People of Paris" is published in *Holiday Magazine's* August edition.[265]

August 10–17: Steinbeck is in Chicago to attend the Democratic National Convention and covers the event for the *Louisville Courier-Journal.*

August 20–23: Steinbeck attends the Republican National Convention in San Francisco.[266]

September: Steinbeck performs services as a speechwriter for Adlai Stevenson and the USIA. Steinbeck also records a number of pieces for Radio Free Europe.

November 19: John finishes the manuscript for *The Short Reign of Pippin IV.*[267]

December or January (Early) 1957: President Eisenhower asks William Faulkner to head his "People to People" program. (Date is estimated from source letter.)[268]

1957

January (Early): Steinbeck prepares for another trip to the UK, funded by articles he will write for the *Louisville Courier-Journal.*

January 7: Steinbeck visits the Morgan Library in New York City.[269]

January 17: Steinbeck writes Arthur Larson, Director of the USIA, regarding sending books to Eastern Europe and admonishing the denial of a passport to signer and civil rights activist Paul Robeson.[270]

January 19: Steinbeck has lunch with Chase Horton.[271]

March: "My War with the Ospreys" is published in *Holiday Magazine's* March edition.[272]

March 25: Steinbeck and Elaine set sail for Naples on the *Saturnia.*[273]

April: *The Short Reign of Pippin IV* is published.

April 12: The CIA is sent information about Steinbeck from the FBI. This report is also sent to the CIA's Office of Security to a redacted source on April 15th.[274]

April 26: Steinbeck is in Rome and writes Elizabeth Otis and Chase Horton regarding his Malory research.[275]

May 9: Steinbeck is in Florence.[276]

May 17: Steinbeck spends the evening with Professor Armando Sapori.[277]

May 27: The film version of *The Wayward Bus* is released in America.[278]

June: *Esquire* publishes Steinbeck's "The Trial of Arthur Miller."[279]

July 4: Steinbeck is in Stockholm.[280]

July 13: Steinbeck is in London.[281]

July 17: "Red Novelist's Visit Produces Uneasy Talk" is published by the *Louisville Courier-Journal*.[282]

July 18: Steinbeck meets Eugene Vinaver in Manchester for the first time.[283]

July 19: Steinbeck spends the night at the Royal Crewe Arms in Blanchland.[284]

July 20: Steinbeck writes Eugene Vinaver about their first meeting.[285] The postscript of this letter has been removed from *Steinbeck: A Life in Letters*. John also visits Rothbury and Hadrian's Wall.[286]

July 21: Steinbeck travels along Hadrian's Wall and down into Wales.[287]

July 22: Steinbeck travels to Tresanton Saint Mawes near Falmouth.[288]

July 23: Steinbeck returns to Manchester.[289]

July 25: John and Elaine return to New York on the *Queen Elizabeth*.[290]

August 30: Steinbeck boards Pan American flight 857 from San Francisco to Tokyo.[291]

September 1–10: Steinbeck attends a meeting of the International Association of Poets, Playwrights, Editors, Essayists and Novelists in Tokyo. John leaves Tokyo on the 10th on Pan American flight 856.[292]

September (Late): Steinbeck returns to his Sag Harbor home to continue work on the Malory project.

October 4: The Soviets launch the first artificial Earth satellite, *Sputnik 1*, into low Earth orbit.

1958

February 12: The United Nations contacts Steinbeck to ask if he will travel to the "Near-East to do some kind of definitive work on a film about the refugee situation there." Steinbeck declines the offer to continue work on the Malory project.[293]

May: Steinbeck is in London.[294]

June 4: Chase Horton speaks to Joseph Campbell.[295]

June (Early): Steinbeck and Elaine travel to England for research on the Malory project.

June 10–13: Steinbeck travels by train from London to Glastonbury. While in Glastonbury, he stays in the George and Pilgrim and meets Robert Bolt. John returns to London on the afternoon of the 13th.[296]

July (Early): Steinbeck and Elaine return to New York from the UK.

September: *Once There Was a War* is published.

September (Late): Steinbeck sends a finished draft of the Malory project to Chase Horton and Elizabeth Otis for review.

November 6: John replies to a letter by Stuart L. Hannon, assistant to the director of Radio Free Europe. Steinbeck grants Radio Free Europe the right to air/publish his comments on Boris Pasternak's (author of *Dr. Zhivago*) Nobel Prize for Literature award.[297]

1959

January 31: Steinbeck has a phone conversation with Chase Horton.[298]

March–October: John travels in England and Wales, researching background for a modern English version of Malory's *Morte d'Arthur*.[299]

March 5–11: Steinbeck sails from New York to Plymouth, UK, aboard the *Liberte*.

April 30: Steinbeck is in Cadbury.[300]

May 2: Steinbeck visits Glastonbury and the ruins of the Abbey.[301]

May 13: Steinbeck is disheartened by an initial review of his *Le Morte d'Arthur* rewrite by Chase Horton and Elizabeth Otis.[302]

June 24: Steinbeck is in Cadbury for Mid-Summer's Eve and believes he saw the ghost of King Arthur.[303]

July: An FBI informant relays that Steinbeck has received a check in the amount of $188.70 from the New York account of the National Bank of Bulgaria. The check is supposedly forwarded to Steinbeck via his literary agent at McIntosh and Otis.[304]

July 2: John and Elaine visit Plush Folly in Dorset.[305]

August 26: Steinbeck spends the day at Amesbury with Sir Philip Antrobus.[306]

October 1–14: Steinbeck is in London.[307]

October 22: Steinbeck returns to New York from the UK aboard the *Flandre*.

December 3: A minor stroke hospitalizes John for two weeks.[308]

1960

January 11–25: John and Elaine vacation in Caneel Bay.[309]

March–July: Steinbeck drafts the final versions of *The Winter of Our Discontent*.[310]

May 1: While conducting a reconnaissance mission for the CIA, Francis Gary Powers' U-2 is shot down over the Soviet Union.

September 23–November: Steinbeck tours the United States with his poodle, Charley.[311]

1961

January 20: Steinbeck and Elaine attend President Kennedy's inaugural address with John Kenneth Galbraith and his wife.[312]

February 20: Steinbeck is in the British West Indies. (Dates of travel are unknown, but the source notes Steinbeck was here during this period.)[313]

February 28: Steinbeck is in Barbados. (Dates of actual travel are unknown, but the source denotes Steinbeck was here during this period.)[314]

March: "Conversation at Sag Harbor" is published in *Holiday Magazine's* March edition.[315]

March–April: John travels to San Diego to perform duties for the Mohole Expedition. The team plans to drill a 12,000-foot hole off the coast of Mexico. John has to return from the expedition due to a torn hernia.[316]

April: *The Winter of Our Discontent* is published.[317]

April 17–19: The Bay of Pigs Invasion occurs.

May 24: John and Elaine have dinner with Dag Hammarskjöld.[318]

July: "In Quest of America Part One" is published in *Holiday Magazine's* July edition.[319]

August 13: East Germany closes the border between East and West Berlin and begins construction of the Berlin Wall four days later.

September (Early): Prior to the 5th, Dag Hammarskjöld meets with John. Hammarskjöld wrote letters of introduction to Heads of State whom he thought Steinbeck might wish to call on during his time abroad. These included the president of the United Arab Republic, Gamal Abdel Nasser; Prime Minister of Israel, David Ben Gurion; vice president of India, Dr. S. Radakrishnan; and Prime Minister of Burma, U. Nu. Hammarskjöld also sent a letter of introduction to Professor Martin Buber in Jerusalem.[320]

September 8: John, Elaine, and John's sons set sail for England aboard the *Rotterdam*.[321]

September–June 1962: Steinbeck spends ten months in Europe.

November: Steinbeck suffers a minor stroke/heart attack in Milan.[322]

December: "In Quest of America Part Two" is published in *Holiday Magazine's* December edition.[323]

December 24: John and Elaine have an audience with Pope John XXIII at the Vatican.[324]

1962

February: "In Quest of America Part Three" is published in *Holiday Magazine's* February edition.[325]

February 27: John celebrates his 60th birthday on the Isle of Capri.[326]

July: *Travels with Charley* is published.

June (Late): Steinbeck writes journalist Max Freedman regarding John's ideas about subversive activities to undermine Communist control of the Berlin Wall.[327]

July 21: Journalist Max Freedman contacts President Kennedy's assistant Evelyn Lincoln about Steinbeck's Berlin War proposals.[328]

August 21: President Kennedy writes to journalist Max Freedman regarding Steinbeck's proposals on the Berlin Wall.[329]

October 14–28: Tensions between the Soviets and Americans result in the two-week Cuban Missile Crisis.

October 25: Steinbeck is awarded the Nobel Prize for Literature and holds a press conference.[330]

November 5: John takes publicity photos at his home in Sag Harbor.[331]

November 17: John takes more publicity photos in Sag Harbor.[332]

December 10: Steinbeck delivers Nobel Prize acceptance speech in Stockholm.[333]

1963

May: Steinbeck and Edward Albee are in Washington for briefings on their upcoming Soviet Union trip.

October 6: The *New York Herald Tribune* publishes "Reflections of a Lunar Eclipse."

October–December: Steinbeck travels to Scandinavia, Eastern Europe, and Russia on United States Information Agency cultural tour, with playwright Edward Albee.

November 15: Steinbeck poses for Martiros Saryan, Lenin Prize laureate painter of Russia in Moscow.[334]

November 22: President Kennedy is assassinated in Dallas, Texas, and Lyndon Johnson is sworn in as President of the United States. Steinbeck and Albee are still behind the Iron Curtain. Steinbeck decides that the pair should finish the mission President Kennedy had sent them on to honor the memory of the fallen president.

December 17: Steinbeck is debriefed by the State Department for three days after his return to the States. Albee and Steinbeck are known to have met with Lucius Battle after returning to Washington.[335] After the debriefing, Steinbeck and Elaine meet President Johnson at a White House dinner.[336]

1964

January 3: USIA interview with Steinbeck and Edward Albee is broadcast on VOA.[337]

February: Steinbeck meets with Jacqueline Kennedy regarding a biography of John F. Kennedy. The project never came to fruition.[338]

February 27: CIA requests information about Steinbeck from the FBI.[339]

April 23: Steinbeck is in New York with presidential advisor Jack Valenti.[340]

August 21: Steinbeck has an eight-minute telephone conversation with President Johnson about attending the Democratic National Convention and speechwriting.[341]

September 14: John is presented with the United States Medal of Freedom by President Johnson.[342]

October 14: Longtime friend and Steinbeck's publisher Pat Covici dies.

1965

January (Early): Steinbeck and Elaine travel from Ireland to London and then go on to Paris.

January 23: Steinbeck's sister Mary Steinbeck Dekker dies in California.[343]

April (Late): LBJ invites John and Elaine for a weekend at the White House.

June 20: Steinbeck writes Douglas Fairbanks Jr. to arrange a visit to the Duchess of Buccleuch's family library with Eugene Vinevar.[344] Also a report is sent to FBI Associate Director Clyde Tolson and Deputy Director Cartha DeLoach on Steinbeck's background.[345]

October 5: Steinbeck attends "Businessman's Dinner" at the White House with President Johnson.[346]

November: Steinbeck was back in Northumberland, with Eugene Vinaver of Manchester, examining manuscripts in the Alnwick Castle library.

December (Late): Steinbeck spends Christmas with John Houston at his house in St. Clearan's, Ireland.[347]

December 31: Steinbeck's "Letters to Alicia" article published in *Newsday* tells of a possible new Malory manuscript at Alnwick Castle.

1966

March 9: An invitation to the Bohemian Club's summer retreat, known as Bohemian Grove, is sent to John.[348]

March 18: John declines invitation to Bohemian Grove.[349]

April: President Johnson appoints Steinbeck to the Council of the National Endowment for the Arts.[350]

May 16: Steinbeck and son John IV visit President Johnson at the White House.

July 1: John attends a whale boat race between the US Coast Guard and Norway at Sag Harbor.[351]

October: Steinbeck and Elaine receive status as war correspondents for *Newsday* to cover the Vietnam conflict.

October 12: *America and Americans* is published by Viking Press.[352]

December to April 1967: Steinbeck's extensive visit to South Vietnam for fact-finding and to visit John IV.

1967

April (Late): Steinbeck and Elaine leave Vietnam and visit Thailand and Laos.

May: Steinbeck and Elaine report to President Johnson about their experience in Vietnam at a White House meeting.[353]

October 23: Steinbeck has back surgery.

December: Steinbeck vacations with Elaine to the Virgin Islands.

1968

March 18: The FBI sends a name check on Steinbeck to Mildred Stegall, President Johnson's White House aide.[354]

August 21: Steinbeck returns to his Sag Harbor home.

December 20: Steinbeck dies in New York of arteriosclerosis.

1969

Journal of a Novel: The "East of Eden" Letters is published.

1975

Steinbeck: A Life in Letters is published by Viking Press.

1976

The Acts of King Arthur and His Noble Knights is published by Viking Press.[355]

Timeline Sources

[1] Steinbeck T., Phone Interview with Thom Steinbeck, 2008.

[2] Harmon, 2011.

[3] Blankenship, 2008.

[4] Blankenship, 2008.

[5] Harmon, 2011.

[6] Schultz & Li, 2005.

[7] Harmon, 2011.

[8] Harmon, 2011.

[9] Harmon, 2011.

[10] Harmon, 2011.

[11] House Special Committee on Un-American Activities, 1938, p. 1996.

[12] Schultz & Li, 2005.

[13] Schultz & Li, 2005.

[14] United States Department of Labor, 1937.

[15] The Broadway League, 2012.

[16] The Broadway League, 2012.

[17] Harmon, 2011.

[18] Harmon, 2011.

[19] Roosevelt, Memorandum for the Director of the Budget, 1939.

[20] Harmon, 2011.

[21] Wartzman, 2009, p. 32 and United Press, 1938.

[22] FBI, John Steinbeck File #9-4583 and #100-106224 Part 1, 2012, p. 39.

[23] Steinbeck J., Telegram to the Committee to Aid Agricultural Organizations, 1939.

[24] Office of the President of the United States, 1939.

[25] Office of the President of the United States, 1939.

[26] Harmon, 2011.

[27] Benson, *The True Adventures of John Steinbeck, Writer*, 1990, p. 415.

[28] Benson, *The True Adventures of John Steinbeck, Writer*, 1990, p. 415.

[29] IMDB.com INC, 2012.

[30] IMDB.com INC, 2012.

[31] Benson, *The True Adventures of John Steinbeck, Writer*, 1990, pp. 441, 449.

[32] IMDB.com INC, 2012.

[33] Steinbeck J., *Steinbeck: A Life in Letters*, 1975, p. 200.

[34] Steinbeck J., *Steinbeck: A Life in Letters*, 1975, p. 200.

[35] Steinbeck J., *Steinbeck: A Life in Letters*, 1975, p. 201.

[36] Steinbeck J., *Steinbeck: A Life in Letters*, 1975, p. 201.

[37] Benson, *The True Adventures of John Steinbeck, Writer*, 1990, p. 453.

[38] Benson, *The True Adventures of John Steinbeck, Writer*, 1990, p. 453.

[39] Benson, *The True Adventures of John Steinbeck, Writer*, 1990, p. 455.

[40] Steinbeck J., Letter to Joe Hamilton, 1940.

[41] Schultz & Li, 2005, p. 345.

[42] Steinbeck J., June 24, 1940, Letter to President Franklin D. Roosevelt, 1940.

[43]Roosevelt, June 25, 1940, Memorandum from FDR to General Watson, 1940.

[44]Benson, *The True Adventures of John Steinbeck, Writer*, 1990, p. 461.

[45]Steinbeck J., August 13, 1940, Letter to FDR, 1940.

[46]Manning, Winter 2001.

[47]Roosevelt, September 3, 1940, Memorandum to General Watson, 1940. Benson's biography claims this meeting took place on 12 Sept 1939. This must represent a typo within the text.

[48]Benson, *The True Adventures of John Steinbeck, Writer*, 1990, p. 465.

[49]Benson, *The True Adventures of John Steinbeck, Writer*, 1990, p. 471.

[50]Benson, *The True Adventures of John Steinbeck, Writer*, 1990, p. 471.

[51]Office of the President of the United States, 1941.

[52]Steinbeck J., *Steinbeck: A Life in Letters*, 1975, pp. 220–221.

[53]United States National Archives and Records Administration, 2012.

[54]Benson, *The True Adventures of John Steinbeck, Writer*, 1990, p. 483.

[55]Benson, *The True Adventures of John Steinbeck, Writer*, 1990, p. 489.

[56]IMDB.com INC, 2012.

[57]Steinbeck J., *Steinbeck: A Life in Letters*, 1975, p. 237.

[58]Benson, *The True Adventures of John Steinbeck, Writer*, 1990, p. 491.

[59]Office of the President of the United States, 1941.

[60]Manning, Winter 2001.

[61]Harmon, 2011.

[62]Steinbeck J., *The Moon Is Down*, 1995, pp. vii–viii.

[63]The Broadway League, 2012.

[64]Steinbeck J., *Steinbeck: A Life in Letters*, 1975, p. 246.

[65]FBI, John Steinbeck File #9-4583 and #100-106224 Part 1, 2012.

[66]Gerard, 2010.

[67]IMDB.com INC, 2012.

[68]FBI, John Steinbeck File #9-4583 and #100-106224 Part 1, 2012.

[69]Larson, Summer 1948.

[70]Steinbeck J., *Steinbeck: A Life in Letters*, 1975, p. 246.

[71]Steinbeck J., *Steinbeck: A Life in Letters*, 1975, p. 248.

[72]FBI, John Steinbeck File #9-4583 and #100-106224 Part 1, 2012.

[73]Harmon, 2011.

[74]FBI, John Steinbeck File #9-4583 and #100-106224 Part 1, 2012, p. 21.

[75]FBI, John Steinbeck File #9-4583 and #100-106224 Part 1, 2012.

[76]IMDB.com INC, 2012.

[77]Steinbeck J., *Steinbeck: A Life in Letters*, 1975, p. 250. Source for both March 27th and 29th.

[78]Steinbeck J., *Steinbeck: A Life in Letters*, 1975, p. 251.

[79]FBI, John Steinbeck File #9-4583 and #100-106224 Part 1, 2012.

[80]Headquarters of SOS European Theater of Operations United States Army, 1943.

[81]Headquarters of Service and Supply European Theater of Operations United States Army, 1943.

[82]FBI, John Steinbeck File #9-4583 and #100-106224 Part 1, 2012.

[83]Steinbeck J., *Steinbeck: A Life in Letters*, 1975, p. 258.

[84]Steinbeck J., *Steinbeck: A Life in Letters*, 1975, p. 259.

[85]Steinbeck J., *Steinbeck: A Life in Letters*, 1975, pp. 260–61.

[86]Fairbanks, 1993, pp. 194–95.

[87]Fairbanks, 1993, p. 196.

[88]Parini, 1995, p. 277.

[89]Steinbeck J., *Steinbeck: A Life in Letters*, 1975, p. 263.

[90]Benson, *The True Adventures of John Steinbeck, Writer*, 1990.

[91]Steinbeck J., *Steinbeck: A Life in Letters*, 1975.

[92]Benson, *The True Adventures of John Steinbeck, Writer*, 1990, p. 537.

[93]Parini, 1995, p. 279.

[94]Steinbeck J., *Steinbeck: A Life in Letters*, 1975, p. 266.

[95]IMDB.com INC, 2012.

[96]FBI, John Steinbeck File #9-4583 and #100-106224 Part 1, 2012.

[97]O'Neal, 1944.

[98]FBI, John Steinbeck File #9-4583 and #100-106224 Part 2, 2012, p. 5.

[99]FBI, John Steinbeck File #9-4583 and #100-106224 Part 1, 2012, p. 47.

[100]FBI, John Steinbeck File #9-4583 and #100-106224 Part 1, 2012, p. 46.

[101]Benson, *The True Adventures of John Steinbeck, Writer*, 1990, pp. 546–548.

[102]FBI, John Steinbeck File #9-4583 and #100-106224 Part 1, 2012, p. 47.

[103]Steinbeck J., *Steinbeck: A Life in Letters*, 1975, p. 268.

[104]Office of the President of the United States, 1944.

[105]Throughout the years a number of invitations to this party have been offered for private sale bearing the signatures of B.W. Huebsch, Berthold Viertel, and Steinbeck. One such recent offering was from Los Angeles' Goldberg Coins and Collectables.

[106]Harmon, 2011.

[107]Office of the President of the United States, 1944.

[108]Railsback & Meyer, 2006.

[109]IMDB.com INC, 2012.

[110]Steinbeck J., *Steinbeck: A Life in Letters*, 1975, p. 273.

[111]Harmon, 2011.

[112]IMDB.com INC, 2012.

[113]Steinbeck J., *Steinbeck: A Life in Letters*, 1975, p. 281.

[114]CIA, 2012.

[115]Steinbeck J., *Steinbeck: A Life in Letters*, 1975, p. 285.

[116]Harmon, 2011.

[117]Schultz & Li, 2005.

[118]Steinbeck J., *Steinbeck: A Life in Letters*, 1975, p. 293.

[119]United States Department of Justice, 1946.

[120]FBI, John Steinbeck File #9-4583 and #100-106224 Part 1, 2012.

[121]Harmon, 2011.

[122]Steinbeck J., *A Russian Journal*, 1948, p. 3.

[123]Benson, *The True Adventures of John Steinbeck, Writer*, 1990, p. 602.

[124]Steinbeck J., *A Russian Journal*, 1948, p. 69.

[125]Steinbeck J., *Steinbeck: A Life in Letters*, 1975, p. 298.

[126]Steinbeck J., *Steinbeck: A Life in Letters*, 1975, p. 299.

[127]United States Department of Justice, 1947.

[128]Harmon, 2011.

[129]FBI, John Steinbeck File #9-4583 and #100-106224 Part 1, 2012.

[130]Steinbeck J., *Steinbeck: A Life in Letters*, 1975, pp. 309–10.

[131]Benson, *The True Adventures of John Steinbeck, Writer*, 1990.

[132]Benson, *The True Adventures of John Steinbeck, Writer*, 1990.

[133]Benson, *The True Adventures of John Steinbeck, Writer*, 1990.

[134]Steinbeck J., *Steinbeck: A Life in Letters*, 1975, p. 313.

[135]Steinbeck J., *Steinbeck: A Life in Letters*, 1975, p. 317.

[136]FBI, John Steinbeck File #9-4583 and #100-106224 Part 1, 2012, p. 4.

[137]Steinbeck J., *Steinbeck: A Life in Letters*, 1975, pp. 319–321.

[138]Steinbeck J., *Steinbeck: A Life in Letters*, 1975, p. 333.

[139]Steinbeck J., *Steinbeck: A Life in Letters*, 1975, p. 338.

[140]Steinbeck J., *Steinbeck: A Life in Letters*, 1975, p. 338.

[141]Steinbeck J., *Steinbeck: A Life in Letters*, 1975, p. 339.

[142]Steinbeck J., *Steinbeck: A Life in Letters*, 1975, p. 344.

[143]Steinbeck J., "The Miracle of Tepayac," 1948.

[144]Steinbeck J., *Steinbeck: A Life in Letters*, 1975, p. 346.

[145]IMDB.com INC, 2012.

[146]Douglass, 2007.

[146, 147]Steinbeck J., *Steinbeck: A Life in Letters*, 1975, p. 355, 365

[148]Steinbeck J., *Steinbeck: A Life in Letters*, 1975, p. 381.

[149]Steinbeck J., *Steinbeck: A Life in Letters*, 1975, p. 388.

[150]Steinbeck J., *Steinbeck: A Life in Letters*, 1975, p. 397.

[151]Steinbeck J., *Steinbeck: A Life in Letters*, 1975, p. 401.

[152]Steinbeck J., *Steinbeck: A Life in Letters*, 1975, p. 401.

[153]Steinbeck J., *Steinbeck: A Life in Letters*, 1975, p. 402.

[154]Steinbeck J., *Steinbeck: A Life in Letters*, 1975, p. 411.

[155]The Broadway League, 2001.

[156]Recorded Speeches and Utterances by Eleanor Roosevelt, 1933–1962, 2012.

[157]Steinbeck J., *Steinbeck: A Life in Letters*, 1975, p. 415.

[158]Pan American World Airways, INC, 1951.

[159]Steinbeck J., *Journal of a Novel: The East of Eden Letters*, 1969, p. 3.

[160]Steinbeck J., *Journal of a Novel: The East of Eden Letters*, 1969, pp. 5–6.

[161]Steinbeck J., *Journal of a Novel: The East of Eden Letters*, 1969, p. 15.

[162]Steinbeck J., *Journal of a Novel: The East of Eden Letters*, 1969, p. 19.

[163]Steinbeck J., *Journal of a Novel: The East of Eden Letters*, 1969, p. 21.

[164]Steinbeck J., *Journal of a Novel: The East of Eden Letters*, 1969, p. 26.

[165]Steinbeck J., *Journal of a Novel: The East of Eden Letters*, 1969, pp. 29–30.

[166]Steinbeck J., *Journal of a Novel: The East of Eden Letters*, 1969, p. 32.

[167] Steinbeck J., *Journal of a Novel: The East of Eden Letters*, 1969, p. 35.

[168] Steinbeck J., *Journal of a Novel: The East of Eden Letters*, 1969, pp. 43–44.

[169] Davis, 2006.

[170] Steinbeck J., *Journal of a Novel: The East of Eden Letters*, 1969, p. 57.

[171] Steinbeck J., *Journal of a Novel: The East of Eden Letters*, 1969, p. 61.

[172] Steinbeck J., *Journal of a Novel: The East of Eden Letters*, 1969, p. 71.

[173] Steinbeck J., *Journal of a Novel: The East of Eden Letters*, 1969, p. 72.

[174] Steinbeck J., *Journal of a Novel: The East of Eden Letters*, 1969, p. 81.

[175] Steinbeck J., *Steinbeck: A Life in Letters*, 1975, p. 420.

[176] Steinbeck J., *Journal of a Novel: The East of Eden Letters*, 1969, p. 94.

[177] Steinbeck J., *Steinbeck: A Life in Letters*, 1975, p. 421.

[178] Benson, *The True Adventures of John Steinbeck, Writer*, 1990, p. 687.

[179] Steinbeck J., *Journal of a Novel: The East of Eden Letters*, 1969, p. 143.

[180] Steinbeck J., *Journal of a Novel: The East of Eden Letters*, 1969, p. 144.

[181] Harmon, 2011.

[182] Steinbeck J., *Journal of a Novel: The East of Eden Letters*, 1969, p. 162.

[183] Steinbeck J., *Journal of a Novel: The East of Eden Letters*, 1969, p. 169.

[184] Steinbeck J., *Journal of a Novel: The East of Eden Letters*, 1969, p. 173.

[185] Steinbeck J., *Journal of a Novel: The East of Eden Letters*, 1969, p. 172.

[186] Steinbeck J., *Steinbeck: A Life in Letters*, 1975, p. 431.

[187] House Committee on Un-American Activities, 1952, p. 2408.

[188] Steinbeck J., Letter to CIA Director Walter Bedell Smith, 1952.

[189] United States Information Agency, 1952.

[190] Smith W. B., 1952.

[191] IMDB.com INC, 2012.

[192] United States Information Agency, 1952.

[193] United States Information Agency, 1952.

[194] FBI, John Steinbeck File #9-4583 and #100-106224 Part 1, 2012, pp. 57–60.

[195] Benson, *The True Adventures of John Steinbeck, Writer*, 1990, p. 708.

[196] Schultz & Li, 2005.

[197] House Committee on Un-American Activities, 1952, pp. 2409–16.

[198] Steinbeck J., *Steinbeck: A Life in Letters*, 1975, p. 443.

[199] Steinbeck J., *Steinbeck: A Life in Letters*, 1975, p. 443.

[200] Associated Press, 1952.

[201] Steinbeck J., *Steinbeck: A Life in Letters*, 1975, p. 444.

[202] Steinbeck J., *Steinbeck: A Life in Letters*, 1975, p. 448.

[203] Steinbeck J., *Steinbeck: A Life in Letters*, 1975, pp. 448–449.

[204] Steinbeck J., *Steinbeck: A Life in Letters*, 1975, pp. 448–449.

[205] Steinbeck J., *Steinbeck: A Life in Letters*, 1975, pp. 448–449.

[206] Steinbeck J., *Steinbeck: A Life in Letters*, 1975, p. 450.

[207] Steinbeck J., *Steinbeck: A Life in Letters*, 1975, p. 450.

[208] United States Department of Justice, 1952.

[209] Benson, *The True Adventures of John Steinbeck, Writer*, 1990, p. 725.

[210]Benson, *The True Adventures of John Steinbeck, Writer*, 1990, p. 725.

[211]Steinbeck J., *Steinbeck: A Life in Letters*, 1975, p. 451.

[212]Steinbeck J., *Steinbeck: A Life in Letters*, 1975, p. 452.

[213]Steinbeck J., *Steinbeck: A Life in Letters*, 1975, p. 454.

[214]Steinbeck J., "A Duel without Pistols," 1952.

[215]Steinbeck J., "The Soul and Guts of France," 1952.

[216]Air France, 1952.

[217]Steinbeck J., *Steinbeck: A Life in Letters*, 1975, p. 456.

[218]Reil, 1952.

[219]Steinbeck J., *Steinbeck: A Life in Letters*, 1975, p. 461.

[220]Steinbeck J., "The Secret Weapon We Were Afraid to Use," 1953.

[221]Steinbeck J., "I Go Back to Ireland," 1953.

[222]Steinbeck J., *Steinbeck: A Life in Letters*, 1975, p. 469.

[223]House Committee on Un-American Activities, 1953, p. 2330.

[224]Steinbeck J., *Steinbeck: A Life in Letters*, 1975, p. 472.

[225]Schultz & Li, 2005.

[226]FBI, John Steinbeck File #9-4583 and #100-106224 Part 1, 2012.

[227]FBI, John Steinbeck File #9-4583 and #100-106224 Part 1, 2012.

[228]Corbis Corporation, 2012.

[229]Steinbeck J., *Steinbeck: A Life in Letters*, 1975, p. 475.

[230]Steinbeck J., *Steinbeck: A Life in Letters*, 1975, p. 476.

[231]Steinbeck J., *Steinbeck: A Life in Letters*, 1975, p. 477.

[232]Steinbeck J., *Steinbeck: A Life in Letters*, 1975, p. 479.

[233]Steinbeck J., *Steinbeck: A Life in Letters*, 1975, p. 479.

[234]Steinbeck J., *Steinbeck: A Life in Letters*, 1975, p. 479.

[235]Harmon, 2011.

[236]Steinbeck J., *Steinbeck: A Life in Letters*, 1975, p. 481.

[237]Biemiller, 2012.

[238]Schultz & Li, 2005.

[239]Morsberger, 2007.

[240]Schultz & Li, 2005, p. 384.

[241]Steinbeck J., *Steinbeck: A Life in Letters*, 1975, p. 495.

[242]Steinbeck J., *Steinbeck: A Life in Letters*, 1975, p. 499.

[243]Steinbeck J., *Steinbeck: A Life in Letters*, 1975, p. 500.

[244]Steinbeck J., *Steinbeck: A Life in Letters*, 1975, p. 501.

[245]Schultz & Li, 2005.

[246]Schultz & Li, 2005.

[247]Schultz & Li, 2005, p. 384.

[248]Corbis Corperation, 2012.

[249]Schultz & Li, 2005.

[250]Steinbeck, Hammarskjöld, & Hovde, "The Dag Hammarskjöld–John Steinbeck Correspondence," 1997, p. 105.

[251]IMDB.com INC, 2012.

[252]Schultz & Li, 2005, p. 384.

[253]Schultz & Li, 2005, p. 384.

[254]Steinbeck J., *Steinbeck: A Life in Letters*, 1975, p. 505.

[255]Steinbeck J., *Steinbeck: A Life in Letters*, 1975, p. 514.

[256]Steinbeck J., *Steinbeck: A Life in Letters*, 1975, p. 516.

[257]The Broadway League, 2012.

[258]Biemiller, 2012.

[259]Steinbeck J., *Steinbeck: A Life in Letters*, 1975, p. 520.

[260]Biemiller, 2012.

[261]Biemiller, 2012.

[262]Steinbeck J., *Steinbeck: A Life in Letters*, 1975, p. 527.

[263]Horton C., 1959.

[264]Horton C., 1959.

[265]Biemiller, 2012.

[266]Steinbeck J., *Steinbeck: A Life in Letters*, 1975, p. 536.

[267]Steinbeck J., *Steinbeck: A Life in Letters*, 1975, p. 541.

[268]Steinbeck J., *Steinbeck: A Life in Letters*, 1975, p. 546.

[269]Steinbeck J., *The Acts of King Arthur and His Noble Knights*, 1976, p. 356.

[270]Steinbeck J., *Steinbeck: A Life in Letters*, 1975, p. 546.

[271]Horton C., 1959.

[272]Biemiller, 2012.

[273]Steinbeck, Hammarskjöld, & Hovde, "The Dag Hammarskjöld–John Steinbeck Correspondence," 1997, p. 107.

[274]FBI, John Steinbeck File #9-4583 and #100-106224 Part 2, 2012, p. 28.

[275]Steinbeck J., *Steinbeck: A Life in Letters*, 1975, p. 552.

[276]Steinbeck J., *The Acts of King Arthur and His Noble Knights*, 1976, p. 366.

[277]Steinbeck J., *The Acts of King Arthur and His Noble Knights*, 1976, p. 367.

[278]IMDB.com INC, 2012.

[279]Steinbeck J., "The Trial of Arthur Miller," 1957. Oddly enough, the Greenwood Publishing book, *A John Steinbeck Encyclopedia* (Railsback & Meyer, 2006), lists the date of this publication as June 1967.

[280]Steinbeck J., *The Acts of King Arthur and His Noble Knights*, 1976, p. 367.

[281]Steinbeck J., *The Acts of King Arthur and His Noble Knights*, 1976, p. 368.

[282]DeMott, *Steinbeck's Reading: A Catalogue of Books Owned and Borrowed*, 1984, p. 172.

[283]Steinbeck J., *The Acts of King Arthur and His Noble Knights*, 1976, p. 368.

[284]Steinbeck J., *The Acts of King Arthur and His Noble Knights*, 1976, p. 368.

[285]Steinbeck J., *Steinbeck: A Life in Letters*, 1975, p. 557.

[286]Steinbeck J., *The Acts of King Arthur and His Noble Knights*, 1976, p. 368.

[287]Steinbeck J., *The Acts of King Arthur and His Noble Knights*, 1976, p. 368.

[288]Steinbeck J., *The Acts of King Arthur and His Noble Knights*, 1976, p. 368.

[289]Steinbeck J., *The Acts of King Arthur and His Noble Knights*, 1976, p. 368.

[290]Benson, *The True Adventures of John Steinbeck, Writer*, 1990, p. 818.

[291]Pan American World Airways, INC, 1957.

[292]Pan American World Airways, INC, 1957.

[293]Steinbeck, Hammarskjöld, & Hovde, "The Dag Hammarskjöld–John Steinbeck

Correspondence," 1997, p. 112.

294 Steinbeck J., *The Acts of King Arthur and His Noble Knights*, 1976, p. 382.

295 Horton C., 1959.

296 Steinbeck J., *Steinbeck: A Life in Letters*, 1975, p. 586.

297 Steinbeck J., *Steinbeck: A Life in Letters*, 1975, p. 602.

298 Horton C., 1959.

299 Railsback & Meyer, 2006.

300 Steinbeck J., *The Acts of King Arthur and His Noble Knights*, 1976, p. 412.

301 Steinbeck J., *The Acts of King Arthur and His Noble Knights*, 1976, p. 412.

302 Steinbeck J., *Steinbeck: A Life in Letters*, 1975, p. 633.

303 Horton C., 1959.

304 FBI, John Steinbeck File #9-4583 and #100-106224 Part 1, 2012.

305 Steinbeck J., *The Acts of King Arthur and His Noble Knights*, 1976, p. 434.

306 Steinbeck J., *The Acts of King Arthur and His Noble Knights*, 1976, p. 444.

307 Steinbeck J., *The Acts of King Arthur and His Noble Knights*, 1976, p. 444.

308 Schultz & Li, 2005.

309 Schultz & Li, 2005.

310 Railsback & Meyer, 2006.

311 Schultz & Li, 2005.

312 Benson, *The True Adventures of John Steinbeck, Writer*, 1990.

313 Steinbeck, Hammarskjöld, & Hovde, "The Dag Hammarskjöld–John Steinbeck Correspondence," 1997, p. 123.

314 Steinbeck, Hammarskjöld, & Hovde, "The Dag Hammarskjöld–John Steinbeck Correspondence," 1997, p. 124.

315 Biemiller, 2012.

316 Schultz & Li, 2005.

317 Harmon, 2011.

318 Steinbeck, Hammarskjöld, & Hovde, "The Dag Hammarskjöld–John Steinbeck Correspondence," 1997, p. 125.

319 Biemiller, 2012.

320 Steinbeck, Hammarskjöld, & Hovde, "The Dag Hammarskjöld–John Steinbeck Correspondence," 1997, p. 128.

321 Steinbeck, Hammarskjöld, & Hovde, "The Dag Hammarskjöld–John Steinbeck Correspondence," 1997, p. 128.

322 Schultz & Li, 2005.

323 Biemiller, 2012.

324 Schultz & Li, 2005.

325 Biemiller, 2012.

326 Meltzer, 2008, p. 194.

327 Steinbeck J., Letter to Max Freedman, 1962.

328 Freedman, 1962.

329 Kennedy, 1962.

330 Schultz & Li, 2005.

331 Corbis Corporation, 2009.

[332]Corbis Corporation, 2009.

[333]Benson, *The True Adventures of John Steinbeck, Writer*, 1990.

[334]Corbis Corporation, 2012.

[335]Corbis Corporation, 2012.

[336]Potter, 2003.

[337]United States Information Agency, 1964.

[338]Schultz & Li, 2005.

[339]FBI, John Steinbeck File #9-4583 and #100-106224 Part 1, 2012.

[340]Office of the President of the United States, 1964.

[341]Johnson L. B., 1964.

[342]Harmon, 2011.

[343]Schultz & Li, 2005.

[344]Steinbeck J., *Steinbeck: A Life in Letters*, 1975.

[345]FBI, John Steinbeck File #9-4583 and #100-106224 Part 1, 2012.

[346]Office of the President of the United States, 1965.

[347]Railsback & Meyer, 2006.

[348]Steinbeck J., Autographed Letter Signed 03/18/1966.

[349]Steinbeck J., Autographed Letter Signed 03/18/1966.

[350]Schultz & Li, 2005.

[351]Corbis Corporation, 2012.

[352]Harmon, 2011.

[353]Railsback & Meyer, 2006.

[354]FBI, John Steinbeck File #9-4583 and #100-106224 Part 1, 2012.

[355]Steinbeck J., *Steinbeck: A Life in Letters*, 1975.

As one would expect in a digital age, there are a good number of references that have come from authoritative internet sources, chiefly newspaper articles, in this text. For the ease of finding digital sources with long or ponderous web addresses, these links have been truncated using the Tiny URL (www.tinyurl.com) service. Typing the Tiny URL link into the address line of your internet browser will take you directly to the source listed in the bibliography. The endnote section of this text contains references from digital editions of books. With the myriad of eReaders available, the location of specific citations would be impossible to convey in traditional formats. In these cases, the traditional convention of listing page numbers could not be followed. Most eReaders are equipped with a search function and entry of a few keywords will result in finding a specific citation.

The final peculiarity within the bibliography and endnotes section is that of Steinbeck's FBI file. The most commonly available version of this text is a PDF document available at either the FBI's "Vault" website or at www.SteinbeckCitizenSpy.com. The FBI has broken these files into two parts and each citation references the applicable part and the page number corresponding to the PDF's page number.

Air France. (1952-31-August). *New York Passenger Lists, 1820–1957 Record for John Steinbeck.* Retrieved 2012-25-August from Ancestry.com: http://tinyurl.com/9nrekgs.

Albee, E. (2012-14-May). Phone Interview with Edward Albee, (B. Kannard, Interviewer).

Allegretti, J. (2006). "Review of: Critical Companion to John Steinbeck: A Literary Reference to His Life and Work". *The Steinbeck Review.*

Allinson, S. (2000). *Undercover: Ernest Hemingway.* From Military.com: http://tinyurl.com/becdou3.

Andrews, C. (1995). *For the President's Eyes Only: Secret Intelligence and the American Presidency from Washington to Bush.* New York: Harper and Collins.

Applebome, P. (2011-13-March). "Adieu, Sweet Life of '20s Luxury." *New York Times.* From http://tinyurl.com/apagr6d.

Associated Press. (1949-21-June). "Russia May Soon Unveil Own A-Bomb, Says Smith." *Ogden Standard Examiner*, p. 1.

Associated Press. (1952-28-April). "Ridgway Named NATO Commander." *The News and Courier*, p. 1.

Associated Press. (1974-31-December). "Hunt Admits Being Chief of Domestic Spy Group." *The Spokesman-Review*, p. 2.

Associated Press. (2007-25-July). "Woman Sued Castro in Father's Death." *USA Today.* From http://tinyurl.com/a934ehz.

Austin, R. (Director). (1982). *Magnum PI: "Did You See the Sunrise?"* [Television Series].

Barahona, D. (2007-1-March). "The Freedom House Files." *Monthly Review*. From http://tinyurl.com/am7937h.

Barnouw, E. (1970). *A History of Broadcasting in the United States: The Image Empire* (Vol. 3). Oxford: Oxford Press.

Battle, L. (1997-16-January). Interview with Ambassador Lucius Battle (N. S. George Washington University, Interviewer)

Battle, L. (2000-29-October). *Los Angeles Times* Interview with Lucius Battle. (N. Kempster, Interviewer).

BBC News. (2008-August 14). "US Celebrities Spied During WWII." *BBC News*. Retrieved from http://tinyurl.com/bypoc2w.

Bell, L. (1970). "The Failure of Nazism in America." *Political Science Quarterly, 85*(4), 585.

Bell, R. E. (1991). *Women of Classical Mythology: A Biographical Dictionary*. ABC-CLIO.

Benson, J. (1990). *The True Adventures of John Steinbeck, Writer*. New York: Penguin.

Benson, J. (2002). *Looking For Steinbeck's Ghost*. Reno, NV: University of Nevada Press.

Berliner, E. (2012-12-Septermber). Interview with *Silurian News* Editor Eve Berliner (B. Kannard, Interviewer).

Bernstein, C. (1977-20-October). "The CIA and the Media." *Rolling Stone*. From http://tinyurl.com/bjaefsa.

Berryville, T. G. (1991-9-December). "Civil Defense Doomsday Hideaway." *Time Magazine*.

Bideleux, R., & Jeffries, I. (2007). *A History of Eastern Europe: Crisis and Change*. Routledge.

Biemiller, C. (2012). *John Steinbeck's Travels with Charley: In Search of America* was First Published in Curtis Publishing's *Holiday Magazine*. From Carl Biemiller, Author for Young Children: http://www.biemiller.com/steinhol.htm.

Billboard Magazine. (1948-3-July). "'Field and Stream' Swims Towards TV." *Billboard Magazine*.

Billboard Magazine. (1950-25-March). "Henry White Named to TV Post at CBS." *Billboard Magazine*.

Blankenship, L. (2008-16-November). E-Mail Interview with Salinas Masonic Lodge #204 Past Master Leroy Blankenship. (B. Kannard, Interviewer)

Blumenson, M. (1969). *Mediterranean Theater of Operations: Salerno to Cassino*. United States Department of the Army.

Bohemian Club. (2012). *John Steinbeck - Autographed Letter Signed 03/18/1966 Document 285255*. Retrieved 2011-11-November from History for Sale: http://tinyurl.com/7oofknt.

Bresler, R. J. (2004). *Freedom of Association: Rights and Liberties Under the Law*. ABC-CLIO.

Britt, G. (Ed.). (1974). *Shoeleather and Printers' Ink: Experiences and Afterthoughts by New York Newspapermen on the Fiftieth Anniversary of Their Old-Timers' Society, Selected from Issues of Silurian News*. New York: Quadrangle/The New York Times Book Co.

Broadway League. (2001). *Burning Bright*. From Internet Broadway Database: http://www.ibdb.com/production.php?id=1872.

Broadway League. (2012). Internet Broadway Database. From Richard H. Gordon: http://www.ibdb.com/person.php?id=93023.

Broadway League. (2012). *Of Mice and Men*. From Internet Broadway Database: http://www.ibdb.com/production.php?id=12320.

Broadway League. (2012). *Pipe Dream*. From Internet Broadway Database: http://www.ibdb.com/production.php?id=2560.

Broadway League. (2012). *The Moon Is Down*. From Internet Broadway Database: http://www.ibdb.com/production.php?id=1185.

Broadway League. (2012). *Tortilla Flat*. From Internet Broadway Database: http://www.ibdb. com/production.php?id=10711.

Brown, E. L. (1977). "The Divine Name 'Pan.'" *Transactions of the American Philological Association, 107*, 57–61.

California Legislature. (1948-25-March). Fourth Report of the Senate Fact-Finding Committee on Un-American Activities: Communist Front Organizations. Sacramento: California State Senate.

Callaghan, D. (1939-13-December). Letter to Marguerite Le Hand. *OF 3858: Steinbeck, John 1939–1940*. Hyde Park, New York: Franklin D. Roosevelt Library and Museum.

Callaghan, D. (1939-13-December). Letter to Marguerite Le Hand. *OF 3858: Steinbeck, John 1939–1940*. Hyde Park, New York: Franklin D. Roosevelt Library and Museum.

Cedillo, J. A. (2007). *Los Nazis en Mexico*. Mexico City: Random House Mondadori.

Center for Cryptologic History. (n.d.). *The Verona Story*. Washington: National Security Agency's Center for Cryptologic History.

Chalou, G. C. (1992). *The Secrets War: The Office of Strategic Services in World War II*. Washington, D.C., National Archives and Records Administration.

Chalquist, C. M. (2004). *The Noble Tale of Sir John of Steinbeck*. Retrieved 2011-21-November from Terrapsych: http://www.terrapsych.com/steinbeck.html.

Chermak, S., & Bailey, F. (2007). *Crimes and Trials of the Century Vol 2*. Westport, Connecticut: Greenwood Press.

Childs, M. (1949-13-April). *Washington Calling*. Sheboygan Press, p. 14.

CIA. (1950). *Foreign Economic Intelligence Requirements Relating to the National Security*. Langley: CIA.

CIA. (2007-25-April). *Intelligence and Analysis: History*. Retrieved 2012-27-August from CIA: http://tinyurl.com/b8wmgyh.

CIA. (2007-4-May). *Support to Mission: Organization*. Retrieved 2012-29-August from CIA: http://tinyurl.com/atjh9f8.

CIA. (2008-31-December). *DCI Walter Bedell Smith Creates the Directorate for Intelligence*. Retrieved 2012-27-August from CIA: http://tinyurl.com/beq76sf.

CIA. (2008-22-May). *The CIA Campus: The Story of Original Headquarters Building*. Retrieved from CIA: http://tinyurl.com/bc7pms2.

CIA. (2011-19-April). *CIA Declassifies Oldest Documents in U.S. Government Collection*. Retrieved 2011-22-April from CIA: http://tinyurl.com/ax2ufzx.

CIA. (2012-12-August). *An End and a Beginning*. From CIA: http://tinyurl.com/ae5ba3m.

CIA. (2012-25-October). *Application Process*. From CIA: http://tinyurl.com/ah83hz2.

Clark, E. E. (2003). *Indian Legends of the Pacific Northwest*. Berkeley, CA: University of California Press.

Cobiron, B. (2012-September-October). E-Mail Conversations with Bernard Corbiron. (B. Kannard, Interviewer).

Coers, D. V. (1991). *John Steinbeck Goes to War: The Moon Is Down as Propaganda*. Tuscaloosa, Alabama: University of Alabama Press.

Cogan, D. (Director). (2008). *Secrecy* [Motion Picture].

Colby, C. (Director). (2011). *The Man Nobody Knew: In Search of My Father, CIA Spymaster William Colby* [Motion Picture].

Cook, J. (2009-13-October). *The Story Behind Walter Cronkite's Destroyed FBI File*. From Gawker: http://tinyurl.com/bhuw2pm.

Corbis Corporation. (2009). *John Steinbeck Peering Through Telescope.* Retrieved 2009-18-February from Corbis: http://tinyurl.com/bj2pet7.

Corbis Corporation. (2009). *Nobel Prize Winning Author John Steinbeck.* Retrieved 2009-18-February from Corbis: http://tinyurl.com/bfmfr5c.

Corbis Corporation. (2012). *Author John Steinbeck and His Wife.* Retrieved 2012-8-June from Corbis: http://tinyurl.com/axnbayk.

Corbis Corporation. (2012). *John Steinbeck Posing for Portrait.* From Corbis Images: http://tinyurl.com/a27of6b.

Corbis Corporation. (2012). *Portrait of John Steinbeck.* Retrieved 2012-8-June from Corbis: http://tinyurl.com/am44kxf.

Corbis Corporation. (2012). *Raymond Massey with Colleagues.* Retrieved 2012-8-June from Corbis: http://tinyurl.com/adsc4kk.

Corbis Corporation. (2012-8-June). *Three Authors Standing and Talking.* From Corbis: http://tinyurl.com/bavw3mu.

Coriden, G. (1992-18-November). The Association for Diplomatic Studies and Training Foreign Affairs Oral History Project (C. S. Kennedy, Interviewer) From http://tinyurl.com/ap7fwb7.

Cornell University Law School. (2012). *2 USC § 192–Refusal of Witness to Testify or Produce Papers.* From Cornell University Law School: http://www.law.cornell.edu/uscode/text/2/192.

Cote, W. E. (2002-22-September). "Correspondent or Warrior? Hemingway's Murky World War II 'Combat' Experience. *The Hemingway Review, 22*(1). .

Counterattack Magazine. (1952). *Red Channels: The Report of Communist Influence in Radio and Television.* New York: *Counterattack Magazine.*

Cowen, T. (2010). *Good and Plenty: The Creative Successes of American Arts Funding.* Princeton, New Jersy: Princeton University Press.

Crewdson, J. M. (1977-27-December). "CIA Established Many Links To Journalists in U.S. and Abroad." *New York Times*, p. 1.

Cron, I. M. (2011). *Jesus, My Father, the CIA, and Me: A Memoir of Sorts.* Nashville, Tennessee: Thomas Nelson.

Crosswell, D. K. (2010). *Beetle: The Life of General Walter Bedell Smith.* Lexington, Kentucky: The University of Kentucky Press.

Cummings, R. H. (2010). *Radio Free Europe's "Crusade for Freedom": Rallying Americans behind Cold War Broadcasting.* Jefferson, North Carolina: McFarland.

Cummings, R. H. (Summer 2008). "Balloons over East Europe: America's Covert Radio and Leaflet Operations in the Cold War." *Falling Leaf: The Quarterly Journal of the PsyWar Society*, 197.

Davidson, P. (1993-25-November). "Diego Rivera's Dirty Little Secret." *The Independent.* From http://tinyurl.com/yjx95aq.

Davis, R. L. (2006). *Zachary Scott: Hollywood's Sophisticated Cad.* Jackson, MS: University Press of MS.

Dawidoff, N. (1995). *The Catcher Was a Spy: The Mysterious Life of Moe Berg.* New York: Vintage Press.

Day, J. (1995). *The Vanishing Vision: The Inside Story of Public Television.* Berkley, CA: University of California Press.

De Courcy, A. (2010-28-January). *Why Did J.D. Salinger Spend the Last 60 Years Hiding in a Shed Writing Love Notes to Teenage Girls?* Retrieved 2010-28-January from *Guardian* (UK): http://tinyurl.com/a8ss5ry.

Deborah, D. (1979). *Katherine the Great.* New York: Sheridan Square Press.

DeMott, R. (1984). *Steinbeck's Reading: A Catalogue of Books Owned and Borrowed.* New York and London: Garland Publishing.

DeMott, R. (1988). "In Memoriam: Chase Horton (1897–1985)." *Steinbeck Quarterly,* 21(Summer-Fall 1988), 69-72.

Diaz, P. (Director). (2007). *Speaking Freely Volume 3: Ray McGovern* [Motion Picture].

Diggins, J. P. (1993). *Up from Communism.* New York: Columbia University Press.

Dilanian, K. (2012-24-January). "Ex-CIA Officer Charged with Disclosing Classified Information." *Los Angeles Times.* http://tinyurl.com/a8s69lp.

Donovan, W. (1941-15-December). Memorandum for the President. Hyde Park, New York: Franklin D. Roosevelt Library and Museum.

Douglass, P. (2007). "Interview with Corinne Cooke." *Steinbeck Review* (Spring), 95–101.

During, S. (1999). *The Cultural Studies Reader* (Second ed.). London: Routledge Press.

Edelman, H. (2005). "Frederick A. Praeger: Apostle of Anti-Communism Who Built Two Publishing Houses." *LOGOS: The Journal of the World Book Community,* 16(2).

Eisenhower, D. D. (1954-7-July). *Dwight D. Eisenhower to John Foster Dulles, 7 July 1954.* (J. H. Press, Ed.) From The Presidential Papers of Dwight D. Eisenhower: http://tinyurl.com/bjp8m4z.

Endicott, S., & Hagerman, E. (1998). *The United States and Biological Warfare: Secrets from the Early Cold War and Korea.* Bloomington, Indiana: Indiana University Press.

Estes, D. (1977). "Kondo Masaharu and the Best of All Fisherman." *The Journal of San Diego History.* From http://www.sandiegohistory.org/journal/77summer/kondo.htm.

Everitt, D. (2007). *A Shadow of Red: Communism and the Blacklist in Radio and TV.* Chicago: Ivan R. Dee.

Fairbanks, D. J. (1993). *A Hell of a War.* London: Robson Books.

FBI. (Retrieved 2012). Albert Einstein File #61-7099 Part 9. FBI. From http://tinyurl.com/agr3xd6.

FBI. (Retrieved 2012). Albert Einstein File #61-7099 Part 11. FBI. From http://tinyurl.com/a67dyfn.

FBI. (Retrieved 2012). Bettie Page FBI File. FBI. From http://vault.fbi.gov/bettie-page.

FBI. (Retrieved 2012). Desi Arnaz FBI File. FBI. From http://vault.fbi.gov/Desi%20Arnaz.

FBI. (Retrieved 2012). Ernest Hemingway File # 64-23312 Part 1. FBI. From http://vault.fbi.gov/ernest-miller-hemingway.

FBI. (Retrieved 2012). Ernest Hemingway File # 64-23312 Part 2. FBI. From http://vault.fbi.gov/ernest-miller-hemingway.

FBI. (Retrieved 2012). Ernest Hemingway File # 64-23312 Part 3. FBI. From http://vault.fbi.gov/ernest-miller-hemingway.

FBI. (1946). History of the SIS (Vol. 1). Washington, D.C., FBI. From http://tinyurl.com/a76w2zw.

FBI. (1946). History of the SIS (Vol. 3). Washington, D.C., FBI. From http://tinyurl.com/bxu9due.

FBI (Retrieved 2012). John Steinbeck File #9-4583 and #100-106224 Part 1. FBI. From http://tinyurl.com/azc8n22.

FBI (Retrieved 2012). John Steinbeck File #9-4583 and #100-106224 Part 2. FBI. From http://tinyurl.com/azp2prx.

FBI (Retrieved 2012). John Updike FBI File. FBI. From http://vault.fbi.gov/john-updike.

FBI (Retrieved 2012). Lilly Hellman File # 100-28760 and 100-28760 Sub A. FBI. From http://tinyurl.com/a4fz9ro.

FBI (Retrieved 2012). Pearl S. Buck FBI File. FBI. From http://vault.fbi.gov/Pearl%20Buck.

FBI (Retrieved 2012). Walter Elias Disney File #HQ-94-4-4667. FBI. From http://vault.fbi.gov/walter-elias-disney.

Finkelman, P. (Ed.). (2006). *Encyclopedia of American Civil Liberties* (Vol. 1). CRC Press.

Freedman, M. (1962-21-July). *Letter to Evelyn Lincoln.* From John F. Kennedy Presidential Library and Museum: http://tinyurl.com/b532lna.

Freedom House. (2012). *Our History.* From Freedom House: http://www.freedomhouse.org/content/our-history.

Friedman, S. (2008-28-June). *Cold War and Insurgency Propaganda Banknotes.* From Psywar.org: http://www.psywar.org/coldwarcurrency.php.

Gannett Government Media Corporation. (2012). *James P. Shaw Awards and Citations.* Retrieved 2012-5-Feb from *Military Times*: http://tinyurl.com/anzzyu7.

Gannett Government Media Corporation. (2012). *Michael Chinigo Awards and Citations.* Retrieved 2012-5-Feb from *Military Times*: http://tinyurl.com/bapzb9n.

Garrett, Major John. (1999). *Task Force Smith: A Lesson Never Learned.* Fort Leavenworth: School of Advanced Military Studies United States Army Command and General Staff College.

Gerard, A. (2010-December). *Steinbeck's Guns.* Retrieved 2012-7-June from 10964 *The Palisades Newsletter*: http://palisadesny.com/history/steinbecks-guns.

Gilbert, J. G. (1995). *Opposite Attraction: The Lives of Erich Maria Remarque and Paulette Goddard.* New York: Pantheon Books.

Goldstein, P. (1999-22-March). "Many Refuse to Clap as Kazan Receives Oscar." *Los Angeles Times.* From http://tinyurl.com/bbpnh9b.

Gonzalez, D. (2005-25-February). "A Cuban Revolution, in Reading." *New York Times.* From http://tinyurl.com/9283yge.

Goodman, A., & Goodman, D. (2007). *Static: Government Liars, Media Cheerleaders, and the People Who Fight Back.* New York: Hyperion.

Gottfried, M. (2004). *Arthur Miller: His Life and Work.* Cambridge, MA: Da Capo Press.

Greenwald, G. (2012-29-August). "Correspondence and Collusion between the New York Times and the CIA." *The Guardian* (UK). From http://tinyurl.com/cuhkof3.

Griffin, W. (2003-20-September). "Cold War, Cold Comfort Ceremony to Mark 1963 Disappearance of Maine Woman's Dad." *Bangor Daily News.*

Guttman, J. (1994-January). "Specialist in Diversion." *World War II Magazine.*

Guttman, J. (2012-16-April). Questions to Jon Guttman from Weidner Publication Group Editor Gerald Swick. (G. Swick, Interviewer)

Hackett, D. A. (1997). *The Buchenwald Report.* Boulder, Colorado: Westview Press.

Hardy, D. M. (2012-1-May). Letter to Brian Kannard re: Subject Steinbeck, John Ernst (MDR). United States Department of Justice.

Harmon, R. B. (2011). *Steinbeck in Schools: Chronology.* Retrieved 2011-18-December from The Martha Heasley Cox Center for Steinbeck Studies: http://tinyurl.com/aqwsbkc.

Hayashi, T. (Ed.). (1972). "Steinbeck and the Arthurian Theme." *Steinbeck Monograph Series*, 5.

Hayashi, T. (1982). "Elizabeth R. Otis as I Remember Her." *Steinbeck Quarterly,* 15(Winter-Spring 1982), 6.

Haynes, J. E., & Klehr, H. (2000). *Venona: Decoding Soviet Espionage in America.* Cambridge: Yale University Press.

Haywood, N. (2011-November). Email Exchange, November 2011 (B. Kannard, Interviewer).

Haywood, N. (2012-29-August). Night Vision Radio with Guest Nic Haywood (R. Barnett, Interviewer) From http://www.latalkradio.com/Rene.php.

Headquarters of Service and Supply European Theater of Operations United States Army. (1943-26-July). Notes on Staff and Command Conference.

Headquarters of Service and Supply European Theater of Operations United States Army. (1943-2-August). Notes on Staff Conference.

Hemingway, Ernest. Letter to John. (1944-3-March). Boston, Massachusetts: John F. Kennedy Presidential Library and Museum.

Henry, A. (1911). *History of Dentistry in Cleveland.* Cleveland, Ohio: Ohio Publishing House of the Evangelical Association.

Herbert Kline, "Filmmaker, 89; Recorded Crises in 30's Europe." (1999-17-February). *New York Times.* From http://tinyurl.com/aoo9e2o.

Heritage Auctions. (2009). *2009 May Grand Format Political & Americana Auction.* From Heritage Auctions: http://tinyurl.com/atue3nu.

Herman, A. (1999). *Joseph McCarthy: Reexamining the Life and Legacy of America's Most Hated Senator.* New York: Free Press.

Herrera, H. (1983). *A Biography of Frida Kahlo.* New York, NY: Harper Collins.

Hewitt, V. A. H. (1943). *The Italian Campaign Western Naval Task Force Action Report of the Salerno Landings September-October 1943.* United States Department of Navy.

Hinds, M. J. (2008). *John Steinbeck: Banned, Challenged, and Censored.* Berkeley Heights, New Jersey: Enslow Publishers.

Horton, C. (1959). *Personal Journal of Chase Horton.* Research Journal held in New York Public Library Special Records Section.

Horton, J. nephew (2012-21-January). Phone Interview with Jospehine Horton's nephew (B. Kannard, Interviewer).

Horton, S. (2011-16-June). "Did the Bush Administration Use the CIA to Attack a Domestic Critic?" *Harper's Magazine.* From http://tinyurl.com/a5x9wtm.

House Committee on Un-American Activities. (1952-19–21-May). *Communist Infiltration of the Hollywood Motion-Picture Industry Part 8.* Washington, D.C., United States Government Printing Office.

House Committee on Un-American Activities. (1947-20–28-October). *Hearings Regarding the Communist Infiltration of the Motion Picture Industry.* Washington, D.C., United States Government Printing Office.

House Committee on Un-American Activities. (1952). *Hearings Regarding the Communist Infiltration of the Motion Picture Industry Part 7.* Washington, D.C., United States Government Printing Office.

House Committee on Un-American Activities. (1953). *Investigations of Communist Activities in the Los Angeles Area Part 6.* Washington, D.C., United States Government Printing Office.

House Special Committee on Un-American Activities. (1938-November and December). *Investigation of Un-American Propaganda Activities in the United States Volume 5.* Washington, D.C., United States Government Printing Office.

Howells, R. (2011). *Inside the Priory of Sion: Revelations from the World's Most Secret Society —Guardians of the Bloodline of Jesus.* London: Watkins Press.

Hughes, R. (1989). *John Steinbeck: A Study in Short Fiction.* Boston: G.K. Hall and Co.

Hyde, H. M. (1982). *Secret Intelligence Agent.* New York: St. Martin's Press.

IMBD.com INC. (2012). *Roland Kibbee.* From IMDB: http://www.imdb.com/name/nm0452134.

IMDB.com. (2012). *Richard H. Gordon.* From IMDB: http://www.imdb.com/name/nm1012871.

IMDB.com INC. (2012). *A Medal for Benny.* Retrieved 2012-6-June from IMDB: http://www.imdb.com/title/tt0037906.

IMDB.com INC. (2012). *Burgess Meredith.* From IMDB: http://www.imdb.com/name/nm0580565.

IMDB.com INC. (2012). *East of Eden.* Retrieved 2012-6-June from IMDB: http://www.imdb.com/title/tt0048028.

IMDB.com INC. (2012). *Lifeboat.* Retrieved 2012-6-June from IMDB: http://www.imdb.com/title/tt0037017.

IMDB.com INC. (2012). *Of Mice and Men.* Retrieved 2012-6-June from IMDB: http://www.imdb.com/title/tt0031742.

IMDB.com INC. (2012). *The Forgotten Village.* Retrieved 2012-6-June from IMDB: http://www.imdb.com/title/tt0033623.

IMDB.com INC. (2012). *The Grapes of Wrath.* Retrieved 2012-6-June from IMDB: http://www.imdb.com/title/tt0032551.

IMDB.com INC. (2012). *The Moon Is Down.* Retrieved 2012-6-June from IMDB: http://www.imdb.com/title/tt0036170.

IMDB.com INC. (2012). *The Red Pony.* Retrieved 2012-6-June from IMDB: http://www.imdb.com/title/tt0041792.

IMDB.com INC. (2012). *The Wayward Bus.* Retrieved 2012-6-June from IMDB: http://www.imdb.com/title/tt0051182.

IMDB.com INC. (2012). *Tortilla Flat.* Retrieved 2012-6-June from IMDB: http://www.imdb.com/title/tt0035460/releaseinfo.

IMDB.com INC. (2012). *Viva Zapata!* Retrieved 2012-6-June from IMDB: http://www.imdb.com/title/tt0045296/releaseinfo.

International Committee of the Fourth International. (2012-3-February). *David North Speaks in Berlin: "In Defense of Leon Trotsky and Historical Truth."* From World Socialist Web Site: http://tinyurl.com/ajg35xm.

Ira & Larry Goldberg Coins & Collectibles at Live Auctioneers.com. Retrieved 2013-3-May from http://www.liveauctioneers.com/item/7197725.

Irving, D. (1996). *Nuremberg: The Last Battle.* London: Focal Point.

James Cummings Bookseller. (2013) *Steinbeck in Cuernavaca.* Retrieved 2013-4-March from http://tinyurl.com/lvecwxz.

Janicek, K. (2012-20-August). *Tapes Found in AP Reporter's Cold War Show Trial.* From Yahoo News: http://tinyurl.com/a3yslyb.

Johnson, L. B. (1964-21-August). *LBJ Recording of Telephone Conversation, WH Series, JOHN STEINBECK, 8:45P, 08/21/1964.* From National Archives: http://research.archives.gov/description/191320.

Johnson, L. K. (2006). *Strategic Intelligence.* Westport, Connecticut: Greenwood Press.

Jones, N. (2011-20-April). *CIA Releases 1917 Invisible Ink Recipe Due to MDR Request, Not Kindness of Heart.* Retrieved 2011-22-April from Unredacted: The National Security Archive Unedited and Uncensored: http://tinyurl.com/b92mlaw.

Kachere, P. (2012-25-August). "CIA's Freedom House: A House of Destruction." *The Sunday Mail.* From http://tinyurl.com/b2p2vh5.

Kahn, E. J. (1965). *The World of Swope* (1st ed.). New York: Simon and Schuster.

Kazan, E. (1988). *Elia Kazan: A Life.* New York: Doubleday.

Kelley, M. (2009-23-September). "Cronkite Records Destroyed by FBI." *USA Today.* From http://www.usatoday.com/news/nation/cronkite.htm.

Kennedy, J. F. (1962-21-August). *Letter to Max Freedman.* From John F. Kennedy Presidential Library and Museum: http://tinyurl.com/b532lna.

Kershaw, A. (2004). *Blood and Champagne: The Life and Times of Robert Capa.* Cambridge, Massachusetts: Da Capo Press.

Konstam, A. (2007). *Salerno 1943: The Allied Invasion of Italy.* Barnsley, UK: Pen & Sword.

Kramer, P. (1981). "Nelson Rockefeller and British Security Coordination." *Journal of Contemporary History,* 16(1), 73–88.

Lanchin, M. (2012-27-August). "Trotsky's Grandson Recalls Ice Pick Killing." *BBC.* From http://www.bbc.co.uk/news/magazine-19356256.

Landsberg, B. (1998-June). *Landmark Accidents: Cleared for the Approach.* Retrieved 2012-15-August from Aircraft Owners and Pilots Association: http://tinyurl.com/bxcqnx3.

Langbart, D. A., & Haines, G. K. (1993). *Unlocking the Files of the FBI: A Guide to Its Records and Classification System.* Lanham, MD: Rowman & Littlefield Publishers.

Larson, C. (Summer 1948). "The Domestic Motion Picture Work of the Office of War Information." *Hollywood Quarterly,* 434–443.

Le Parti Communiste Internationaliste. (1952-30-May). "Into Action to Gain the Liberation of Jacques Duclos." (M. Abidor, Ed.) *Le Parti Communiste Internationaliste.*

Lee, F. R. (2003-28-June). "A Library In Cuba: What Is It?" *New York Times.* From http://tinyurl.com/9dx7l4v.

LeFabre, W. (1993). *America, Russia, and the Cold War, 1945–80.* New York: McGraw-Hill.

Liggett, B. (2005-13-April). "Press, Politics and Poker—Howard Bayard Swope." *Poker Player.* From http://tinyurl.com/atqz3rq.

Lincoln, H., Baigent, M., & Leigh, R. (1982). *Holy Blood, Holy Grail.* New York: Delacorte.

Lincoln, H., Baigent, M., & Leigh, R. (1983). *The Messianic Legacy.* New York: Delta Press.

Lodge of Edinburgh (Mary's Chapel) No.1. (1999). *The Lodge of Edinburgh (Mary's Chapel) No.1: Quatercentenary of Minutes 1599–1999.* Edinburgh: The Lodge of Edinburgh (Mary's Chapel) No.1.

Luce, H. (Ed.). (1952-28-January). *Life Magazine.*

Lunding, H. (1970). *Stemplet Fortroligt* (3rd ed.). Gyldendal.

Lynn, K. (1993). *Hemingway.* Cambridge, MA: Harvard University Press.

Lyons, R. D. (1994-4-June). "Frederick A. Praeger Dies at 78; Published Books on Communism." *New York Times.*

MacFarland, K. D., & Roll, D. L. (2005). *Louis Johnson and the Arming of America: The Roosevelt and Truman Years.* Bloomington: University of Indiana Press.

MacLeish, A. (1941-24-January). Letter to Josephus Daniels. Hyde Park, New York: Franklin D. Roosevelt Library and Museum.

Malkin, L. (2008). *Krueger's Men: The Secret Nazi Counterfeit Plot and the Prisoners of Block 19*. Paris: Back Bay Books.

Manning, M. (Winter 2001). "The Cover." *Libraries and Culture*, 36(1), pp. 267–74.

Marolda, E. J. (Ed.). (1998). *FDR and the U.S. Navy*. New York: Palgrave Macmillan.

Martinez, L. (2012, May 23). *CIA Identifies, Memorializes Fallen Covert Officers*. Retrieved from ABC News: http://tinyurl.com/b3vvkqh.

Masonic Service Association. (2010). *Masonic Membership Statistics*. From Masonic Service Associations of North America: http://www.msana.com/msastats.asp.

Matthews, J. (2003-September). *Capri*. From University of Maryland University College Around Naples Encyclopedia: http://tinyurl.com/a7zwjvm.

Maurer, N. (2010). *The Empire Struck Back: The Mexican Oil Expropriation of 1938 Reconsidered*. Harvard Business School.

Mayo Clinic. (2011-8-April). *Post-traumatic Stress Disorder (PTSD)*. From The Mayo Clinic: http://tinyurl.com/ar9pa7j.

McBride, J. (2006). *What Ever Happened to Orson Welles? A Portrait of an Independent Career*. Lexington, Kentucky: The University Press of Kentucky.

Meeks, J.D. (2009) *From the Belly of the HUAC: The HUAC Investigations of Hollywood, 1947–1952*. Ann Arbor, Michigan: ProQuest, UMI Dissertation Publishing

Meltzer, M. (2008). *John Steinbeck: A Twentieth-Century Life*. New York: Viking.

Menninger, C. W. (2012-10-December). *People to People Beginnings*. From People to People International: http://tinyurl.com/be5dn8j.

Meredith, J. H. (1999-22-March). "Hemingway's U.S. 3rd Army Inspector General Interview during World War II." *The Hemingway Review*. Retrieved 2012-12-Feb from The Free Library: http://tinyurl.com/bbskkxh.

Miller, M. (1943). *Land Where Time Stands Still*. Binghamton, NY: Vail-Ballou Press.

Miller, R. M. (1985). *Harry Emerson Fosdick: Preacher, Pastor, Prophet*. Oxford: Oxford Press.

Milward, A. S. (1984). *The Reconstruction of Western Europe: 1945–51*. New York: Routledge.

Monier, A., Ahlgren, G., & Monier, S. (1993). *Crime of the Century: The Lindbergh Kidnapping Hoax*. Wellesley, Maine: Branden Books.

Montague, L. L. (1992). *General Walter Bedell Smith As Director of Central Intelligence, October 1950-February 1953*. Pittsburgh: Penn State Press.

Morsberger, R. A. (2007). "Introduction: The Short Reign of Pippin IV: A Fabrication. In J. Steinbeck, *The Short Reign of Pippin IV: A Fabrication*." New York: Penguin Books.

National Defense University. (1997). *Allied Command Structures in the New NATO*. Darby, Pennsylvania: Diane Publishing Company.

National Security Agency. (1944-20-February). Covername JOSE to go to Cuba. Reference to GNOM-Covername for Ramon Mercader, who murdered Trotsky. National Security Agency. From http://tinyurl.com/b2nkz5s.

National Security Archive. (1995). *The National Security Archives at George Washington University*. Retrieved 2012-6-January from FOIA Basics.

National Security Archive. (2010-12-February). *The National Security Archives of George Washington University*. Retrieved 2012-15-August from Project Azorian: The CIA's Declassified History of the Glomar Explorer: http://tinyurl.com/b6go8ll.

Navasky, V. S. (1980). *Naming Names*. New York: Hill and Wang.

New York Times. (1967-September). "Obituary: Mrs. Horton, 79, Co-Owner of Bookstore in the 'Village'." *New York Times*.

New York Times. (1981-17-October). "Donald R. Heath, 87; Served as a U.S. Envoy." *New York Times.*

New York Times. (1992-20-Auguest). "Obituary Stanley Woodward Sr., Former U.S. Envoy, 93." *New York Times.*

94th Congress. (1975). *Hearings Before the Select Committee to Study Governmental Operations with Respect to Intelligence Activities: Volume II.* Washington D.C., United States Government Printing Office.

94th Congress. (1976). *Supplementary Detailed Staff Reports on Intelligence Activities and the Rights of Americans: Final Report of the Select Committee to Study Governmental Operations with Respect to Intelligence Activities Book III.* Washington D.C., United States Government Printing Office.

Nobilem, P., & Rosenbaum, R. (1976-9-July). "The Circus Aftermath of JFK's Best and Brightest Affair." *New Times.*

Norton, G. (1953-January). "Hurricanes of 1952." *Monthly Weather Review*, p. 12. From http://tinyurl.com/a7ehf66.

Nyksha. (1919-30-September). A Bohemian Bookshop. *El Paso Herald*, p. 6.

O'Donnell, P. K. (2004). *Operatives, Spies, and Saboteurs.* New York: Simon and Schuster.

O'Connor, B. (1939-8-December). Letter to Marguerite Le Hand. *OF 3858: Steinbeck, John 1939–1940.* Hyde Park, New York: Franklin D. Roosevelt Library and Museum.

Official 509th Parachute Infantry Association. (2006). *509th Parachute Infantry Timeline.* From Official 509th Parachute Infantry Association: http://www.509thgeronimo.org/509thTimeline.htm.

Office of the President of the United States. (1939-9-February). 1581-Miscel. Franklin D. Roosevelt Library and Museum.

Office of the President of the United States. (1939-5-April). P.P.F. 9-C. *OF 3858: Steinbeck, John 1939–1940.* Hyde Park, New York: Franklin D. Roosevelt Library and Museum.

Office of the President of the United States. (1941-24-January). P.P.F. 86. *OF 3858: Steinbeck, John 1939–1940.* Franklin D. Roosevelt Library.

Office of the President of the United States. (1941-15-December). Personal Secretary File: Subject File: Office of Strategic Services: Donovan Reports. *OF 3858: Steinbeck, John 1939–1940.* Franklin D. Roosevelt Library and Museum.

Office of the President of the United States. (1944-7-August). P.P.F. 8853. *OF 3858: Steinbeck, John 1939–1940.* Franklin D. Roosevelt Library and Museum.

Office of the President of the United States. (1944-27-June). Personal Secretary File: Subject File: Democratic National Convention. *OF 3858: Steinbeck, John 1939–1940.* Franklin D. Roosevelt Library and Museum.

Office of the President of the United States. (1964-23-April). *LBJ Recording of Telephone Conversation, WH Series, Speaker: SIGNAL CORPS OPERATOR, Time: Unknown, 04/23/1964.* From National Archives: http://research.archives.gov/description/189715.

Office of the President of the United States. (1965-5-October). *President's Daily Diary Entry.* Retrieved 2012-28-July from National Archives: http://research.archives.gov/description/192459.

Office of the President of the United States. (2011). *Franklin D. Roosevelt Day by Day: June 26, 1940.* From Franklin D. Roosevelt Library and Museum: http://tinyurl.com/apbskcy.

Office of the President of the United States. (2011). *Franklin D. Roosevelt Day by Day: July 26, 1940.* From Franklin D. Roosevelt Museum and Library.

Office of the Secretary of the Navy. (2002-7-January). SECNAV Instruction 1650.1G. *Navy and Marine Corp Award Manual*. Washington, D.C., Department of the Navy.

Ohio Department of the Adjutant General. (1926). *The Official Roster of Ohio Soldiers, Sailors, and Marines in the World War, 1917–18*. Columbus, Ohio: The F. J. Heer Printing Co.

O'Neal, B. D. (1944-26-February). Letter from Birch D. O'Neal to J. Edgar Hoover.

Oregon State University Libraries Special Collections & Archives Center. (2011-30-March). *Pauling Obtains His FBI File*. From The Pauling Blog: http://tinyurl.com/axn54v2.

OSS Society, Inc. (2005-Summer). *OSS Society Newsletter*.

Otis, E. R. (1982). "Autobiography." *Steinbeck Quarterly, 15* (Winter-Spring 1982), 9.

Paley Center for Media. (2012). *The Paley Center for Media: History*. From The Paley Center for Media: http://tinyurl.com/bdtqbhw.

Pan American World Airways, INC. (1951-8-January). *New York Passenger Lists, 1820-1957 Record for John Steinbeck*. Retrieved 2012-25-August from Ancestry.com: http://tinyurl.com/cmcnwco.

Pan American World Airways, INC. (1957-30-August). *Honolulu, Hawaii, Passenger and Crew Lists, 1900–1959*. Retrieved 2012-25-August from Ancestry.com: http://tinyurl.com/8w8oe4f.

Pan American World Airways, INC. (1957-10-September). *Honolulu, Hawaii, Passenger and Crew Lists, 1900–1959 Record for John E Steinbeck*. Retrieved 2012-25-August from Ancestry.com: http://tinyurl.com/9j34ufp.

Parini, J. (1995). *John Steinbeck: A Biography*. New York: Henry Holt & Co.

Parker-Stainback, M. (2008-February). *Nazi Connections in Mexico Enabled Trotsky's Assassination*. From Inside Mexico: http://tinyurl.com/avvpprm.

Patton, G. S. (1996). *The Patton Papers 1940–1945*. (M. Blumenson, Ed.) Cambridge, Massachusetts: Da Capo Press.

Persico, J. E. (2001). *Roosevelt's Secret War*. New York: Random House.

Phillips, P. M. (1994). *A Relative Advantage: Sociology of the San Francisco Bohemian Club*. Davis, California: University of California Davis.

Picknett, L., & Prince, C. (2006). *The Sion Revelation*. New York: Touchstone Books.

Pike, J. (2011-11-July). *Weather Mountain*. Retrieved 2012-15-August from Global Security: http://tinyurl.com/bjkmtx6.

Potter, L. A. (2003). "Letter from President Lyndon B. Johnson to John Steinbeck." *Social Education*, 196–199.

Poveda, T., Powers, R., Rosenfeld, S., Theoharis, A. G., & Powers, R. G. (1998). *The FBI: A Comprehensive Reference Guide*. Westport, Connecticut: Greenwood Press.

Praeger, F. (1963-14-January). Letter to Allen Dulles, 14 January 1963. Princeton University Dulles Archive.

Procter, B. (2007). *William Randolph Hearst: The Later Years, 1911–1951*. Oxford: Oxford University Press.

Podvig, P. (2013). "Did Star Wars Help End the Cold War? Soviet Response to the SDI Program". Working paper of Russian Nuclear Forces Project. 2013-March.

Prutsch, U. (2010). "Americanization of Brazil or a Pragmatic Wartime Alliance?: The Politics Of Nelson Rockefeller's Office Of Inter-American Affair in Brazil During World War II." *Passagens: International Journal of Cultural Policy and Legal History*, 2(4), 181–216.

Putnam, T. (Spring 2006). "Hemingway on War and Its Aftermath." *Prologue Magazine*, 38(1).

Radio Daily. (1949-11-April). "Swope Joins RCA Alter Exit From CBS." *Radio Daily*, pp. 1, 37.

Railsback, B., & Meyer, M. J. (2006). *A John Steinbeck Encyclopedia*. Westport, Connecticut: Greenwood Press.

Raines, B. (2003). *Navy Beach Jumpers, the 1940's*. From US Navy Beach Jumpers Association: http://www.beachjumpers.com/History/1940sBR.htm.

Rankin, M. A. (2010). *Mexico, la patria: Propaganda and Production during World War II*. Lincoln, Nebraska: University of Nebraska Press.

Ravo, N. (1999-6-June). "Obituary: Philip H. Reisman Jr., 82, Writer of Documentaries and Dramas." *New York Times*.

Recorded Speeches and Utterances by Eleanor Roosevelt, 1933–1962. (2012-12-August). From Franklin D. Roosevelt Presidential Library and Museum: http://tinyurl.com/bbf8d7a.

Reich, C. (1996). *The Life of Nelson A. Rockefeller: Worlds to Conquer 1908–1958*. New York: Doubleday.

Reil, R. (1952-25-September). Letter to Elizabeth Otis.

Reisman, P. (2007-29-January). *My Dad and the CIA*. From *The Journal News* (Gannett): http://tinyurl.com/aa4v3d4.

Remak, J. (1957-March). "Friends of the New Germany: The Bund and German-American Relations." *Journal of Modern History, 29(1)*.

Resch, J. P. (2004). *Americans at War: Society, Culture, and the Homefront*. Macmillan Reference USA. From Book Rags.

Riebling, M. (2009). *Wedge: From Pearl Harbor to 9/11: How the Secret War Between the FBI and CIA Has Endangered National Security*. New York: Simon and Schuster.

Ringle, K. (1974-2-December). "Hush-Hush Mt. Weather Is a Crisis Facility." *Washington Post*.

Rivera, D., & March, G. (1992). *My Art, My Life: An Autobiography*. Mineola, New York: Dover Publications.

Robarge, D. (2007-27-June). *CIA's Chief Historian Gives Perspective on Newly Released Documents*. Retrieved 2012-15-August from CIA: http://tinyurl.com/aba6yv6.

Romero, D. (1946-December). "Egmont Arens: Industrial 'Humaneer'." *Mechanix Illustrated*.

Rooney, A. (1999-22-June). Archive of American Television Interview with Andy Rooney (D. Carlton, Interviewer).

Rooney, A. (2003). *Common Nonsense*. New York: Public Affairs.

Roosevelt, F. D. (1939-22-June). Memorandum for the Director of the Budget. *OF 3858: Steinbeck, John 1939–1940*, Hyde Park, New York: Franklin D. Roosevelt Library and Museum.

Roosevelt, F. D. (1940-25-June). June 25, 1940 Memorandum from FDR to General Watson. *OF 3858: Steinbeck, John 1939–1940*, Hyde Park, New York: Franklin D. Roosevelt Library and Museum.

Roosevelt, F. D. (1940-3-September). September 3, 1940 Memorandum to General Watson. *OF 3858: Steinbeck, John 1939–1940*. Hyde Park, New York: Franklin D. Roosevelt Library and Museum.

Rose, P. (2007-14-April). *Two Strategic Intelligence Mistakes in Korea, 1950*. Retrieved 2012-27-August from CIA: http://tinyurl.com/ap337z9.

Ross, S. H. (2002). *Strategic Bombing by the United States in World War II: The Myths and the Facts*. New York: McFarland.

Rowe, J. J. (1940-20-August). August 20, 1940, Memorandum to General Edwin Watson. Hyde Park, New York: Franklin D. Roosevelt Library and Museum.

Rowe, J. J. (1940-20-August). August 20, 1940, Memorandum to the President (FDR). Hyde Park, New York: Franklin D. Roosevelt Library and Museum.

Ruffing, S., & Nicholson, J. (1996, 2006). *Mark F. Ethridge Papers, 1931–1981*. From University of North Carolina Libraries: http://tinyurl.com/aycjzxf.

Saunders, F. S. (1995-22-October). "Modern Art was CIA 'Weapon'." *The Independent*.

Schuler, F. E. (1998). *Mexico Between Hitler and Roosevelt: Mexican Foreign Relations in the Age of Lazaro Cardenas, 1934–1940*. Albuquerque: University of New Mexico Press.

Schultz, J., & Li, L. (2005). *Critical Companion to John Steinbeck: A Literary Reference to His Life and Work*. New York: Facts on File.

Schwartz, R. A. (1999). *How the Film and Television Blacklists Worked*. Miami: Florida International University.

Schwartz, S. (1995-13-May). "Colonel Boris T. Pash." *San Francisco Chronicle*. From http://tinyurl.com/a6un5cl.

Schwartz, S. (2006-6-August). "Near Washington, Preparing for the Worst." *Washington Post*.

Scott, P. D. (1996). *Deep Politics and the Death of JFK*. Berkley: Univ. of California Press.

Shribman, D. M. (2012-1-March). "Even Academics Like Ike Now." *The National Interest*.

Smith, J. (1984-29-January). "Robert Thayer, Naval Officer, Diplomat, Dies." *Washington Post*.

Smith, R. H. (2005). *OSS: The Secret History of America's First CIA*. Guilford, CT: Lyons Press.

Smith, W. B. (1952-6-February). Letter from CIA Director Walter Bedell Smith to John Steinbeck.

Snider, B. L. (2012). *The Agency and the Hill: CIA's Relationship with Congress, 1946–2004*. CreateSpace.

Snider, L. B. (n.d.). *Congressional Oversight of Intelligence: Some Reflections on the Last 25 Years*. Duke University Law School.

Society of the Silurians. (2011). *About The Society of the Silurians*. From The Society of the Silurians: http://www.silurians.org/about.

Steinbeck, E. (1989-13-April). Audio Interview with Elaine Steinbeck (D. Swaim, Interviewer). From http://tinyurl.com/bkvm4wj.

Steinbeck, J. (1939-2-February). Telegram to the Committee to Aid Agricultural Organizations. *OF 3858: Steinbeck, John 1939–1940*. Hyde Park, New York: Franklin D. Roosevelt Library and Museum.

Steinbeck, J. (1940-13-August). August 13, 1940, Letter to FDR. Hyde Park, New York: Franklin D. Roosevelt Library and Museum.

Steinbeck, J. (1940-24-June). June 24, 1940, Letter to President Franklin D. Roosevelt. *OF 3858: Steinbeck, John 1939–1940*. Franklin D. Roosevelt Library and Museum.

Steinbeck, J. (1940-June). Letter to Joe Hamilton. *OF 3858: Steinbeck, John 1939–1940*. Hyde Park, New York: Franklin D. Roosevelt Library and Museum.

Steinbeck, J. (1945-June). Letter to Burgess Meredith and Paulette Goddard. James Cummings Bookseller. http://tinyurl.com/lvecwxz.

Steinbeck, J. (1945). *Cannery Row*. New York: Viking Press.

Steinbeck, J. (1948). *A Russian Journal* (1999 Penguin Classics ed.). New York: Penguin.

Steinbeck, J. (1948-25-December). "The Miracle of Tepayac." *Collier's Weekly*, pp. 22–23.

Steinbeck, J. (1952-23-August). "A Duel without Pistols." *Collier's Weekly*, pp. 13–15.

Steinbeck, J. (1952-28-January). "Letter to CIA Director Walter Bedell Smith."

Steinbeck, J. (1952-30-August). "The Soul and Guts of France." *Colliers Weekly*, pp. 26–28, 30.

Steinbeck, J. (1953-31-January). "I Go Back to Ireland." *Collier's Weekly*, pp. 49–51.

Steinbeck, J. (1953-10-January). "The Secret Weapon We Were Afraid to Use." *Collier's Weekly*, pp. 9–12.

Steinbeck, J. (1957). *The Short Reign of Pippin IV: A Fabrication*. New York: Viking.

Steinbeck, J. (1957-June). "The Trial of Arthur Miller." *Esquire Magazine*.

Steinbeck, J. (1962-June). *Letter to Max Freedman*. From John F. Kennedy Library and Museum: http://tinyurl.com/b532lna.

Steinbeck, J. (1962-June). The Wall: Letter to John F. Kennedy. John F. Kennedy Presidential Library and Museum. From http://tinyurl.com/asv9apq.

Steinbeck, J. (1963-6-October). "Reflections of a Lunar Eclipse." *New York Herald Tribune*.

Steinbeck, J. (1964-4-August). Letter to Nancy Pearson: August, 4, 1964. From http://tinyurl.com/aq7wauo.

Steinbeck, J. (1969). *Journal of a Novel: The East of Eden Letters*. New York: Penguin.

Steinbeck, J. (1975). *Steinbeck: A Life in Letters*. (E. Steinbeck, & R. Wallsten, Eds.) New York: Viking.

Steinbeck, J. (1976). *The Acts of King Arthur and His Noble Knights*. New York: Del Rey.

Steinbeck, J. (1990). *Working Days: The Journals of The Grapes of Wrath*. (R. DeMott, Ed.) New York: Penguin.

Steinbeck, J. (1995). *The Moon Is Down*. New York: Penguin.

Steinbeck, J. (2003). *America and Americans and Selected Nonfiction*. New York: Penguin Classics.

Steinbeck, J. (2006). *The Grapes of Wrath*. New York: Penguin Classics; Reissue edition.

Steinbeck, J. (2007). *Once There Was a War*. New York: Penguin.

Steinbeck, J. (2008). *The Winter of Our Discontent*. New York: Penguin.

Steinbeck, J. (n.d.). *Autograph Letter Signed 03/18/1966*. Retrieved 2011-19-December from History for Sale: http://tinyurl.com/a4ffdqo.

Steinbeck, J. (n.d.). *East of Eden*. New York: Viking.

Steinbeck, J. I., & Steinbeck, N. (2001). *The Other Side of Eden: Life with John Steinbeck*. Prometheus Books.

Steinbeck, J., Hammarskjöld, D., & Hovde, C. F. (1997). "The Dag Hammarskjöld–John Steinbeck Correspondence," *Development Dialogue: The Journal of the Dag Hammarskjöld Foundation*, pp. 97–129.

Steinbeck, T. (2003). *Down to a Soundless Sea*. New York: Ballantine Books.

Steinbeck, T. (2008-10-November). Phone Interview with Thomas Steinbeck (B. Kannard, Interviewer)

Steinbeck, T. (2013-15-February). Phone Interview with Thomas Steinbeck (B. Kannard, Interviewer).

Steinbeck, T. (2013-25-February). Phone Interview with Thomas Steinbeck (B. Kannard, Interviewer).

Steinbeck, T. (2013-26-March). Phone Interview with Thomas Steinbeck (B. Kannard, Interviewer).

Steinbeck, T. (2013-14-April). Phone Interview with Thomas Steinbeck (B. Kannard, Interviewer).

Steinbeck, T. (2013-13-May). Phone Interview with Thomas Steinbeck (B. Kannard, Interviewer).

Steinbeck, T. (2013-18-May). Phone Interview with Thomas Steinbeck (B. Kannard, Interviewer).

Steinbeck, T. (2013-28-May). Phone Interview with Thomas Steinbeck (B. Kannard, Interviewer).

Steinbeck, T. (2013-1-July). Phone Interview with Thomas Steinbeck (B. Kannard, Interviewer).

Stout, D. (2008-18-May). "Lucius Battle, Diplomat and Official, Dies at 89." *New York Times*.

Sturges, R. S. (1990). *Medieval Interpretation: Models of Reading in Literary Narrative, 1100–1500*. Southern Illinois University Press.

Sweeny, M. S. (2001). *Secrets of Victory: The Office of Censorship and the American Press and Radio in World War II*. Chapel Hill: University of North Carolina Press.

Tavernise, S. (2011-24-November). "As Fewer Americans Serve, Growing Gap Is Found Between Civilians and Military." *New York Times*.

Taylor, J. (Director). (1983). *Frontline: "Space: The Race for High Ground"* [Motion Picture].

TC. (2012). Interview with Former CIA Operations Officer (B. Kannard, Interviewer).

Teukolsky, R. (n.d.). "Regarding Scientist X." *Berkley Science Review, 1*(17).

The Daily Beast. (2011-10-May). *10 Revelations about Robert Redford*. From The Daily Beast: http://tinyurl.com/afm9685.

The Daily Worker. (1924-5-February). "Workers' School in New York City Opens Second Term." *The Daily Worker*.

Theoharis, A., Immerman, R., Johnson, L., Olmsted, K., & Prados, J. (2006). *The CIA: Security Under Scrutiny*. Westport, Connecticut: Greenwood Press.

Thomas, E. (2002). *Robert Kennedy: His Life*. New York: Simon & Schuster.

Thomas, L. (2008-28-March). *"Air of Freedom": Poetry and National Security*. From Chicken Bones: A Journal for Literary and Artistic African-American Themes: http://tinyurl.com/aa9nrvt.

Time Magazine. (1940-1-January). "German Scuttle and Run from British Sea Might." *Time Magazine*, pp. 11–15.

Time Magazine. (1948-19-July). "Radio: Video v. Housework." *Time Magazine*.

Time Magazine. (1952-13-October). "National Affairs: Eisenhower on Communism." *Time Magazine*.

Time Magazine. (1973-28-May). "Operating at Home." *Time Magazine*.

Time Magazine. (1974-15-July). "The CIA: Some Foolish Mistakes." *Time Magazine*.

Trento, J. (2001). *The Secret History of the CIA*. New York: MJF Books.

Troy, T. M. (2007-14-April). *The Cultural Cold War: The CIA and the World of Arts and Letters*. From CIA: http://tinyurl.com/yfeaatq.

Tweedy, M. (2011, December 2). Letter from Michael Tweedy December, 2, 2011 (B. Kannard, Interviewer).

United Nations. (2001-25-May). *NGO Committee Hears Arguments for, against Freedom House*. From United Nations: http://tinyurl.com/bk9kh5p.

United Press. (1938-25-October). "Communists' Farm Activity Aired in Probe." *The Pittsburgh Press*, p. 1.

United Press. (1953-30-September). "Actor Tells of Red Role." *Reading Eagle*, p. 50.

United States Department of Justice. (1946-19-November). *New York Passenger Lists, 1820–1957 Record for John Steinbeck*. Retrieved 2012-26-August from Ancestry.com: http://tinyurl.com/8qx5zjt.

United States Department of Justice. (1947-5-October). *New York Passenger Lists, 1820–1957 Record for John E Steinbeck*. Retrieved 2012-26-August from Ancestry.com: http://tinyurl.com/8r3cvj5.

United States Department of Justice. (1952-25-August). *New York Passenger Lists, 1820–1957 Record for John E Steinbeck*. Retrieved 2012-26-August from Ancestry.com: http://tinyurl.com/8hg8mfj.

United States Department of Justice. (1997). *Title 9 Criminal Resource Manual 1663*. From United States Department of Justice: http://tinyurl.com/a935439.

United States Department of Justice. (n.d.). *What is FOIA*. Retrieved 20-20-August from FOIA.gov: http://www.foia.gov/about.html.

United States Department of Labor. (1937-27-July). *New York Passenger Lists, 1820–1957 Record for John Ernst Steinbeck*. Retrieved 2012-26-August from Ancestry.com: http://tinyurl.com/8fzyvkc.

United States Department of State. (1944). *Foreign Service List 1944*. Washington, D.C., United States Office of Printing.

United States Department of State. (1951). *Foreign Service List 1951*. Washington, D.C., United States Office of Printing.

United States Department of State. (1953). *Foreign Service List 1953*. Washington, D.C., United States Government Printing Office.

United States Department of State. (1956). *Foreign Service List 1956*. Washington, D.C., United States Government Printing Office.

United States Department of State. (2012-8-June). *Art in Embassies; US Department of State*. From History: http://art.state.gov/history.aspx.

United States Department of the Navy. (1946-January). German Espionage and Sabotage Against the United States. *Office of Naval Intelligence Review*, 1(3), 33–38. From http://tinyurl.com/ajm9s7c.

United States Department of Veterans Affairs. (n.d.). BIRLS Death File, 1850–2010. United States Department of Veterans Affairs.

United States Equal Employment Opportunity Commission. (2009-13-August). *FOIA Handbook: XI. Summary of Exemptions*. Retrieved 2012-1-March from United States Equal Employment Opportunity Commission: http://archive.eeoc.gov/foia/hb-11.html.

United States Information Agency. (1952-31-January). *Interview with John Steinbeck, 01/31/1952*. From National Archives: http://research.archives.gov/description/119028.

United States Information Agency. (1952-11-February). *Interview with John Steinbeck, 02/11/1952*. From National Archives: http://research.archives.gov/description/119037.

United States Information Agency. (1952-26-February). *Interview with John Steinbeck, 2/26/1952*. From National Archives: http://research.archives.gov/description/120000.

United States Information Agency. (1964-3-January). *Interview with John Steinbeck and Edward Albee*. From National Archives: http://research.archives.gov/description/123543.

United States National Archives and Records Administration. (2000). *Disposition of Federal Records: A Records Management*. United States Government Printing Office.

United States National Archives and Records Administration. (2012-12-August). *Executive Orders Disposition Table*. From National Archives: http://tinyurl.com/bza9wed.

United States War Department. (1942-21-January). FM 30–26: Regulations for Correspondents Accompanying U.S. Army Forces in the Field. Washington, D.C., United States War Department.

University of Texas. (2011). *Egmont Arens*. From the Greenwich Village Bookshop Door: A Portal to Bohemia 1920–1925: http://tinyurl.com/bc2lnas.

University of Virginia. (1950-16-March). "Radio Network Gives Contest." *The Cavalier Daily*, p. 1. From http://tinyurl.com/bo3sv66.

USS *Knight*. (1943). *USS Knight Action Reports September 1943*. United States Department of Navy.

Vanderwood, P. J. (1992). "The Image of Mexican Heroes in American Films." *Film Historia*, 2(3), 221–244.

Vaughn, R. (2004). *Only Victims: A Study of Show Business Blacklisting*. New York: Limelight Editions.

Wald, M. L. (2012-16-October). "Halting a Slow Fade to History: 'Argo,' as Seen by the Iran Hostage Crisis Survivors." *New York Times*. From http://tinyurl.com/axxebgq.

Wallace, R., Melton, H. K., & Schlesinger, H. R. (2009). *Spycraft: The Secret History of the CIA's Spytechs, from Communism to Al-Qaeda*. New York: Penguin.

Waller, D. (2011). *Wild Bill Donovan*. New York: Simon and Schuster.

Walt Disney Company. (2012). *Paul Winkler*. Retrieved 2012-1-August from Disney Insider: http://tinyurl.com/av3yrhz.

Ward, E. R. (n.d.). *Two Rivers, Two Nations, One History: The Transformation of the Colorado River Delta*. University of Georgia.

Warfield, A. M. (1966-26-July). Memorandum for Acting Director of Personnel [CIA].

Warner, M. (1995-Fall). "Salvage and Liquidation: The Creation of the Central Intelligence Group." *Studies in Intelligence*.

Wartzman, R. (2009). *Obscene in the Extreme: The Burning and Banning of John Steinbeck's the Grapes of Wrath*. Public Affairs.

Webster, W. (1991-2-July). *Chronology of CIA's Senior Management Structure*. Retrieved 2012-27-August from Federation of American Scientists: http://tinyurl.com/aysocs4

Weiss, P. (1989-November). "Masters of the Universe Go to Camp: Inside the Bohemian Grove." *Spy Magazine*.

Wenzer, K. C. (1996). *Anarchists Adrift: Emma Goldman and Alexander Berkman*. Saint James, New York: Brandywine Press.

West, R. (1981-5-October). "The Power of 21." *New York Magazine*.

Wetzsteon, R. (2003). *Republic of Dreams: Greenwich Village: The American Bohemia, 1910–1960*. New York: Simon and Schuster.

Whaley, B. (2012). John Steinbeck and the Calling of Masonry. *Salinas Lodge #204*.

Wheeler, D. D. (2012). A Guide to the History of Intelligence 1800–1918 (Draft). *Journal of US Intelligence Studies*.

Whelan, R. (1994). *Robert Capa: A Biography*. Lincoln, Nebraska: University of Nebraska Press.

Whitfield, M. (2012-12-May). "Judge: Keep Part of CIA's Bay of Pigs History Secret." *The Miami Herald*.

Wilford, H. (2003). *The CIA, the British Left and the Cold War: Calling the Tune?* Oxford: Psychology Press.

Wilford, H. (2009). *The Mighty Wurlitzer: How the CIA Played America*. Cambridge, Massachusetts: Harvard University Press.

Willis, C. S. (Director). (2009). *Nova: The Spy Factory* [Motion Picture].

Wilson, J. D. (2010-30-August). At Work with Donovan. *Center for the Study of Intelligence, 37*(3), 71–79. From http://tinyurl.com/9szqerr.

Winks, R. (1987). *Cloak and Gown: Scholars in the Secret War 1939–1961*. New York: William Morrow and Company.

Wise, D. (1994). *Mole-Hunt: How the Search for a Phantom Traitor Shattered the CIA*. New York: Avon Books.

Wright, L. (2008-2-June). "The Rebellion Within." *The New Yorker*. From http://tinyurl.com/5ayfpw.

Wynn, N. A. (2009). *The A to Z of the Roosevelt-Truman Era*. Scarecrow Press.

Zuidema, J. (2008-8-November). *SEAL Predecessors Hold Annual Reunion; Recount Service, Sacrifices*. Retrieved 2012-13-Feb from United States Navy Website: http://tinyurl.com/angbyc2.

Introduction

[1]While not appropriate for the introduction of this text, I would like to make it clear that at no time did Thomas Steinbeck, or anyone else, directly influence the contents of this book. Thomas offered source material and advice for my work, but to believe that Thomas somehow directed the contents of this book would be an incorrect conclusion. A man of Thomas's integrity would find such an idea as abhorrent as I find the idea of altering my text to suit a specific individual.

[2]Thomas and I disagree on two points—John's relationship with the FBI and Elaine Steinbeck's knowledge of John's covert life. Thomas contends that J. "Edna" Hoover (as Thomas would commonly refer to the former head of the FBI) hated his father and would have done most anything to burn the elder Steinbeck down. I believe that John had wanted his family to see an adversarial relationship with the Bureau, but I'm not convinced the evidence holds to long-term animosity between Steinbeck and Hoover. If such existed, Hoover surely would have called Steinbeck before HUAC no matter what the CIA might have wished. Steinbeck dodging the HUAC bullet is covered later in this text. As for Elaine, Thomas's statement later in the introduction gives a clear idea of his stance on Elaine's foreknowledge. I believe it is possible she knew and present an argument for such later in the text.

[3]Hardy, 2012.

[4]Dilanian, 2012.

Chapter 1: The Winter of Our Discontent

[1]This chapter is a fictionalized look at the morning of January 28, 1952.

Chapter 2: Of Mice and Men

[1]At: http://vault.fbi.gov/John%20Steinbeck.

[2]United States Department of Justice.

[3]National Security Archive, 1995.

[4]Whitfield, 2012.

[5]United States Equal Employment Opportunity Commission, 2009 The current Executive Order is number 12958, signed by President Bush on March 25, 2003. The verbiage of the exemption was basically the same when the Steinbeck FBI file was released under the FOIA.

[6]CIA, 2011.

[7]Jones, 2011.

[8]FBI, 1946, p. 1.

[9]Examination of these files represents literally thousands of pages of documentation. At times, the files are scans of photocopies of mimeographed pages. The experience of sifting through the pages was eye watering to say the least, and it is possible that something slipped past my examination. If there are CIA exemptions in these files someone finds, please contact me and I will amend this text.

[10]FBI, p. 46.

[11]FBI, p. 70.

[12]Langbart & Haines, 1993.

[13]Benson, *The True Adventures of John Steinbeck, Writer*, 1990, p. 406.

[14]TC, 2012.

[15]Tavernise, 2011.

[16]TC, 2012.

[17]Examples of the CIA's disclosure policy are numerous enough to be considered common knowledge. TC also would not comment on specifics about "walk-ins" other than it was common during the time frame and general examples as to their use and relationship with the Agency.

[18]Martinez, 2012. This number is current through the end of May 2012.

[19]TC, 2012.

[20]Steinbeck J., *Steinbeck: A Life in Letters*, 1975, p. 403.

[21]Steinbeck J., *A Russian Journal*, 1948, p. 29.

[22]Steinbeck J., *Steinbeck: A Life in Letters*, 1975, p. 266.

[23]Applebome, 2011.

[24]Liggett, 2005.

[25]The Society of the Silurians, 2011.

[26]Britt, 1974, p. 309.

[27]Berliner, 2012.

[28]Steinbeck: Steinbeck J., *A Russian Journal*, 1948, p. 6 Swope: Kahn, 1965, p. 357.

[29]Griffin, 2003.

[30]Steinbeck J., The Wall: Letter to John F. Kennedy, 1962.

[31]Irving, 1996, p. 101.

[32]Eisenhower, 1954.

[33]Radio Daily, 1949.

[34]Kahn, 1965, p. 388.

[35]The Paley Center for Media, 2012.

[36]Deborah, 1979, p. 175.

[37]Wilford, *The Mighty Wurlitzer: How the CIA Played America*, 2009, p. 227.

[38]Freedom House, 2012.

[39]Freedom House, 2012.

[40]Andrews, 1995, p. 203.

[41]Miller R. M., 1985, p. 192.

[42]Troy, 2007. This article is actually a book review of *Intelligence in Recent Public Literature* by Frances Stonor Saunders. Mr. Troy served in the CIA's Directorate of Intelligence and largely agrees with the book's findings in respect to front organizations. This endorsement speaks volumes to Stonor Saunders' findings.

[43]A number of sources in recent years have confirmed the link. *Katherine the Great* by Deborah Davis and *The Mighty Wurlitzer* by Hugh Wilford have delved into this topic beyond any reasonable doubt.

[44]Cowen, 2010, p. 71.

[45]Diggins, 1993, p. 245.

[46]Day, 1995, pp. 102, 106.

[47]The Broadway League, 2001.

[48]The book *Eight Is Enough* spawned the wildly popular '70s TV show by the same name. Considering the show's lead character Tom Bradford is based on Braden. It's difficult to imagine Dick Van Patten as a spy . . .

[49]Saunders, 1995.

[50]Saunders, 1995.

[51]Horschak, 2008.

[52]Kachere, 2012.

[53]United Nations, 2001.

[54]Lee, 2003.

[55]Gonzalez, 2005.

[56]Freedom House, 2012.

[57]Childs, 1949.

[58]Heritage Auctions, 2009.

[59]MacFarland & Roll, 2005.

[60]The title of Secretary of War changed to that of Secretary of Defense with the National Security Act of 1947.

[61]LeFabre, 1993.

[62]Garrett, Major John, 1999.

[63]Shribman, 2012.

[64]Associated Press, 1949.

[65]CIA, 2008.

[66]TC, 2012.

[67]CIA, 2008. The CIA even has a picture of the sign that hung outside the E Street compound on its Flikr feed at http://www.flickr.com/photos/ciagov/5416190823/in/set-72157625851180039. The story behind the sign is fairly amusing. According to the photo's caption: "For several years there was no sign at the entrance of the original CIA Headquarters Buildings. President Eisenhower was on his way to church one Sunday morning. He wished to drop his brother Milton off at CIA for a meeting with DCI Allen Dulles. Because there was no sign, the White House driver had great difficulty finding the entrance. This upset the President. The following day President Eisenhower called Dulles and ordered a sign placed at the entrance. It was the President's view that the E Street address was well known as CIA Headquarters and that the absence of a sign fooled no one."

[68]Cummings, Radio Free Europe's "Crusade for Freedom": Rallying Americans Behind Cold War Broadcasting, 2010, p. 238.

[69]Rose, 2007.

[70]CIA, 2007.

[71]CIA, 2008.

[72]Webster, 1991.

[73]Bernstein, 1977.

[74]TC, 2012.

[75]FBI, John Steinbeck File #9-4583 and #100-106224 Part 1, 2012, p. 57.

[76]For January 31st: United States Information Agency, 1952 For February 11th: United States Information Agency, 1952 For February 26th United States Information Agency, 1952.

[77]United States Department of State, 1951.

[78]TC, 2012.

[79]Steinbeck J., *Steinbeck: A Life in Letters*, 1975, p. 527.

[80]FBI, John Steinbeck File #9-4583 and #100-106224 Part 2, 2012, pp. 28–39.

81CIA, 2007.

82Railsback & Meyer, 2006, p. 23.

83Whelan, 1994, p. 287.

84Riebling, 2009, p. 148.

85Wallace, Melton, & Schlesinger, 2009.

86It is likely this should read SSA instead of SAA. SSA is the FBI's abbreviation for Special Supervisory Agent.

87FBI, John Steinbeck File #9-4583 and #100-106224 Part 2, 2012, p. 50.

88Kelley, 2009.

89Cook, 2009.

90http://vault.fbi.gov/John%20Steinbeck.

91This document can be downloaded in PDF format at: http://www.archives.gov/records-mgmt/publications/disposition-of-federal-records and covers statutes of the United States Code that apply to record retention.

92United States National Archives and Records Administration, 2000, p. 66.

93United States National Archives and Records Administration, 2000, p. 161.

94United States Department of Justice, 1997. The necessary measure of protection for government documents and records is provided by 18 U.S.C. §2071. Section 2071a contains a broad prohibition against destruction of government records or attempts to destroy such records. This section provides that whoever: willfully and unlawfully; conceals, removes, mutilates, obliterates or destroys; or attempts to conceal, remove, mutilate, obliterate or destroy; or carries away with intent to conceal, remove, mutilate, obliterate or destroy; any record, proceeding, map, book, paper, document or other thing deposited in any public office may be punished by imprisonment for three years, a $2,000 fine, or both.

95There is a long-shot possibility to the NARA having been notified of the disposition of file 9-4583. The NARA can conduct an inventory of an agency/department's records. The file may have been uncovered during this process, but it is unlikely. According to the NARA handbook, "In records management, an inventory is a descriptive listing of each record series or system, together with an indication of location and other pertinent data. It is not a list of each document or each folder but rather of each series or system. Its main purpose is to provide the information needed to develop the schedule." (United States National Archives and Records Administration, 2000, p. 40) It does not sound as if this process would uncover any individual files of historical importance.

96The Hubble Space telescope was able to visually confirm the existence of extrasolar planets in 2008.

Chapter 3: The Wool Gatherer

1De Courcy, 2010.

2Steinbeck J., *Cannery Row*, 1945.

3Steinbeck J., *The Acts of King Arthur and His Noble Knights*, 1976.

4Steinbeck T., Phone Interview with Thomas Steinbeck, 2008.

5Steinbeck T., Phone Interview with Thomas Steinbeck, 2008.

6Steinbeck J., *The Acts of King Arthur and His Noble Knights*, 1976, p. 437.

7 Steinbeck T., *Down to a Soundless Sea*, 2003.

8 Steinbeck T., *Down to a Soundless Sea*, 2003.

9 Steinbeck T., Phone Interview with Thomas Steinbeck, 2008.

[10]Salinas' Free and Accepted Masonic Lodge #204 currently holds their stated meetings on the second Tuesday night of each month. Practices like this rarely change in Masonic Lodges and there is no reason to believe the day has changed since Steinbeck's boyhood. Should the day and time of the month have changed, Masonic Lodges hold stated meetings once a month on a regular day.

[11]Benson, *The True Adventures of John Steinbeck, Writer*, 1990.

[12]Being both a Mason and a father of a young son, I can attest that the never-ending stream of normal life questions a lad poses to his father are compounded exponentially when the boy's father is a Mason.

[13]The Lodge of Edinburgh Mary's Chapel No.1, 1999, p. 5 For clarification, this Lodge is located in Edinburgh, Scotland. I had the opportunity to visit this Lodge in 1999, and am grateful to the Brothers there for their kindness to a fellow traveling man.

[14]The observations of the history and culture of Masonry are my own. At the time of publication, I had been a Master Mason and a 32nd Degree Scottish Rite Mason for fifteen years.

[15]Some have speculated that this is the origin of the Friday the 13th being an unlucky day.

[16]Blankenship, 2008.

[17]Whaley, 2012.

[18]Steinbeck T., Phone Interview with Thomas Steinbeck, 2008.

[19]Steinbeck T., Phone Interview with Thomas Steinbeck, 2008.

[20]Steinbeck J., *East of Eden*, Steinbeck J., *The Winter of Our Discontent*, 2008, pp. 68, 132, 218, 224, respectfully.

[21]Steinbeck J., *The Grapes of Wrath*, 2006, pp. 73, 202.

[22]Once again, I draw on my personal experiences as a Mason to make this statement. By and large, the groups of men I have known in my association with Masonic Lodges have been of the highest moral and ethical caliber. However, living in the South, I have also seen Brothers with antiquated views on certain subjects. The notions of a few do not taint the overall organization of Masonry and in such cases, one agrees to disagree with differing worldviews.

[23]Whaley, 2012.

[24]Steinbeck T., Phone Interview with Thomas Steinbeck, 2008.

[25]During the 1950s, Freemasonry was the largest fraternal organization in America. The Masonic Service Association of North America places the number of Masons in 1950 America at a little over 3.6 million. The male population of the United States was around 76 million. Not adjusting for age (Masons have to be of "legal age" which at the time would be 18 or 21), a little less than 5% of American males were Masons in 1950. One can extrapolate that in any given industry, at least 5% of employees were Masons. In my experience with Masonry, a higher percentage of Masons are attracted to these type of jobs and I personally would estimate the number at 10% of employees in these fields.

[26]This would be difficult to track given that the identities of the majority of intelligence officers are classified. Given the assumptions in the previous endnote, one can estimate similar percentages.

Chapter 4: The Grapes of Wrath

[1]Steinbeck J., *Steinbeck: A Life in Letters*, 1975, p. 202.

[2]The University of Chicago holds a number of letters and telegrams between the two men discussing their work with the National Foundation for Infantile Paralysis.

[3]O'Connor, 1939.

[4]Callaghan, Letter to Marguerite Le Hand, 1939.

[5]Callaghan, Letter to Marguerite Le Hand, 1939.

[6]Persico, 2001, p. 16.

[7]Estes, 1977.

[8]Cedillo J. A., 2007.

[9]Rivera & March, 1992, p. 140.

[10]Davidson, 1993.

[11]Herrera, 1983.

[12]Cedillo J. A., 2007.

[13]International Committee of the Fourth International, 2012.

[14]Rivera & March, 1992, p. 139.

[15]Parker-Stainback, 2008.

[16]Davidson, 1993.

[17]*Time Magazine*, 1940.

[18]Rivera & March, 1992.

[19]Parker-Stainback, 2008.

[20]Cedillo J. A., 2007.

[21]The People's Commissariat for Internal Affairs, from the Russian *Narodnyy Komissariat Vnutrennikh Del*, abbreviated NKVD was the secret police organization of the Soviet Union that directly executed the rule of power of the Soviets.

[22]Parker-Stainback, 2008.

[23]Lanchin, 2012.

[24]Benson, *The True Adventures of John Steinbeck, Writer*, 1990, p. 384.

[25]Benson, *The True Adventures of John Steinbeck, Writer*, 1990, p. 453.

[26] Benson, *The True Adventures of John Steinbeck, Writer*, 1990, p. 354.

[27]Rivera & March, 1992.

[28]Davidson, 1993.

[29]Steinbeck J., Letter to Joe Hamilton, 1940.

[30]Steinbeck J., Letter to Joe Hamilton, 1940.

[31]Ward.

[32]Procter, 2007, p. 49.

[33]Steinbeck J., Letter to Joe Hamilton, 1940.

[34]FBI, 1946, p. 141. The company name of the agent's cover story has been redacted from this text.

[35]FBI, 1946, p. 471.

[36]United States Department of the Navy, 1946.

[37]Rankin, 2010, p. 18.

[38]Cedillo J. A., 2007.

[39]Steinbeck J., Letter to Joe Hamilton, 1940.

[40] Steinbeck, J., June 1945 Letter to Burgess Meredith and Paulette Goddard.

[41]Steinbeck J., June 24, 1940, Letter to President Franklin D. Roosevelt, 1940.

[42]Office of the President of the United States, 2011.

[43]Steinbeck J., Letter to Joe Hamilton, 1940.

[44] Steinbeck J., August 13, 1940, Letter to FDR, 1940.

[45] Office of the President of the United States, 2011.

[46] Prutsch, 2010.

[47] Prutsch, 2010.

[48] Prutsch, 2010.

[49] Wilford, *The Mighty Wurlitzer: How the CIA Played America*, 2009, p. 16.

[50] Dawidoff, 1995.

[51] Kramer, 1981.

[52] Steinbeck J., "Reflections of a Lunar Eclipse," 1963.

[53] Steinbeck J., August 13, 1940 Letter to FDR, 1940.

[54] Rowe, August 20, 1940 Memorandum to the President FDR, 1940

[55] Rowe, August 20, 1940 Memorandum to General Edwin Watson, 1940 The shorthand was deciphered by two separate legal secretaries conversant in multiple forms of shorthand thanks to Leesa Smith.

[56] Roosevelt, September 3, 1940 Memorandum to General Watson, 1940.

[57] As a side note, the OSS had considered the plan in 1942 and it was once again presented to President Truman, by the OSS, in 1945. At neither time was the counterfeiting campaign adopted.

[58] Steinbeck J., "The Secret Weapon We Were Afraid to Use," 1953, pp. 9–10.

[59] Malkin, 2008.

[60] CIA, 1950, pp. 3–6.

[61] Steinbeck J., "The Secret Weapon We Were Afraid to Use," 1953, p. 9.

[62] "The Soul and Guts of France" in particular is an anti-Communist propaganda piece.

[63] The media references for SDI are too numerous to list. While not very cricket as far as references go, anyone who paid attention to the news during the 1980s can attest to the flap the Star Wars program caused.

[64] Taylor, 1983.

[65] Wilford, *The Mighty Wurlitzer: How the CIA Played America*, 2009, pp. 31–32.

[66] Cummings, *Radio Free Europe's "Crusade for Freedom": Rallying Americans Behind Cold War Broadcasting*, 2010.

[67] Cummings, "Balloons Over East Europe: America's Covert Radio and Leaflet Operations in the Cold War," Summer 2008.

[68] Friedman, 2008.

[69] Podvig, 2013. While the exact cost, and efficacy, of the Star Wars program held on Soviet military decisions from 1983 to the fall of Communism in 1991 are debatable. The fact remains that through the development of a number of Soviet weapon systems from 1983 to 1990 were in direct response to SDI. So one can safely say the Soviets did spend resources in combating a nonexistent SDI threat. Another good example of Soviet reaction to impotent American weapon systems is the Soviets production of some 1200 MiG-25 fighter aircraft in response to the XB-70 supersonic bomber project. Two prototypes of the XB-70 were produced and one crashed during a test flight. If one gives a very conservative estimate of research and development, plus production costs of $1 million per aircraft, one can see how seriously the Soviets reacted to perceived threats.

[70] National Public Radio, 2003.

[71] Benson, *The True Adventures of John Steinbeck, Writer*, 1990, p. 477.

72Steinbeck J., "Reflections of a Lunar Eclipse," 1963.

73Coers, 1991, p. 7.

74Benson, *The True Adventures of John Steinbeck, Writer*, 1990, p. 488. Benson has made this assertion and it has stuck ever since.

75Benson, *The True Adventures of John Steinbeck, Writer*, 1990, p. 487.

76Coers, 1991.

77Steinbeck J., *The Moon Is Down*, 1995, pp. vii–viii.

78Benson, *The True Adventures of John Steinbeck, Writer*, 1990, p. 486.

79Waller, 2011.

80Railsback & Meyer, 2006, p. 258.

81Benson, *The True Adventures of John Steinbeck, Writer*, 1990, p. 489.

82Steinbeck J., "Reflections of a Lunar Eclipse," 1963.

83Waller, 2011, p. 100. Waller does not cite a specific source for this assertion. This text also mentions that a New York appraiser came up with the counterfeiting German Mark scheme. In January of 1942, a Colorado publisher also presented the idea to Donavon, but there is also no citation for this either.

84Coers, 1991, p. 7.

85Coers, 1991, p. 24.

86Sweeny, 2001.

87Steinbeck J., The Wall: Letter to John F. Kennedy, 1962.

88Lunding, 1970, pp. 68–72.

89Donovan, 1941.

90Bell L., 1970.

91Remak, 1957.

92FBI, John Steinbeck File #9-4583 and #100-106224 Part 1, 2012, p. 17.

93FBI, John Steinbeck File #9-4583 and #100-106224 Part 1, 2012, p. 16.

94FBI, John Steinbeck File #9-4583 and #100-106224 Part 2, 2012, p. 50.

95Steinbeck J., *Steinbeck: A Life in Letters*, 1975, p. 246.

96Winks, 1987.

97FBI, John Steinbeck File #9-4583 and #100-106224 Part 2, 2012, p. 32.

98Gerard, 2010.

99Steinbeck T., Phone Interview with Thomas Steinbeck, 2013-18-May.

100Steinbeck T., Phone Interview with Thomas Steinbeck, 2013-18-May.

101Steinbeck T., Phone Interview with Thomas Steinbeck, 2013-18-May.

102Benson, *The True Adventures of John Steinbeck, Writer*, 1990.

103Steinbeck J., *Steinbeck: A Life in Letters*, 1975, p. 250.

104Ross, 2002.

105Steinbeck J., *Steinbeck: A Life in Letters*, 1975, p. 246.

106FBI, John Steinbeck File #9-4583 and #100-106224 Part 1, 2012, p. 24.

107FBI, John Steinbeck File #9-4583 and #100-106224 Part 1, 2012, p. 25.

108FBI, John Steinbeck File #9-4583 and #100-106224 Part 1, 2012, p. 24.

109Trento, 2001, p. 193.

110Schwartz S., "Colonel Boris T. Pash," 1995.

111Trento, 2001, p. 193.

Steinbeck: Citizen Spy • Page 316

[112]Truman was not informed about the Manhattan Project until after FDR's death.

[113]Teukolsky.

[114]Headquarters of Service and Supply European Theater of Operations United States Army, 1943, p. 14. Earlier in the same report, Col. Pickens relays that Steinbeck has "started his movie." The assumption is that the later quote relates directly to Steinbeck's efforts.

Chapter 5: Once There Was a War

[1]Zuidema, 2008.

[2]Hewitt, 1943, p. 160.

[3]Fairbanks, 1993, p. 194.

[4]North was an heir to the Ringling Brothers—Barnum and Bailey Circus.

[5]Fairbanks, 1993, p. 194.

[6]Benson, *The True Adventures of John Steinbeck, Writer*, 1990, p. 532.

[7]Benson, *The True Adventures of John Steinbeck, Writer*, 1990, p. 530.

[8]Official 509th Parachute Infantry Association, 2006.

[9]Hewitt, 1943, p. 159.

[10]Chalou, 1992, p. 188.

[11]The account of the September 8–9, 1943, comes primarily from Fairbanks account and that of Steinbeck biographer Jackson Benson. Out of all the evidence I had at my disposal, these seem to be the most accurate accounts. Even as gifted a biographer as Benson is, there are still some fine points that have eluded him. For example, Benson mentions that Steinbeck was at Salerno and then spent a few weeks with the Beach Jumpers. I'm sure this is an editorial mistake, but the timeline of events does not bear this out. The invasion of Salerno began on the September 9, 1943. Steinbeck's movements and actions of the BJs are well documented within his letters, World War II documents, and Steinbeck returning to London on September 22nd. This simply goes to illustrate how inaccurate the science of reconstructing someone's life can become at times.

[12]Benson, *The True Adventures of John Steinbeck, Writer*, 1990, p. 533.

[13]Fairbanks, 1993, p. 196.

[14]Benson, *The True Adventures of John Steinbeck, Writer*, 1990.

[15]The legislation was passed for the Silver Star being issued to United States Army members on July 9, 1918, 65th Congress, Section II, Chapter 143, page 873. Members of the Navy and Marine Corps have been eligible to receive the Silver Star for qualifying acts from December 6, 1941, to the present. The language in the proceeding quotation is inclusive for all branches of the United States military.

[16]Office of the Secretary of the Navy, 2002.

[17]Gannett Government Media Corporation, 2012. Shaw was awarded the Silver Star on 15 November 1943. The citation reads as follows: "The President of the United States of America takes pleasure in presenting the Silver Star to Mr. James P. Shaw a United States Civilian, for gallantry in action while serving as Field Director, American Red Cross, attached to the [Classified] Infantry, in action on 11 July 1943, near Licata, Sicily. On that date, an enemy dive-bomber scored a direct hit on a landing craft, which had almost reached its position for debarkation. Mr. Shaw, who was already ashore, immediately left his position of comparative security, waded back into the rough water and assisted many men to safety. He continued to assist until the last man had been brought to shore and the wounded cared for. All of these acts were performed at the risk of his life because of

attacking enemy airplanes, the explosion of ammunition on the damaged craft, and the turbulent and treacherous water. The gallantry of Mr. Shaw on this occasion is a distinct credit to himself and the American Red Cross."

[18]Gannett Government Media Corporation, 2012. Chinigo was awarded the Silver Star on 15 November 1943. The citation reads as follows: "The President of the United States of America takes pleasure in presenting the Silver Star to Mr. Michael Chinigo, a United States Civilian, for gallantry in action. Mr. Chinigo, in his capacity as an accredited correspondent assigned to the 3rd Infantry Division, landed with the first group of assault troops on the shores of Sicily on 10 July 1943. Disregarding his personal safety, he moved forward with advance groups, under heavy enemy fire, interrogating prisoners as they were taken, and assisting the wounded. Later, he accompanied a patrol that entered Palermo in advance of the occupation by our troops, contacted the Chief of Police and went with him to inform the Italian troops that the American forces had taken the city. Accompanying a patrol on another occasion, he entered Messina prior to its occupation, and returned with two truckloads of Italian prisoners. Mr. Chinigo's absolute disregard for personal safety, his voluntary actions and willingness to be of service above and beyond the call of duty reflect highest credit upon himself and his profession."

[19]United States War Department, 1942, p. Section 3d. The specific regulation reads: "Correspondents will not exercise command, be placed in a position of authority over military personnel, nor will they be armed."

[20]United States War Department, 1942, p. Section 3e.

[21]United States War Department, 1942, p. Section 4d.

[22]Rooney, Archive of American Television Interview with Andy Rooney, 1999.

[23]Lynn, 1993.

[24]Cote, 2002.

[25]Putnam, Spring 2006.

[26]Meredith, 1999.

[27]Hewitt, 1943, p. 159.

[28]USS *Knight*, 1943, p. September 12th.

[29]Benson, *The True Adventures of John Steinbeck, Writer*, 1990, p. 530.

[30]Matthews, 2003.

[31]Fairbanks, 1993, p. 198.

[32]USS *Knight*, 1943, p. September 12th.

[33]Guttman, Specialist in Diversion:, 1994.

[34]Matthews, 2003.

[35]USS *Knight*, 1943.

[36]Parini, 1995, p. 277.

[37]Blumenson, 1969.

[38]Benson, *The True Adventures of John Steinbeck, Writer*, 1990, p. 540.

[39]Steinbeck J., *Once There Was a War*, 2007.

[40]Parini, 1995, p. 277.

[41]Mayo Clinic, 2011.

[42]Parini, 1995, p. 278.

[43]Steinbeck J., *Steinbeck: A Life in Letters*, 1975, p. 262.

[44]Steinbeck J., *Steinbeck: A Life in Letters*, 1975, p. 263.

[45]Steinbeck J., *Steinbeck: A Life in Letters*, 1975, p. 258.

[46]Meredith, 1999.

[47]Raines, 2003.

[48]Benson, *The True Adventures of John Steinbeck, Writer*, 1990. These were Steinbeck's own words describing the cable in a letter to his wife Gwyn, dated September 25, 1943.

[49]Benson, *The True Adventures of John Steinbeck, Writer*, 1990.

[50]Resch, 2004.

[51]Fairbanks, 1993, pp. 192–195.

[52]Guttman, Questions to Jon Guttman from Weidner Publication Group Editor Gerald Swick, 2012.

[53]Guttman, "Specialist in Diversion," 1994.

[54]FBI, John Steinbeck File #9-4583 and #100-106224 Part 1, 2012, p. 44.

[55]Wise, 1994.

[56]FBI, 1946.

[57]O'Neal, 1944.

[58]Center for Cryptologic History.

[59]National Security Agency, 1944.

[60]FBI, John Steinbeck File #9-4583 and #100-106224 Part 2, 2012, p. 5.

[61]Benson, *The True Adventures of John Steinbeck, Writer*, 1990, pp. 546–548. The meeting is not dated, but it would have happened sometime between Steinbeck returning from Mexico on March 15th and Hemingway leaving for Europe in late April or early May of 1944.

[62] FBI, 2012, p. 2.

[63]Allinson, 2000.

[64]Center for Cryptologic History.

[65]FBI. Ernest Hemingway File # 64-23312 Part 1, 2012, p. 37. It is worth noting that sometime between October 2012 and July 2013, the FBI has "updated" Hemingway's file on their "Vault" site. The file used as reference for this book can be found at http://www.steinbeckcitizenspy.com.

[66]FBI. Ernest Hemingway File #64-23312 Part 1, 2012, p. 49.

[67]Hemingway, 1943.

[68]United States Department of State, 1944.

[69]Steinbeck T., Phone Interview with Thomas Steinbeck, 2013-1-July.

Chapter 6: The Trial of Arthur Miller

[1]Finkelman, 2006, p. 780.

[2]Patton, 1996.

[3]Chermak & Bailey, 2007, p. 171.

[4]House Committee on Un-American Activities, 1947, p. 401.

[5]House Committee on Un-American Activities, 1947.

[6]House Committee on Un-American Activities, 1947, p. 83.

[7]As much as it might be construed as humor, there really was an American Vegetarian Party formed in 1947 by John Maxwell, a vegetarian restaurant owner, and Symon Gould, an editor for *American Vegetarian*. The two ran for president and vice president respectively in 1948.

[8]Cornell University Law School, 2012.

[9] Bresler, 2004, p. 170.

[10] The first real law to address political affiliation discrimination was the Civil Service Reform Act of 1978.

[11] *Counterattack Magazine*, 1952, p. 2.

[12] *Counterattack Magazine*, 1952, p. 109.

[13] IMDB.com INC, 2012.

[14] FBI, John Steinbeck File #9-4583 and #100-106224 Part 1, 2012, p. 31.

[15] House Special Committee on Un-American Activities, 1938, p. 1996.

[16] House Special Committee on Un-American Activities, 1938, p. 1997.

[17] Wartzman, 2009, p. 32.

[18] FBI, John Steinbeck File #9-4583 and #100-106224 Part 1, 2012, p. 24.

[19] FBI, John Steinbeck File #9-4583 and #100-106224 Part 2, 2012, p. 5.

[20] California Legislature, 1948, p. 49.

[21] House Committee on Un-American Activities, 1947, pp. 155–56.

[22] *The Daily Worker*, 1924.

[23] House Committee on Un-American Activities, 1947, p. 391.

[24] These numbers do not count uncredited films these men worked on. Since it is not known if the members of HUAC were privy to this information, uncredited works were not included in the calculations. Film credit sources are taken from IMDB.com.

[25] FBI, John Steinbeck File #9-4583 and #100-106224 Part 2, 2012, p. 4. The MPAA's statement mirrors, but is separate than, the Waldorf Statement of 1947.

[26] Navasky, 1980, p. 61.

[27] Steinbeck J., "The Trial of Arthur Miller," 1957.

[28] Vanderwood, 1992.

[29] Navasky, 1980, p. 272.

[30] Goldstein, 1999.

[31] Steinbeck J., *Steinbeck: A Life in Letters*, 1975, p. 443.

[32] Benson, *The True Adventures of John Steinbeck, Writer*, 1990, p. 722.

[33] Benson, *Looking For Steinbeck's Ghost*, 2002, p. 26.

[34] TC, 2012. This was a general impression I received when asking TC about HUAC and also represents the other scant accounts of a CIA/HUAC relationship. The source in note 36 of this chapter also illustrates an overview of a standoffish position between the Agency and HUAC. A contra-position is held within the research of Jack Meeks in his work *From the Belly of the HUAC: The HUAC Investigations of Hollywood, 1947–1952*, pg. 130. Meeks holds the four CIA agents did name checks on 923 individuals on April 13, 1948. Meeks cites a visitor log for those viewing HUAC files, but does not disclose how he knew the individuals were from the Agency. Given the strictures placed on the CIA in the National Security Act of 1947, it is unlikely that CIA officers would have signed a logbook as such, although the possibility does exist.

[35] Riebling, 2009, p. 96.

[36] Johnson L. K., 2006, p. 7.

[37] Herman, 1999, p. 227.

[38] Snider B. L., 2012, p. 314.

[39] Snider B. L., 2012, p. 315.

[40]TC, 2012. Angleton's Tuesday night ritual also included going to a Georgetown drug store to read magazines instead of purchasing them.

[41]Poveda, Powers, Rosenfeld, Theoharis, & Powers, 1998, p. 157.

[42]Kazan, 1988, pp. 462–63.

[43]House Committee on Un-American Activities, 1952, p. 3462.

[44]Wynn, 2009, p. 106.

[45]House Committee on Un-American Activities, 1953, p. 2330.

[46]IMBD.com INC, 2012.

Chapter 7: A Russian Journal

[1]Steinbeck J., *A Russian Journal*, 1948, p. 3.

[2]Steinbeck J., *A Russian Journal*, 1948, p. 69.

[3]Benson, *The True Adventures of John Steinbeck, Writer*, 1990, p. 601.

[4]FBI, John Steinbeck File #9-4583 and #100-106224 Part 2, 2012, p. 35.

[5]Steinbeck J., *A Russian Journal*, 1948, pp. 36–37.

[6]Benson, *The True Adventures of John Steinbeck, Writer*, 1990, p. 461.

[7]Steinbeck J., *Once There Was a War*, 2007.

[8]Steinbeck J., *A Russian Journal*, 1948, pp. 122–123.

[9]TC, 2012.

[10]A paragraph explanation of American intelligence from the end of the Civil War to the present is an oversimplification. A number of texts exist in the bibliography that give the topic the attention it deserves. *For the President's Eyes Only* by Christopher Andrew is great overview text for those interested in a more in-depth study.

[11]Bernstein, 1977.

[12]Bernstein, 1977.

[13]The counterargument is that the Pentagon Papers were a plant to positively color the CIA's Vietnam experience.

[14]Bernstein, 1977.

[15]Parini, 1995, p. 321.

[16]FBI, John Steinbeck File #9-4583 and #100-106224 Part 1, 2012.

[17]Prutsch, 2010.

[18]McBride, 2006, pp. 73–74.

[19]FBI, John Steinbeck File #9-4583 and #100-106224 Part 2, 2012, p. 37.

[20]Kershaw, 2004, p. 197.

[21]Wald, 2012.

[22]Milward, 1984, p. 46.

[23]Kershaw, 2004, pp. 197–199.

[24]*Billboard Magazine*, 1948.

[25]*Billboard Magazine*, 1950. At this time, Steinbeck had stepped down as President of World Video and White had taken the company's reins.

[26]Benson, *The True Adventures of John Steinbeck, Writer*, 1990, p. 611.

[27]The Broadway League, 2012.

[28]IMDB.com, 2012.

[29]Cron, 2011, p. 19.

[30]University of Virginia, 1950.

[31]Ravo, 1999.

[32]Barnouw, 1970, pp. 101–102.

[33]Reisman, 2007 Of note, Phil Reisman III is a journalist in his own right and never responded to numerous requests for an interview.

Chapter 8: East of Eden

[1]Steinbeck J., *Steinbeck: A Life in Letters*, 1975, p. 313.

[2]Steinbeck J., *A Russian Journal*, 1969, p. 57.

[3]Steinbeck J., *Steinbeck: A Life in Letters*, 1975, p. 434.

[4]Steinbeck J., *A Russian Journal*, 1969, p. 175.

[5]Parini, 1995, p. 355.

[6]Wright, 2008.

[7]Norton, 1953.

[8]Benson, *The True Adventures of John Steinbeck, Writer*, 1990, pp. 707–08.

[9]Steinbeck J., *Steinbeck: A Life in Letters*, 1975, p. 446.

[10]United States Department of Justice, 1952.

[11]Air France, 1952.

[12]Steinbeck J., *Steinbeck: A Life in Letters*, 1975, p. 434.

[13]Steinbeck J., *Steinbeck: A Life in Letters*, 1975, p. 446.

[14]Scott P. D., 1996, pp. 174–75.

[15]Tweedy, 2011.

[16]A reprint of this letter is at: Steinbeck J., *Steinbeck: A Life in Letters*, 1975, p. 557.

[17]Le Parti Communiste Internationaliste, 1952.

[18]Steinbeck J., *Steinbeck: A Life in Letters*, 1975, p. 448.

[19]Benson, *The True Adventures of John Steinbeck, Writer*, 1990, p. 725.

[20]Steinbeck J., "The Soul and Guts of France," 1952, p. 26.

[21]Steinbeck J., "The Soul and Guts of France," 1952, p. 27.

[22]Endicott & Hagerman, 1998, pp. 75–77.

[23]Steinbeck J., "The Soul and Guts of France," 1952, p. 28.

[24]Reil, 1952.

[25]Walt Disney Company, 2012.

[26]Cobiron, 2012 I had a number of email conversations with Mr. Cobiron from the beginning of Sept. to early Oct. 2012 about his book, which is unfortunately not available in English.

[27]Steinbeck J., *Steinbeck: A Life in Letters*, 1975, p. 450.

[28]Steinbeck J., "A Duel without Pistols," 1952, p. 14.

[29]Steinbeck J., "A Duel without Pistols," 1952, p. 13.

[30]Steinbeck J., "The Secret Weapon We Were Afraid to Use," 1953.

[31]*Time Magazine*, 1952.

Chapter 9: Burning Bright

[1]Henry, 1911.

[2]Ohio Department of the Adjutant General, 1926.

[3]Heath, 2011.

[4]*New York Times*, 1967.

[5]Thomas L., 2008

[6]Wenzer, 1996, p. 61.

[7]Wetzsteon, 2003, p. 80.

[8]Heath, 2011.

[9]University of Texas, 2011.

[10]Arens would be best known for his career as an industrial designer. His iconic designs of common household appliances are actually on display at New York's MoMA.

[11]Horton, J. nephew, 2012. Josephine Horton's nephew spoke with me on the condition I not print his name in this text. Honoring his wishes, I have withheld his name.

[12]Horton, J. nephew, 2012.

[13]Horton, J. nephew, 2012.

[14]Horton, J. nephew, 2012.

[15]Horton, J. nephew, 2012.

[16]Horton C., 1959.

[17]Horton C., 1959.

[18]Benson, *The True Adventures of John Steinbeck, Writer*, 1990, pp. 877–878.

[19]Horton C., 1959.

[20]Having gone over a number of original letters from Steinbeck, I could have used someone like Mary Morgan to help me pick through Steinbeck's scrawling script.

[21]US Department of Veterans Affairs.

[22]Edelman, 2005.

[23]Hackett, 1997, pp. xv–xvii

[24]Theoharis, Immerman, Johnson, Olmsted, & Prados, 2006.

[25]Lyons, 1994.

[26]TC, 2012. When asked about Frederick Praeger, TC was not familiar with the man. However, TC was well familiar with Praeger Publishing and commented that their books were heavily used by the Agency.

[27]Praeger Publishing is now an imprint of Greenwood Publishing Group owned by ABC-CLIO. A request for book listings from 1949–1959 was denied by the current Praeger imprint citing: "Unfortunately, due to multiple company acquisitions, we no longer have access to the records that would have provided that information." The search for titles that would be of interest to Steinbeck was then conducted via a number of book services and catalogs and may not be 100% exhaustive.

[28]A number of examples exist in the New York Public Library's holdings of Chase Horton's journal and letters where Steinbeck and Horton discuss the how uneless Ashe's research is to their endeavors.

[29]DeMott, *Steinbeck's Reading: A Catalogue of Books Owned and Borrowed*, 1984, pp. 85–86.

[30]Held in the New York Public Library's Special Collections Division.

[31]Associated Press, 1974.

[32]Endicott & Hagerman, 1998, p. 140.

[33]These archives are available online at http://findingaids.princeton.edu/collections/MC019. There are numerous examples of meetings in Dulles' day planner for meetings with the aforementioned individuals.

[34]Praeger, 1963.

[35]Praeger, 1963.

[36]During, 1999, p. 574.

[37] Bernstein, 1977.

[38] Bernstein, 1977.

[39] By the time of Campbell's hiring, the *Louisville Courier-Journal* had won the Pulitzer in 1918, 1928, and 1956. Since 1964, the newspaper has picked up another six Pulitzers.

[40] Benson, *The True Adventures of John Steinbeck, Writer*, 1990, p. 786.

[41] Ruffing & Nicholson, 1996, 2006.

[42] DeMott, *Steinbeck's Reading: A Catalogue of Books Owned and Borrowed*, 1984, p. xlvi.

[43] Goodman & Goodman, 2007, pp. 97–98.

[44] Greenwald, 2012.

[45] Greenwald, 2012.

Chapter 10: The Short Reign of Pippin IV

[1] Picknett & Prince, 2006, p. 84.

[2] Steinbeck J., *The Short Reign of Pippin IV: A Fabrication*, 1957, p. 44.

[3] Morsberger, 2007.

[4] Allegretti, 2006, pp. 143–146.

[5] Morsberger, 2007.

[6] Steinbeck T., Phone Interview with Thomas Steinbeck, 2008.

[7] Steinbeck T., Phone Interview with Thomas Steinbeck, 2008.

[8] CIRCUIT stands for *Chevalerie d'Institutions et Règles Catholiques d'Union Indépendante et Traditionaliste* and translates in English as "Knighthood of Catholic Rule and Institution and of Independent Traditionalist Union."

[9] Haywood, Night Vision Radio with Guest Nic Haywood, 2012.

[10] Haywood, Email Exchange, November 2011.

[11] FBI, John Steinbeck File #9-4583 and #100-106224 Part 1, 2012, pp. 58–60 FBI, John Steinbeck File #9-4583 and #100-106224 Part 2, 2012, pp. 1–5.

[12] Morsberger, 2007.

[13] Steinbeck T., Phone Interview with Thomas Steinbeck, 2013-18-May.

[14] Steinbeck T., Phone Interview with Thomas Steinbeck, 2013-1-July.

[15] Steinbeck T., Phone Interview with Thomas Steinbeck, 2013-18-May.

[16] Morsberger, 2007.

[17] Morsberger, 2007.

[18] Steinbeck J., *The Short Reign of Pippin IV: A Fabrication*, 1957, p. 1.

[19] *The Daily Beast*, 2011.

[20] Haywood, Night Vision Radio with Guest Nic Haywood, 2012.

[21] Brown, 1977.

[22] I contacted the staff at Château de Neuville about the existence of the statues in relation to *The Short Reign of Pippin IV*. Their reply was in a curt French manner that relayed they had no idea what I was talking about.

[23] Lincoln, Baigent, & Leigh, 1982.

[24] Morsberger, 2007.

[25] National Defense University, 1997, p. 50.

Chapter 11: The Secret Weapon We Were Afraid to Use

[1] Menninger, 2012.

[2] Albee, 2012.

[3] Albee, 2012.

[4] This is an often-heard quote from a family member that will remain unnamed, but sums up the anti-Catholic feelings about Kennedy rather well.

[5] Steinbeck J., The Wall: Letter to John F. Kennedy, 1962.

[6] Albee, 2012.

[7] Albee, 2012.

[8] Benson, *The True Adventures of John Steinbeck, Writer*, 1990, p. 944.

[9] Albee, 2012.

[10] Albee, 2012.

[11] Potter, 2003.

[12] Corbis Corporation, 2012. The picture from Corbis places Battle there and Edward Albee confirmed he was a part of the debriefing process.

[13] Wilford, *The Mighty Wurlitzer: How the CIA Played America*, 2009, p. 157.

[14] Thomas E., 2002, p. 418.

[15] Coriden, 1992.

[16] FBI, John Steinbeck File #9-4583 and #100-106224 Part 2, 2012, p. 52.

[17] FBI, John Steinbeck File #9-4583 and #100-106224 Part 2, 2012, p. 50.

[18] Haynes & Klehr, 2000, p. 342.

[19] Steinbeck J., Letter to Nancy Pearson: August, 4, 1964. This letter is unpublished and at the time of publication was on sale by Bromer Booksellers for a paltry $14,000.

Chapter 12: The Wayward Bus

[1] Landsberg, 1998.

[2] Pike, 2011.

[3] Ringle, 1974.

[4] Andrews, 1995, p. 401.

[5] Andrews, 1995, p. 401.

[6] Robarge, 2007.

[7] National Security Archive, 2010.

[8] Andrews, 1995, p. 401.

[9] Andrews, 1995, p. 403.

[10] Colby, 2011.

[11] TC, 2012. These were general impressions TC observed of his fellow intelligence officers and is echoed in the cited works of Andrews and Trento.

[12] On the surface, this statement might seem overreaching, if one does not consider George Tenet's July 2001 refusal to testify before a House of Representatives subcommittee. In a letter to Congressman Stephen Horn on July 17th, Tenet states:

In response to your letter inviting me to testify at a July 18, 2001 Subcommittee hearing, I regret to say that neither I nor any CIA representative will testify.

My decision is fully compatible with the wishes of the Chairman of the House Permanent Select Committee on Intelligence who urged me not to testify at the 18 July hearing. The House Intelligence Committee referred CIA to the recently passed House rule that stipulates clearly and unequivocally that the Intelligence Committee has "exclusive" responsibility to review and study the Intelligence Community's sources and methods.

Let me be clear. CIA has not questioned nor will it ever question the right of the Congress to have answers to questions it has asked.

The letter goes on to explain the CIA has jumped through all of the Legislative Branch's oversight hoops and shouldn't have to testify about anything. The full letter can be viewed at the American Federation of Scientists website at: http://www.fas.org/irp/news/2001/07/tenet.html.

[13]The Foreign Intelligence Surveillance Act (FISA) and Foreign Intelligence Surveillance Court (FISC) were inspired by the recommendations of the Church Committee, along with guidelines for the CIA reporting to various Senate and Congress subcommittees.

[14]While technically out the door, Colby was asked by President Ford to remain DCI until George Bush could take the post. Ford was scheduled to visit China early in 1976 and having Bush, who was the Ambassador to China at the time, leave for Washington wouldn't have made for a smooth trip. Colby stayed on as DCI until after Ford's return to the States.

[15]94th Congress, 1976, p. 574.

[16]CIA, 2012.

[17]94th Congress, 1975, pp. 62–63.

[18]Wilford, *The CIA, the British Left, and the Cold War: Calling the Tune?*, 2003, pp. 95–98.

[19]Reich, 1996, p. 559.

[20]Albee, 2012.

[21]Oregon State University Libraries Special Collections & Archives Research Center, 2011.

[22]Austin, 1982.

[23]Albee, 2012.

[24]Grace, 2008

Creative Commons Photo Credits

CPSIA information can be obtained at www.ICGtesting.com
Printed in the USA
LVOW01s1502270515

440110LV00016B/716/P